HANDS-ON
LOTUS 1-2-3
(RELEASE 2.2)

**WADSWORTH SERIES IN
COMPUTER INFORMATION SYSTEMS**

Understanding Database Management Systems, Second Edition, Joseph A. Vasta

The COBOL Handbook, Linda Belcher

A Complete Course in Structured COBOL Programming, John C. Molluzzo

Information Systems in Management, Third Edition, James A. Senn

Four Software Tools (with WordStar 5.5, Lotus 1-2-3, and dBASE III Plus), Second Edition, Tim Duffy

Four Software Tools Plus: Applications and Concepts, Tim Duffy

Four Software Tools (with WordPerfect, Lotus 1-2-3, and dBASE III Plus), Tim Duffy

Four Software Tools (with WordPerfect, VP-Planner, and dBASE III Plus), Tim Duffy

Four Software Tools, Alternate Edition (with WordStar, VP-Planner, and dBASE III), Tim Duffy

Hands-On Lotus 1-2-3 (with an introduction to IBM PC DOS), Tim Duffy

Hands-On Lotus 1-2-3 (Release 2.2) (with an introduction to IBM PC DOS), Tim Duffy

Hands-On dBASE III Plus (with an introduction to IBM PC DOS), Tim Duffy

Hands-On WordStar 5.5 (with an introduction to IBM PC DOS), Tim Duffy

A Casebook: Four Software Tools, Tim Duffy and Wendy Duffy

Structured COBOL Programming, John C. Molluzzo

Big Blue BASIC, Second Edition, Peter Rob

Contemporary Systems Analysis and Design, Raymond T. Clarke and Charles A. Prins

Applied Structured BASIC, Roy Ageloff and Richard Mojena

IBM PC BASIC, Peter Rob

Essentials of Structured BASIC, Roy Ageloff and Richard Mojena

Programming in dBASE II and dBASE III, Peter Rob

Introduction to Microcomputer Programming, Peter Rob

Tim Duffy
Professor of Accounting in Information Systems
Illinois State University

HANDS-ON
LOTUS 1-2-3
(RELEASE 2.2)

**DOS for IBM PC and MS DOS
Spreadsheets Using Lotus 1-2-3 (Release 2.2)**

Wadsworth Publishing Company
Belmont, California
A Division of Wadsworth, Inc.

Computer Science Editor: Frank Ruggirello
Editorial Assistant: Carol Carreon
Production Editor: Deborah Cogan
Managing Designer: Donna Davis
Print Buyer: Martha Branch
Copy Editor: Rene Lynch
Interior and Cover Design and Art Editing: Vargas/Williams/Design
Technical Illustration: Perfect Plot
Composition: Graphic Typesetting Service, Los Angeles

© 1990 by Wadsworth, Inc. All rights reserved. No part of this book may be reproduced, stored in a retrieval system, or transcribed, in any form or by any means, electronic, mechanical, photocopying, recording, or otherwise, without the prior written permission of the publisher, Wadsworth Publishing Company, Belmont, California 94002, a division of Wadsworth, Inc.

IBM is a registered trademark of the International Business Machines Corporation.

Lotus and 1-2-3 are trademarks of Lotus Development Corporation.
Lotus charts adapted from Arthur Andersen & Co. materials.

VP-Planner Plus is a trademark and Paperback Software is a registered trademark of Paperback Software International, Berkeley, CA, U.S.A.

Printed in the United States of America   49

4 5 6 7 8 9 10—94 93

Library of Congress Cataloging-in-Publication Data

Duffy, Tim.
    Hands-on Lotus 1-2-3 (Release 2.2) : DOS for IBM and MS DOS, spreadsheets using Lotus 1-2-3 (release 2.2) / Tim Duffy.
      p.   cm. — (Wadsworth series in computer information systems)
    ISBN 0-534-13476-9
    1. Lotus 1-2-3 (Computer program)   2. Business—Data processing.
3. Electronic spreadsheets.   I. Title.   II. Series.
HF5548.4.L67D85   1990
650′.028′55369—dc20
                                      89-49253
                                        CIP

························· To Bubba

CONTENTS

Preface   xiii

PART I   DOS   O.1

Chapter 1   Introduction to Computers and the Disk Operating System (DOS)   O.2

Chapter Objectives   O.3
What Is a Computer?   O.4
What Is a Computer System?   O.4
Software Categories   O.6
Application Programs   O.6
Operating Systems: IBM PC DOS and MS DOS   O.7
Commonly Used DOS Commands   O.16
Disk Commands   O.17
File Commands   O.17
Time Commands   O.17
Internal and External Commands   O.18
Format Notation   O.18
Rules Common to All DOS Commands   O.18
Information About Specific DOS Commands   O.18
Disk Commands   O.20
File Commands   O.25
Time Commands   O.31
DOS Command Summary   O.32
DOS Commands by Function and Type   O.32
Chapter Review   O.33
Key Terms and Concepts   O.33
Chapter Quiz   O.34
Computer Exercises   O.38

Chapter 2   Advanced DOS Concepts   O.40

Chapter Objectives   O.41
Batch Files: The DOS Automator   O.42
How Batch Files Work   O.42
Rules for Creating Simple Batch Files   O.43
Creating Batch Files   O.43
Executing a Batch File   O.44
Sample Batch Files   O.45
Introduction to Disk Directories   O.45
Directories and Directory Commands   O.46
PATH: Executing Commands Without Changing Directories   O.51
Configuring Your System   O.52
Chapter Review   O.54
Key Terms and Concepts   O.54
Chapter Quiz   O.54
Computer Exercises   O.57

viii Contents

PART II SPREADSHEETS USING LOTUS 1-2-3 S.1

Chapter 3 **Fundamentals of Spreadsheets and Lotus 1-2-3** **S.2**

Chapter Objectives **S.3**
Introduction to Spreadsheets **S.4**
Why Use Spreadsheet Software? S.4
Spreadsheet Syntax S.7
Problem-Solving Steps Using Spreadsheets S.9
Introduction to Lotus 1-2-3 **S.9**
Parts of 1-2-3 S.9
Lotus 1-2-3 Add-ins S.10
Starting Lotus 1-2-3 S.10
Lotus 1-2-3 Screen S.11
Navigating Around the 1-2-3 Worksheet S.14
How Lotus 1-2-3 Uses Other Keys S.15
Data Entry S.18
Entering Formulas S.19
Circular References S.20
Built-in Functions S.20
Correcting Errors on the Worksheet S.21
The Undo Feature of Lotus 1-2-3 S.22
Getting Help S.23
Entering a Sample Lotus 1-2-3 Worksheet S.25
Saving and Retrieving Worksheet Files S.32
Chapter Review **S.34**
Key Terms and Concepts **S.35**
Chapter Quiz **S.35**
Computer Exercises **S.39**

Chapter 4 **More on Ranges, Copying, Formatting, Printing, and Functions** **S.46**

Chapter Objectives **S.47**
Range **S.48**
The Copy Command **S.49**
Formatting **S.51**
Adding and Deleting Rows and Columns **S.53**
Moving Cell Contents **S.55**
Settings Sheet **S.57**
The Print Command **S.58**
Print Menu S.59
Print Default Settings S.63
1-2-3 and the Print Line Counter S.63
Forced Page Breaks S.63
Using Multiple Printers with 1-2-3 S.64
Passing Print Files to Other Software Packages S.65
1-2-3 Functions **S.66**
More on Data Entry **S.67**
Changing a Column Width S.67

Changing the Width of Several Columns   S.68
Dates   S.69
Text   S.70
Repeating Text   S.70
1-2-3 Sample Function Worksheet   **S.71**
1-2-3 Sample Function Spreadsheet   **S.72**
Chapter Review   **S.79**
Key Terms and Concepts   **S.79**
Chapter Quiz   **S.80**
Computer Exercises   **S.83**

Chapter 5   Maintaining and Enhancing Your Worksheets   S.86

Chapter Objectives   **S.87**
Controlling Your Worksheet Environment   **S.88**
Worksheet Zero Command   S.88
GoTo Command   S.88
System Command   S.88
Changing the Directory   S.89
Column Hide   S.90
Finding Circular References and Status Commands   S.91
Password-Protecting Your Worksheets   S.93
Range Transpose   S.94
Range Value   S.94
Range Search   S.96
Range Names   **S.98**
Name Menu   S.98
Naming Instructions   S.99
More Range Name Examples   S.100
Use of Dummy Columns or Rows in Expanding Ranges   S.104
Sorting   **S.106**
Sort Menu   S.106
Worksheet Practice with the Sort Command   S.107
Titles   **S.111**
Titles Menu   S.112
Titles Instructions   S.112
Relative and Absolute Addressing   **S.112**
Automatic Worksheet Recalculation   **S.116**
More on Functions   **S.116**
@PMT   S.116
@IF and Logical Operators   S.117
@DATE and Arithmetic   S.119
Worksheet Practice   **S.120**
Loan Amortization Worksheet   S.120
Car Loan Evaluation Worksheet   S.126
Cell Contents Listing for Amortization Worksheet   S.129
Cell Contents Listing for Car Loan Worksheet   S.130
Chapter Review   **S.130**
Key Terms and Concepts   **S.131**
Chapter Quiz   **S.131**
Computer Exercises   **S.134**

Chapter 6   Professional Use of Worksheets   S.150

Chapter Objectives   S.151
Templates   S.152
Planning   S.152
Implementing Template Functions in the Design   S.153
Designing the Logic   S.153
Developing the Template   S.154
Final Testing   S.154
Final Documentation   S.154
Support and Maintenance   S.155
Windows   **S.155**
Worksheet and Cell Protection   **S.157**
Protecting the Worksheet   S.157
Unprotecting the Worksheet   S.158
Utilizing the Data Fill Feature   **S.159**
1-2-3 and Sensitivity Analysis   **S.160**
Manual Sensitivity Analysis Example   S.161
Table Command of 1-2-3   S.161
Sensitivity Analysis Changing One Basic Assumption   S.163
Sensitivity Analysis Changing Two Basic Assumptions   S.168
Linking Files   **S.172**
Establishing a Link   S.174
Limitations of File Linking   S.175
Sample Worksheet for Linking Files   S.176
Cell Contents of Car Loan Sensitivity Analysis   S.178
Cell Contents for the File Link Sample Worksheet   S.182
Chapter Review   **S.183**
Key Terms and Concepts   **S.184**
Chapter Quiz   **S.184**
Computer Exercises   **S.187**

Chapter 7   Graphing with 1-2-3   S.192

Chapter Objectives   S.193
Steps in Building a Graph and Printing the Graph   **S.194**
Graph Menu   **S.195**
Graph Settings Sheet   S.196
Type   S.196
X   S.197
ABCDEF   S.197
Reset   S.197
View   S.197
Save   S.198
Options   S.198
Name   S.200
Group   S.200
Generating Graphs   **S.202**
Simple Bar Graphs   S.202
Entering Titles   S.203
Changing Data Ranges   S.204

Side-by-Side Bar Graphs   S.206
Converting to Line Graphs   S.207
Entering Legends   S.208
Reconverting to Bar Graphs   S.208
Pie Charts   S.208
Exploded Pie Chart   S.210
Stacked Bar Charts   S.211
Generating a Table of Graph Names   S.212
XY Graphs   S.213
Introduction to Graph Printing   S.216
PrintGraph Menu   S.218
Step-by-Step PrintGraph Instructions   S.222
Chapter Review   S.224
Key Terms and Concepts   S.224
Chapter Quiz   S.225
Computer Exercises   S.227

Chapter 8   Data Management   S.230

Chapter Objectives   S.231
1-2-3 Data Management Versus dBASE   S.232
Introduction to 1-2-3 Data Management   S.232
1-2-3 Database Commands   S.234
Query Menu   S.234
Query Settings Sheet   S.235
Building a Database and Accessing Information   S.235
The Criterion Range   S.236
Find Command and Editing/Changing Records   S.238
Output and Extract   S.239
Unique and Delete   S.241
1-2-3 Statistical Functions for Database   S.243
Chapter Review   S.245
Key Terms and Concepts   S.246
Chapter Quiz   S.246
Computer Exercises   S.249

Chapter 9   Spreadsheet Macros   S.252

Chapter Objectives   S.253
Introduction to Macros   S.254
Special Keys   S.256
Building More Macros   S.258
Creating a Macro with a Regular Range Name   S.258
Using 1-2-3's LEARN Mode for Entering Macros   S.259
Examining a Sample Macro   S.262
Rules for Entering Macros   S.264
Placement of Macros   S.264
Macro Documentation   S.264
Entering Some Simple Macros   S.265
Planning for Macros   S.267

Errors in Macros   S.267
Macro Debugging   S.267
Special Macro Commands   S.268
/XG, /XI, and /XQ—{branch}, {if}, {left}, and {quit}   S.268
/XC and /XR   S.270
/XN and /XL—{getlabel} and {getnumber}   S.270
Lotus 1-2-3 Command Language   S.271
/XM or {menubranch}   S.272
Printing the Worksheet   S.273
Chapter Review   S.275
Key Terms and Concepts   S.276
Chapter Quiz   S.276
Computer Exercises   S.279

Chapter 10

Using the Lotus 1-2-3 Add-ins   S.284

Chapter Objectives   S.285
Hardware and Software for 1-2-3 Add-ins   S.286
Hardware Requirements   S.286
Using Add-in Software   S.286
Allways   S.287
Desktop/Spreadsheet Publishing Definitions   S.287
Interaction Between 1-2-3 and Allways   S.288
Invoking Allways   S.289
Specifying a Range Before a Command   S.289
Allways Keys   S.290
Examples Using Allways   S.291
Macro Library Manager   S.302
Limitations of Macro Library Manager   S.303
Saving the Macro Library   S.303
The Macro Library Manager Menu   S.303
Building a Macro Library   S.304
Chapter Review   S.306
Key Terms and Concepts   S.306
Chapter Quiz   S.306
Computer Exercises   S.309

Appendix A

Lotus 1-2-3 Command Menus, Functions, and Command Language   A.1

Appendix B

Allways Command Menus   A.23

Glossary   A.27

Index   A.39

PREFACE

The spreadsheet is the piece of software that has single-handedly caused American business to take the microcomputer seriously as a problem-solving tool.

Electronic spreadsheet software dramatically improves the user's accuracy, efficiency, and productivity. For example, once a worksheet has been prepared, other options ("what if" alternatives) can be easily considered simply by making the appropriate changes and instructing the spreadsheet to recalculate all entries to reflect those changes.

Mastery of electronic spreadsheets is becoming a crucial skill for individuals who plan to embark on careers as diverse as agriculture, education, business, and so on. And an introductory spreadsheet course not only benefits a student upon graduation, but also helps that individual in many other courses that he or she may have to take in college. Thus, one of the most important one-hour courses today's college student can take is a course covering electronic spreadsheets.

OBJECTIVE OF TEXTBOOK

The objective of this text is to teach students to solve realistic problems using spreadsheet software. It is not necessary to go into extreme detail about spreadsheets, since the primary goal of most applications courses is to get students to the point where they feel comfortable using the computer to solve problems. The spreadsheet package selected for this text is Lotus 1-2-3 Release 2.2.

Lotus 1-2-3 is still, without a doubt, the standard against which all other spreadsheet packages are measured. In spite of many of the work-alikes which have entered the marketplace, Lotus 1-2-3 remains the best-selling spreadsheet package for business. Many employers now expect their newly hired college graduates to have at least a working knowledge of this important business tool.

HARDWARE REQUIREMENTS

An IBM PC/PS2 or IBM-compatible computer, with two floppy disk drives (or one floppy drive and a fixed disk) and 320K of RAM memory, is required. You will also need a monitor capable of displaying graphics (VGA, EGA, color, or monochrome with a graphics adapter) in order to view any graphs that are generated. The printer (with graphics capabilities if it is to be used to print 1-2-3 graphs) is also required for printing graphs or worksheets. Allways requires 512K and a fixed disk.

STRUCTURE OF TEXT

This textbook works best in a "hands-on" environment; that is, the step-by-step exercises in the text make most sense when an individual is sitting at a computer, or has easy access to one, so that an immediate response to some action can be generated. (A symbol like the one in the left margin highlights all hands-on material.)

The text assumes that the software has already been configured for use. If a package has not been configured to a specific machine, please refer to the Lotus 1-2-3 Release 2.2 documentation.

SAMPLE FILES AND LEARNING AIDS

A number of sample diskette worksheet files have been provided for use with text lessons and exercises. At the end of each chapter, exercises are offered to provide quick feedback to students on their progress. In addition to the written exercises, hands-on computer exercises are included in chapters to provide students with feedback through various challenging applications of material covered in each chapter.

At the end of the text, Appendix A presents a graphic depiction of the various menus used in Lotus 1-2-3. Appendix A also contains a summary of commonly used 1-2-3 functions as well as a summary of advanced macro commands. Appendix B contains Allways command menus. An extensive glossary of computer terms used in the text appears at the back of the book, as do keyboard templates for 1-2-3.

IN-DEPTH PROJECTS

Also included with this textbook, are in-depth worksheet projects for student use. The objective of these projects is to pull together key aspects of the Lotus 1-2-3 Release 2.2 spreadsheet software.

TEACHING AIDS

A disk containing all of the finished worksheets at the end of each spreadsheet chapter as well as solutions to the in-depth projects is available to instructors. As an extra bonus, this disk also contains a Lotus 1-2-3 GRADBOOK template that adopters can use for tracking their grades. The GRADBOOK template is completely macro driven and makes the tedious process of tracking grades much easier.

ACKNOWLEDGMENTS

It seems hard to believe that it has been over five years since I started the first edition of *Four Software Tools*. Five years ago I was not aware of all of the strenuous efforts required in producing a college/university-level textbook. Since that time, however, I have developed a sincere appreciation of exactly what is required to make a text a success at the college/university level. This "success formula" includes family, friends, colleagues, and many individuals in the publishing business. I remain deeply indebted to my wife, Wendy, who initially encouraged me to start my first version of *Four Software Tools*. Without her encouragement, the original text would probably never have been finished.

I would also like to express a sincere word of appreciation to the reviewers of this manuscript as well as to reviewers of prior manuscripts.

The efforts of individuals at the publishing company also play an important role in the success or failure of a text. The editorial staff has traditionally been a favorite of this author. As a result of these warm feelings, I would like to acknowledge Frank Ruggirello, Serina Beauparlant, Reita Kinsman, and Carol Carreon. All of these individuals have made preparing manuscripts for Wadsworth a much more pleasant chore.

The production staff also plays an important role in making or breaking a publishing project. I would like to congratulate Debbie Cogan for making this project as painless as possible. Her attention to detail and professional manner were very much appreciated.

An overlooked ingredient in the success of many textbooks is the sales staff of a publishing firm. I remain firmly convinced that the sales staff of Wadsworth Publishing Company is one of the best in the world. This is based on first-hand experience that has been gained by working with many of these individuals in various convention sales booths. I want to especially thank Peggy Hopp, Lisa Bettendorf, Ragu Raghavan, Jerry Levine, Reita Kinsman, Bill Pollock, Bob Ross, and Doni Marquart. Many of these individuals, including those not mentioned because of space considerations, will always be considered to be personal friends.

A dedication is not complete without including my son, Michael. Michael makes any writing project a challenge. It seems to be more and more difficult to reserve large blocks of time to the writing endeavor. Michael makes it very apparent that his dad should be able to find ample time to take him to play on the playground. He feels that no day is complete without at least an hour playing at Fairview playground.

Finally, I would like to dedicate this text again to my editor, Frank Ruggirello. I continue to feel that "Bubba" is the premier computer science editor in the publishing world. His knowledge of the marketplace continues to amaze and astound me. In addition to counting Frank as an editor, I also consider Frank and his wife, Suzanna, to be personal friends. The Giants tickets, with seats behind home plate, are also appreciated (not to mention the Giants/Cubs play-off tickets). Frank's informal dress, gruff exterior, and contrived/infamous temper, truly belie a steadfast friend.

PART I

DOS

CHAPTER 1

INTRODUCTION TO COMPUTERS AND THE DISK OPERATING SYSTEM (DOS)

CHAPTER OBJECTIVES

After completing this chapter, you should be able to:

- List the parts of the computer
- List the three classifications of software
- List the five classifications of application software
- List and describe the various parts of DOS
- List and describe the rules for filenames
- Prepare a diskette for use
- Start (boot) the computer system
- Describe how DOS uses the prepared disk
- Use "wild cards"
- Use various DOS commands

The computer has had a greater impact on our society than has any other device invented in the second half of the twentieth century. As late as the mid-1970s, computers were used by relatively few people. For many people today, computers are as much a part of a daily life as automobiles, telephones, and electric lights.

WHAT IS A COMPUTER?

A **computer** is a general-purpose electronic device that performs high-speed arithmetic and logical operations according to internal instructions, which are executed without human intervention.

The key terms and implications of this definition are examined below:

Electronic. Electricity is the computer's lifeblood. In a high-speed computer, electricity pulses at half the speed of light through the intricate silicon-chip circuits that serve as the machine's brain cells.

Arithmetic Operations. Computers can perform the **arithmetic operations** of addition, subtraction, multiplication, and division.

Logical Operations. Computers can perform such **logical operations** as comparing one datum with another. This allows the computer operator to determine if the datum is less than, equal to, or greater than another datum.

Instructions Contained Internally. Computers can store instructions used to manipulate data. A complete set of instructions for performing some type of operation is called a **program.** For example, a payroll program enables a computer to calculate an organization's payroll, taking into account a variety of factors such as salary levels, overtime hours, and part-time employment.

Internal Storage. A program requires some **internal storage** capability in order to manipulate data. Like its human counterpart, this storage system is called memory. **Memory** holds the computer's operating system, the program being executed, the data operated on, and any intermediate results that are created by the program.

General Purpose. By retrieving a variety of programs from memory and executing them, a computer can perform an almost limitless number of tasks—from calculating a business's monthly expenses to drawing architectural blueprints.

WHAT IS A COMPUTER SYSTEM?

A **computer system** has four functional parts: input, processing, storage, and output (Figures 1.1 and 1.2). The input portion of a computer system permits the user to enter instructions or data into the computer, just as the five senses allow people to receive information about the world. Numerous **input devices** are used, the most popular being the keyboard.

The computer's processing or "thinking" unit is called the **central processing unit (CPU).** The CPU processes data and performs arithmetic and logical calculations. It is divided into three parts: primary storage (or memory), the control unit, and the arithmetic/logic unit (Figure 1.3).

The **primary storage** holds the executing program's instructions, the data being processed, and intermediate calculations generated by the program. This memory is short-term and retains data only while the program is running;

Figure 1.1
The four functional parts of a computer system

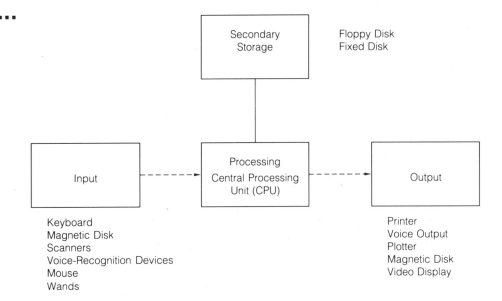

Figure 1.2
A typical hardware configuration for a microcomputer system (Courtesy of IBM)

the memory is lost when the computer's power is turned off. The control unit directs the computer's actions by holding each instruction as it is being executed, decoding that instruction, and then directing the other CPU components on what actions to take. The arithmetic/logic unit performs the arithmetic operations of addition, subtraction, multiplication, and division, and any comparisons required by the program.

In contrast to primary storage, **secondary storage** is separate from the CPU and can store data indefinitely (the memory is not lost when the power is turned off). Specific secondary memory can be inputted into the computer any time the operator needs that information for some task. Just as a student can open a particular reference book whenever necessary, an accountant can access a client's billing history by putting the proper magnetic disk into his or her computer.

Today, the magnetic disk is the most popular form of secondary storage.

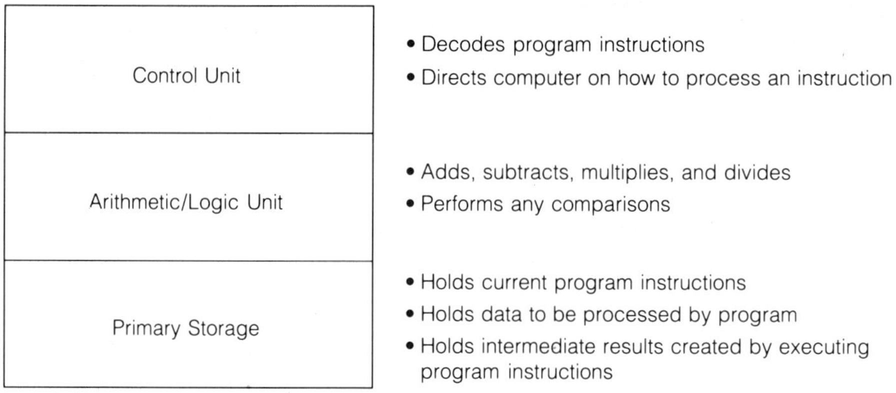

Figure 1.3
The three parts of the CPU are the control unit, the arithmetic/logic unit, and primary storage

Control Unit	• Decodes program instructions • Directs computer on how to process an instruction
Arithmetic/Logic Unit	• Adds, subtracts, multiplies, and divides • Performs any comparisons
Primary Storage	• Holds current program instructions • Holds data to be processed by program • Holds intermediate results created by executing program instructions

The bulk of data processed by a computer resides in secondary storage and is moved into primary storage only when needed for processing. This means that data are constantly being transferred from secondary storage to primary storage and back again. The process of transferring data into a computer is known as the **read process.** The process of transferring data out of a computer back to secondary storage is known as the **write process.** Data not required by the CPU for processing are stored in secondary storage.

Output devices store and present data in forms that can be read by either humans or machines. In short, they "communicate" processed information in ways comparable to our use of speech, writing, and mathematical notation to communicate information and ideas. Commonly used humanly readable devices are the monitor, printer, and plotter. A common machine-readable device is the magnetic disk, which stores data as magnetic charges. When needed, these data are read by the computer and processed by a program, then displayed on a screen or printed.

SOFTWARE CATEGORIES

The three general categories of software are programming languages, application programs, and operating systems (Figure 1.4). All three software types are needed to make computers usable to the average person.

APPLICATION PROGRAMS

Most people find it reassuring that they need not know how to program in order to use a microcomputer effectively. For most of their needs, microcomputer users can buy off-the-shelf software called application programs.

Application programs are precoded sets of generalized computer instructions that are designed to resolve particular data-processing needs. The computer operator need only select the right application program for the job, just as you would need to choose the proper tool to tighten a bolt. A general ledger package, a mailing list program, and PacMan are all examples of application programs.

Application software can be divided into five core applications: electronic spreadsheets, word processing, communications, database management, and graphics (Figure 1.5).

Figure 1.4
Types of software

Figure 1.5
Types of application software

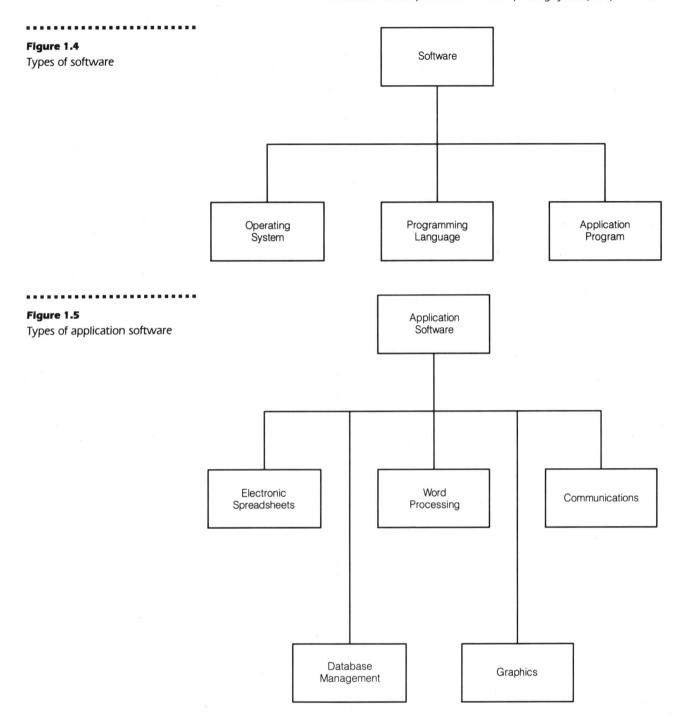

OPERATING SYSTEMS: IBM PC DOS AND MS DOS

Operating system software coordinates the computer's hardware and supervises the input, output, storage, and processing functions. Operating systems allow the user to issue commands to the computer, such as "open a file," "copy screen to print," or "copy file *x* from this disk to that disk." Without this software, a user would need a degree in computer science to operate a microcomputer effectively.

Every computer has an operating system, which varies with the type of computer (e.g., microcomputer or mainframe, IBM or Apple). The operating

Figure 1.6
Component parts of DOS

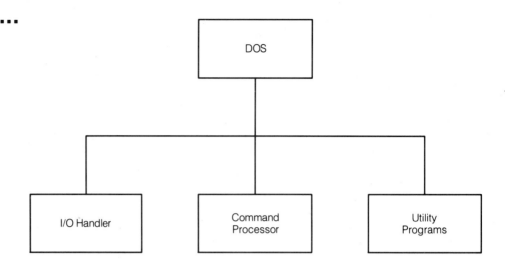

system must be activated when the computer is turned on; otherwise the operator cannot interact with the computer. Some operating systems activate automatically; others require the user to insert a diskette containing the operating system.

The IBM Personal Computer **disk operating system (DOS)** is a collection of programs designed to make it easy for users to create and manage files, run programs, and use the system devices attached to the computer. This section provides rudimentary information about various DOS commands required for daily use of the IBM PC. (For more information, refer to the Disk Operating System reference manual, written by Microsoft.) Knowledge of DOS is critical because this software dictates how programs are executed on IBM and IBM-compatible microcomputers. The operating system sets many practical limits on a computer's usefulness.

The software firm **Microsoft** developed PC DOS for IBM when the computer manufacturer decided to make a microcomputer. Microsoft markets virtually the same operating system, under the name **MS DOS,** to many of the manufacturers of IBM-compatible computers. The two operating systems are identical for all intents and purposes.

Parts of DOS PC DOS contains three program parts: the I/O (input/output) handler, the command processor, and utility programs (Figure 1.6).

The I/O handler manages input and output, encoding and decoding all data transferred between application programs and peripherals such as monitors, keyboards, disk drives, and printers. It also contains routines for preparing data to be stored on a disk, whether the data consist of a program, a document, or something else. The I/O handler comprises "hidden" files called IBMBIO.COM and IBMDOS.COM, which we will discuss shortly.

The command processor has built-in functions (also called subprograms) that handle most DOS tasks, including copying files, running programs, and examining a disk's table of contents to determine what files are stored on it. The file COMMAND.COM contains the command processor.

Utility programs perform "housekeeping" tasks that don't readily fit in the command processor. Utility programs are referred to as external files because they are stored separately on disks. Utilities handle such tasks as formatting disks, comparing files and/or disks, and reporting the available free space on a disk.

The above DOS programs are stored on a disk in four pieces:

1. The **boot record** contains the program responsible for loading the rest of DOS into the PC. The boot record is contained on every formatted disk, regardless of whether it contains DOS.
2. The **IBMBIO.COM** program acts as the I/O handler, managing all input and output to and from the computer.
3. The **IBMDOS.COM** program acts as the DOS file manager and contains file-related functions that can be used by DOS to store and retrieve files.
4. The **COMMAND.COM** program accepts DOS commands and runs the appropriate programs.

Only the COMMAND.COM program appears in the disk directory. The others are hidden program files that reside on the disk but are not shown when the directory command is issued.

When DOS is placed on a disk, it consumes considerable storage space. In fact, DOS requires about 78K of storage space, leaving about 282K of storage available on a typical disk for programs and data. DOS does not have to be placed on data disks, but it should be placed on any disks that will be used to run application programs.

Boot Process Starting a computer has long been known as the **boot process,** a term derived from the old expression "pulling oneself up by the bootstraps." There are two basic ways to initiate the boot process: the **cold start,** starting the computer when the power is off, and the **system reset,** or **warm start.** To warm start a computer, the user depresses three keys and holds them in sequence: Ctrl, Alt, and Del.

When a computer is cold or warm started, the CPU executes the bootstrap loader, a small program contained in ROM. The bootstrap executes. It checks the disk directory to ensure that the disk has, in consecutive storage locations, the IBMBIO.COM and IBMDOS.COM programs, which are then loaded in order into RAM.

The IBMBIO.COM program executes next. It checks to see what peripherals are attached to the computer and prepares the units for use. For example, the IBMBIO.COM initializes a printer, signaling it to stand by to receive information. After IBMBIO.COM has finished, the IBMDOS.COM program performs **initialization** work that allows data to be passed to a disk and stored. Next, the COMMAND.COM file is brought in from the disk and placed in RAM, completing the boot process.

After the boot process is completed, DOS checks for an AUTOEXEC.BAT file on the boot disk. **AUTOEXEC.BAT** files are commands that the user wants the computer to execute automatically each time it is started, such as starting an application program. If there is such a file, DOS executes its commands.

If the computer does not find an AUTOEXEC.BAT file, the computer displays a screen prompt requesting the date. The date may be entered using as delimiters (punctuation indicating where one part of a command ends and the next part begins) either dashes (the mm-dd-yy format) or slashes (the mm/dd/yy format). If a date is not entered and the Return key is pressed, the system will default to 1-01-80, and any files saved during this session will have the default date as the creation or change date. Next, the computer asks for the time, which is entered using colons (the hh:mm format) as delimiters.

The entry 10:42 indicates that the time is 10:42. After the operator has entered the date and time, the computer displays these three lines at the top of the screen:

```
The IBM Personal Computer DOS
Version 3.30  (C)Copyright International Business Machines Corp 1981, 1987
              (C)Copyright Microsoft Corp. 1981, 1986
```

A> is the DOS prompt. The appearance of A> signals that DOS is waiting for a command to be entered. The date and time entered are recorded in the directory for any files that are created or changed during this session.

Starting DOS If the computer power is off (cold start):

1. Insert the DOS disk or the program disk with DOS (label side up and thumb on label) in disk drive A (the left-hand disk drive).
2. Close the drive door.
3. If peripherals are attached, turn their power switches to the ON position.
4. Turn the system unit power switch (located on the right-hand side, toward the rear of the machine) to the ON position.

If the computer power is already on (system reset or warm start):

1. Insert the DOS disk or the program disk with DOS (label side up and thumb on label) in disk drive A.
2. Close the drive door.
3. Press and hold down both the Ctrl and Alt keys; then press the Del key. Release the three keys.

Both of these procedures load DOS into memory. Starting the computer and loading DOS takes from 3 to 45 seconds, depending on how much memory the PC has.

When first turned on in a cold start, a computer performs a memory check to ensure that all of the RAM locations are capable of storing and retrieving data correctly. This memory check is not performed during a system reset. The memory check consumes most of the computer's start-up time, and the more memory a machine has, the longer the test takes.

Default Drive The "A" in A> (the DOS prompt) designates the **default disk drive** to DOS, telling it which disk to use to retrieve a file or execute a command. Unless the user specifies another drive, DOS will search only the default-drive disk for filenames. The default can be viewed as the drive currently in use.

DOS tries to start a computer by trying to find DOS on drive A. If it cannot find DOS there, it checks to see if there is a hard disk with DOS. If DOS is on the disk in drive A, the default drive is A>. If DOS is on the hard disk, the default drive is C>. Additional drives attached to the computer are specified by consecutive letters of the alphabet: B for the second disk drive, C for the third, and so on.

The user can change the default drive by keying (entering) the designation letter of the desired drive in either upper- or lowercase letters—DOS always translates the letter into upper case. A colon must be keyed after the letter.

For example, to change to disk drive B, the user would change the prompt as follows:

```
A>_      Original drive
A>B:_    New drive designation
B>_      New prompt
```

B is now the default (current) drive, and henceforth DOS will search only the disk located in disk drive B to execute commands or find filenames that are entered, unless the user specifies another drive.

Directory DOS disk files are kept in a **directory,** which contains filenames, file extensions, file size, and the dates and times when the files were created or last updated. The directory of a disk can be listed by using the DIR command. For example, a disk directory might yield the following list:

```
A>dir
Volume in drive A has no label
Directory of A:\

        COMMAND   COM   17792   10-20-83   12:00p
        PROCEDUR        17408   11-23-84   12:03a
        INTRNOUT         3968   11-23-84   12:02a
        AIS             32256    1-01-80   12:52a
        INTRNOUT  BAK    3968   11-22-84    1:01p
        AISOUTL          2816   10-24-84   12:09a
        ARTICLE         14592   11-01-84   12:02a
        INTAUDI         11136   11-15-84    3:26p
        INTERN    BAK   12032   12-04-84    5:36p
        INTCOVER  BAK     768   12-11-84   12:06a
        INTCOVER          768   12-11-84   12:02a
        INTERN          12032   12-05-84   12:01a
        ISECON    BAK   15488    1-01-80   12:03a
        ISECON          15488              12:09a
         14 File(s)  173056 bytes free
```

Notice that the directory listings have one or more spaces between the filename and the file extension. This is because the DOS directory does not show delimiters. To access a file, the user must place the period between the filename and the extension.

Next to the directory is a system area known as the **file allocation table (FAT).** Its job is to keep track of which sectors store particular files and to inventory available space on the disk so that new files can be created and stored in unused areas. Each disk has one directory and two copies of the FAT. If the system has a problem reading the first copy of the FAT, it reads the second.

Filenames A *file* is a collection of related information that can be data (data file) or instructions for manipulating data (program file). Users keep track of the files on a disk by name. Each filename must be unique. If a disk has a MICRO.1 filename and the user stores a second file named MICRO.1, the computer will destroy the original MICRO.1 and replace it with the second.

Within space and special character limitations, users can name files anything they wish. Disk **filenames** can be one to eight characters in length and

Figure 1.7
Components of a filename

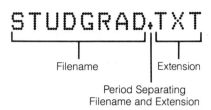

can be followed by a one- to three-character **filename extension,** separated by a period. A student data file for grades, for example, might be called STUD-GRAD.TXT. The components of this name are labeled in Figure 1.7.

The following characters can be used for filenames:

```
A–Z     !     }
0–9     '     –
$       (     ^
&       )     ~
#       -     `
@       {
```

All other characters are invalid. An invalid character is assumed to be a delimiter, which truncates the filename. Embedded spaces (blanks within the filename or filename extension) are not allowed.

Filenames should reflect the data held in the files. For example, a student drafting an English term paper on a computer could title the file ENGTP—an abbreviation for English term paper.

When used, the optional filename extension should immediately follow the filename. The same character set allowed for filenames can be used for filename extensions. All other characters are invalid. DOS can locate a file with a filename extension only if the user enters both the filename and its extension. The only exceptions to this rule are the DOS file extensions BAT, EXE, or COM.

Generally, special characters should not be used in filenames because some software packages do not accept them. In addition, Microsoft may use special characters as DOS commands in future versions of the operating system program. For example, the %, <, >, and \ characters were allowable in DOS 1.0 and DOS 1.1 but are invalid in all versions of the software from DOS 2.0 on.

A 360K disk can store as many as 112 files, or a single disk can store a single document of 360K as long as it is the only file on the entire disk. A hard disk, however, does not have this limitation, and DOS allows a file to be up to 32 billion bytes in size.

Global Filename Characters, or Wild Cards Global filename characters, also known as **wild cards,** enable users to execute commands against files whose names have one or more characters in common. The two wild cards used in DOS are **?** and *****. A ? character in a filename or extension indicates that any character can occupy that position. For example, a computer will respond to the command

```
DIR REPORT?.?
```

by listing all directory entries on the default drive having filenames of seven characters and beginning with REPORT. The listed entries may have any character in the seventh position. Files that would be listed by the above DIR command include

```
REPORTA
REPORTB
REPORTB.2
```

An asterisk in a filename or extension indicates that any character can occupy that position and any remaining positions in the filename or extension. For example, a computer will respond to the command

```
DIR W*.*
```

by listing all directory entries on the default drive having filenames beginning with W and having any or no extension. The filenames in this example may be from one to eight characters in length, and the extensions may be from one to three characters in length. (The second * in the above command tells DOS to list any files that start with a W with or without a file extension.) Files that would be listed by the above DIR command include

```
WS          COM
WSOVLY1     OVR
WINSTALL    COM
WORK01
```

Preparing a Disk Data are stored on a disk's narrow, concentric recording rings called tracks, which are further divided into sectors. Before a disk can store data, it must be organized. This is done by the formatting (initializing) process, which magnetically marks the boundaries of the tracks and sectors. These magnetic tracks demarcate the information boundaries on the disk, somewhat like traffic lanes dictating the routes and directions of cars.

Every operating system has specific formatting needs. For DOS to recognize a disk and track files on it, the disk must be formatted to DOS standards. The FORMAT utility program that resides on the DOS disk performs this task. An operator only has to format a disk the first time it is used.

FORMAT verifies the storage integrity of every sector of a disk. It finds and write-protects tracks that have bad (nonrecordable) sectors, sets up the directory, establishes the FAT, and puts the boot record program at the beginning of the disk. It can also create a copy of DOS on a new disk if that option is specified in the original command.

There are two commands to format a disk. The first, which both formats the disk and places DOS on the disk, must be used if the user wants to store application software to the disk. The second command formats the disk but does not place DOS on it and should be used for disks that will only store data.

```
FORMAT B:/S
FORMAT B:
```

Versions of DOS Since first creating PC DOS and MS DOS, Microsoft has written several versions of the operating system. These versions include DOS 1.1, 2.0, 2.1, 3.0, 3.1, 3.2, 3.3, and 4.0. The digit to the left of the decimal indicates the version of the operating system; the digit to the right of the decimal indicates the release of the operating system. The 1.0, 2.0, and 3.0 versions represent the first releases of their respective versions.

Version 1.x (1.0, 1.1, and so on) was the original operating system for the IBM PC computer and compatibles. This operating system truly represents the infancy of the PC. Many of the commands that now appear in the operating system did not even exist in this version. Also, many commands that were in this first version have been significantly altered to perform other tasks in addition to those originally expected of them. This first version of DOS supported only floppy disk drives.

Version 2.x, a major upgrade of version 1.x, was the operating system Microsoft developed specifically for the IBM XT microcomputer. This version of DOS was the first to support a hard disk drive and the first that allowed the creation of directories and subdirectories for storing programs and files in separate areas on a disk. It also allowed operators to reassign the use of disk drives (for example, the operator could designate drive B as the default drive).

Version 3.x, the next major DOS improvement, appeared about the same time as the IBM AT microcomputer. Although Version 3.x does not take advantage of the full power of the 80286 microprocessor chip and was not designed specifically for the AT, it still enhanced the power of the new computer. Version 3.x provides a number of advanced features, some of which are creating its own RAM disk; supporting networking, or connection of several computers to share resources (version 3.2); and supporting 3.5-inch disk drives (version 3.2).

Version 4.x has added a DOS shell to allow the user to operate DOS more easily. This DOS shell provides a graphics/menu interface that allows a user to "point" to files that are to be operated on. Each succeeding DOS version has been able to perform increasingly complex tasks and, consequently, has required a corresponding increase in memory. The following depicts the growth of DOS:

DOS Version	Disk Space (bytes)	Memory (bytes)
1.1	13,663	12,400
2.0	39,660	24,576
2.1	40,320	26,576
3.0	58,926	37,024
3.1	62,122	37,040
3.2	68,668	43,712
3.3	78,555	54,992
4.0	106,431	55,088

How DOS Uses the 5.25-Inch Double Density Disk Most disk drives record 48 tracks per inch (tpi) on diskette, but only a ⅚-inch strip of disk actually holds tracks. With 48-tpi drives, then, only 40 usable tracks are actually created. These tracks are labeled 0 through 39.

Each track is usually divided into eight or nine sectors. An IBM PC, unless told to do otherwise, will automatically divide a track into nine sectors, creating 720 total sectors on a disk (40 tracks × 9 sectors × 2 sides). Of these 720 sectors, 12 are reserved by the system to be used as follows:

Four sectors to hold the FAT (two copies, with two sectors per copy)
Seven sectors to hold the directory
One sector to hold the boot program in the boot record

Figure 1.8

Tracks, sectors, and clusters on a disk

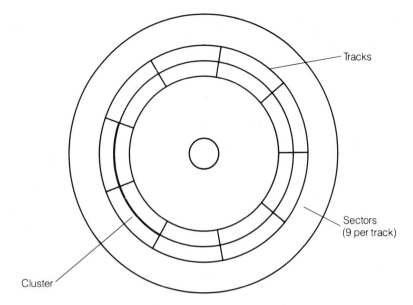

Therefore, 708 sectors (with a total user storage of 362,496 bytes) remain available on a disk formatted without the operating system.

Space within a track is allocated in increments called **clusters** (Figure 1.8). A cluster on a single-sided disk is one sector; a cluster on a double-sided disk consists of two adjacent sectors. The operating system will allocate just one cluster to a file, then wait until that cluster is filled before assigning another.

Another important disk concept is the **cylinder** (Figure 1.8). A floppy disk contains 40 tracks on each side of the disk, with each track on the top side lying directly above the corresponding track on the bottom side. All like-numbered tracks on all recording surfaces constitute a cylinder. On floppy disks, two tracks make up each cylinder; on a hard disk, there may be up to 10 tracks to a cylinder.

DOS refers to the bottom of the disk as side 0 and the top as side 1. On a double-sided disk, DOS starts storing data on the outermost track (referred to as track 0) of side 0, filling sectors 0 through 8. It then goes to side 1 to use track 0, sectors 0 through 8; then back to side 0 to use track 1, sectors 0 through 8; and so on. This process continues until the entire disk is full. (If the disk is single-sided, of course, DOS does not switch sides.)

The cylinder concept allows the disk drive to access information much faster than would otherwise be possible. The read/write heads need only be activated electronically from one side to another until the cylinder of storage is filled, at which point the read/write head can position itself mechanically to the next cylinder. Mechanical delay is always more time-consuming than electronic delay.

Control Keys Control keys are used whenever commands or input lines are entered. When two keys are required to convey a command—for example, Ctrl-Break—the first key must be pressed and held down while the second key is pressed. Control keys include the following:

Enter	Makes a line or command available to the computer
Ctrl-Break	Stops a program that is executing
Ctrl-S	Temporarily stops output to the

	screen so that it can be examined (restart the output by again pressing Ctrl-S)
Shift-PrtSc (or Ctrl-P)	Toggles the printer echo either ON or OFF
Esc	Cancels the current line (many programs also use this key to stop processing or to get out of some difficulty)
Backspace	Moves the cursor back one position
Function keys	Used by various packages to cut down on the number of keystrokes required to enter a command
Num Lock	Activates either the numeric key pad or the Arrow keys and other special function keys

DOS Editing Keys DOS editing keys allow the user to make changes to the last DOS command entered, a feature that can save many keystrokes. The instruction buffer, referenced with some of the keys below, is a temporary holding area that retains the user's last command so that it can be quickly executed again.

Del	Skip one character in the current line
Esc	Cancel the current line without changing the data in the instruction buffer
F1	Copy and display one character from the instruction buffer to the cursor position in the current line
F2	Copy all characters from the instruction buffer up to a specified character and place them in the current line
F3	Copy all remaining characters from the instruction buffer up to the current line
F4	Skip all characters in the instruction buffer up to a specified character
F5	Place the current line in the instruction buffer for more editing
Ins	Insert characters at the current cursor location using this toggle

The F3 key is probably the most important of the keys listed above. Pressing it summarily reissues the prior command held in the instruction buffer.

COMMONLY USED DOS COMMANDS

To facilitate coverage of these commands, they have been broken down into three basic families of commands. Each of these families of commands is first discussed briefly. This brief discussion is then followed by a more in-depth discussion of each command. The three families of DOS commands to be discussed are disk commands, file commands, and time commands.

DISK COMMANDS

- The **CHKDSK command** is used to examine the directory and the file allocation table (FAT) of a disk as well as to produce disk and memory status reports. CHKDSK can also be used to repair errors in the directories or the FAT. This is the only command that allows you to verify the amount of RAM that has been installed for the computer (up to 640K).
- The **DISKCOPY command** allows you to copy the entire contents of the disk that is in the specified source drive onto the disk that is in the specified target drive—exactly as the information appears on the source disk.
- The **FORMAT command** is used to initialize the disk in the designated or default drive so that it conforms to a recording format that DOS can use. As it executes, FORMAT analyzes the entire disk for defective sectors, initializes the directory, sets up space for the file allocation table, and records the boot program in the boot record.

FILE COMMANDS

- The **COPY command** allows you to copy one file or a number of files with the same name characteristics (this is accomplished by the use of wild cards) to another disk. It also allows you to copy one or more files and create a new file with a different name on the same disk. In the latter case, a different name must be given in the new COPY command.
- The **DIR command** allows you to obtain lists of files contained in the directory or of specified files or families of files using wild cards. A line is displayed for each file and includes the filename, extension (if any), file size, and date and time of creation (or updating). Again, this command is used to copy files or families of files and would not typically be used to copy an entire disk of files to another disk.
- The **ERASE command** is used to delete a specific file or group of files from the disk in the designated drive. (If no drive is specified, the default is used.)
- The **RENAME command** allows you to change the name of an existing file to a new name.
- The **TYPE command** is used to display the contents of a file to the screen. It allows you to view a file without first starting another program that might normally be used in processing that file.
- The **XCOPY command** is used to copy files quickly. This command is faster than the COPY command because it reads multiple files into a buffer that is equal in size to the amount of available memory.

TIME COMMANDS

- The **DATE command** allows you to change the date that has been stored by DOS (today's date). Ultimately, the date is stored in the directory entry for any records or files that are created or altered and resaved during a session with the computer.

- The **TIME command** is used to change the time that is currently held by DOS. This time is placed in the directory entry for any file that is created or updated and then stored to disk.

INTERNAL AND EXTERNAL COMMANDS

DOS has two types of commands: internal and external. An **internal command** is executed immediately because it is built into the command processor COMMAND.COM. An **external command** resides on disk as a separate file (an external command is also sometimes referred to as a *utility*) and must be read from the appropriate disk device before it can be executed. This means that if the file is not at the default drive location, you must indicate the location of the file by placing the drive identifier in front of the command/filename so that DOS will be able to find the file and execute the instructions contained in it. For example, if the FORMAT command is used to format a disk in drive B and if the FORMAT.COM file resides in the default drive A, issue the following command:

```
A>FORMAT B:
```

However, if the FORMAT.COM file resides on a disk other than the default drive (for example, on drive C), the default drive is A, and if you wish to format the disk in drive B, use the following command:

```
A>C:FORMAT B:
```

FORMAT NOTATION

Format notation refers to the rules that must be followed when entering commands for DOS. These rules are sometimes referred to as *syntax*. The following rules indicate how DOS commands are to be entered.

RULES COMMON TO ALL DOS COMMANDS

1. Any words shown in capital letters must be entered exactly as shown. They can, however, be entered as any combination of upper- and lowercase letters because DOS automatically changes all letters to upper case.
2. Supply any items shown in lowercase letters.
3. Items in square brackets ([ ]) are optional.
4. Ellipsis points (. . .) indicate that the item they accompany can be repeated as many times as desired.
5. All punctuation (except brackets)—commas, equal signs, question marks, colons, slashes, and so on—must be included where shown.

Commands are usually followed by one or more **parameters**—information of any kind that is entered in addition to the command name. For example, the name of the file to be copied and the destination drive for the copy are parameters for the COPY command.

A **delimiter** is a character that shows where one part of a command ends and another part begins. Common delimiters are the space, comma, semicolon, equal sign, and Tab key, although generally only the space (usually represented in instruction manuals as the character ▯) is used. A period is not a delimiter. Commands and parameters must always be separated by delimiters.

Examples

```
ERASE FILE01
RENAME OLDFILE NEWFILE
```

No part of a filename can be separated by a delimiter.

Examples

```
B: REPORT.DOC    [correct]
A: REPORT DOC    [incorrect twice]
```

You can end commands while they are running by pressing CtrlBreak. It may take a while for the command to affect the computer. The CtrlC command works in the same fashion.

Operationally, drives can act in either of two roles: A **source drive** is one that data are transferred from, and a **target drive** is one that data are transferred to. Depending on the particular operation involved, a drive may function as either the source drive or the target drive.

HINTS/HAZARDS

Some adopters of this textbook may be using a networked device. Such individuals cannot use the following commands covered in this text.

```
CHKDSK
DISKCOPY
FORMAT
LABEL
RECOVER
SYS
```

If you do try to use such a command, DOS responds with the following message:

```
Cannot <command> to a network device
```

The <command> entry is the name of the command that you entered at the keyboard.

INFORMATION ABOUT SPECIFIC DOS COMMANDS

Information about each DOS command described on the following pages is divided into five areas: (1) the command itself is named; (2) the purpose (function) of the command is presented; (3) the syntactical format of the command is detailed, with any optional parameters; (4) the nature of the command is given, identifying whether it is part of DOS (internal) or is a utility (external); and (5) any remarks or explanations about the command are given.

DISK COMMANDS

CHKDSK (Check Disk) Command

Function: This command allows you to analyze the directory and the FAT of a disk and produces disk and memory status reports. CHKDSK can also repair errors in the directories or FAT.

Format: `CHKDSK [d:][filename][/F][/V]`

Type: External

Remarks and Examples:

CHKDSK temporarily makes the drive specified in d: the default drive. If CHKDSK ends prematurely (because, for example, you replied A to a disk error message), the default drive changes to the drive that CHKDSK was checking.

CHKDSK will not automatically correct errors found in the directory or FAT unless you specify the /F parameter. If the /F parameter is not specified, CHKDSK functions but does not actually make corrections, allowing you to analyze the possible consequences of making a correction. It is generally inadvisable to make corrections unless there is a major problem; if the error is in the directory or FAT itself, a large part of the data on the disk can be lost.

If the /V parameter is specified, a series of messages (one for each file) identifying the status of each file will be displayed.

CHKDSK FILENAME tells if the file specified (in this case, FILENAME) has been stored in contiguous sectors on disk. When a disk has recently been formatted, the 512 individual byte sectors used to store files store input files contiguously. After some files have been erased and other files added, however, DOS still attempts to store any new files or additions to existing files in the first vacant sector. Occasionally, a large file ends up being stored in a number of nonadjacent sectors as a result. Such a file, referred to as a **fragmented file**, slows DOS's reading speed because the read/write heads will have to be moved physically to a number of different locations on disk.

If the number of noncontiguous locations reported by CHKDSK is large, re-forming the file by using the COPY command may improve performance.

CHKDSK does not prompt you to insert a disk in the specified drive; it automatically assumes that the disks are in the appropriate drives and begins to execute shortly after the Enter key has been pressed.

The status report displayed by CHKDSK contains the following pieces of information:

1. Disk report:
   Total disk space
   Number of bytes used for hidden or system files
   Number of bytes used for user files
   Bytes used by tracks containing bad sectors
   Bytes available for use

2. RAM report
   Bytes of total memory (RAM)
   Bytes of available (unused) memory

After the diskette has been checked, error messages (if any) are displayed, and a status report like the following appears:

```
362496 bytes total disk space
 22528 bytes in 2 hidden files
135168 bytes in 1 user files
 (4608 bytes in bad sectors)
204800 bytes available on disk
262144 bytes total memory
249744 bytes free
```

Notice that two hidden files were reported in the above status report. These are the DOS system files IBMBIO.COM and IBMDOS.COM, which are hidden from normal directory searches.

You should run CHKDSK occasionally for each disk to ensure the integrity of the file structures.

Examples of some uses of CHKDSK follow:

1. Run the CHKDSK program that resides on drive A against the disk in drive B.

    A>CHKDSK B:

2. Tell CHKDSK to correct any errors in the above example automatically.

    A>CHKDSK B:/F

3. Find out if the file REPORT has much fragmentation.

    A>CHKDSK REPORT

4. Find out if any of the files on the disk in drive A are fragmented.

    A>CHKDSK *.*

5. With B as the default drive, execute CHKDSK from drive A against the disk in drive B.

    B>A:CHKDSK

DISKCOPY (Copy Diskette) Command

Function: This command allows you to copy the contents of the diskette that is in the specified source drive onto the diskette that is in the specified target drive—exactly as the information appears on the source disk.

Format: DISKCOPY [d:][d:][/1]

Type: External

Remarks and Examples:

The first parameter specified is the *source drive*, and the second is the *target drive*. The /1 parameter causes DISKCOPY to copy only side 0 (the first side) of the diskette, regardless of whether the diskette is single- or double-sided. The same drives (or different ones) can be specified as source and target. If the drives are the same, a single-drive copy operation is performed. At appropriate times, a prompt to insert the diskette is displayed; when this has been done, DISKCOPY prompts the user to press any key in order to continue.

The following command causes DOS to load in the DISKCOPY file from the default disk drive.

```
A>DISKCOPY A: B:
```

The contents of a disk to be placed in drive A are to be copied to a disk to be placed in drive B. The following message is displayed:

```
Insert source disk in drive A:
Insert target disk in drive B:
Strike any key when ready:
```

The DISKCOPY program then checks to see if the disk in drive B is formatted. If it isn't, DISKCOPY formats it. It then performs the copy process and after copying displays the following prompt:

```
Copy another (Y/N)?_
```

If Y is depressed, the next copy is done on the originally specified drives, and DISKCOPY again prompts the user to insert the source and target disks. If N is depressed, the command ends.

The following command is different from the one above in that it expects the source disk to be in drive B and the target disk to be in drive A:

```
DISKCOPY B: A:
```

Because preexisting files on the target disk are destroyed when the copy process begins, it is important that you understand how the command works and that you develop consistency when using DOS copy commands. This will result in fewer instances of accidental data destruction.

If both parameters are omitted, a single-drive copy operation is performed using the default drive. On a single-drive system, all prompts are for drive A, regardless of any drive specifiers that have been entered.

Disks subjected to a great deal of file creation and deletion activity become fragmented because diskette space is allocated to files on the basis of where the first available opening is. Because a diskette with fragmented files can degrade performance by requiring excessive head movement and rotational delays in finding, reading, or writing a file, the CHKDSK*.* command should be used on busy disks from time to time to identify the extent of fragmentation. If a lot of fragmentation exists, use the COPY command to eliminate it.

The following command, for example, can be used to copy all the files (in unfragmented order) from the diskette in drive A to the diskette in drive B:

```
COPY A:*.* B:
```

HINTS/HAZARDS   It is safest to use preformatted disks when using DISKCOPY. You should also make certain that there are no bad sectors on the target disk. Since the copy generated is a mirror image, good data can end up being placed in a bad sector during a DISKCOPY operation.

HINTS/HAZARDS   When you use the DISKCOPY command, be certain that you are consistent in specifying the source and target drives. Otherwise, you may insert your original disk in the target drive and a blank, formatted disk in the source drive. In this situation, you end up with two blank, formatted disks along with a severe case of heartburn.

FORMAT Command

Function: This command is used to initialize the diskette in the designated or default drive so that it conforms to a recording format that DOS can use. FORMAT analyzes the entire diskette for defective sectors, initializes the directory, sets up space for the file allocation table, and records the boot program in the boot record.

Format: `FORMAT [d:][/S][/1][/8][/V][/B][/4]`
`[/t:yy][/n:xx]`

Type: External

Remarks and Examples:

All new diskettes must be formatted. An unformatted disk is unrecognizable to DOS.

If the /S parameter is specified in the FORMAT command, the operating system files IBMBIO.COM, IBMDOS.COM, and COMMAND.COM are copied from the default diskette onto the newly formatted disk. Using the /S parameter creates a system disk, with all the operating system files necessary to boot the system. The external utility programs, however, must be copied from a DOS master disk.

If you specify the 1 parameter, the target diskette is formatted for single-sided use.

The /8 parameter tells FORMAT to prepare the disk with eight sectors per track, instead of the default number of nine per track. You should let DOS use the default number so that you gain the additional 40K of disk space.

The /V parameter, which prompts the user for a volume label, cannot be used with the /8 parameter. You will be prompted for the volume name and can enter up to 11 characters. Thereafter, the volume name will appear when the DIR and CHKDSK commands are executed, further identifying the disk for you.

The /B parameter creates a disk with eight sectors per track and leaves room for IBMBIO.COM and IBMDOS.COM to be placed on the disk at a later time with the SYS command. Because it does not record these files onto the disk, any version of the IBM operating system can be placed there.

Formatting destroys any previously existing data on the disk. Do *not* format a disk that contains data you will need later, or they will be lost forever.

During the formatting process, discovery of any defective sectors in a track results in the whole track's being marked RESERVED. This prevents any sectors in the **reserved track** from being allocated to a data file.

The DOS system files are marked as hidden files. FORMAT produces a status report that indicates (on separate lines) the following information:

   Total disk space

   Space currently allocated to system files

   Space marked as defective

   Amount of space available for future files

The following command causes the diskette in drive B to be formatted and the operating system files to be copied:

```
A>FORMAT B:/S
```

The system begins by issuing the following message:

```
Insert new diskette for drive B:
and strike any key when ready
```

After you insert the appropriate diskette and strike any key, the system issues the following message while disk formatting is taking place.

```
Formatting...
```

Once the formatting is complete, the system issues this message:

```
Formatting...Format complete
System transferred

362496 bytes total disk space
 40960 bytes used by system
 (4608 bytes in bad sectors)
316928 bytes available on disk

Format another (Y/N)?_
```

Enter Y to format another diskette; enter N to end the FORMAT program.

The FORMAT B:/S command causes DOS to be placed on a nine-sectored track disk, creating what is known as a **system disk**. This is desirable when the disk is to contain programs for use; it permits the system to be booted from the disk.

If the disk is to be used only to store data (a so-called **slave disk**), the FORMAT B: command should be selected. This command performs all the tasks mentioned above except placing the files IBMBIO.COM, IBMDOS.COM, and COMMAND.COM on the disk. The system cannot be booted from such a disk; if booting is attempted, DOS will display the following message:

```
Non-System disk or disk error
Replace and strike any key when ready
```

Depending on the version of DOS and the type of disk drives that you have, you can specify the type of disk to be formatted. The /4 parameter is used to format a 5.25-inch 360K disk using a high density disk drive; otherwise DOS formats the disk as a 1.2Mb diskette. Do not use this parameter if you have regular 320K disk drives.

The /t and /n parameters are supported beginning with DOS 3.3. The /t:yy parameter allows you to tell DOS the number of tracks on a 3.5-inch disk. This parameter formats a 3.5-inch diskette to the number of tracks specified. For 720K disks and 1.44 Mb disks, this value is 80 (/t:80).

The /n:xx parameter allows you to specify the number of sectors per track if it is different from the default setting. For example, this parameter can be used to format a 3.5-inch 720K disk in a 3.5-inch 1.44Mb drive. In this situation, the command would be FORMAT B:/N:9 to specify nine sectors per track instead of the drive's default of 18 sectors per track.

HINTS/HAZARDS

Never format a double density disk as a high density disk. The surface quality of a double density disk is not good enough to retain the packed magnetic charges created by a high density disk drive. If you try to format a double density disk in this way, the result may be that you lose important files.

FILE COMMANDS

COPY Command

Function: This command allows you to copy one file or a number of files with the same name characteristics to another disk. It also allows you to copy one or more files and create a new file with a different name on the same disk. In the latter case, a different name must be given to the new copy.

Format:
```
COPY [/A/B]filespec[/A][/B]
     [d:][filename[.ext]][/a][/B]
```
or
```
COPY [/A/B]filespec[/A][/B]
     [d:][filename[.ext]][/A][/B][/V]
```

Type: Internal

Remarks and Examples:

The parameter filespec is the source file. The parameter [d:][filename[.ext]] is the target file.

Only the commonly used aspects of the COPY command are discussed here. For more coverage, refer to the DOS manual.

In the following example, the file REPORT is copied onto the disk contained in drive B. Because no name for the new file is specified, it has the same name as the original file. For the same reason, the source drive and the target drive must be different; otherwise an error message is displayed.

```
A>COPY REPORT B:
```

In the following example, the file FILE01 is copied from the disk in disk drive B onto the disk in default drive A, with no change in the filename.

```
A>COPY B:FILE01
```

In the following example, all files from the diskette in the default drive are copied onto the diskette in drive B. The filenames remain unchanged, and each is displayed as its file is copied. This method is very useful if the files on the default drive diskette (drive A) are fragmented.

```
A>COPY *.* B:
```

In the following example, file FILE01 is copied, and the copy is renamed FILE01.BAC. Because a drive is not specified, the default drive is used. Both files now reside on the same disk.

```
A>COPY FILE01 FILE01.BAC
```

In the following example, file FILE01 is copied, and the copy on the disk in drive B is renamed FILE01.BAC. But because a target drive is specified, two copies of the file are made. One resides on the disk in drive A and has the name FILE01; the other resides on the disk in drive B and has the name FILE01.BAC.

```
A>COPY FILE01 B:FILE01.BAC
```

In the following example, file FILE01.ABC is copied from the diskette in drive A onto the diskette in drive B, and the copy is named FILE01.XXX.

```
A>COPY FILE01.ABC B:*.XXX
```

DIR (Directory) Command

Function: This command allows you to obtain lists of all files contained in the directory or of specified files or families of files. A line is displayed for each file and includes the filename, extension (if any), file size, and date and time of creation (or updating).
Format: `DIR [d:][filename[.ext]][/P][/W]`
Type: Internal
Remarks and Examples:

The /P parameter causes the display to pause after 23 lines have been displayed. The message `Strike a key when ready...` is then displayed.

The /W parameter (wide parameter) produces a five-column-wide display of the directory. Only the filename and extension for each file are displayed.

The wildcard characters ? and * can also be used with the filename and extension parameters.

In the following example, all directory entries on the default drive are listed.

```
A>DIR
```

In the following example, all directory entries on the diskette in drive B are listed.

```
A>DIR B:
```

A typical directory listing might look like this:

```
A>DIR
    Volume in drive A has no label
    Directory of A:\
COMMAND    COM    17792   10-20-83   12:00p
WSOVLY1    OVR    41216    6-21-84    3:30p
WSMSGS     OVR    29056    4-12-83
WINSTALL   OVR    38528    3-02-83
WS         INS    43776    3-02-83
WSU        COM    21376    1-01-80   12:04a
WINSTALL   COM     1152    3-02-83
WST        COM    21376    6-21-89    3:29p
INSTALL    EXE    36352    3-28-84    8:00a
AUTOEXEC   BAT       11    1-01-80   12:01a
MM         INS     2816    3-28-84    8:01a
WSD        COM    21376    6-21-89    3:30p
WS         COM    21376    6-21-89    3:28p
MAILMRGE   OVR    13568    3-28-84    8:03a
SYSTEM1             128    1-01-89   12:00a
PISANI              640    1-30-89   12:07a
CHKDSK     COM     6400   10-20-83   12:00p
LETTER              128    1-01-89    4:21a
PRINT               128    1-01-89   12:03a
DIR1                  0    1-01-89   12:52a
      20 File(s)  11264 bytes free
```

The filename, extension, size of the file, creation date, and time of creation are given for each file on the diskette. The amount of available storage on the disk is given at the end of the directory listing.

In the following example, all directory entries on the disk in the default drive that start with a W are listed.

```
A>DIR W*.*
```

The listing elicited by the above instruction might look like this:

```
    Volume in drive A has no label
    Directory of A:\
WSOVLY1    OVR    41216    6-21-84    3:30p
WSMSGS     OVR    29056    4-12-83
WINSTALL   OVR    38528    3-02-83
WS         INS    43776    3-02-83
WSU        COM    21376    1-01-80   12:04a
WINSTALL   COM     1152    3-02-83
WST        COM    21376    6-21-84    3:29p
WSD        COM    21376    6-21-84    3:30p
WS         COM    21376    6-21-84    3:28p
       9 File(s)  11264 bytes free
```

Only files that begin with a W are included in this directory listing.

In the following example, all directory entries on the diskette in the default drive that have an extension of .COM are listed.

```
A>DIR *.COM
```

The listing elicited by the above instruction might look like this:

```
Volume in drive A has no label
Directory of A:\
COMMAND    COM    17792   10-20-83   12:00p
WSU        COM    21376    1-01-80   12:04p
WINSTALL   COM     1152    3-02-83
WST        COM    21376    6-21-89    3:29p
WSD        COM    21376    6-21-89    3:30p
WS         COM    21376    6-21-89    3:28p
CHKDSK     COM     6400   10-20-83   12:00p
MORE       COM      384   10-20-83   12:00p
       8 File(s)  8192 bytes free
```

The DIR/P command causes a directory listing to be displayed to the screen one page at a time. After 23 lines have been displayed, the following message appears at the bottom of the screen:

```
Strike a key when ready ..._
```

The DIR/W command is used to get a display of only the file names and extensions of the disk files. The names are displayed in five columns, and the amount of available storage is also given.

```
Volume in drive A has no label
Directory of A:\
COMMAND  COM   WSOVLY1       OVR   WSMSGS   OVR   WINSTALL   OVR   WS
WSU      COM   WINSTALL      COM   WST      COM   INSTALL    EXE   AUTOEXEC BAT
MM       INS   WSD           COM   WS       COM   MAILMRGE   OVR   SYSTEM1
PISANI         CHKDSK        COM   LETTER         PRINT            DIR1
      20 File(s)  11264 bytes free
```

ERASE Command

Function: This command is used to delete a specific file or group of files from the disk in the designated drive. (If no drive is specified, the default drive is used.)

Format: `ERASE filespec`
or
`DEL filespec`

Type: Internal

Remarks and Examples:

The shortened form **DEL** can be used in place of ERASE.

The global characters ? and * can be used in the filename and in the extension. *Global characters should be used with caution,* however, because several files can easily be erased with a single command. If proper care is not taken in using this command, a user may inadvertently delete all of the files on a diskette.

To erase all files on a diskette, enter the following:

```
ERASE [d:]*.*
```

The system files IBMBIO.COM and IBMDOS.COM cannot be erased because they are hidden files and are not accessible to you.

If *.* is used to erase all the files on a disk, DOS issues the following message to verify that all files are to be erased:

```
Are you sure (Y/N)?
```

You then press Y and depress Enter to erase or press N and depress Enter to cancel the command.

In the following example, the file FILE01.PRG is erased from the diskette in drive A:

```
A>ERASE FILE01.PRG
```

HINTS/HAZARDS

The regular version of PC DOS does not have the ability to restore a file once it has been erased from disk. DOS utilities such as the Norton Utilities, Mace Utilities, and PC Tools all have a program that performs this task. Also, a number of such utilities have been placed on bulletin boards as public domain software. If you do accidentally erase a file, do not save any data to the disk; make a copy of the disk using DISKCOPY before you try to recover the deleted file. If you make a mistake recovering the file, the deleted file will still be on your back-up disk.

You may have a special version of DOS that has an "unerase" utility. For example, the 3.3 Plus version of MS DOS, provided with Zenith computers, contains the command GDU to recover accidentally deleted files. GDU is an external command with the format `GDU [d:]filename`.

RENAME (or REN) Command

Function: This command allows you to change the name of an existing file specified in the first parameter to the new name and extension specified in the second parameter.
Format: `REN[AME] filespec filename [.ext]`
Type: Internal
Remarks and Examples:

The abbreviated form REN can be used for the RENAME command. The global characters ? and * can also be used with this command.

In the following example, file FILE03 on drive B is renamed NEWFILE:

```
RENAME B:FILE03 NEWFILE
```

In the following example, file FILE03 on drive B is renamed FILE03.XY:

```
REN B:FILE03 *.XY
```

TYPE Command

Function: This command causes the contents of the requested file to be displayed on the screen.
Format: TYPE filespec
Type: Internal
Remarks and Examples:

    Depress Ctrl-PrtSc if you want the contents of a file to be printed as they are being displayed. Depress CtrlS to cause the output to pause, and then press any other key to continue scrolling.

    Text files appear in a legible format; other files, however, such as object program files, may contain nonalphabetic or nonnumeric characters that render them unreadable.

    In the following example, file FILE03.PRG on the diskette in drive B is displayed on the screen:

TYPE B:file03.prg

XCOPY Command

Function: This command is an adapted version of the COPY command. Instead of reading and writing one file at a time, XCOPY reads multiple files into a buffer that is equal in size to the amount of available memory. Once the files have been read into memory, XCOPY writes the files to the receiving disk. XCOPY can be used for a single file, groups of files, or all of the files on a disk or directory.
Format: XCOPY [filename][/A][D:mm-dd-yy][/E] [/M][/P][/S][/V][/W]
Type: External
Remarks and Examples:

    The /A parameter results in only those files with a set archive bit being copied.

    The /D:mm-dd-yy parameter results in only those files created or modified on or after the specified date being copied.

    The /E parameter creates corresponding subdirectories, if any exist in the area being copied, to the receiving area of the disk.

    The /M parameter results in files being copied that have a set archive bit and, once the copy has executed, resets the archive bit on the source file.

    The /P parameter causes a prompt from DOS to be displayed to the operator before a file is copied.

    The /S parameter copies files from all subdirectories within the specified directory in addition to the directory's files.

    The /V parameter turns on the verify feature of DOS for any XCOPY operation.

    The /W parameter results in prompts to insert different disks before the XCOPY command executes.

    The XCOPY command does not copy any hidden files that reside on a disk or in a directory, nor will it overwrite existing files with the same name that have been set to read-only status via the ATTRIB command.

TIME COMMANDS

DATE Command

Function: This command allows you to change the date that has been stored by DOS (today's date). Ultimately, the date is placed in the directory entry for any files that are created or altered and resaved during this session.

Format: `DATE [mm-dd-yy]`

Type: Internal

Remarks and Examples:

If a valid date is entered with the DATE command, the new date is accepted by DOS. Otherwise, the DATE command produces the following prompt:

```
Current date is day mm-dd-yy
Enter new date:_
```

The system displays the day of the week in the day location. Don't worry that you have never told it the day of the week; DOS has a formula for calculating this piece of information.

To leave the date unchanged, press Enter.

The valid delimiters within the date are hyphens (-) and slashes (/). This means that the dates 4-23-89 and 4/23/89 are both correct. DOS also allows you to mix these delimiters, so the date 4/23-89 also works.

Any date is acceptable as today's date as long as the digits are in the correct ranges for each field. This means, for example, that you can't enter 16 for a month (12 is the maximum) or 35 for a day (31 is the maximum). DOS also does not allow you to enter a date prior to 1-1-80.

If a mistake is made, the error message `INVALID DATE` is displayed.

HINTS/HAZARDS

You can save a keystroke by entering the new date to be used by DOS following the DATE command. For example, to change the system date to January 15, 1991, you enter the following command at the keyboard:

```
DATE 1-15-91
```

TIME Command

Function: This command permits you to change or enter a new time for the system. This date then becomes a part of any directory entry of a new file.

Format: `TIME [hh:mm:ss.xx]`

Type: Internal

Remarks and Examples:

Upon receiving a valid time entry from the user, DOS stores that information until the system is shut down or until a new time is entered. In the latter case, the system displays the following prompt:

```
Current time is hh:mm:ss.xx
Enter new time:_
```

In this prompt, hh stands for hours, mm for minutes, ss for seconds, and xx for hundredths of a second.

To leave the time as currently set, press Enter.

A 24-hour clock pattern is used. This means that 1:00 P.M. is entered as 13:00. Most people are concerned only with hours and minutes; the seconds and hundredths do not have to be used.

If partial time information (for example, just hours) is entered, the remaining fields are shown as zeros.

The valid delimiters for time fields are colons (:)—separating hours, minutes, and seconds—and the period (.)—separating seconds and hundredths of a second.

If an invalid time or invalid delimiter is entered, the `Invalid time` message will be displayed.

In the following example, when the Enter key is depressed, the time recorded by the system is changed to 18:25:00.00.

```
A>TIME
Current time is 00:25:16.65
Enter new time:18:25_
```

DOS COMMAND SUMMARY

CHKDSK	Checks the status of a disk and prepares the status report
COPY	Copies one or more files
DATE	Changes the system date
DEL	Deletes one or more files
DIR	Lists the files in the directory
DISKCOPY	Copies a complete diskette
ERASE	Deletes one or more files
FORMAT	Prepares a disk for use
RENAME	Renames disk files
TIME	Changes the system time
TYPE	Displays file contents on the monitor screen
XCOPY	Provides quick copying via RAM buffer

DOS COMMANDS BY FUNCTION AND TYPE

Time: DATE, TIME
File: COPY, DEL, DIR, ERASE, RENAME, TYPE, XCOPY
Disk: CHKDSK, DISKCOPY, FORMAT

Internal Commands	External Commands (Utilities)
COPY	CHKDSK
DATE	DISKCOPY

Internal Commands	External Commands (Utilities)
DEL	FORMAT
DIR	XCOPY
ERASE	
RENAME	
TIME	
TYPE	

CHAPTER REVIEW

The three basic types of software for microcomputers are operating systems, programming languages, and application programs. Users do not have to know how to program to make effective use of today's microcomputers.

Application programs are prewritten programs that are used to solve specific user problems. The five basic problem areas addressed by application software are electronic spreadsheets, word processing, database management, communications, and graphics. A number of these general applications can be combined in one piece of software by a process known as integration. Integration allows the operator to pass data/information quickly from one application to another and to manipulate or process it without having to leave one application and start another.

The disk operating system (DOS), a critical piece of software that is loaded into the machine at start-up time, allows the user to perform once laborious tasks (formatting a disk, copying files, or listing the directory of a disk) with ease.

Information stored on a disk is contained in files. Each file must have a unique file name. File names follow rather rigid naming conventions.

DOS uses disk drives in executing commands. It also uses information contained on special areas of the disk or in files. Global (wild card) characters can be used to access some of this information if it is file-related.

The two basic types of DOS commands are internal and external. Internal commands are part of the DOS file COMMAND.COM. To execute one of these, you need only enter the command from the keyboard. External commands reside on disk as separate, external files. For one of these to be executed, the disk it is on must reside in the default drive or in a drive that you specify with a drive identifier.

Each DOS command has characteristics in common with other DOS commands; DOS also makes use of a common format notation. Disk-oriented commands all have unique features that can only be expressed adequately when discussed in detail.

KEY TERMS AND CONCEPTS

A> (DOS prompt)
application programs
arithmetic operations
AUTOEXEC.BAT
boot process
boot record
central processing unit (CPU)

CHKDSK command
clusters
cold start
COMMAND.COM
computer
computer system
control keys

COPY command
cylinder
DATE command
default disk drive
DEL
delimiter
DIR command
directory
DISKCOPY command
disk operating system (DOS)
DOS editing keys
ERASE command
external command
file allocation table (FAT)
filename extension
filenames
FORMAT command
format notation
fragmented file
global filename characters
IBMBIO.COM
IBMDOS.COM
initialization
input devices
internal command
internal storage

logical operations
memory
Microsoft
MS DOS
operating system
output devices
parameters
primary storage
program
read process
REN
RENAME command
reserved track
secondary storage
slave disk
source drive
system disk
system reset
target drive
TIME command
TYPE command
warm start
wild cards
write process
XCOPY command

CHAPTER QUIZ

Multiple Choice

1. Which of the statements below is false with respect to copying files using IBM PC DOS?
   a. DISKCOPY is the command used to re-form fragmented files.
   b. COPY can create a copy of a file on the same disk, but a different name must then be used.
   c. COPY can be used to create a back-up file on another disk.
   d. DISKCOPY creates an exact copy of a disk's contents. It does this sector by sector and track by track.

2. The FORMAT command does all but which of the following tasks?
   a. Divides each track into eight or nine sectors.
   b. Marks any track having a bad sector(s) as reserved.
   c. Builds the directory.
   d. Builds the FAT.
   e. Performs all the above tasks.

3. Which of the following entries might not appear on a report generated by CHKDSK?
   a. The total amount of installed RAM
   b. The total amount of disk storage
   c. The amount of available disk storage
   d. The number of bytes in bad sectors
   e. All of the above can appear.

4. Which of the commands below cannot use the * or ? wild cards?
   a. ERASE
   b. COPY
   c. CHKDSK
   d. DISKCOPY
   e. DIR
   f. All of these commands can use wild cards.

5. Which of these commands will cause the contents of the file FILE1 on a disk in drive A to be copied to a disk in drive B?
   a. A>COPY FILE1 A:
   b. B>COPY A:FILE1
   c. A>COPY FILE1 A:FILE1.BAK
   d. Both a and b
   e. All of the above will accomplish the task.

True/False

6. If you do not give a drive specifier in a command, DOS assumes that the command you have just entered is to be executed against the default drive.

7. An external command must reside on the default disk unless a drive specifier is given.

8. The COMMAND.COM file contains the external DOS commands.

9. The ERASE and DEL commands can be used interchangeably.

10. The computer can be booted from a slave disk.

Answers

1. a   2. e   3. e   4. d   5. b   6. t   7. t   8. f   9. t   10. f

Exercises

1. Define or describe each of the following:
   a. internal command
   b. external command
   c. COPY versus DISKCOPY
   d. system versus slave disk

2. List the five core software applications.
   a.

   b.

   c.

   d.

   e.

3. _____ allows you to pass data quickly from one application to another.

4. The company named _____ wrote the DOS for the IBM PC.

5. List and describe the four parts of IBM PC DOS.
   a.

   b.

   c.

   d.

6. List and describe the parts of a filename. Place an asterisk to the left of the required part(s).
   a.

   b.

7. List the pieces of information given by the directory command for each file.
   a.

   b.

   c.

   d.

   e.

8. The _____ command is used to prepare a disk for use.

9. A _____ start requires that the power to the machine be off beforehand.

10. The disk that is automatically searched is the _____ disk.

11. Of the 720 sectors created on the disk, only 702 are available to the user. The remaining sectors are taken up by _____, _____, and _____.

12. Like-numbered tracks from both recording surfaces are called _____.

13. The wildcard character _____ is used to identify a variable in only one position.

14. If a file was originally created with a file extension, that extension must be used any time that the file is referenced in the future. The exceptions to this rule are when the extension is

a.

b.

c.

15. Up to _____ files can be stored on a single disk.

16. Two adjacent sectors that are used for storing data in a file are called a(n) _____.

17. List three internal DOS commands.
    a.

    b.

    c.

18. List three external DOS commands.
    a.

    b.

    c.

19. Give the following FORMAT commands (assume A as the default):
    a. Format the disk in drive A, placing the operating system on it.
    b. Format the disk in drive A without placing the operating system on it.
    c. Format the disk in drive B, placing the operating system on it.
    d. Format the disk in drive B without placing the operating system on it.

20. Without changing the default drive, give the following COPY commands:
    a. Copy file FILE1 from the default disk A and create file FILE1.BAK on drive A.
    b. Copy file FILE1 from the default disk A onto the disk in drive B.
    c. Copy file FILE1 from disk B and copy it onto the disk in default drive A, using the same name.
    d. Copy file FILE1 from disk B and copy it onto the disk in default drive A, using the name FILE1.BAK.

21. The default drive is A. Enter the command that would erase file FILE1 from the disk in drive B, without changing the default drive.

22. The DOS command that is used to re-form fragmented files is the _____ command.

23. The DOS command that is used to list the directory of a disk is the _____ command.

24. Two commands that can be used to delete unwanted files are
    a.

    b.

25. The command used to create a "carbon" copy of the disk in drive A onto the disk in drive B is _____.

26. Two commands that can be used to tell you the amount of available space on a disk are
    a.

    b.

27. The format notation [ ] means that these parameters are _____ when using this command.

28. The copy command that also copies all the files of one disk onto another disk is the COPY _____.

29. The parts of a computer are:
    a.

    b.

    c.

30. The five types of application software are:
    a.

    b.

    c.

    d.

    e.

COMPUTER EXERCISES

1. Enter the following DIR commands:
   a. Display the directory, one page at a time.
   b. Display the directory using the wide parameter option.

2. Change the date and time of the system. Use the DATE and TIME commands to verify that the change was properly made.

3. What is the date on the SEMPCINT.DOC file? What command do you have to use to get the date?

4. Run CHKDSK on your diskette. Fill in the following blanks:
   _____ bytes total disk space
   _____ bytes in _____ hidden files

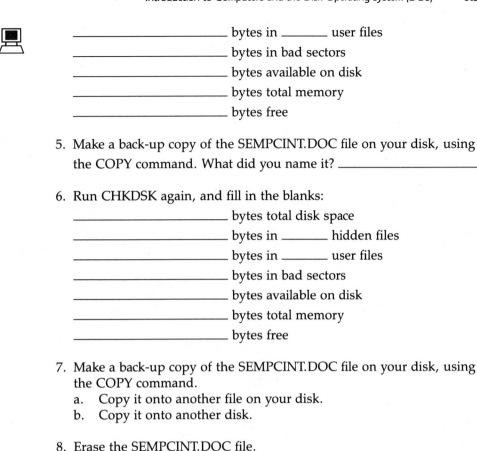

_____ bytes in _____ user files
_____ bytes in bad sectors
_____ bytes available on disk
_____ bytes total memory
_____ bytes free

5. Make a back-up copy of the SEMPCINT.DOC file on your disk, using the COPY command. What did you name it? _____.

6. Run CHKDSK again, and fill in the blanks:
_____ bytes total disk space
_____ bytes in _____ hidden files
_____ bytes in _____ user files
_____ bytes in bad sectors
_____ bytes available on disk
_____ bytes total memory
_____ bytes free

7. Make a back-up copy of the SEMPCINT.DOC file on your disk, using the COPY command.
   a. Copy it onto another file on your disk.
   b. Copy it onto another disk.

8. Erase the SEMPCINT.DOC file.

9. List (TYPE) the contents of the back-up file of SEMPCINT.DOC on your screen. Give the instruction that you used:
   _____ .

CHAPTER

2

ADVANCED DOS CONCEPTS

CHAPTER OBJECTIVES

After completing this chapter, you should be able to:

- **Tell what a batch file does**
- **Use both types of batch files**
- **Create batch files**
- **Create batch files with replaceable parameters**
- **Discuss the concept of directories**
- **Use common directory commands**
- **Use the active directory**
- **Use the CONFIG.SYS file to configure your system**

BATCH FILES: THE DOS AUTOMATOR

The disk operating system (DOS) gives you tremendous power on your computer. DOS allows you to perform tasks on files such as copying, deleting, renaming, listing files as they occur in the directory, and listing files in sorted order. DOS also allows you to customize the operating environment to meet your specific needs. Customization involves placing any number of DOS commands in a file and then executing the commands contained in that file. The file that contains these DOS commands is known as a **batch file.**

A batch file then feeds its DOS commands to DOS. Once DOS receives a command from a batch file, it executes it and tries to access any other commands in that file. A batch file can have any filename but is required to have a .BAT file extension. The .BAT file extension indicates to DOS that the file contains system commands rather than text, machine language, or any other data.

What are the advantages of using a batch file? Batch files can save you large amounts of time. You can tell DOS to execute all DOS commands in the file by typing the batch file's name. Since the commands are already correctly entered into the file, you don't have to worry about making mistakes in any of the DOS commands or filenames.

Why is the term *batch* used in referring to a batch file? The term goes back to the early days of data processing when batches of machine-readable documents or system commands were submitted to a computer. The computer's operating system would process a batch of operating system instructions at one time, while a computer program would process a batch of machine-readable documents at one time. With early computers, information could not be entered interactively as it was needed. Instead, information was recorded on punched cards, magnetic disks, or magnetic tapes and then entered into the machine. There was very little interaction between the operator and the machine or between a user and the computer.

Batch files on today's microcomputers contain frequently executed sequences of DOS commands. Such sequences include booting the machine, entering date and time, and then starting a program; copy commands for backup for critical files; and using batch files to make it easier for beginners to use the microcomputer.

HOW BATCH FILES WORK

There are two types of batch files. The first executes automatically upon booting the system (AUTOEXEC.BAT); the second can be executed only by entering its name from the keyboard. When you are executing the second type of batch file, you do not have to include the .BAT file extension.

When DOS executes the commands in a batch file, it follows the same steps that it uses in executing any DOS command. It checks to see if the command is contained in the COMMAND.COM file (internal command). If the command is not an internal command, it checks to see if the command is contained on the default disk (unless a drive identifier was used). It assumes that such a command contains either a .COM or .EXE file extension. If DOS is unable to find a .COM or .EXE file, it checks to see if there is a file on the indicated disk with an appropriate .BAT file extension. When DOS encounters any one of these circumstances, it starts to execute that command/batch file.

The user does not have to wait for all of the commands in a batch file to be executed before stopping the process. You can stop a batch file at any time by entering a Ctrl + Break command or a Ctrl + C command. Either of these commands brings the following message:

```
Terminate batch job (Y/N)?_
```

If you press the N key, the batch file continues processing. If you press the Y key, DOS returns you to the default disk with the standard DOS prompt (i.e., A>, B>).

An AUTOEXEC.BAT batch file executes during the boot process immediately after DOS has been loaded into RAM memory. Note that you can have only one AUTOEXEC.BAT file on a disk at any one time. If there happen to be more than one, DOS executes the first AUTOEXEC.BAT file that it finds in the directory. Here is a sample AUTOEXEC.BAT batch file:

```
REM start-up procedure
DATE
WS
```

Notice that the batch file contains only three commands. **REM** displays the message start-up procedure on the screen. The DATE command prompts the user for the date. After the date has been entered, the WS command starts the WordStar word processing program. Thus, this batch file allows an individual, without much knowledge of a computer, to use a WordStar disk that contains DOS and this batch file and, without having to learn any DOS commands, do word processing. Remember, it does not matter to DOS whether a command is in uppercase letters, lowercase letters, or a combination of the two.

RULES FOR CREATING SIMPLE BATCH FILES

The following rules are imposed by DOS when you name and create a batch file:

- You can create batch files by using either the DOS COPY command to copy commands to a batch file or by using a word processor in nondocument or programming mode.
- Please note that when you use the COPY option, DOS erases all the data in a file and starts fresh. You cannot modify an existing batch file with the COPY command.
- The filename of a batch file must be entered according to standard DOS procedures; that is, it can have one to eight allowable characters.
- The file extension *must* be .BAT.
- The filename cannot be the same as a DOS internal command or as any file with a .COM or .EXE file extension, because DOS cannot differentiate between such commands and may execute the internal command instead of the .BAT command. If another file residing on the disk has the batch filename but a different file extension, DOS executes the file that it finds first in the directory.

CREATING BATCH FILES

Batch files can be created in a number of ways, two of which are covered here: using the COPY CON: facility of DOS or using the nondocument mode of a word processor. The **COPY CON:** procedure uses the DOS copy feature to copy all commands entered at the keyboard to the batch file. The COPY CON: convention is most appropriate when you are creating a small batch file. If you have to make changes to a large batch file, a word processor is better because you don't want to destroy your existing text and start from the beginning. The following steps would be required to create the AUTOEXEC.BAT file:

1. A>COPY CON:AUTOEXEC.BAT
2. REM start-up procedure
3. DATE
4. TIME
5. ^Z

Let's examine each of these steps. The COPY CON: portion of step 1 tells DOS that a file is to be created from entries generated at the keyboard. The AUTOEXEC.BAT tells DOS the name of the file to be created.

Steps 2–4 contain the commands that are to be placed in the file. DOS knows you are finished with a line when you press the Enter key.

Step 5 contains a ^Z entry. The ^Z indicates the end of the file to DOS. DOS now knows to record all commands in the file to disk. The ^Z is achieved not by entering the characters ^Z but by pressing the F6 function key. When you press the F6 key, DOS stores the file to disk under the name used in the COPY CON: command (AUTOEXEC.BAT).

A frequent problem in using the COPY CON: facility is error correction. Once you press Enter, you cannot make changes in a line. If you make mistakes, continue entering the various DOS commands and make any changes using the nondocument mode of a word processor.

This batch file could be entered using the nondocument or programming mode of a word processing language. Nondocument mode does not embed any special ASCII control sequences in a file. After the AUTOEXEC.BAT file has been opened, the above commands can be entered exactly as they appear.

There is no difference in how the two files execute. The only difference is in how they are created. Most people, once they are familiar with a word processor, prefer to create batch files with their nondocument mode, because errors are much easier to correct.

EXECUTING A BATCH FILE

The following rules apply when you are ready to tell DOS to execute a batch file:

- DOS assumes that the batch file resides on the default drive unless you indicate otherwise by using a drive identifier (for example, C:SAMPLE.BAT).
- To start a batch file, simply enter the filename. You do not have to enter the .BAT file extension.
- Once the batch file is located by DOS, the operating system begins executing commands residing in the batch file one at a time. When one command has been executed, DOS automatically loads the next command and tries to execute it.
- If DOS loads an instruction and is unable to interpret it, a `Syntax error` message is displayed.
- Once a batch file has begun execution, you can stop it by entering a Ctrl + Break or Ctrl + C DOS interrupt command. Once one of the above commands is entered, DOS displays the following message:

```
Terminate batch job (Y/N)?_
```

If you answer N, the batch file continues to execute, and the next command is read and executed. If you answer Y, the stream of commands coming from the batch file is interrupted, and you are returned to DOS (a system prompt is displayed to the screen). If you have removed the disk, DOS will prompt you to reinsert the disk containing the batch file. If you simply want to stop the execution, enter another interrupt command (Ctrl + Break or Ctrl + C); otherwise, reinsert the original disk and press any key to continue.

SAMPLE BATCH FILES

Many of today's IBM or IBM-compatible computers have expanded memory cards that allow you to add up to 640K of regular RAM to your microcomputer. This extra RAM allows you to turn part of your RAM into an electronic disk that can be used to store program files and pass them, with tremendous speed, to the CPU. If you use programs such as WordStar that require a lot of disk I/O, a RAM disk can give you much faster processing.

The following batch file allows you to create a RAM disk as you boot the system. This particular example makes use of a utility provided by the Quadram Corporation on their multifunction card. Of course, this batch file has to be named AUTOEXEC.BAT and would be stored on the disk containing all of the WordStar program files.

```
QM2 QD=10, QC=0, QS=0, BATCH
COPY *.*C:
C:
WS
a:
```

Let's examine these statements. The first calls the Quadram utility QM2 and tells it, among other things, to create a RAM disk. This becomes device C:. The next statement takes all of the files that appear on the disk in drive A and copies them, one at a time, to the RAM disk. The next statement makes the RAM disk (default C>) the default drive. The fourth statement starts WordStar. The last statement changes the default drive to A when you exit WordStar.

The next example of a batch file contains the statements necessary for starting VP-Planner Plus.

```
DATE
VPP
```

The first command prompts you for the date and then resets the computer's system date from the data that you enter at the keyboard. The second command starts VP-Planner Plus.

INTRODUCTION TO DISK DIRECTORIES

Before we look at directories, let's review how DOS prepares a regular double-sided disk via the FORMAT command. When DOS is finished formatting a disk, it prepares the **directory** and places it in seven sectors. This directory can hold up to 112 files. DOS, in essence, limits the number of files that you can place on your disk. DOS also limits the number of files that a directory can hold on other types of disks. A list of the type of disk and its maximum number of files follows:

Disk Type	Maximum Number of Files
Single sided	64
Double sided	112
High density (AT)	224
Hard disk	512

Although DOS appears to limit the number of files that can be stored on a disk, this is not really the case. Can you imagine that a high density disk with 1.2 mb of storage or a hard disk with 10 to 20 mb, or more, is able to store only a limited number of files? You can circumvent this apparent limitation on any disk by using subdirectories. Directories can be used on diskettes, but they are most frequently used on hard disks and high density diskettes.

The main directory is referred to as the **root directory,** and any additional directories are **subdirectories.** Subdirectories allow you to store more information (files) on a disk and to organize your disk more effectively. This means that you can place your word processing programs and files in a subdirectory for word processing or your database management programs and database files in a database subdirectory. Such an organization is shown in Figure 2.1.

Each of the subdirectories depicted in Figure 2.1 can be divided into other subdirectories. The database directory might be subdivided into two subdirectories, one for holding business-related data files and the other for personal data files.

DIRECTORIES AND DIRECTORY COMMANDS

A subdirectory is like a root directory except that it is itself a file and contains DOS housekeeping entries in a regular directory; also, it does not have the size limitation of the root directory. A subdirectory can expand indefinitely (or until there is no more disk space).

Since a subdirectory is a file, it must be named. However, it cannot be built like other files but instead uses the following commands:

Command	Purpose
Make Directory **(MKDIR) [MD]**	Build a file to contain the new directory entries.
Change Directory **(CHDIR) [CD]**	Move to another directory and make that the active directory.
Remove Directory **(RMDIR) [RD]**	Delete the file containing the directory.
TREE	Display all directories on the disk.

The first three directory commands are internal commands. They can be executed either by their complete DOS name (in parentheses) or by their abbreviated name [in brackets]. The TREE (found only in PC DOS) is an external command and resides as a separate file on disk. The syntax of these commands is discussed in greater detail at the end of the chapter.

Before you make a subdirectory, you should plan how you want to store data on your disk. You may decide to store programs and information by application type such as depicted in Figure 2.1, or you may plan to store

Figure 2.1
Three subdirectories under the root directory

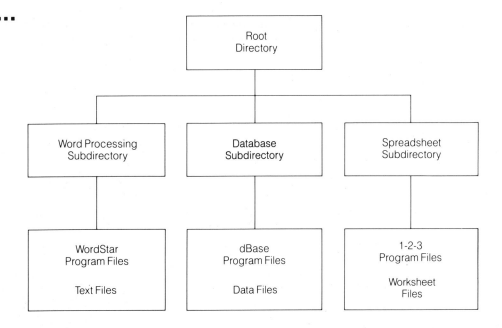

programs and information by project. A third possibility is to combine these two techniques, storing information by project within an application.

The Make Directory (MD) Command   Once you have an idea of how you want to store your information, you can build the subdirectories that will hold the information. This is accomplished via the MKDIR (MD) command.

If you want to work along with an example, format a system disk and copy these files to it:

CHKDSK.COM
FORMAT.COM
DISKCOPY.COM
MORE.COM
SYS.COM
TREE.COM
SORT.EXE
ANSI.SYS

A directory listing of the files on the disk would now appear as follows:

```
Volume in drive A is TIM DUFFY
Directory of A:\

COMMAND     COM      17792     10-20-83     12:00p
CHKDSK      COM       6400     10-20-83     12:00p
FORMAT      COM       6912     10-20-83     12:00p
DISKCOPY    COM       2576     10-20-83     12:00p
MORE        COM        384     10-20-83     12:00p
SYS         COM       1680     10-20-83     12:00p
TREE        COM       1513     10-20-83     12:00p
SORT        EXE       1408     10-20-83     12:00p
ANSI        SYS       1664     10-20-83     12:00p
         9 File(s)   294912 bytes free
```

You are now ready to build three subdirectories for storing information: word processing (WP), spreadsheets (SS), and database management (DB). Each is created by using the MD commands:

```
A>MD WP
A>MD DB
A>MD SS
```

After each command is entered, drive A starts up to record information for that subdirectory's file. You can now issue a DIR command, and the following information will be displayed on your screen:

```
Volume in drive A is TIM DUFFY
Directory of A:\

COMMAND    COM        17792       10-20-83      12:00p
CHKDSK     COM         6400       10-20-83      12:00p
FORMAT     COM         6912       10-20-83      12:00p
DISKCOPY   COM         2576       10-20-83      12:00p
MORE       COM          384       10-20-83      12:00p
SYS        COM         1680       10-20-83      12:00p
TREE       COM         1513       10-20-83      12:00p
SORT       EXE         1408       10-20-83      12:00p
ANSI       SYS         1664       10-20-83      12:00p
WP                    <DIR>        3-29-89      12:05a
DB                    <DIR>        3-29-89      12:05a
SS                    <DIR>        3-29-89      12:05a
       12 File(s)   291840 bytes free
```

Notice that this listing shows that DOS is treating the directories as files. The original listing had nine files, but after you created the subdirectories, it has 12 files. You can differentiate a subdirectory from a file by the <DIR> message (abbreviation for directory), which is displayed in place of the extension and file size data. Notice that the date on which the subdirectory was created (the system date stored in the machine at start-up time) is also listed.

Also notice that the bytes-free entry has changed since the three subdirectories were created. Each subdirectory takes a minimum of 1K, or 1,024 characters, of storage.

The Change Directory (CD) Command Once your subdirectories have been created, you can reach a subdirectory via the CD (Change Directory) command. To move from the root directory to the database (DB) subdirectory, you enter the CD DB command. To make sure that you have moved to the right subdirectory, you can issue the DIR command to see where you are. The following output will be displayed on your monitor:

```
Volume in drive A is TIM DUFFY
Directory of A:\DB

   .           <DIR>       3-29-89      12:08a
   ..          <DIR>       3-29-89      12:08a
       2 File(s)   291840 bytes free
```

The output of this DIR command is just a bit different from the output of the root directory. Notice that the second line of this directory listing contains

A:\DB. This denotes the subdirectory that is considered by DOS to be active. You can always tell when you are at the root directory because the output of the DIR command will give the default drive followed only by a backslash, for example, A:\.

You can also use the CD command to find out where you are in a subdirectory tree, since the CD causes DOS to respond with the current active directory:

```
CD         (Command)
A:\DB      (Response)
```

If you were at the root directory, the same command would produce a different response:

```
CD
A:\
```

You can also use the CD command to leave the subdirectory and return to the directory above in the hierarchy by entering CD .. or CD\, but if you use the first option, be sure to put a space between the CD and the two periods. Entering one of these commands moves you from the current subdirectory to the directory immediately above it. In this case, if you are at the DB subdirectory, you are taken to the root directory.

The Active (Current) Directory The active (current) directory concept is especially important in a hard disk or high density disk environment. After you have moved to a subdirectory in your hard disk, you can switch the default drive to one of your diskette drives, and DOS will remember which is the active subdirectory. If you copy files from the diskette to the hard disk drive that contains the active (current) subdirectory, they will be placed in that subdirectory.

For example, suppose that your current active subdirectory is on drive B. Also suppose that you have changed your default drive from B to A but want to copy a file called MEMO.TXT back to your active subdirectory on drive B. All that is required is to enter the following command:

```
A>COPY MEMO.TXT B:
```

Since DOS remembers which is the active subdirectory, it automatically copies the file to that subdirectory.

When you are copying information from one directory to another, remember that both the directory and the filename must be used. For example, if you want to copy the FORMAT.COM file from the root directory to the DB directory, you enter the following DOS command:

```
A>COPY FORMAT.COM \DB
```

This command translates as follows: Take the file called FORMAT.COM and copy it to the DB subdirectory; use the existing name. Now, if you want to refer to the FORMAT.COM file as it exists in the DB subdirectory while you are in the root directory, enter \DB\FORMAT.COM. When you refer to files in directories other than the active directory, you must use their full names. The subdirectory is part of that name.

While remaining at the root directory, you can copy the FORMAT.COM file from the DB subdirectory to the WP subdirectory by using the following command:

```
A>COPY \DB\FORMAT.COM \WP
```

Again, you must specify all of the sending information, which in this case is the name of the subdirectory and the name of the file, and all of the receiving information, which (unless you are going to change the name of the file) is only the receiving directory. The complete name for a file, including the complete subdirectory name, is referred to as the **path.**

The TREE Command You may someday use a microcomputer system that is not familiar to you, in which case you may not know what subdirectories are on a disk or which files are in which subdirectory. Then the PC DOS TREE command will be extremely helpful. The TREE command is an external file that must reside on one of the disks. In this example, it is in the root directory. The TREE command generates the following output:

```
DIRECTORY PATH LISTING FOR VOLUME TIM DUFFY
Path: \SS
Sub-directories: None
Path: \WP
Sub-directories: None
Path: \DB
Sub-directories: None
```

This information might not be enough for you. The TREE command also has a /F parameter that lists any files found in a directory in addition to the directory name. The TREE /F command generates the following display:

```
DIRECTORY PATH LISTING FOR VOLUME TIM DUFFY
Path: \SS
Sub-directories: None
Files:           None
Path: \WP
Sub-directories: None
Files:           FORMAT.COM
Path: \DB
Sub-directories: None
Files:           FORMAT.COM
```

The Remove Directory (RD) Command Assume that the DB subdirectory is no longer needed. Since you do not want to waste the disk space taken up by this directory and its files, you want to erase it. However, the ERASE command cannot be used to remove a directory. You must use the RMDIR (RD) command. First, all files must be deleted from the directory with the ERASE *.* command. If you forget to remove any file from the subdirectory, DOS will display the following error message:

```
Invalid path, not a directory
or directory not empty
```

If you receive this error message, simply go to that directory and erase the rest of the files from it; position back to the directory above; then issue the RD command to remove the subdirectory.

PATH: EXECUTING COMMANDS WITHOUT CHANGING DIRECTORIES

Assume that you have a computer system with a hard disk (device C) and two diskette drives (devices A and B). While you are working on drive A, you want to execute the DOS command CHKDSK. This command, however, resides in the subdirectory DOSFILES that you created to hold the external DOS files. (This saves room on the root directory and also provides storage that is easy for you to remember.) The problem is that you must switch to the DOSFILES subdirectory, issue the DOS command CHKDSK, and then switch back to your current drive or directory and resume work. This process takes several Change Directory (CD) commands, which you would like to avoid.

The **PATH command** provides the capability to automatically search specified drives or directories if the desired file cannot be found in the active disk or directory. It can be used for any file with a .EXE, .COM, or .BAT file extension.

PATH Command

Function: The PATH command searches specified drives and directories for commands or batch files that are not found on the current drive or directory.
Format: `PATH [d:]path[[;[d:]path...]]`
or
`PATH;`
Type: Internal
Remarks and Examples:

The PATH command allows you to specify a list of drives and subdirectory names separated by semicolons. When you now enter a command that is not found in the current active disk or subdirectory, DOS searches the named drives and subdirectories in the sequence you entered them; the current drive or subdirectory is left unchanged.

Entering PATH with no parameters displays the current path. Entering PATH; (with only a semicolon) resets the search path to the current drive and subdirectory, which is the DOS default.

A path can be any valid series of subdirectories separated by a backslash. Each separate path must be separated by semicolons, and the search by DOS for the program or batch file will be in the order of the drives and subdirectories specified in the PATH command. If the file cannot be found in the current directory and the designated paths, a `Bad command or filename` message will appear. If you give a bad drive name or subdirectory, DOS will skip that parameter without displaying an error message.

If, in the example above, you want to tell DOS to automatically go to the DOSFILES subdirectory if it is unable to find a specified program or batch file in the active drive or subdirectory, you should give the following PATH command:

`PATH c:\dosfiles`

Now when a command is entered, DOS first searches the active disk and subdirectory; if it is unable to locate the desired program file, it searches the DOSFILES subdirectory to see if it is located there. If it finds the appropriate file, the command is executed; if it is unable to locate the file, the message `Bad command or filename` appears on the monitor.

You may want DOS to search two subdirectories for command files. For example, you might want DOS to examine the DOSFILES subdirectory and the UTILITY subdirectory as well. This is accomplished via the following command:

```
PATH c:\dosfiles;c:\utility
```

Now when a command is entered, DOS first searches the active disk or subdirectory. If it is unable to locate the desired program file, it searches the DOSFILES subdirectory to see if the file is located there; if it is not, it searches the UTILITY subdirectory. If it finds the file, the command is executed; if it is unable to locate the file, the message `Bad command or filename` appears on the monitor.

CONFIGURING YOUR SYSTEM

DOS, beginning with version 2.0, enables you to use commands that customize or configure your computer system. Any time that you start DOS via a boot operation, DOS searches the root directory of the active drive for a file named **CONFIG.SYS**. If the CONFIG.SYS file is found, DOS reads that file and uses the commands in it to customize its environment. If CONFIG.SYS is not found, DOS uses default values.

The CONFIG.SYS file can be created in a number of ways: You can use the COPY command to create it, you can use the EDLIN editor, or you can use your word processing package. This file can contain various commands, but only the commands commonly used to configure your system are covered here: ASSIGN, BREAK, BUFFERS, and FILES.

ASSIGN The **ASSIGN statement** can be used in a CONFIG.SYS file to reassign device names. You must have the ASSIGN.COM file on your boot disk.

BREAK The **BREAK option** can be either on or off and allows you to instruct DOS to check for a control break (Ctrl-Break) when a program requests DOS to perform any tasks. The default for DOS is off. If you want DOS to search for Ctrl-Break whenever it is requested, use the command BREAK = ON. This is especially useful if you wish to break out of a program compile (such an operation produces few or no standard device operations).

Format: `BREAK = [ON|OFF]`

BUFFERS The **BUFFERS option** permits you to determine the number of disk buffers that DOS is to allocate in memory when it starts (the default is two for a PC and three for an AT). A buffer is part of RAM that is used by the computer to hold information that has been read, is to be written to disk, or is to be printed.

Format: `BUFFERS = x`

The *x* represents a number between 1 and 99 and is the number of disk buffers that DOS allocates in RAM when it starts. Each of these buffers requires 512 bytes of RAM. Since DOS automatically starts with two buffers, only 1,024 bytes are used for buffers. This 1K of buffer storage may not be enough for such simple operations as looking at the directory of a diskette or a subdirectory of a hard disk, especially if there are many small files. A small number of buffers results in much shifting of data in this reserved area. Therefore, a directory listing takes much less time when more buffers are allocated in RAM.

Database applications also require more buffer space. A small number of buffers (for example, the default value 2) means that the response of the database in retrieving data from disk is going to be slow. Any database program that makes use of relative addressing (a topic to be covered later in the text) requires a larger number of buffers to increase performance.

How many buffers should you set aside? This is determined by the size of your computer and the types of processing applications that you want to perform. Since each buffer takes up 512 bytes, you probably don't want to specify 50 of them when you have a machine with only 128K of storage. Allocating too many buffers can have a negative effect on the performance of your machine. When you increase the number of buffers too much, DOS spends too much time searching the buffers for data. For most applications about 20 buffers are sufficient.

FILES The **FILES command** allows you to specify the maximum number of files that can be open at any one time (the default value assigned by DOS is 8).

Format: `FILES = x`

The *x* can be any number between 8 and 255. The default value is 8, which means that no more than eight files can be open at any one time. What does this mean to you? Any file access, whether it is a read, write, or close, is performed by telling DOS which file such a task is to be performed against.

When a file is opened, DOS reserves a fixed amount of memory called a *control block* to handle I/O for this file. The size of this area depends on the value specified in the FILES = command. A number commonly used for this option is 15. This is especially valid when you are using a program, such as dBASE III Plus, that allows you to have several data files open at any one time.

Creating the CONFIG.SYS File One of the easiest ways to create a CONFIG.SYS file is to use the COPY command of DOS. This is accomplished by issuing the COPY CON:CONFIG.SYS command. This command places you in the line-by-line editor of DOS, and you can enter any commands that you want. Be sure, however, that the command is correct before you press the Enter key, since you cannot go back and correct any errors. When you have finished entering the desired commands, depress the F6 key (a ^Z appears) to indicate to DOS that you have finished.

The following lines represent the commands necessary to create a CONFIG.SYS file that will set the number of buffers to 20 and the number of files to 15, and that will create a 256K RAM disk with 256 byte sectors and a directory containing 64 entries.

```
COPY CON:CONFIG.SYS
BUFFERS = 20
FILES = 15
DEVICE = VDISK.SYS 256 256 64^Z
```

CHAPTER REVIEW

Three advanced topics are covered in this chapter: batch file commands, directory commands, and commands used for configuring the system.

Batch files allow you to save DOS commands to a file with a .BAT file extension and then execute those commands by entering the name of the batch file. The commands in the batch file are executed one at a time by DOS as though you were entering them from the keyboard.

There are two types of batch files: The first type is AUTOEXEC.BAT, and the second type is a file with a .BAT file extension. The major difference between the two types of files is that an AUTOEXEC.BAT file is automatically executed by DOS when the boot process has finished and a regular batch file must be invoked by entering the name of the file.

Directories and subdirectories are used to divide disk storage space into functional units. This allows you to place all word processing files in one directory, all spreadsheet files in another directory, and all data management files in still another directory. Directories are most appropriate on a hard disk but can be used as easily on diskettes. The major advantage of directories, besides allowing you to group similar files, is that the file number limitations that DOS places on the root directory can be avoided by building a subdirectory.

A number of directory commands are available in DOS. The MKDIR (MD) command allows you to build a directory. The CHDIR (CD) allows you to move in a downward or upward direction from one directory to another. Once all files have been erased from a directory, the RMDIR (RD) command can be used to delete a directory.

The CONFIG.SYS file can be used to configure your system. The CONFIG.SYS file can contain instructions to DOS on how many files to have open at one time. It can also provide information to DOS about how many disk buffers for receiving disk I/O to have active at any one time. The CONFIG.SYS file can also contain the VDISK command used to construct a RAM disk. The instructions contained in the CONFIG.SYS file are used by DOS during the boot process to configure the system.

KEY TERMS AND CONCEPTS

ASSIGN statement
batch file
BREAK option
BUFFERS option
CHDIR (CD)
CONFIG.SYS
COPY CON:
directory
FILES command
MKDIR (MD)
path
PATH command
REM
RMDIR (RD)
root directory
subdirectory
TREE

CHAPTER QUIZ

Multiple Choice

1. Which of the following statements about batch files is true?
    a. Batch files are automatically executed by DOS.
    b. Batch files contain special instructions in binary for DOS.
    c. DOS automatically searches the root directory of the system disk from which the boot process occurred for an AUTOEXEC.BAT file.

d. A batch file can only be named AUTOEXEC.BAT.
e. None of the above statements is true.

2. A batch file cannot contain
   a. frequently executed DOS commands.
   b. commands needed upon booting the computer.
   c. commands that are used to configure the system by setting up disk I/O buffers.
   d. commands used to start a software package.
   e. All of the above commands can be in a batch file.

3. A root directory is
   a. the first directory created to hold a subdirectory's files.
   b. the first directory that you make on disk.
   c. a directory that has subdirectories beneath it.
   d. the directory that is automatically created by DOS when it initializes a disk.
   e. None of the above statements is true.

4. Which of the following directory commands is used to display your location in a subdirectory?
   a. MD
   b. CD
   c. RD
   d. TREE
   e. None of the above

5. Which command is used to create more buffers in RAM using the CONFIG.SYS file?
   a. RAMDISK
   b. VDISK
   c. BUFFERS
   d. RAMBUFFER
   e. None of the above

True/False

6. The CONFIG.SYS file is located and the commands in it are executed any time that you start a new program.

7. Batch commands are executed one at a time by DOS.

8. The root directory of a disk is always limited by the number of files that can be stored in it.

9. Most of the DOS commands that deal with disk directories are internal commands.

10. Once the standard drivers have been loaded by DOS, DOS searches the boot disk to see if a CONFIG.SYS file resides on it and finishes the start-up process

Answers

1. c   2. c   3. d   4. b   5. c   6. f   7. t   8. t   9. t   10. t

Exercises

1. Define or describe each of the following:
   active directory
   root directory
   batch file
   file path

2. The _____ batch file is automatically executed once the boot process has finished.

3. The _____ command is used to build a batch file without invoking a word processor.

4. A batch file can be interrupted by entering the _____ series of keystrokes.

5. The _____ key is depressed once you have finished entering the batch file from DOS.

6. The character that is used to indicate replaceable parameters is _____.

7. The directory created automatically on any disk device during the format process is called the _____ directory.

8. A double sided 5.25-inch disk can store a maximum of _____ files without using directories.

9. Directories are created by using the _____ DOS command.

10. Directories are erased by using the _____ DOS command.

11. Before a directory can be removed, all files must be removed using the DOS _____ command.

12. The directory command that is part of PC DOS but not MS DOS is the _____ command.

13. A directory is actually viewed by DOS as a _____ of data.

14. When you issue a DIR command, a directory has a _____ entry in place of the file extension and file size entries.

15. The _____ command is used to find out where you are in a series of directories and subdirectories.

16. The file named _____ contains instructions that tell DOS how to configure the system.

17. The _____ command tells DOS how much memory to use for disk I/O operations.

18. The _____ command tells DOS how many files can be open at any one time.

COMPUTER EXERCISES

The following exercises are necessary to create files that are needed later in the text. Any time that you see the ^Z entry you are to depress the F6 function key.

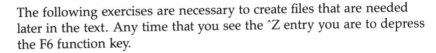

1. For running the student version of VP-Planner Plus, create a batch file called RUNVP.BAT using the following steps:

```
COPY CON:RUNVP.BAT
DATE
VPP^Z
```

2. On the system disk that you use to boot your computer, place the following CONFIG.SYS file. This diskette with the CONFIG.SYS file should then be used to boot your computer any time that you want to use dBASE III Plus.

```
COPY CON:CONFIG.SYS
FILES = 15
BUFFERS = 20^Z
```

PART II

SPREADSHEETS USING LOTUS 1-2-3

CHAPTER 3

FUNDAMENTALS OF SPREADSHEETS AND LOTUS 1-2-3

CHAPTER OBJECTIVES

After completing this chapter, you should be able to:

- **List concepts common to worksheets**
- **Define common spreadsheet terminology**
- **List feaures that are common to all spreadsheet packages**
- **List the three parts of Lotus 1-2-3**
- **Understand the various aspects of the 1-2-3 screen**
- **Manipulate the 1-2-3 pointer**
- **Enter various commands using / keystrokes as well as various key combinations**
- **Enter a 1-2-3 worksheet**

INTRODUCTION TO SPREADSHEETS

The spreadsheet is the piece of software that has single-handedly caused American business to take the microcomputer seriously as a problem-solving tool. An electronic spreadsheet is simply the electronic equivalent of the accounting worksheet. Both the electronic worksheet and the accounting worksheet consist of a matrix composed of rows and columns that allow a person to organize information in an easy-to-understand format.

The terms *spreadsheet* and *worksheet* can be distinguished as follows: A **spreadsheet** is the set of program instructions, such as VisiCalc or Lotus 1-2-3, that produces a worksheet; a **worksheet** is a model or representation of reality that is created using a spreadsheet software package. Spreadsheets can be used in completing any data manipulation involving numbers and text that is usually performed with pencil, paper, and calculator. Uses of spreadsheets in business include:

- Budget preparation
- Working trial balances
- Business modeling
- Sales forecasting
- Investment analysis
- Payroll
- Real estate management
- Taxes
- Investment proposals

Electronic spreadsheet software greatly improves the user's accuracy, efficiency, and productivity. Once a worksheet has been prepared, other options ("what if" alternatives) can be easily considered by simply making the appropriate changes and instructing the spreadsheet to recalculate all entries to reflect these changes. The user can thus spend more time on creative decision making.

WHY USE SPREADSHEET SOFTWARE?

Suppose that you have a friend, Ed, who owns a grocery store with the following departments: Deli, Bakery, Liquor, Grocery, Produce, and Meat. It's the end of the year, and Ed would like to compare the sales of the various departments for last year and this year, keeping track of the overall change in sales (either positive or negative) and the percentage change in sales for each of the departments.

You have volunteered to help Ed develop this report manually. To ease the calculation process and ensure that the correct numbers are included in each calculation, you have decided to use some standard lined paper divided into a number of columns. This type of paper is often referred to as worksheet paper.

In designing the report, you decide that the easiest way to present the data is to have the names of the departments along the vertical axis of the report and the column headings along the horizontal axis. You can now enter last year's and this year's sales figures for each department (see Figure 3.1).

Once you have entered the data properly, you can use your calculator to compute the change in sales from last year to this year by subtracting the sales for last year from the sales for this year and then record the difference for each department in the Change column.

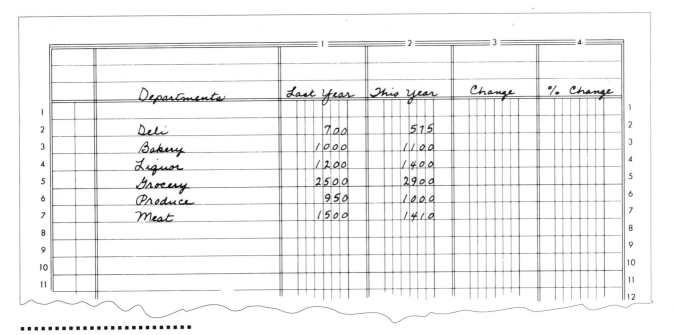

Figure 3.1
Manual worksheet containing labels and sales figures

Figure 3.2
Manual worksheet with Change column calculated

In many business applications, negative numbers are represented within parentheses rather than with a minus sign. For example, to calculate the change for the Deli department, you enter the equation 575 − 700 in your calculator and receive the answer −125. Enter the −125 as (125) on your report. Once you have finished with all of the Change calculations, your report should look like that in Figure 3.2.

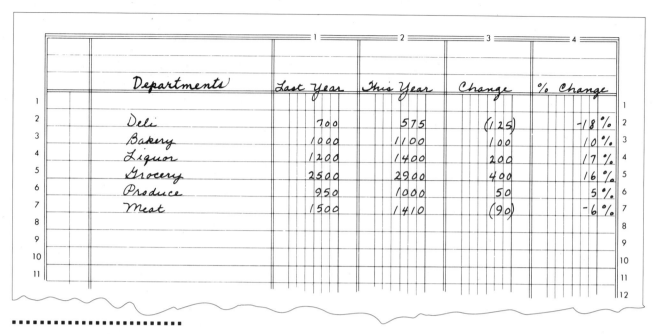

Figure 3.3
Manual worksheet with % Change calculation results shown

You are now ready to compute the % Change entries. This is accomplished by dividing the Change figure by the Last Year sales entry for each department and converting the result to a percent. For example, to arrive at the % Change for the Deli department, you must divide −125 by 700. The result, −.1786, must now be converted to a whole percent. Since percentages are really just decimal fractions, the value to be placed in your report is −18%. After you have performed the just-described steps for each department, your report should look like that in Figure 3.3.

You must now generate a total for each of the four columns containing numbers: Last Year, This Year, Change, and % Change (calculate Change and % Change as before). This involves adding all of the numbers in a column together, recording the sum value, clearing the calculator, and starting over for the next column of numbers. Once you have generated the column totals, your report should appear like that in Figure 3.4.

Your report for Ed is now completed and you can present it to him to use in his decision making. What if, however, the sales for three departments change? Then, to use the report effectively, you would have to entirely redo it. Or what if Ed wants you to determine the impact of a 10% increase in this year's sales for each department? The ability to respond quickly to changes and reflect them in a report, as well as to respond to various "what if" questions, is what gives a spreadsheet package its tremendous power.

Suppose that instead of building this report manually you use a computerized spreadsheet package. The computer-generated report will appear to be amazingly similar to your manual report. All of the column headings, department names, and sales figures for each department have to be entered. The calculation instructions (formulas) on how the spreadsheet package is to manipulate the figures are also entered. However, since the instructions are the same within a column, once a formula is entered, you can reuse it by copying it down the column. For example, you enter a formula for calculating the Change data once and then copy that formula down the column. You do the same for the % Change formula. All that is left is to tell your spreadsheet

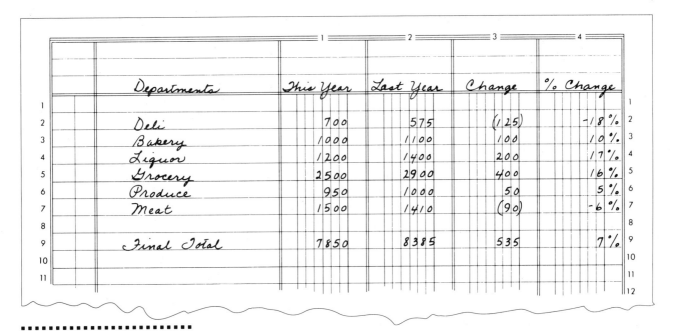

Figure 3.4
Manual worksheet with totals shown

package to calculate the total for the Last Year column of numbers. Since the other columns also have to be summed, you can copy the formula to them.

The real advantage of using a spreadsheet is that since it is formula driven, when a change is made to any of the sales figures, the spreadsheet automatically recalculates the report and generates the appropriate answers without any additional work on your part. Spreadsheet software thus makes answering "what if" questions easy.

SPREADSHEET SYNTAX

Each spreadsheet package allows the user to identify a unique address or **cell** at the intersection of a row and a column. A **row** is on a horizontal axis; a **column** is on a vertical axis. Worksheet cells are referred to by their Column/Row designation, and each may contain a label, a number, or a formula.

A **label** is alphanumeric text used to provide headings for the rows and columns, to make the worksheet easier to understand. Labels may be numeric (for example, quarters 1, 2, 3, and 4) or alphabetic (for example, the word *quarter*). A **number** is a numeric value entered in a cell. It may be either a constant or a variable; in the latter case it is the result of some type of mathematical calculation.

The **formula** contained in a cell creates relationships between values in other specified cells. For example, if the contents of cells E1, E2, E3, and E4 were to be added together, with the result to be placed in cell E7, the formula +E1 + E2 + E3 + E4 would be placed in cell E7. Formulas used in cells can be more complex than just simple sums; they can contain financial calculations such as net present value or statistical expressions such as variance or standard deviation.

Understanding that formulas allow computations based on the value in one cell to determine values in other cells makes spreadsheets easy to use. It is imperative that anyone wishing to make effective use of spreadsheets be able to express relationships in terms of values—for example, gross margin = sales − cost of goods sold, or taxes = gross income × 35 %. Once such a relationship has been defined and placed in a numeric format, any situation involving that relationship can be analyzed via an electronic worksheet.

One major strength of the electronic spreadsheet is that it presents and works with data in the familiar tabular format that is used to present or depict almost all data. A personal budget, for example, uses this tabular format: The budget categories are placed in a column, and the various time periods are placed as headings across the top row. Moreover, the spreadsheet is able to project and evaluate numerous alternatives to a single plan—the ubiquitous "what if" form of analysis—making it an important aid in decision making. The interrelationship of the cells enables the viewer to see immediately what effect changing the contents of one or more cells has on the rest of the worksheet.

Spreadsheets can be used in two basic ways: with your own worksheet, if you have a unique application or just have the time and want the practice (and if the application to be modeled is not very complex); or with a template. A **template** is much the same as an application program; someone has already done all the logical planning, designing, and implementing involved in building the template. Consequently, the individual using the template only has to enter some data and receive the results.

VisiCalc, an acronym for Visible Calculator, was the first spreadsheet introduced for microcomputers. It was designed by Dan Bricklin and Robert Frankston at a time when Bricklin was a student in the Harvard MBA program; he became interested in developing VisiCalc after growing tired of playing "what if" games in case studies that primarily required financial analysis. At the time, some software packages available for mainframe computers were capable of performing this type of manipulation, but they were difficult to use. One apocryphal story has Bricklin discussing the possible application of such a concept to the newly emerging microcomputers with one of his MBA professors and being told that the idea would never be marketable.

Another person associated with VisiCalc was Dan Flystra, also a student in the MBA program at Harvard, who purchased the marketing rights to the product and founded Personal Software—later renamed VisiCorp (now defunct).

VisiCalc was originally designed to run on the Apple II computer and was responsible for many purchases of Apple computers by business. Since the introduction of the program, many different spreadsheet packages have been produced for microcomputers. Many of these reflect tremendous improvements in power and capability over the original VisiCalc. Probably the best known of these is the Lotus 1-2-3 spreadsheet program. Just as VisiCalc was responsible for business purchases of Apple microcomputers, Lotus 1-2-3 was responsible for many business purchases of IBM PC microcomputers.

Lotus 1-2-3 is the progeny of Mitch Kapor, a colorful character who taught himself programming after a number of other job endeavors. His first spreadsheet success was VisiTrend/Plot, a statistical and graphics package that he designed and programmed; it was purchased by VisiCorp and was capable of receiving data from VisiCalc.

With the money he earned from the sale of VisiTrend/Plot, plus some venture capital, Kapor set out to beat VisiCorp at its own game. He realized that the VisiCalc–VisiTrend/Plot hookup was cumbersome, since it required passing data, leaving one program, and then starting the other. He felt that this whole process could be made transparent to the end user.

Kapor and his staff designed Lotus 1-2-3 specifically for the IBM PC microcomputer; it was introduced early in 1983. A tremendous publicity campaign (and the superior quality of the software) helped Lotus 1-2-3 become an immediate success in the business community.

PROBLEM-SOLVING STEPS USING SPREADSHEETS

In approaching a problem, especially a complex problem, you should try to develop a plan for handling it as early in the process as possible. Much additional work can be avoided by prior planning; your end product will look better, and you will avoid redoing work. The planning process steps are (1) determining the purpose, (2) planning, (3) building and testing, and (4) documenting.

Determining the Purpose The first step is to determine exactly what the purpose or goal of the worksheet is. In other words, what do you want it to do for you? What inputs will you need to provide to the worksheet? What outputs do you want the spreadsheet to generate? Are printed reports needed to make the information provided by the worksheet useful?

Planning The second step is to plan a blueprint of your worksheet on paper. This blueprint should maintain the same rectangular format presented by the screen you are using and should include all screens that will have explanations to you or other users. Remember that you may be using this spreadsheet only once a year and may not remember all the nuances of your spreadsheet logic after such a long separation. You should also plan how you will manipulate your data.

Building and Testing The third step is to build and test your worksheet. If you have planned everything properly, this step should go smoothly. Testing the spreadsheet involves making sure that it manipulates the data correctly. A lot of things can go wrong—for instance, a formula might reference an incorrect cell, or it might be entered incorrectly—but a number of packages that you can process against a spreadsheet help in this procedure. Two of them, Spreadsheet Auditor and Docucalc, display the spreadsheet (as it appears on the screen), the cell values, and the corresponding formulas within cells used to manipulate data.

Documenting The final step is to finish the documentation for using the worksheet. Some of this documentation is included within the worksheet itself, but many other concepts may have to be covered to allow a user other than the worksheet's author to operate it effectively. In addition, limitations on inputs and outputs must be communicated, and, if the worksheet is to be used as a template within an organization, its date of creation and its author's name and telephone number must be provided.

INTRODUCTION TO LOTUS 1-2-3

The **Lotus 1-2-3** software package, as the name implies, has three logical and totally integrated parts: spreadsheet, data management, and graphing. **Integration** means that you do not have to leave the spreadsheet program, for instance, to get to the graphing or data management programs.

PARTS OF 1-2-3

Spreadsheet The extremely powerful **Lotus spreadsheet** manipulates the tabular accountinglike data. You can enter numbers, labels, or formulas into the worksheet. For example, you can list 12 numbers in a column and define one cell to hold the sum of those numbers; thereafter, when any one of these numbers is changed, the sum is automatically updated to reflect the change.

Data Management The **data management feature** of Lotus 1-2-3 allows you to sort, summarize, and extract (make reports of) portions of the individual records contained in a file. The major difference between this type of data management and other types is that in Lotus 1-2-3 the entire file is contained in a worksheet.

Graphics The **graphics feature** allows you to take information that you have entered in a worksheet and display it graphically to the screen (assuming you have graphics screen capability) or to the printer. You can display information in the form of a pie chart, bar chart, stacked bar chart, line graph, or XY graph. A regular monochrome monitor, however, will not display a graph; rather, the computer will simply beep.

LOTUS 1-2-3 ADD-INS

Add-in software packages provide users of Lotus 1-2-3 with capabilities that are not found in the spreadsheet package. These add-in packages were introduced beginning with Release 2.01 of Lotus 1-2-3 and were especially emphasized with the introduction of Release 2.2 of 1-2-3. Two of these packages are provided with any purchase of Release 2.2.

Allways Allways is a spreadsheet publishing add-in for 1-2-3 that allows you to create presentation-quality printouts of worksheets and graphics. It also allows you to merge text and graphics on one page. Chapter 10 of this text is devoted to this particular package.

Macro Library Manager This feature allows you to create libraries of macros that can be incorporated in your worksheet. You can now easily create a macro in one worksheet and then use it in another.

STARTING LOTUS 1-2-3

Lotus 1-2-3 is a menu-driven software package, meaning that lists of options (*menus*) are displayed for you to choose from. Lotus 1-2-3 allows you to make a selection by either entering the first character of the option at the keyboard or positioning the pointer using a Right or Left Arrow key and then depressing Enter.

Starting Lotus 1-2-3 is a straightforward process. Simply place the Lotus system disk in disk drive A and your data disk in disk drive B. Turn on the computer (if the computer is already on, simply enter LOTUS). If you are using a computer with a fixed disk, issue the appropriate CD command (i.e. CD\ 123 or CD 123). The computer will then display the **Lotus Access System** (see Figure 3.5). This is the first example of a 1-2-3 menu structure. The first line, with the 1-2-3, PrintGraph, Translate, and other entries, is the menu line containing the various options from which to choose. The second line contains a description of the highlighted menu option. Since the highlighted option is 1-2-3, the message Use 1-2-3 is displayed. As you move the pointer from one entry to another via the Right and Left Arrow keys, the message changes to reflect the new, highlighted menu option. At this time, either enter a 1 or depress the Enter key. After some disk processing, a copyright screen will

Figure 3.5
The Lotus Access System

```
1-2-3  PrintGraph   Translate   Install   Exit
Use 1-2-3

              1-2-3 Access System
              Copyright  1986, 1989
           Lotus Development Corporation
                All Rights Reserved
                   Release 2.2

The Access System lets you choose 1-2-3, PrintGraph, the Translate utility,
and the Install program from the menu at the top of this screen.  If
you're using a two-diskette system, the Access System may prompt you to
change disks.  Follow the instructions below to start a program.

o  Use → or ← to move the menu pointer (the highlighted rectangle
   at the top of the screen) to the program you want to use.

o  Press ENTER to start the program.

You can also start a program by typing the first character of its name.

Press HELP (F1) for more information.
```

Figure 3.6
1-2-3 copyright screen

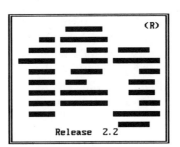

```
                           Copyright  1985, 1989
                        Lotus Development Corporation
                           All Rights Reserved
                              1S00064-0028323

Licensing Information:

   User Name: Tim Duffy
Company Name: Personal Copy of Lotus 1-2-3

         Use, duplication, or sale of this software, except as
         described in the Lotus License Agreement, is strictly
              prohibited.  Violators may be prosecuted.
```

appear indicating that you are in Lotus 1-2-3 (see Figure 3.6). After a short wait, the screen depicted in Figure 3.7 will be displayed, and the directory of the default disk drive will be read by the system.

LOTUS 1-2-3 SCREEN

At first, the worksheet screen may appear to contain little, but looks in this case are deceiving. The following pieces are part of the worksheet screen: control panel, mode indicator, border, worksheet with pointer/cursor, current date and time, error message area, and indicators.

Figure 3.7

The Lotus 1-2-3 worksheet screen

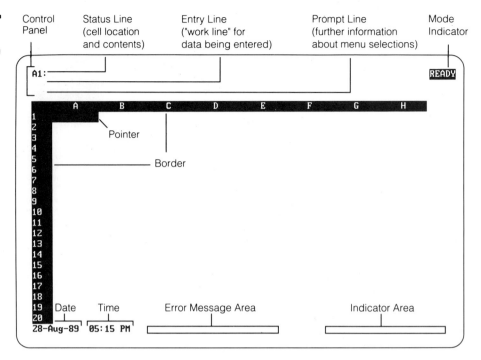

Control Panel The **control panel** is contained on the top three lines of your screen and consists of (1) the status line, (2) the entry line, and (3) the prompt line. The **status line** tells where you are, displaying the cell address, data format (if any), cell width, and cell contents; information is given about how the data in that particular cell are being processed by Lotus and about whether the cell contains a label, a value, or a formula. The status line has the following format:

The cell address is always followed by a colon—A1:.

Information about a cell formatted using the / Range Format command appears in parentheses—(C2).

A cell that has a column width different from the rest of the worksheet appears within brackets—[15].

The protection status appears. If a PR appears in the cell, you cannot change this cell's contents. If a U appears, this cell's contents can be changed.

The cell contents appear to the right of any of the above entries.

The **entry line** corresponds to a "scratch" area that contains any data you happen to enter. It also contains any "pre-entered" information destined for the cell location given in the status line. This information is not placed in either the cell or the status line until the Enter key is pressed. The entry line may also contain a menu of options for performing various operations on your worksheet. The Main Menu can be invoked any time by entering the slash (/) command.

The **prompt line** contains further options or an explanation of a specific command when a 1-2-3 menu is displayed.

Mode Indicator The **mode indicator,** in the upper right-hand corner of the screen, displays status information about what 1-2-3 is doing. The following are some mode indicators you will see while you are working in this book:

READY	Lotus 1-2-3 is waiting for you to tell it to do something.
VALUE	You are entering a number or formula to be contained in a cell.
LABEL	You are entering text information to be contained in a cell.
EDIT	You are changing the contents of a cell via the edit feature of 1-2-3.
POINT	You are pointing to a cell or to a range of cells.
MENU	You have a menu displayed before you and are selecting from it.
HELP	You are using the 1-2-3 help feature.
ERROR	Something went wrong, and 1-2-3 is waiting for you to depress the Enter or Esc key to acknowledge the error.
WAIT	1-2-3 is calculating the spreadsheet or performing a read/write operation and cannot accept more commands.
FIND	1-2-3 is using its data management feature to perform a find operation.
FILES	You are using a command that displays a listing of files.
LEARN	You entered the **Learn command** (Alt + F5) to turn on the Macro Learn feature to record your keystrokes in a specific grouping of cells.
MEM	This indicator tells you that the amount of unused computer memory has dropped below 4096 bytes. If you continue to enter additional data in this worksheet, you may receive a "Memory full" error message.
OVR	The Ins key is activated and results in characters entered from the keyboard that will replace existing characters in the cell.
RO	This worksheet has a read-only status. This means you cannot save any changes you make unless some individual on the network that has write privileges saves this worksheet and thereby allows you to have write privileges.
UNDO	This indicator tells you that the Undo feature of 1-2-3 is activated, which allows you to recover from errors committed in building or using the worksheet. This feature will be covered later in this chapter.

Border The **border** labels the rows and columns of your worksheet. The columns are labeled with letters of the alphabet (A, B, C, and so on), and the rows are labeled with numbers (1, 2, 3, and so on).

Worksheet The **Lotus worksheet** contains whatever space is available to the user for problem solving. The worksheet has three key parts: cell, pointer, and window. As was noted earlier, a cell is the intersection of a row and column and is referred to by its cell address Column/Row. For example, B5 refers to the cell located at the intersection of column B and row 5. A cell can contain either a label, a value, or a formula.

The **pointer,** also sometimes referred to as the cursor, is the reverse-video bar (light background with dark characters). Its width depends on the width of the cell being referenced. The contents of the referenced cell are displayed in the status line of the control panel.

The 1-2-3 worksheet is large compared to many other spreadsheet packages. It contains 256 columns (A, B, C, D, . . . , IV) and 8,192 rows for a grand total of 2,097,152 cells. How large a piece of paper would you need to hold this size spreadsheet? If each cell were ¼ inch high and 1 inch wide, a piece of paper that could hold all of these rows and columns would have to be 170.6 feet high and 21.3 feet wide. The 1-2-3 worksheet is, indeed, large.

It goes without saying that all these cells cannot be displayed at one time on your small display screen. Instead, only small, rectangular sections of these 2,097,152 cells can be displayed at one time. The display, referred to as the **window,** always has 20 rows; the number of columns displayed depends on the column width.

Current Date and Time The **current date** and **current time** are displayed here. Remember that for this information to be correct you must respond to the DATE and TIME prompts when you boot the computer system.

Error Message Indicator **Error messages** appear in the lower left-hand corner of the screen, giving a brief explanation of what has gone wrong. They are accompanied by a beep from the computer when a Lotus 1-2-3 rule has been broken. After you have read the message and wish to return control to the worksheet, simply depress the Esc or Enter key.

Indicators The old IBM keyboard does not tell you whether the Scroll Lock, Caps Lock, and Num Lock keys are on or off. The Lotus 1-2-3 **indicators** for each of these provide this information. If one of these keys is on, a message in reverse video will be displayed in the lower right-hand corner of the screen. Other indicators, CALC and UNDO, will be discussed later.

NAVIGATING AROUND THE 1-2-3 WORKSHEET

Because Lotus 1-2-3 was designed specifically for the old IBM PC, it makes full use of all the keys on the keyboard—an especially important feature when it comes to moving the pointer quickly around the worksheet. Most pointer movement commands are accomplished by using the ten-key pad found on the right-hand side of the keyboard; Lotus 1-2-3 automatically places these keys in cursor movement mode rather than in numeric mode. The movement keys work as follows:

- The **Down Arrow** moves the pointer down one cell position (down one row).

- The **Up Arrow** moves the pointer up one cell position (up one row).
- The **Right Arrow** moves the pointer to the right one cell position (to the right one column).
- The **Left Arrow** moves the pointer to the left one cell position (to the left one column).
- The **Pg Up key** moves the pointer up 20 lines (one page) in its present column.
- The **Pg Dn key** moves the pointer down 20 lines (one page) in its present column.
- The **Home key** moves the pointer to cell position A1.
- The **End key,** when entered prior to an Arrow key, positions the pointer in the same direction as the Arrow key at the next nonblank boundary cell. For example, a worksheet will typically have blocks of cells with data, followed by blocks of blank, empty cells that are in turn followed by other cells with data. If the pointer is in a blank/empty region and the End key is depressed, followed by an Arrow key, the pointer will be moved to the first nonblank cell. If the same command sequence is entered again, the pointer moves to the last nonblank cell in that block. Entering the same command sequence moves the pointer to the next nonblank area. When there are no longer any nonblank cells remaining in one direction of pointer movement, one of 1-2-3's boundaries will have been reached (for example, row 8,192 or column IV).
- The **Tab key,** located above the Ctrl key, moves the pointer to the right one screen (72 characters) at a time. The **Tab plus Shift keys** move the pointer to the left one screen (72 characters) at a time.

The Tab key function can also be performed with two other sets of keystrokes:

Moving to the right one screen at a time (also referred to as a *big right*): Ctrl + Right Arrow

Moving to the left one screen at a time (also referred to as a *big left*): Ctrl + Left Arrow

The above keys move or skip the cursor across the worksheet. In contrast, the **Scroll Lock key** causes the worksheet to move under the cursor, rather than causing the cursor to move across the worksheet.

HOW LOTUS 1-2-3 USES OTHER KEYS

Figure 3.8 shows where the various special-purpose keys are located on the IBM PC keyboard and what they are used for. The remaining special-purpose keys work as follows:

- The **/ key** is used to invoke the 1-2-3 Main Menu. The Main Menu (see Figure 3.9) is used to invoke other menus or commands. The various menus used in 1-2-3 account for over 115 different commands. The menus and the command prompts appear in the control panel of the worksheet screen. A menu item can be selected by positioning the pointer to that item and pressing the Enter key or by entering the first character of the command. When you are dealing with a menu item, the message in the prompt line describes the command or displays a

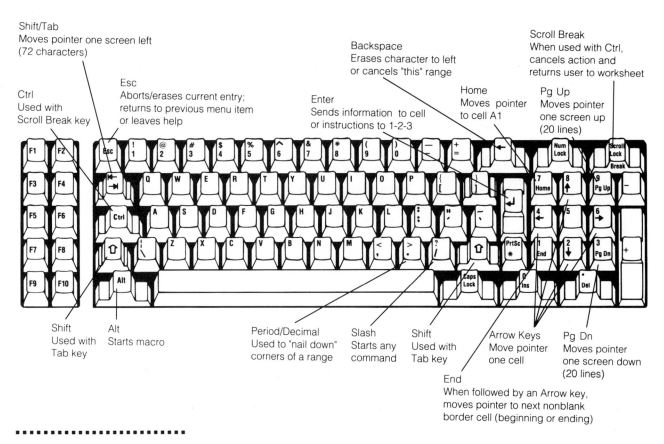

Figure 3.8
IBM PC keyboard labeled for use with Lotus 1-2-3

submenu that will be executed if this option is selected. A menu item once selected may invoke another menu or may execute a command. The various menus contained in 1-2-3 can be seen in Appendix A.

- The **Esc key** is used to back out of a command sequence if you are in a menu. If you are entering data in a cell, anything that appears on the entry line is simply erased when you depress Esc, and the original contents of the cell (if any) are left unchanged.

- The **Ctrl plus Scroll Break keys** are used to cancel any action taking place and return the user to the worksheet. This key sequence can be used to cancel printing, sorting, or any other 1-2-3 operation.

- The **Macro (Alt) key** lets you give letter keys alternative meanings. If you find yourself repeating certain sequences of keystrokes, you can have 1-2-3 save these keystrokes in a **keyboard macro;** then you can direct 1-2-3 to execute them by depressing the Macro key along with the coded one-letter name.

- The **Enter key** tells 1-2-3 that you have finished typing and want to send the information to the cell or give 1-2-3 an instruction.

- The **Backspace key** deletes the character to the left of the pointer and can also cancel the current range.

- The **function keys** are the 10 keys positioned together on the left-hand side or the 12 keys along the top of the keyboard. They are used to perform specially defined 1-2-3 functions with only one keystroke. The 10 function keys perform the following tasks in Lotus 1-2-3:

Figure 3.9
The Lotus 1-2-3 Main Menu invoked by pressing the / key

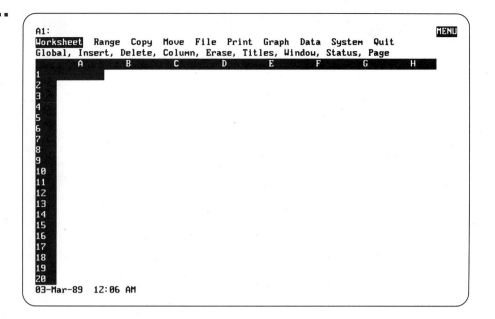

F1	Help	Displays a help screen
F2	Edit	Edits the contents of a cell
F3	Name	Displays defined range names
F4	Abs	Defines a cell as an absolute value
F5	GoTo	Moves the pointer to a cell
F6	Window	Jumps from one window to another
F7	Query	Performs the last query sequence
F8	Table	Performs the last table sequence
F9	Calc	Recalculates all the formulas in the worksheet
F10	Graph	Generates the graph last defined

The function keys can also be used in conjunction with the Alt key. This means that instead of being able to perform only 10 tasks, you now can issue 20 different instructions, using the following commands.

Compose (Alt + F1)	This command can be used in READY, EDIT, and LABEL modes to create special characters that cannot be entered using the regular keys of the keyboard. You can refer to the Lotus 1-2-3 documentation to see these characters.
Step (Alt + F2)	This command turns on STEP mode and allows you to execute a macro a key-

Run (Alt + F3)	stroke at a time. This command is covered in depth in a later chapter. This command can be used in READY mode to display a list of range names so you can select the name of the macro you want to run. This command is covered in depth in a later chapter.
Undo (Alt + F4)	This command is used in READY mode to cancel any changes made to the worksheet since 1-2-3 was last in READY mode.
Learn (Alt + F5)	This command is used to record keystrokes entered from the keyboard as text within a cell, which can then be used as a macro. This command is covered in depth in a later chapter.
App1 (Alt + F7)	This command is used in READY mode to activate the add-in program that has been assigned to this key.
App2 (Alt + F8)	This command is used in READY mode to activate the add-in program that has been assigned to this key.
App3 (Alt + F9)	This command is used in READY mode to activate the add-in program that has been assigned to this key.
App4 (Alt + F10)	This command is used in READY mode to activate the add-in program that has been assigned to this key.

HINTS/HAZARDS — When you are issuing commands that require the Alt key, you can use the Shift key instead of the Alt key.

DATA ENTRY

Data entry is the process of placing values, labels, or formulas into the individual cells of a worksheet. A label cell can be printed or listed onto the screen, but it cannot be involved in a calculation. Therefore, you could say that the type of data stored in a cell dictates how that cell can be manipulated. The spreadsheet software must have some indication of the type of data you wish to store in a cell, and it is forced to make certain assumptions.

If you begin entering data of an alphabetic character within a cell, the spreadsheet will assume that you wish to enter **label data.** When 1-2-3 encounters alphabetic data, it automatically places a single quote (') at the beginning. This presents a problem when you are entering formula-related information, because the formula's reference to the cell location must start with an alphabetic character. You can solve the problem by placing a + symbol before the cell location, so that 1-2-3 recognizes the entry as a formula rather than as a label.

Numeric information is entered simply by typing the digits that it is composed of. [A negative number is represented by placing a minus sign (−) before the number; no such convention is needed if the number is positive.]

This presents a problem when you wish to have **numeric data** treated as a label. For example, how could the years *1984* and *1985* be presented to Lotus 1-2-3 as labels rather than numbers? Lotus 1-2-3 uses a very simple technique: In order to present *1984* as a label, all you need to do is place a single quote (') before the value to be treated as a label. For example, in this case you would enter the characters '1984 and Lotus would treat *1984* as a label.

Formulas explaining how numeric data are to be manipulated are entered as they would be processed algebraically. If the formula is entered properly, the spreadsheet will perform the operation; otherwise, an error message will be displayed in the lower left-hand corner of the screen, and the computer will beep. If this happens, the formula must be edited or reentered.

HINTS/HAZARDS   Any numbers that are entered with a label prefix are treated as text by 1-2-3 and 1-2-3 assigns a numeric value of zero to such a cell. Any calculations that reference this cell will thus generate incorrect results.

ENTERING FORMULAS

Operators   Formulas tell 1-2-3 what mathematical manipulations you want it to perform on specific cell contents. The operations that 1-2-3 can perform are invoked by using the following symbols in a formula:

```
^    Exponentiation
*    Multiplication
/    Division
+    Addition
-    Subtraction
```

Thus, to divide the contents of cell C3 by the contents of cell D3, you would enter the formula +C3/D3.

Precedence (Order of Operations)   The order in which calculations are executed is called **precedence.** Operations are always performed in the following order, left to right within a formula:

First exponentiation

Then any multiplication and division, in the order that they occur

Then any addition and subtraction, in the order that they occur

For example, the formula +A7/A1+B3*D4^3 results in the following:

1. The contents of cell D4 are raised to the third power.
2. The contents of cell A7 are divided by the contents of cell A1.
3. The contents of cell B3 are multiplied by the result of step 1.
4. The result of step 2 is added to the result of step 3.

Parentheses and Precedence   Parentheses can be used to override the above order of operations. At the most general level, operations inside parentheses are performed before those outside; within the parentheses, however, the order of operations is the same as that listed above. When multiple sets of parentheses are used, the operations within the innermost set are executed, followed by those within the next set.

For example, the formula + C3 − (A3 + D3) results in the following:

1. The contents of cell A3 are added to the contents of cell D3.
2. The result of step 1 is subtracted from the contents of cell C3.

For a more complex example, the formula +D3*D4+(C7+E4^3*F6 −(G6/F7+D3^2)+A1) results in the following:

1. The calculation (G6/F7+D3^2) is performed first, because these operations reside in the innermost set of parentheses.
    a. The contents of cell D3 are raised to the second power.
    b. The contents of cell G6 are divided by the contents of cell F7.
    c. The result of step 1a is added to the result of step 1b.
2. The formula now logically appears as +D3*D4+(C7+E4^3*F6 −step1+A1), and the next part of the formula to be executed is (C7+E4^3*F6−step1+A1).
    a. The contents of cell E4 are raised to the third power.
    b. The result of step 2a is multiplied by the contents of cell F6.
    c. The contents of cell C7 are added to the result of step 2b.
    d. The result of step 1 is subtracted from the result of step 2c.
    e. The result of step 2d is added to the contents of A1.
3. The formula now logically appears as +D3*D4+step2.
    a. The contents of cell D3 are multiplied by the contents of cell D4.
    b. The result of step 3a is now added to the result of step 2 to obtain the final result.

CIRCULAR REFERENCES

One problem that almost all users of a spreadsheet like 1-2-3 encounter when entering formulas is the circular reference. A **circular reference** is a formula in a cell that, directly or indirectly, refers back to that same cell. A circular reference in a worksheet is indicated when a CIRC message appears at the bottom of the screen. When the circular reference is corrected, the CIRC message disappears. A circular reference would appear on the screen if the following formula appeared in cell B12:

@SUM(B1.B12)

The circular reference appears because the cell B12 is an operand in the operation as well as the cell designated to hold the answer. A cell cannot be both.

BUILT-IN FUNCTIONS

Built-in functions are processes or formulas that have already been programmed into the spreadsheet software package. These functions save the user a tremendous amount of effort and tedium in writing all the statements needed to perform some type of mathematical manipulation. In the Lotus spreadsheet package, a function is designated by the @ symbol. To sum the values contained in cells A3, B3, C3, D3, and E3 and place the result in cell G3, the following formula would be required in cell G3: `@SUM(A3.E3)`. Some of the more common Lotus 1-2-3 functions follow:

Mathematical	Absolute value, arc cosine, arc sine, arc tangent, cosine, log, exponent, pi, random, round, integer, sine, square root, tangent
Logical	True, false, if/then/else
Financial	Internal rate of return, net present value, future value of an annuity, present value, payment
Statistical	Average, minimum, maximum, standard deviation, variance

CORRECTING ERRORS ON THE WORKSHEET

There are basically five correction methods, plus one start-over method, for dealing with errors you've made while using the Lotus 1-2-3 package:

1. If you make an error while typing something in the "scratch" area of the control panel, use the Backspace key to erase the mistake, and then retype any deleted data.
2. If you have entered something in the worksheet that you want to replace with other data, move the pointer back to that cell, type the new data, and hit Enter. The new entry will take the place of the old.
3. If you have entered data in a cell of the worksheet that you want to blank out, position the pointer to that cell, depress the key sequence /RE, and hit Enter to erase the contents of that one cell.
4. If you start to enter data for a cell and then change your mind, simply depress the Esc key, and the data will not be entered in the cell. If you are inside a menu, you can depress the Esc key to get back to the previous level. If you want to return to the worksheet, depress Ctrl and Break simultaneously.
5. Suppose a cell that has an error in it contains a very long formula or label. You don't want to reenter all of the information because you will more than likely commit some other error in doing so. In this type of situation, you should depress the **Edit key (F2)**. The Edit key places the cell contents on the entry line as well as on the status line. You can now use the following keys and perform "word processing" on the cell contents displayed on the entry line.

Home	Places the cursor at the beginning of the line
End	Places the cursor at the end of the line
Del	Deletes the character under the cursor
Backspace	Deletes the character to the left of the cursor
Esc	Returns the user to the worksheet without changes

Ctrl-Break	Stops what is being done and returns you to the worksheet in READY mode
Arrow key	Moves the cursor in the direction of the arrow

To insert information on a line, position the cursor one position to the right of where you want the new information to go and start typing.

6. If everything is totally wrong and you have a complete mess on your hands, you may just wish to start over with a new worksheet, erasing what's already on the screen. To erase the current worksheet, enter the following commands: /Worksheet Erase Yes. This will erase both the screen and RAM. You cannot recall anything, so use this command sequence carefully.

HINTS/HAZARDS

Many novices just starting out with 1-2-3 make the mistake of clearing a worksheet cell by positioning the pointer to the cell, pressing the Space key, and then pressing the Enter key. Instead of clearing (blanking) the cell, however, a space has been placed in the cell. You can now see the single quote (') in the status line indicating a cell with text data. You must always clear a cell with the / Range Erase command. Any other method results in the cell's still having something in it.

THE UNDO FEATURE OF 1-2-3

The Undo feature of 1-2-3, which could be referred to as the "oops" command, allows you to restore your worksheet as it existed before changes that have been made since the last time you were in READY mode. The Undo feature of 1-2-3 can only be used when the Undo indicator appears at the bottom of your screen. If the Undo indicator does not appear, this feature has been disabled on your copy of 1-2-3. This may have been done to allow you to create a larger worksheet, since the Undo feature divides available RAM memory into two parts, one for the present worksheet and the other for a copy of the contents prior to the last READY mode.

The Undo feature of 1-2-3 can save you tremendous amounts of time when you are making changes to your worksheet. Assume, for instance, that you have entered a complex segment of text or a formula at a cell location. While the pointer is at that cell location at a later session, you inadvertently press the space bar and then issue a pointer movement command to move the pointer, resulting in the cell's prior contents being replaced with a single space. You can restore the worksheet to its prior contents by issuing the Undo command.

Notes on Using the Undo Command The Undo feature works only when you are in 1-2-3 in READY mode. It does not work when you are in any of the other features of 1-2-3, such as PrintGraph, Translate, or Install, or while add-in programs are invoked.

The default for 1-2-3 is to have Undo invoked. You can, however, disable Undo by entering the command / Worksheet Global Default Update to modify the configuration file. Undo will now be off whenever 1-2-3 is started.

To allow you to undo a command and return your worksheet to its prior contents, 1-2-3 reserves approximately 50% of the available RAM in your computer. This means that the amount of memory available for the worksheet that you are currently working on is reduced.

If the Undo feature is not invoked, once you have started 1-2-3 and retrieved a worksheet or once you have attached a 1-2-3 add-in you will not be able to turn on Undo. This is because once memory has been allocated to a worksheet or for using an add-in software package, that memory cannot be reserved to create an Undo buffer (temporary storage area). In this type of situation, you would save the worksheet (/ File Save), erase RAM (/ Worksheet Erase), turn on the Undo feature (/ Worksheet Global Default Other Undo Enable), and then retrieve the worksheet (/ File Retrieve).

The Backup When you are using Undo, 1-2-3 creates a back-up copy of the worksheet whenever you press a key that could lead to changes in the worksheet. Since this is done in RAM, the speed is exceptionally fast and is not noticed by the operator of the computer. Once an undesired change is made, the original version of the worksheet (prior to the change) can be restored using the Undo (Alt + F4) command. 1-2-3, for example, automatically saves the worksheet anytime the Main Menu is invoked by pressing the slash (/) key.

The following commands automatically result in a backup of the worksheet being made by the Undo feature:

Abs (F4)	Graph (F10)
Backspace	Help (F1)
Ctrl-Break	Ins
Del	Learn (Alt + F5)
Enter	Name (F3)
Esc	Step (Alt + F2)
GoTo (F5)	Window (F6)

Limitations of Undo Although 1-2-3's Undo feature allows you to undo commands that affect the worksheet, it does not allow you to undo changes that affect files on disk. For example, Undo will not undo the results of issuing a / File Save command, since this affects a disk worksheet file rather than a worksheet in RAM.

GETTING HELP

From time to time, you may forget where you are in a menu structure (see Appendix A for Lotus 1-2-3 command structure) or you may not understand how a particular command operates. Since 1-2-3 has over 115 built-in commands, it's reasonable to assume that you will not be acquainted with all of them.

To aid you in remembering these commands (or in becoming acquainted with them for the first time), Lotus 1-2-3 provides a built-in tutor, known as the **help facility,** which you can activate by pressing the F1 key. The help facility displays information about the current menu options available to you or about the current command you are working on; it is made context-sensitive by the position of the pointer in a menu or a command sequence from a menu. To get out of help and back to the worksheet, simply press the Esc key.

Figure 3.10
Help screen for READY mode

```
A1:                                                                    HELP

1-2-3 Help Index

About 1-2-3 Help          Linking Files             1-2-3 Main Menu
Cell Formats              Macro Basics              /Add-In
Cell/Range References     Macro Command Index       /Copy
Column Widths             Macro Key Names           /Data
Control Panel             Mode Indicators           /File
Entering Data             Operators                 /Graph
Error Message Index       Range Basics              /Move
Formulas                  Recalculation             /Print
@Function Index           Specifying Ranges         /Quit
Function Keys             Status Indicators         /Range
Keyboard Index            Task Index                /System
Learn Feature             Undo Feature              /Worksheet

To select a topic, press a pointer-movement key to highlight the topic and then
press ENTER.  To return to a previous Help screen, press BACKSPACE.  To leave
Help and return to the worksheet, press ESC.

30-Aug-89  07:21 PM
```

Figure 3.11
Help screen for Main Menu

```
A1:                                                                    HELP
Worksheet Range Copy Move File Print Graph Data System Add-In Quit
Global Insert Delete Column Erase Titles Window Status Page Learn

1-2-3 Commands

Worksheet Commands        Graph Commands
Range Commands            Data Commands
/Copy                     /System
/Move                     Add-In Commands
File Commands             /Quit
Print Commands

To use 1-2-3 commands, type / (slash) or < (less-than symbol) to display the
Main Menu at the top of the screen.

To select a command from the menu, highlight the command and press ENTER or
type the first character of the command.  When you highlight a command, 1-2-3
displays an explanation or submenu in the third line of the control panel.

To back out of a menu one level at a time, press ESC.
To leave a menu and return to READY mode, press CTRL-BREAK.

Using Command Menus                                              Help Index
30-Aug-89  07:22 PM
```

For example, suppose that you needed help while you were at READY mode in your worksheet. If you pressed the Help key (F1), the screen depicted in Figure 3.10 would be displayed to your monitor. Notice that the control panel is displayed at the top of your screen and that the mode indicator says HELP. To leave, press the Esc key. Suppose now that you want more help with entries contained in the Main Menu. After you have invoked the Main Menu via the / key, press the Help key (F1) and a screen like that depicted in Figure 3.11 will appear on your monitor. You can now obtain help related to the Move command by highlighting that option. The Help screen depicted in Figure 3.12 now appears on your screen with information about the Move command. When you have finished, press the Esc key to return to READY mode.

Figure 3.12
Help screen for the Move command

```
A1:                                                                    HELP
Worksheet Range Copy Move File Print Graph Data System Add-In Quit
Move a cell or range of cells

1-2-3 Commands

    Worksheet Commands        Graph Commands
    Range Commands            Data Commands
    /Copy                     /System
    /Move                     Add-In Commands
    File Commands             /Quit
    Print Commands

    To use 1-2-3 commands, type / (slash) or < (less-than symbol) to display the
    Main Menu at the top of the screen.

    To select a command from the menu, highlight the command and press ENTER or
    type the first character of the command.  When you highlight a command, 1-2-3
    displays an explanation or submenu in the third line of the control panel.

    To back out of a menu one level at a time, press ESC.
    To leave a menu and return to READY mode, press CTRL-BREAK.

Using Command Menus                                          Help Index
30-Aug-89  07:22 PM
```

ENTERING A SAMPLE LOTUS 1-2-3 WORKSHEET

Recall our earlier example, in which your friend Ed owned a grocery store and asked you to design a report comparing sales of his various departments. Since Ed knows you are enrolled in a course that covers Lotus 1-2-3, you have been honored with a request to help him prepare a spreadsheet to perform the data manipulation. After carefully examining the problem, you decide that a worksheet like that shown in Figure 3.13 will present the information in an understandable format.

In the course of this project, the following learning objectives in the use of Lotus 1-2-3 will be accomplished:

1. Introduction to pointer movement
2. Entering labels (text)
3. Use of the @SUM function
4. Entering 1-2-3 formulas
5. Changing column width for an entire worksheet
6. Global data format changes
7. Use of the Copy command
8. Use of the Range Format command
9. Use of the Range Erase command
10. Justification of text within a cell
11. Printing a worksheet

Format of Instructions In accomplishing the preceding objectives, you will have to perform a number of processing steps, which are detailed on the following pages. Any time you see a letter followed by a number (for example, B4), it signifies that you are to go to that cell location and enter the data or instruction that follows.

Figure 3.13
Screen showing COMPSALS worksheet

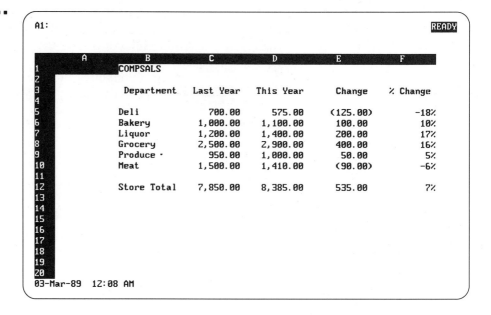

After you have finished entering the data or instruction, depress the Enter key or an Arrow key. Depressing the Enter key takes the information from the entry line and places it in the cell, leaving the pointer on that cell. The pointer can then be moved to another cell via the appropriate Arrow key.

To accomplish the same task with one less keystroke, simply depress an Arrow key when you are finished entering data on the entry line. This action both enters the data in the cell and moves the pointer to the next cell location.

 Step-by-Step Instructions for 1-2-3 Sample Worksheet—COMPSALS

1. Enter row and column labels. Don't worry if some of the labels won't fit in a cell. That will be taken care of later.

B1	COMPSALS
B3	Department
C3	Last Year
D3	This Year
E3	Change
F3	% Change
B5	Deli
B6	Bakery
B7	Liquor
B8	Grocery
B9	Produce
B10	Meat
B12	Store Total

2. Change the column width to 12 for the whole spreadsheet (global). Lotus 1-2-3 brings up a blank worksheet with a column width of 9.

/	Brings up the Main Menu for Lotus 1-2-3.
W	Selects the desired Worksheet selection from the Main Menu. You may select from a menu in either of two ways:

(1) You can move the pointer with Arrow keys to the selection and depress Enter; or (2) you can enter the first letter of the option desired. You will notice that, as you move the pointer along the options, the prompt line changes from option to option. This gives the user additional information about each option.

G	Tells 1-2-3 that the command to be entered will affect the entire worksheet.
C	Signifies that the Column Width command has been selected from the menu.
12	Changes the column width from 9 to 12 positions.
Enter	Tells 1-2-3 to execute the command.

3. Enter totals for the Last Year and This Year columns. Don't enter the commas or decimal points as presented above. You'll tell 1-2-3 what to do with these numbers later.

C5	700
C6	1000
C7	1200
C8	2500
C9	950
C10	1500
D5	575
D6	1100
D7	1400
D8	2900
D9	1000
D10	1410

4. At C12, demonstrate the use of the @SUM function.

C12 [by manual pointer movement]	@SUM(Enters the beginning of the formula
C5 [by manual pointer movement]	Positions the pointer at cell C5
.	Marks the beginning of the range
C10 [by manual pointer movement]	Positions the pointer at cell C10, the last cell to be summed
)	Stops the process with a)
Enter	Executes the sum function

The above steps will produce the value 7850 in cell C12. The use of the @SUM function introduces the use of a function and illustrates 1-2-3's ability to point to data and then enter that pointed address into a formula. The @SUM function also introduces the concept of a **range.** As you no doubt noticed, the pointed range (adjacent cells included in the operation) appeared in reverse video. This convention allows a user to see exactly which cells will be included in an operation.

Note carefully what happens on the screen as you total the This Year column.

5. At D12, use the @SUM function to add the numbers in the This Year column.

D12 [by manual pointer movement]	@SUM(Enters the first part of the formula
D5 [by manual pointer movement]	Positions the pointer at cell D5
.	Marks the beginning of the range
D10 [by manual pointer movement]	Positions the pointer at D10
)	Stops the process with a)
Enter	Executes the sum function

The above steps will produce the value 8385 in cell D12.

6. Use a global change to put two positions to the right of the decimal point and to allow for commas between the hundreds and thousands digits.

/	Brings up the Main Menu for Lotus 1-2-3
W	Selects the Worksheet option from the Main Menu (see task 2 above)
G	Tells 1-2-3 that the command to be entered will affect the entire worksheet
F	Tells 1-2-3 that the format (the manner in which data are presented on the worksheet) is to be selected
,	Tells 1-2-3 that commas are to be placed where you would logically expect them (Negative numbers will be contained in parentheses; a fixed number of decimal places can also be specified.)
2	Tells 1-2-3 that two decimal positions will be displayed
Enter	Tells 1-2-3 to execute the instruction

7. At E5, calculate the change between This Year and Last Year (using the pointer method).

+	Indicates to 1-2-3 that a formula is to be entered
D5 [by manual pointer movement]	Positions the pointer at cell D5
-	Indicates to 1-2-3 that the next cell is to be entered
C5 [by manual pointer movement]	Positions the pointer at cell C5
Enter	Executes the command and places the result in cell E5

You can use the pointer when entering a cell location in a formula. This works well when you don't remember the exact location.

8. Copy (replicate) this formula for the rest of the cells in the column. Copying the formula into the other cells in the column can save a tremendous amount of time and can eliminate typing errors. Make sure that the pointer is at E5.

/		Brings up the Main Menu
C		Selects the Copy option
Enter		Establishes the sending area (You want to copy only the contents of cell E5.)
	Down Arrow to E6	Positions the pointer at the first cell in the range, to receive the formula contained in E5
.		Indicates to 1-2-3 that this is the first cell to be referenced in a range—"nailing down" the beginning
	Down Arrow to E12	Positions the pointer at the last cell in the range to receive the formula contained in E5
Enter		Tells 1-2-3 to execute the Copy command

Don't worry about the garbage in E11. You'll get rid of that later.

You will notice that the other cells now have answers in the change column that correspond to those at the beginning of this lesson. Move the pointer from one cell to another in the column. Notice that the cell addresses have been changed automatically by 1-2-3. This ability to change cell locations automatically during a copy or move is referred to as **relative addressing.**

9. Enter the formula to calculate the percentage change. You'll change the format of the column later. Position the pointer to cell F5.

+E5/C5	Places this formula in cell F5
Enter	Executes the sum function

You should have the value (0.18) in cell F5.

This method demonstrates that you are not required to point if you know the cell addresses. The pointing method, although impressive at first, can actually result in extra work for a worksheet user, especially if the cell locations are far away on the worksheet.

10. Copy this formula for the rest of the column, after first positioning the pointer at cell F5.

/		Invokes the Main Menu
C		Selects the Copy command
Enter		Establishes cell F5 as the only cell holding data to be copied to other cells
	Down Arrow to F6	Positions the pointer at the first cell that is to receive the formula to be copied
.		Indicates to 1-2-3 that this is the first cell to be referenced in a range
	Down Arrow to F12	Positions the pointer at the last cell in the range that is to receive the formula from cell F5
Enter		Tells 1-2-3 that the range has been established and that the command is to be executed

11. To get rid of the two entries at E11 and F11, position the pointer at F11.

	/	Invokes the Main Menu
	R	Selects the Range option from the Main Menu (The Range option should be used whenever you wish to perform operations on only a part of the worksheet, rather than on all of it.)
	E	Tells 1-2-3 that you wish to erase the contents of a range of cells beginning with F11, not the entire worksheet
	Back Arrow	Moves the pointer to the last cell in the range (E11)
	Enter	Tells 1-2-3 that the range has been established and that the command is to be executed

Your spreadsheet should now look like the worksheet in Figure 3.14.

12. Format column F for percentages, beginning with position F5.

	/	Invokes the Main Menu
	R	Selects the Range option from the Main Menu
	F	Selects the Format option to change a portion of the worksheet
	P	Tells 1-2-3 that you wish to use the percent format to display data within a range
	0	Tells 1-2-3 that there are to be no positions to the right of the decimal
	Enter	Marks cell F5 as the beginning of the range
	Down Arrow to F12	Marks the rest of the cells in the range
	Enter	Tells 1-2-3 that the range has been established and that the data format is now to be changed to percent

13. Position the pointer at F3 to right-justify the column labels.

	/	Invokes the Main Menu
	R	Selects the Range option from the Main Menu (You want to right-justify only one row of labels—a range.)
	L	Selects the Label Prefix command
	R	Tells 1-2-3 to right-justify the label within the cell and start the range with cell F3
	Back Arrow to B3	Establishes the range of cells whose labels are to be right-justified
	Enter	Tells 1-2-3 to right-justify the labels within the marked range of cells

14. Save the worksheet onto disk, using the name COMPSALS.

	/	Brings up the Main Menu
	F	Selects the File option (This option is selected any time you wish to read or write data onto a disk.)
	S	Executes the Save command to save a worksheet to the disk in drive B
	COMPSALS	Responds to the Lotus 1-2-3 prompt for the filename (If the file has already been saved before,

Figure 3.14
COMPSALS worksheet

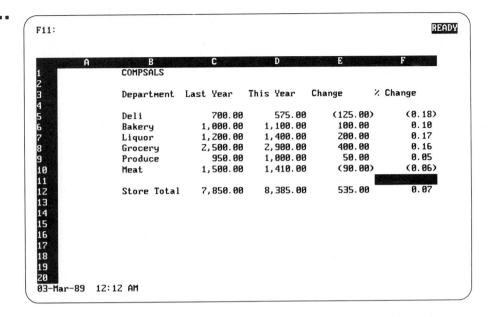

1-2-3 will ask if you want to cancel or replace: Cancel would result in the command being canceled; Replace would overwrite the old file with the present worksheet in RAM.)

Enter	Executes the command

15. Print the worksheet.

/	Brings up the Main Menu
P	Selects the Print option
P	Tells 1-2-3 that the output is to go to the printer
R	Tells 1-2-3 that you wish to tell it what part of the worksheet is to be printed (Remember that there are 524,288 cells.)
A1 [by manual pointer movement]	Gives the first cell location (lower right-hand corner)
.	Tells 1-2-3 that a range is to be established
F12 [by manual pointer movement]	Gives the last cell location (lower right-hand corner)
Enter	Tells 1-2-3 that the range has been established
G AGP	Tells 1-2-3 to begin printing

16. Go to the next page of the printout, so the current page can be removed.

- P Tells 1-2-3 to go to the top of the next page
- A Tells 1-2-3 that it is now at the top of the paper (If you forget to align the printer with this command, your worksheet may have a wide gap in the middle.)

SAVING AND RETRIEVING WORKSHEET FILES

The first time that you work on a worksheet, 1-2-3 prompts you to enter a name for the worksheet when you issue the command to save it to disk. Any worksheet file that you save to disk has the .WK1 file extension. The following commands are used to save a worksheet to disk:

/   Brings up the Main Menu for 1-2-3

F   Selects the File option from the Main Menu (This option is selected any time that you want to save or load a worksheet from disk.)

S   Executes the Save command to save a worksheet to the disk in drive B

The worksheet file can now be loaded at a later time and changes can be made to that worksheet. Use the following commands to load a worksheet:

/   Brings up the Main Menu for 1-2-3

F   Selects the File option from the Main Menu

R   Selects the Retrieve option to read a worksheet file from the disk in drive B (You can now either manually enter the name of the worksheet to be loaded or simply "point" to the appropriate worksheet file using the pointer and then depressing the Enter key.)

Once you finish making any changes to the worksheet, you must again save it to disk. Since you indicated the name of the worksheet to 1-2-3 when you loaded it, 1-2-3 displays that name as the default when you issue the Save command. By pressing the Enter key, you accept that default. If you wish to enter another name, the current name disappears as soon as you press any other alphabetic or numeric key. If you press the Enter key to accept the default name, 1-2-3 displays the following menu:

```
Cancel    Replace    Backup
```

The Cancel command tells 1-2-3 to stop this operation and returns you to READY mode.

The Replace command tells 1-2-3 to go ahead and save the contents of this worksheet to disk. This process destroys the original worksheet file and replaces it with the new worksheet.

The Backup command tells 1-2-3 to save the prior version of the worksheet (the one currently residing on disk) with a .BAK file extension and then save the worksheet in RAM using the original filename.

If you try to exit 1-2-3 without saving changes to disk, 1-2-3 displays the following menu prompt: WORKSHEET CHANGES NOT SAVED! End 1-2-3 anyway? This gives you the opportunity to respond with a No and then issue a / File Save command to save your worksheet. If 1-2-3 did not perform this task, it would be possible to lose many hours of work by simply forgetting to save your worksheet to disk.

Once you have saved a file to disk, you may want to verify that it actually was stored properly. You can verify that a worksheet was stored properly in two ways. First, you can simply reload the worksheet file from disk using the / File Retrieve commands. Second, you can use the List command from the File Menu. Issuing the / File List command results in a menu display from which you select the appropriate type of file that you wish to have displayed. In this case, you would enter the following commands:

Figure 3.15
Type of screen displayed when you enter the / Files List Worksheet instruction

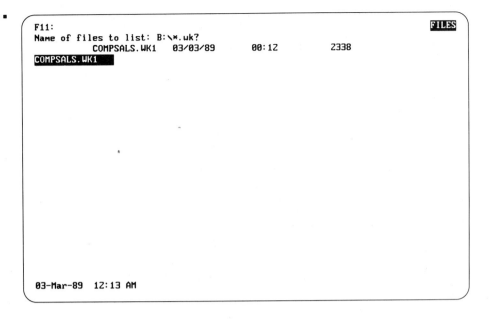

/	Brings up the Main Menu of 1-2-3
F	Selects the File option of the Main Menu
L	Selects the List option of the File Menu
W	Tells 1-2-3 to display all of the worksheet files (those files with a .WK? file extension) to the screen (see Figure 3.15)

When you wish to return to 1-2-3, press the Enter key.

Release 2.x of 1-2-3 stores worksheets with a file extension of .WK1. The older version of 1-2-3 (Release 1A) stored worksheets with an extension of .WKS. These older .WKS worksheet files can be read by Release 2.x of 1-2-3, but when a Save command is executed these files are saved using the .WK1 file extension. This means that when you retrieve a .WKS file and then subsequently save it, that file appears twice: One file contains the .WKS file extension, and the other contains the .WK1 file extension. Once this occurs, you should use the / File Erase Worksheet command to erase the .WKS file. Otherwise you might make important changes, save the file, and later retrieve the unchanged .WKS file.

Your worksheet should now look exactly like the worksheet at the beginning of this lesson. If it doesn't, you have done something wrong. Compare the contents of each cell with the contents listed below:

B1	'COMPSALS
B3	"Department
C3	"Last Year
D3	"This Year
E3	"Change
F3	"%Change
B5	'Deli
C5	700
D5	575
E5	+D5 − C5
F5	(P0) + E5/C5
B6	'Bakery
C6	1000

D6	1100
E6	+D6 − C6
F6	(P0) + E6/C6
B7	'Liquor
C7	1200
D7	1400
E7	+D7 − C7
F7	(P0) + E7/C7
B8	'Grocery
C8	2500
D8	2900
E8	+D8 − C8
F8	(P0) + E8/C8
B9	'Produce
C9	950
D9	1000
E9	+D9 − C9
F9	(P0) + E9/C9
B10	'Meat
C10	1500
D10	1410
E10	+D10 − C10
F10	(P0) +E10/C10
B12	'Store Total
C12	@SUM(C5..C10)
D12	@SUM(D5..D10)
E12	+D12 − C12
F12	(P0) + E12/C12

CHAPTER REVIEW

One of the most frequently used microcomputer applications in business is the electronic spreadsheet, which allows an individual to manipulate any data/information that can be placed in a row-and-column format. Most spreadsheet software packages have a number of features in common, including the ability to copy formulas or text, delete rows or columns, load worksheets from disk, insert rows or columns, change the format of data presentation, move text or formulas from one location to another, print the worksheet, save the worksheet, freeze portions (titles) of the worksheet, and split the screen.

Two of the most popular spreadsheet packages are VisiCalc and Lotus 1-2-3. VisiCalc was originally built for the Apple II microcomputer, and Lotus 1-2-3 was originally built for the IBM PC. Both software packages resulted in dramatically increased sales for their respective machines when they were first introduced.

When you are using a spreadsheet package, you must follow a number of logical steps in planning, developing, and testing your worksheet in order to ensure that the problem is properly modeled.

The Lotus 1-2-3 spreadsheet package is a menu-driven, integrated package composed of the functional parts of spreadsheet, graphics, and data management. Its screen consists of a control panel, border, mode indicator, special indicators, error message indicator, and worksheet area. Various keys of the keyboard are used to move the pointer around the worksheet area.

You can enter data and correct errors by making changes in the control panel area. After data are entered or changes made, they will be reflected in the appropriate cell if you press an Arrow key or the Enter key. Arithmetic manipulation of numeric data contained in cells can be accomplished by entering a formula or by telling 1-2-3 to use one of its built-in functions. A detailed example of worksheet formation involves the practical application of many of these functions.

KEY TERMS AND CONCEPTS

Add-ins
Allways
Alt (Macro) key
Backspace key
backup
border
built-in functions
cell
circular reference
column
control panel
Ctrl plus Scroll Break keys
current date
current time
data entry
data management feature
Down Arrow
Edit key (F2)
End key
Enter key
entry line
error messages
Esc key
formula
function keys
graphics feature
help facility
Home key
indicators
integration
keyboard macro
label

label data
Left Arrow
Lotus Access System
Lotus 1-2-3
Lotus spreadsheet
Lotus worksheet
Macro Library Manager
mode indicator
number
numeric data
Pg Dn key
Pg Up key
pointer
precedence
prompt line
range
relative addressing
Right Arrow key
row
Scroll Lock key
spreadsheet
status line
Tab key
Tab plus Shift keys
template
Undo
Up Arrow key
VisiCalc
window
worksheet
/ key

CHAPTER QUIZ

Multiple Choice

1. Which of the following terms is not related to a worksheet?
   a. Row
   b. Column
   c. DOS prompt
   d. Pointer
   e. Border
   f. All of the above terms are related to a spreadsheet.

2. Which of the following items is not allowed in a cell?
   a. Formula
   b. Label
   c. Function
   d. Number
   e. All of the above are allowed in a cell.
   f. None of the above is allowed in a cell.

3. Which of the following names is not related to spreadsheet software triumphs?
   a. Mitch Kapor
   b. Dan Bricklin
   c. VisiCalc
   d. Steve Jobs
   e. Lotus 1-2-3

4. Which of the following keystrokes does not result in cursor movement?
   a. Arrow key
   b. Pg Up
   c. Alt
   d. Tab
   e. End + an Arrow key
   f. All of the above result in cursor movement.

5. Which of the following items is not found in the control panel?
   a. Entry line
   b. Prompt line
   c. Error line
   d. Status line
   e. All of the above are part of the control panel.
   f. None of the above is part of the control panel.

True/False

6. Integrated packages allow you to pass information from one part to another without any real difficulty.

7. The mode indicator is used to show the current status of the worksheet.

8. A cell is referenced by using the Row/Column designation.

9. The built-in functions in 1-2-3 always start with a @ character.

10. When entering a formula, you need only enter the cell location and an operation symbol—for example, A2 − B7.

Answers

1. c   2. e   3. d   4. c   5. c   6. t   7. t   8. f   9. t   10. f

Exercises

1. Define or describe each of the following:
   a. built-in function
   b. 1-2-3 data management
   c. 1-2-3 graphics
   d. Lotus Access System
   e. control panel
   f. mode indicator
   g. indicators
   h. Edit key (F2)
   i. precedence
   j. on-line help

2. A spreadsheet is the software, while a(n) _____ is the work area.

3. Any cell can be referenced by referring to its corresponding _____ and _____.

4. List each of the types of contents a cell may have:
   a.

   b.

   c.

5. A(n) _____ is similar to a prepackaged program. You enter the data, and it computes the results.

6. List the steps involved in using a spreadsheet to solve a problem.
   a.

   b.

   c.

   d.

7. List the three integrated parts of Lotus 1-2-3.
   a.

   b.

   c.

8. List the three parts of the 1-2-3 control panel.
   a.

   b.

   c.

9. The _____ indicator is used to identify the current status of the Lotus 1-2-3 package.

10. The part of your worksheet that is visible on your screen is referred to as the _____.

11. The second line of the control panel is the _____ line.

12. Explain the use of each of the following cursor movement keys:
    a. Arrow key

    b. Pg Up

    c. Pg Dn

    d. End

    e. Home

    f. Tab

13. The _____ key is used to quit an instruction or back up a step in the menu.

14. The two keys _____ and _____ are used to stop any spreadsheet process or function.

15. A cell that contains text automatically has a(n) _____ placed in it.

16. Why is the concept of precedence important in entering formulas? Explain how 1-2-3 evaluates a formula and executes it using precedence. How can this order of precedence be changed?

17. Why are built-in functions so useful? List some functions that you might find useful, and beside each function give an application of it.
    a.

    b.

    c.

    d.

18. Explain how the use of each of the following keys changes when the EDIT mode is entered by pressing the F2 key.
    a. Home

    b. Del

    c. Backspace

    d. End

    e. Esc

    f. Arrow keys

19. The four keystrokes _____, _____, _____, and _____ are used to erase the entire worksheet.

Fundamentals of Spreadsheets and Lotus 1-2-3 **S.39**

20. Practice using the on-line help facility, which is activated by pressing the F1 key.

21. The two add-in packages that are provided with Lotus 1-2-3 Release 2.2 are _____ and _____.

22. The _____ add-in provides spreadsheet publishing capabilities.

23. The _____ feature of 1-2-3 allows you to restore the contents of a worksheet using the Alt + F4 key sequence.

24. The _____ key can be used in place of the Alt key when issuing a command requiring use of the Alt key.

25. The key sequence used to erase the contents of a cell is _____.

COMPUTER EXERCISES

1. Use the / File Retrieve command to load the worksheet file called CALENDAR, which contains an appointment calendar for keeping track of various appointments. Practice moving the pointer around the worksheet using the following commands.

   Part I

   a. Use the various Arrow keys to move the pointer.
   b. Press the Home key.
   c. Press the Pg Dn key twice.
   d. Press the Pg Up key three times; notice the beep.
   e. Position the pointer at 8:00.
   f. Press the End key, followed by the Down Arrow key.
   g. Press the same two keys again; the pointer should be at row 8192.
   h. Press the End key, followed by the Right Arrow key; the pointer should be at cell IV8192.
   i. Now enter any character at cell IV8192. You should receive a `Memory Full` error message. Even though 1-2-3 has a bountiful number of cell locations, the limited amount of RAM in your computer prevents you from using all of them. Press the Esc key to get rid of the error message.
   j. Press the End key, followed by the Up Arrow key. You should now see `'end of column` at cell IV1. Notice that there is a single quote mark in front of the text. This single quote tells 1-2-3 that the contents of this cell are text data. Although you can enter the single quote, 1-2-3 automatically places it in the cell for you.
   k. Press the Home key.
   l. Press the Tab key twice.
   m. Press the Shift and Tab keys together.
   n. Position the pointer at cell A5. This cell contains the 1-2-3 function @NOW. This function is used to get the date that you entered when you started Lotus 1-2-3. If you did not enter a date, this cell contains 01-Jan-80 (the DOS default).

   Part II

   a. Press the Scroll Lock key.
   b. Use the various Arrow keys to move the pointer.

c. Press the Pg Dn key twice.
d. Press the Pg Up key once.
e. Press the Tab key twice.
f. Press the Shift and Tab keys together.

2. Use the / File Retrieve command to load the worksheet file called PAYMENT, which is a template that allows you to enter the amount of a loan, the interest rate, and the number of years for the loan and then automatically calculates the amount of the payment and the total amount paid over the life of the loan.

    Before you do anything to the worksheet, let's explore some of its features. This worksheet has two areas: The first will hold information about various loans, and the second contains the information about a loan that you are permitted to change. If you try to change any cells, the computer merely beeps and displays the error message Protected Cell. Press Esc to continue. The high-intensity (bright) cells' contents can be changed, but the others can't. Note the PR entry on the status line for protected cells and the U entry of the high-intensity unprotected cells.

    You are therefore allowed to change the loan amount, the interest rate, and the life of the loan in years. Enter the loan amounts without using dollar signs or commas. For example, if a loan is for $10,000, enter it as 10000. The current interest rate is 12%, expressed as a decimal (.12). The final field that you are allowed to change is the length of the loan, which is currently set for 4 years. These two variables appear at the bottom of the screen.

    Notice that as soon as you change the contents of one field the worksheet automatically recalculates itself.

    Enter information about the following loans:
    a. $10,000 at 12% for 4 years
    b. $15,000 at 12% for 4 years
    c. $25,000 at 14% for 6 years
    d. $80,000 at 16% for 20 years
    e. $120,000 at 13% for 15 years

3. Use the / File Retrieve command to load the worksheet file called ERRORS, which contains a number of mistakes that you should correct.
    a. Reenter the following mistakes:
        twilve
        cumpany

    b. Use the F2 Edit command to remedy the following errors:
        The dog jumped ovr the lasy cat
        The childrun sat at hoam

    c. Use the / Range Erase command to delete each of the following:
        xxxxxxxxx
        ****

        \\\\\\\\\

4. You are to create a student's budget schedule that will subtract total expenses from total income for a 4½-month period (one semester) and set net cash amounts for each month. In addition, the schedule should

provide monthly totals for income and expense items, with grand totals as depicted in the example below.

The dollar figures, along with the budget categories in the example below, are only illustrative. You are to pick categories and supply amounts appropriate to your particular situation. You are to use formulas or the sum function to calculate column and row totals as well as the net cash amount.

```
              School Year Budget
TERM:   FALL                                YEAR:  1991
NAME:

INCOME        JANUARY    FEBRUARY    MARCH     APRIL     MAY      TOTAL

WORK            175         400       400       400      200      1575
AWARDS           50         150       150       150       50       550
ALLOWANCE        35          75        75        75       75       335
OTHER             5          25        25        25       25       105

EXPENSES

TUITION         250         550       550       550      250      2150
BOOKS           400           0         0         0        0       400
HOME            100         250       250       250      250      1100
CLOTHING         40         125       125       125       75       490
FOOD             40          90        90        90       40       350
TRANSPORT        20          35        35        35      100       225
OTHER            20          35        35        35       35       160

TOTALS

INCOME          265         650       650       650      350      2565
EXPENSES        870        1085      1085      1085      750      4875

NET CASH       -605        -435      -435      -435     -400     -2310
```

(use formula)

Save the worksheet to a file called CH3EX4.

5. You are the manager of a car dealership. You have six salespeople working for you. Your boss has requested that you take the last two years of sales information for each sales rep and determine the difference between the two years in sales dollars. Your boss has requested the information in the format shown in Figure 3.16.

You are to enter the formulas that will calculate the Change and % Change column entries. Place a total at the bottom of any column containing numeric information.

Set the worksheet column width to 12.
Save the worksheet to a file called CH3EX5.

6. The bandleader has asked you to help in the record keeping for the high school band members' fund-raising drive. The band members are selling candy (at $3.00 per can) to pay for a trip to Washington, D.C. The bandleader has accounting information concerning the number of

Figure 3.16
Car dealership worksheet

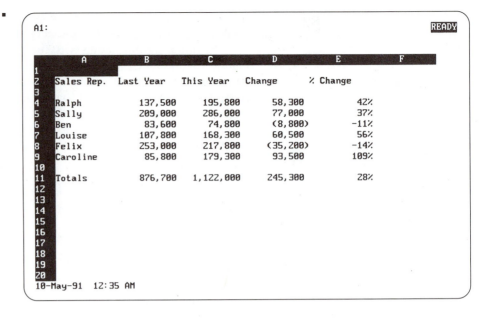

Figure 3.17
Candy sales worksheet

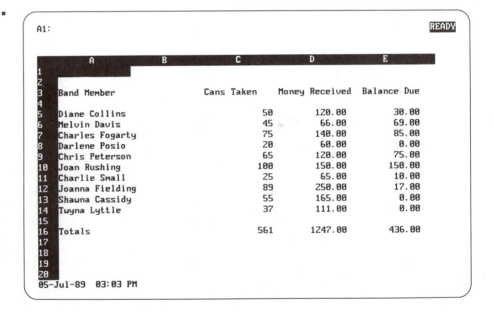

cans of candy checked out by each member and the money turned in by each member (Figure 3.17). You have been asked to determine how much, if anything, each member owes and to provide any information you can on totals.

Save this worksheet file to disk using the name CH3EX6.

 7. The head of the accounting department is interested in a comparative income statement for the last two years and has asked you to prepare the financial statement using the information that follows. You have also been asked to ascertain the dollar change between the various income statement entries. The margin is calculated by subtracting cost from sales.

```
                        ACE Inc.
             Income Statement (unaudited)

                     Last Year      This Year        Change

     INCOME

     Sales            175,000        225,000         50,000
     Cost             120,000        160,000         40,000

     Margin            55,000         65,000         10,000

     EXPENSES

     Materials         22,000         20,000        (2,000)
     Supplies           3,000          3,100           100
     Payroll           19,000         20,000         1,000
     Utilities            950            975            25
     Misc.              1,000          1,125           125
     Rent               6,000          6,000             0

     Total             51,950         51,200         (750)

     NET INCOME         3,050         13,800         10,750
```

Don't worry too much about getting the headings exactly centered. Save this worksheet to a file called CH3EX7.

8. Prepare a worksheet that contains a quarterly summary report for the ABC Company by region, as shown in Figure 3.18. Each of the regions should have a column total. Set the global column width to 12 and right-justify the column headings using the Label Prefix command. Save as CH3EX8.

9. Prepare a worksheet containing the car sales report by sales representative for Nissan Motors, as shown in Figure 3.19. You wish to track sales for six sales representatives and five car models. The global column width should be set to 10. The global column format should be comma with zero decimal positions. A total should be calculated using the @SUM function for each sales representative as well as for the total sales for each model of car. Save as CH3EX9.

10. Prepare a projected profit report for the XYZ Company for a five-year period, as shown in Figure 3.20. The sales for each year should increase 20%. The costs should always be assumed to be 60% of sales, while the profit is always equal to the sales minus the costs. After the worksheet has been finished, plug in a first-year sales figure of $60,000. Save as CH3EX10.

11. Retrieve the CALENDAR worksheet. Once the worksheet is displayed on the screen, issue the command / Worksheet Erase to erase the worksheet. Your screen should now be blank. Once a worksheet is erased, you can issue the Undo command (Alt + F4) to once again view the CALENDAR worksheet. Issue the Undo command again and you see the blank worksheet.

Figure 3.18

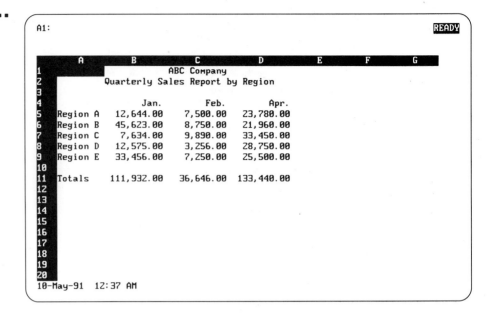

Figure 3.19

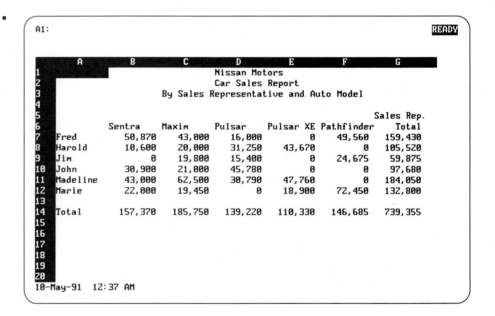

 With the screen showing the CALENDAR worksheet, issue a / File Retrieve command and load the worksheet file called PAYMENT. The payment template should now appear on your screen. Issue the Undo command and the CALENDAR worksheet appears on your screen. Again issue the Undo command and the PAYMENT worksheet appears on your screen.

Issue the Undo command to make the CALENDAR worksheet appear on your screen. Position the pointer to cell B3, issue the command / Range Erase, and press the Enter key. The text APPOINTMENT CALENDAR is now erased from your worksheet; to

Figure 3.20

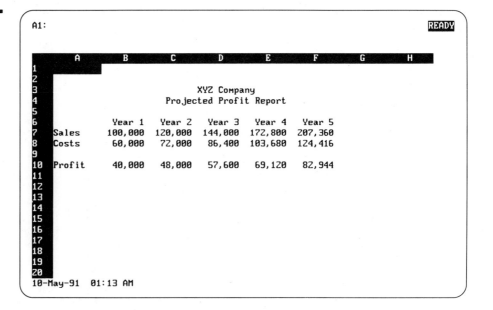

 make this text reappear, issue the Undo command. Notice that since you had made a change to the worksheet the prior contents of the back-up worksheet containing PAYMENT were replaced with the CALENDAR worksheet as it appeared before the / Range Erase command was issued.

CHAPTER 4

MORE ON RANGES, COPYING, FORMATTING, PRINTING, AND FUNCTIONS

CHAPTER OBJECTIVES

After completing this chapter, you should be able to:

- Use ranges effectively
- Use the Copy command
- Use the format conventions of 1-2-3 and know the differences between a range format and a global format
- Add and delete rows and columns
- Use the Move command
- Use the Print command to print a worksheet
- Use 1-2-3 built-in functions

In Chapter 3, you were introduced to a number of different 1-2-3 commands, some of which had virtually self-explanatory names. The concept of a range and the Copy, Format, Move, and Print commands, however, must be covered in more detail. These commands give a 1-2-3 user additional power to simplify actions and to determine how output will appear.

RANGE

When you are using 1-2-3, a statement or a process you wish to perform may require your indicating a range of cells to 1-2-3. A **range** is any specially designated single cell or rectangular group of cells on a worksheet; it is defined by pointing to the cells with the pointer or by typing the addresses of cells at the opposite corners of the range. Remember that a cell is a rectangle and therefore has only four corners.

Figure 4.1a displays a valid range containing three cells:

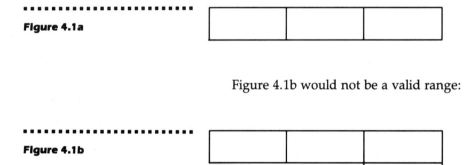

Figure 4.1a

Figure 4.1b would not be a valid range:

Figure 4.1b

You can give the cell locations of any pair of cells on opposite corners in defining a range of 1-2-3. For example, suppose you had a range containing a number of cells and having as its four corners the cells A, B, C, and D; to define the range, you would only have to give the cell addresses of two opposite corners, in whichever order you like—A and C, B and D, D and B, or C and A. Given any of these cell addresses, 1-2-3 will define the range depicted in Figure 4.2:

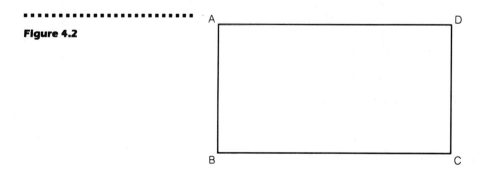

Figure 4.2

From time to time a worksheet will contain range settings from a previous session with 1-2-3 that you no longer desire, such as print settings. You may

More on Ranges, Copying, Formatting, Printing, and Functions   **S.49**

wish to cancel a previous print range and specify another. Any range in any 1-2-3 command can be cancelled by depressing the Backspace key. The new range can now be entered.

With the many spreadsheet commands that utilize ranges, one problem that many 1-2-3 novices face is when to "nail" the pointer down with a period (.) and when to simply extend a range via pointer manipulation commands. This problem is easily solved for you via visual cues by 1-2-3. If you issue a command that does not have the pointer already nailed down, you receive a prompt that contains only one reference to a cell (A1, for example). On the other hand, if the pointer has already been nailed down by 1-2-3, you receive a prompt like A1..A1. This means that all you have to do is simply extend the range via pointer movement commands. If the range displayed by a command is incorrect, press the Backspace key to cancel the range, move the pointer to the appropriate beginning cell, press the period key to nail the range, and extend the range via pointer manipulation commands.

THE COPY COMMAND

The **Copy command,** which takes information that has been entered in one or more cells and copies it to other cells on the worksheet, can save you many keystrokes and much time when you are building a worksheet. You will probably remember using the Copy command as part of your work on the sample COMPSALS worksheet in the last chapter, but you may not yet understand everything that it was doing. The Copy command involves setting up a **sending** cell or cells that contain the data to be copied and then setting up a **receiving** set of cells to which the data will be copied. The following steps are required:

1. Select the Copy command from the Main Menu.
2. Indicate to 1-2-3 which cells are to be in the "From" range—that is, which cells hold data to be copied onto other cells. If only one cell is involved, simply hit the Enter key; if a range of cells is involved, extend the range [the two periods (..) indicate that the beginning of the range is already fixed] and then move the pointer to the last cell in the range (or enter the cell address) and depress the Enter key (see Figure 4.3).
3. Indicate to 1-2-3 which cells are to be in the "To" range—that is, which cells are to receive data currently held in the "From" cells. If only one cell is involved, simply hit the Enter key. If a range of cells is involved, **nail down** the beginning of the range with a period (.), and then move the pointer to the last cell in the range (or enter the cell address) and depress the Enter key (see Figure 4.4).

HINTS/HAZARDS

Once the Enter key is pressed, the indicated cells are copied (see Figure 4.5). Make certain that your "From" cell range does not overlap your "To" cell range. If this happens, 1-2-3 overwrites the previous contents of the cell(s), and the previous contents are irretrievably lost.

As was noted in Chapter 3, 1-2-3 automatically changes the cell references in a formula it is copying to reflect the new cell location of the formula. This is an example of the concept of relative addressing. Other text data are copied

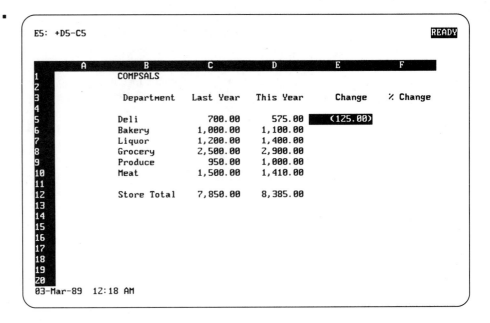

Figure 4.3
The cells to be copied identified to 1-2-3

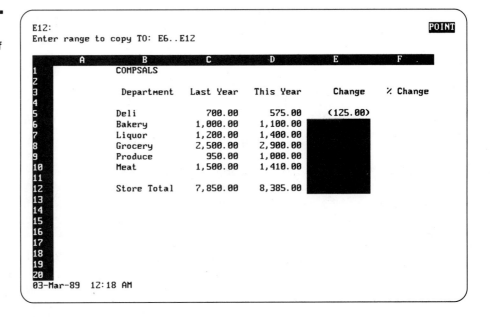

Figure 4.4
The cells to receive the outputs of the copied cell identified to 1-2-3

from one cell to another exactly as they appear. For example, if a cell containing the label *Year* were copied to another cell, the receiving cell would also contain *Year*; and if the text in the sending cell were right-justified, the text in the receiving cell would also be right-justified.

The Copy command contains a time-saving feature you can use when you are copying a range of cells. Imagine that you wish to copy a range of cells two cells (columns) wide by 20 rows deep. You would establish the "From" range as before—by entering the cell addresses or by pointing—and 1-2-3 would then be informed that the sending range consists of two columns and 20 rows. When you tell 1-2-3 the "To" range, however, you can simply identify the address of the upper left-hand cell of the receiving range (or point to this

Figure 4.5
The worksheet after the Copy command has been executed

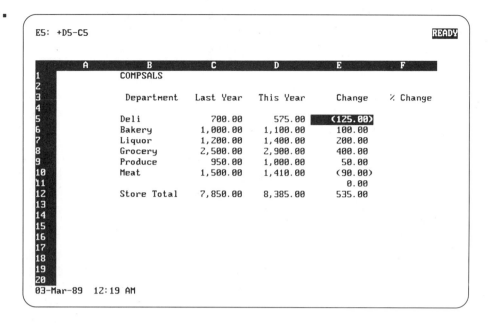

cell) and hit the Enter key. Because 1-2-3 retains in memory what the sending data look like, it assumes that you want it to move the whole range and does so.

FORMATTING

The 1-2-3 spreadsheet package uses the Format command to control the manner in which new numeric information appears in a cell. As you have already seen, you can either **format** the entire worksheet via the / **Worksheet Global Format** option or format a specific part of the worksheet via the / **Range Format** series of commands. It is important to note that the range format takes precedence over the worksheet global format, so any cell containing data not specifically formatted using the Range Format command can be changed using the Worksheet Global Format command.

Cell data can be formatted using the global or range options in various ways, including the following:

Fixed This option displays a fixed number of decimal places (0–15), specified by the worksheet user. Examples: 10, 10.5, −120.00. When this command is used in a / Range Format command, the message (F x) appears in the status line. The x denotes the number of decimal positions.

Scientific This option displays data in the exponential scientific notation format. The worksheet user specifies the number of decimal places in the multiplier (0–15). The exponent (E) is expressed as a power of 10 from +99 to −99. Examples: 1.35E +11, −7.5E −19. When this command is used in a / Range Format command, the message (S x) appears in the status line. The x denotes the number of decimal positions.

Currency This option places a dollar sign ($) before each numeric cell entry and places commas after the thousands and millions places in each entry large enough to have them. Negative numbers are placed in parentheses. The user indicates how many positions to the right of the decimal are desired. Examples: $13.50, ($6.75), $1.050. When this command is used in a / Range Format command, the message (Cx) appears in the status line. The x denotes the number of decimal positions.

, This option is identical to the Currency option, except that no dollar signs are used. When this command is used in a / Range Format command, the message (,x) appears in the status line. The x denotes the number of decimal positions.

General This option, the default numeric display, suppresses trailing zeros after a decimal point. Extremely large or small numbers are displayed in exponential notation format. Examples: 17.66, −4.3, 2.4 +10. When this command is used in a / Range Format command, the message (G) appears in the status line.

+/− This option displays a horizontal bar graph in which the number of symbols is the integer part of the value. Plus signs are used to represent positive integers, and minus signs are used to represent negative integers; if the value is zero, a period (.) is displayed. For example,

```
 6   =  + + + + + +
 4   =  + + + +
-3   =  - - -
10   =  + + + + + + + + + +
-5   =  - - - - -
3.5  =  + + +
```

When this command is used in a / Range Format command, the message (+) appears in the status line.

Percent This option displays the numeric entry in a cell as a percentage (%). The user must specify how many decimal positions are desired. The value contained in the cell is the decimal equivalent multiplied by 100 and followed by a percent sign. Examples: 45%, 12.5%, −23%. When this command is used in a / Range Format command, the message (Px) appears in the status line. The x denotes the number of decimal positions.

Date This option requests you to enter the format of date display desired from among the following possibilities:

1	DD-MMM-YY	(Example:09-Sep-87)
2	DD-MMM	(Example:09-Sep)
3	MMM-YY	(Example:Sep-87)
4	(Long Intn'l)	(Example:09-09-87)
5	(Short Intn'l)	(Example:09-09)

The time entries display a symbol for the following entries when you wish to format a cell containing a date function:

1	(HH:MM:SS AM/PM)	(Example:11:18:53 AM)
2	(HH:MM AM/PM)	(Example:11:18 AM)
3	(Long Intn'l)	(Example:11:18:53)
4	(Short Intn'l)	(Example:11:18)

When the Date command is used in a /Range Format command, the message (Dx) appears in the status line. The x denotes the date format option selected. If the time format was selected, a (Tx) appears in the status line.

Text This option displays the formula, rather than the result of the formula, in a cell. Example: +D3/C3. When this command is used in a /Range Format command, the message (T) appears in the status line.

Hidden This option allows you to inhibit the display of numbers, formulas, and text in a cell so that it does not appear on the screen. When the pointer resides on the cell that has been hidden, the contents of the cell appear in the control panel with the range indicator (H). This option is useful when you wish to embed comments or documentation concerning some aspect of your worksheet but do not wish to have those comments appear when the worksheet is printed. When this command is used in a /Range Format command, the message (H) appears in the status line.

Reset This option is used to change the format of a cell or a range of cells from the existing range format back to the global format.

Remember that the general format option is the default format used by 1-2-3 to start a spreadsheet and that the default column width used by 1-2-3 is nine positions wide. You can determine other default values used by 1-2-3 by entering the command /Worksheet Status.

HINTS/HAZARDS

When you are trying to determine which global format should be used, examine which format is used for the largest portion of the worksheet and make that your global format. Any exceptions to this global format can be addressed using the /Range Format command.

ADDING AND DELETING ROWS AND COLUMNS

From time to time, you may want to add or delete one or more rows or columns on the worksheet. This task involves simply pointing to where you wish to add or delete the row or column. The pointer plays a major role in this process. Columns are added to the *left* of the pointer position, and rows are added *above* the pointer position.

HINTS/HAZARDS

Make certain that there are no important areas of the worksheet offscreen that may be affected by your deleting a row or column. Remember, the entire column or row will be completely destroyed, not just what appears on the screen.

Let's add a column to the COMPSALS worksheet, which currently appears as shown in Figure 4.6. First, position the pointer where the addition or deletion is to take place. For example, if you want to add a column between present

Figure 4.6
COMPSALS worksheet

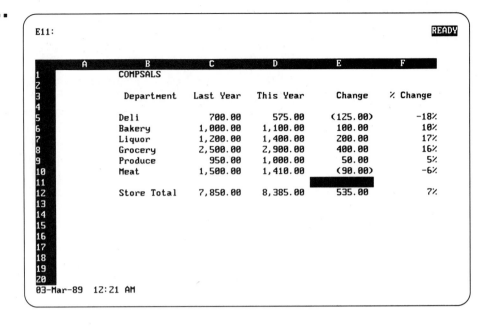

columns B and C, place the pointer anywhere in column C. Then issue the following commands:

/	Gets the Main Menu
W	Takes the Worksheet option
I	Takes the Insert option from the Worksheet Menu
C	Tells 1-2-3 that you wish to insert a column
Enter	Executes the command

The pointer in column C appears in reverse video, indicating that the range is only one column wide. When you depress the Enter key, the old column C will become the new column D. If you had wanted to add two columns, you would have depressed the Right Arrow one time and then the Enter key. The COMPSALS worksheet now looks as shown in Figure 4.7.

Now let's add two rows between the Deli and Bakery lines. First position the pointer anywhere on the Bakery line; then issue the following commands:

/	Gets the Main Menu
W	Takes the Worksheet option
I	Takes the Insert option from the Worksheet Menu
R	Tells 1-2-3 to insert a row
Down Arrow	Extends the range to two rows
Enter	Tells 1-2-3 to add the rows

The COMPSALS worksheet now appears as shown in Figure 4.8. You are now free to use these new rows and columns to enter new departments and to enter summary information for sales from two years ago.

Deleting rows and columns involves essentially the same process, except that you mark the actual ranges (rows or columns) to be deleted instead of inserted.

Figure 4.7
COMPSALS worksheet with column added

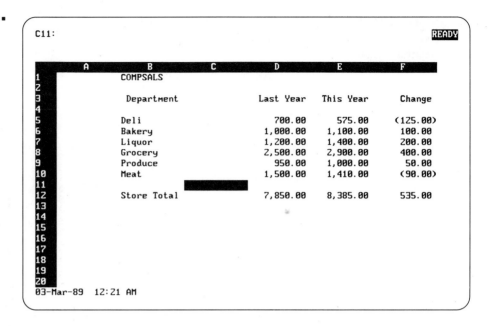

Figure 4.8
COMPSALS worksheet with rows added

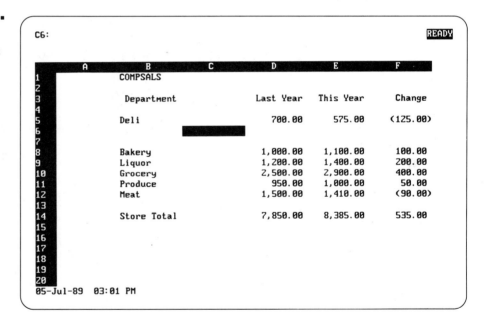

MOVING CELL CONTENTS

You may want to add or delete a column or row from your worksheet, only to discover that another area of your worksheet would be disastrously affected by such an action. This is the time to use 1-2-3's **Move feature,** which allows you to relocate cell contents without disturbing other worksheet areas. The Move feature automatically retains all functional relationships of any formulas; it works by specifying sending and receiving areas on the worksheet (much like the Copy statement, except that in Move the sending contents are destroyed).

Figure 4.9
Loan amortization worksheet

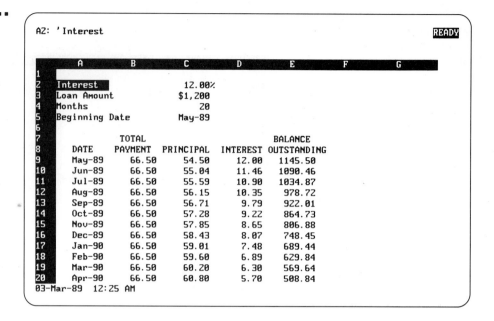

> **HINTS/HAZARDS** Make certain that the receiving range does not overlap any valuable cells in your worksheet. All cells in the receiving range will be destroyed, and you will not be able to retrieve the data previously contained in them.

Suppose that you have a loan amortization worksheet that looks like the one in Figure 4.9. Imagine that you want to center the information contained at the top of the worksheet in order to give the worksheet a more balanced look. To perform this task, which involves moving the information contained in eight cells one column to the right, you would execute the following steps:

/	Invokes the Main Menu
M	Selects the Move option from the Main Menu
A1 [by manual pointer movement]	Positions the pointer at A1 to establish the beginning of the "From" range
.	Nails down the beginning of the "From" range
C5 [by manual pointer movement]	Positions the pointer to the ending cell in the "From" range
Enter	Tells 1-2-3 that the "From" range has been defined
B1 [by manual pointer movement]	Positions the pointer at the beginning of the "To" range
Enter	Tells 1-2-3 to move the cell contents

The worksheet would now appear as shown in Figure 4.10.

Figure 4.10

Loan amortization worksheet with information centered

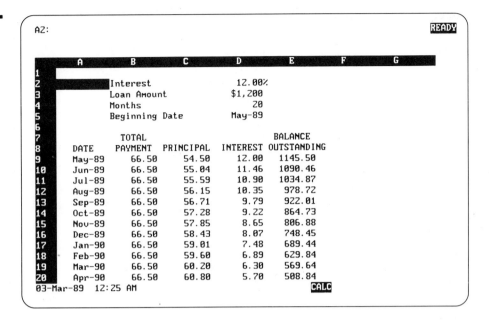

SETTINGS SHEET

Some commands of 1-2-3, such as the Print command, usually require you to use various submenus and their commands to properly tell 1-2-3 exactly how it is to handle a task, such as printing. In this type of situation, it is likely that users will forget or not be certain that they have entered all the commands necessary for performing a task. To alleviate this problem and to assist the user, 1-2-3 displays a special status screen called a **settings sheet** that helps you keep track of which commands you have selected as well as the responses to those commands (see Figure 4.11). A settings screen shows you the current settings for all of the options/commands related to accomplishing a particular task. The control panel containing the contents of the cell at the pointer location, along with the corresponding command menu, also appears above the settings screen. While the settings are displayed on the screen, you cannot make changes to them there, but must respond to the commands contained in the menu at the top of the screen.

With the Print command, for instance, you might want to change the right-hand margin, change the size of print, add a header or footer, and specify a new print range. You can specify these commands using the commands in the Print Menu as well as invoking a submenu using the Options entry of the Print Menu. As you respond to each of the various commands, your responses are immediately placed in the settings sheet, providing you with a summary of the various actions that you have taken.

HINTS/HAZARDS

When you are using a command that makes use of settings screens, your worksheet is not visible because of the status screen. If you wish to see the worksheet without leaving the command you are working with, 1-2-3 allows you to issue the Window command (F6) to make the settings screen disappear so that you can view your worksheet.

Figure 4.11

A print settings screen that appears when the Print command is selected

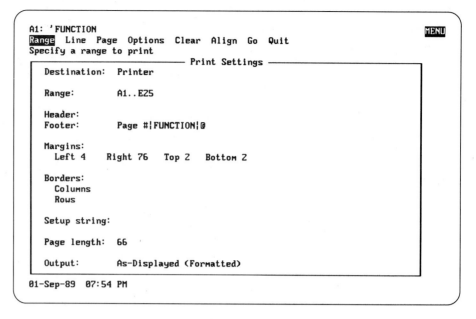

Figure 4.12

The settings screen that appears any time that the / Worksheet Global command has been entered at the keyboard

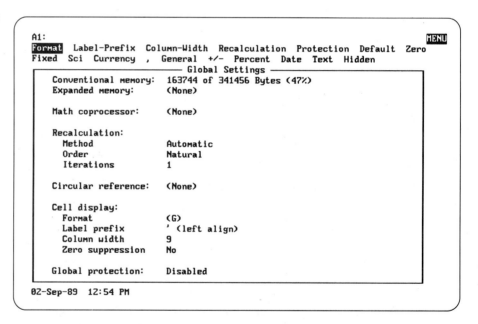

Another commonly viewed settings screen is the Global settings screen (see Figure 4.12), which appears any time a command starting with / Worksheet Global is entered from the keyboard. This settings screen provides you with summary information about the status of several important commands that, when entered, affect the entire worksheet. Many of these commands will be covered later in the text.

THE PRINT COMMAND

When you want to get something out of the computer or off disk so that you can examine it at your leisure, the **Print command** is an invaluable aid. On the other hand, if you don't understand how it generates output, the command can be frustrating to use. The Print command allows you to print either the whole worksheet or parts (ranges) of it. The output can be sent directly to a printer or placed in a disk file, from which it can later be used by a word processing program. The spreadsheets displayed in this book were originally created using 1-2-3, then saved to disk, and then accessed using WordStar's File command.

After you select the Print option from the Main Menu, 1-2-3 prompts you to tell it whether you want the output to go to a printer (the Printer option) or onto a disk file (the File option). If you select the File option, you will be asked to enter the filename, to which 1-2-3 will add the extension .PRN. This is important to remember, because if you wish to access the file later the filename you specify must include the .PRN extension.

PRINT MENU

At this point, 1-2-3 will display the following **Print Menu** in the control panel:

```
Range Line Page Options Clear Align Go Quit
```

Let's examine in turn what each of these options does.

Range The **Print Range option** is selected to tell 1-2-3 which part of the worksheet is to be printed. You can enter the cell addresses of two opposite corners of the range that is to be printed, or you can use the pointer to identify the range to 1-2-3.

Line The **Line Option** tells the printer attached to your computer to advance the paper one line. This command is useful when you want to leave some blank space between ranges that are printing out.

Page The **Page option** advances the paper in the printer to the top of the next page. It is useful if you want printed output to start on a new sheet of paper. After 1-2-3 is finished printing the range of cells that you have indicated, it stops the printer at that location. To advance the page in the printer, simply choose the Page option. This will also result in the printing of any footing lines (discussed later).

Options The Options selection invokes the **Options Menu** (shown below), which allows you to place headings, footings, borders, and so forth on the printout:

```
Header Footer Margins Borders Setup Pg-Length Other Quit
```

Options contained in this menu enable you to temporarily override defaults set by 1-2-3 for printing information. These overrides remain in effect until you change them or restart Lotus 1-2-3. If you save your spreadsheet and later call it back, Lotus 1-2-3 will remember the overrides because they will have become part of the worksheet file.

Header/Footer These options allow you to enter one line of text to be used as a heading or footing for each page of printout generated. You will be prompted for the text and can place up to 240 characters on the line. In either a heading or a footing line, the following special characters can be used to give printing instructions to 1-2-3:

#	Numbers the pages beginning with 1
¦	Splits headings/footings into sections as follows: The first part is left-justified The second part is centered The third part is right-justified
@	Prints today's date

For example, you could place the following text in the footing of the sample worksheet COMPSALS:

```
Page #¦COMPSALS¦@
```

This input would develop a footing with the word *Page* and the page number in the first (left-justified) section. The word COMPSALS would appear in the center part of the footing, its text centered. The date would appear in the third (right-justified) section.

Lotus 1-2-3 always leaves two blank lines between the worksheet and any headings and footings. You can suppress headings and footings by selecting `Options Other Unformatted` and reinstate them by selecting `Options Other Formatted`.

Margins This option, which allows you to change the current margins (left, right, top, and bottom), is especially important if you have a dot matrix printer and want to print the worksheet using compressed print so that you get more characters per line. The maximum value allowed for resetting the right-hand margin is 240 characters.

The None option of the Margins command permits you to clear the current margins and reset the top, left, and bottom margins to 0 and the right margin to 240.

HINTS/HAZARDS When you are printing on 8.5-inch by 11-inch paper and you reset the right-hand margin to a setting greater than the default (76), you will usually want to use a smaller type to get more characters to print. In this instance, you must also remember to use the Setup command to change the type size.

Borders This option allows you to specify horizontal or vertical borders that will be displayed on each page of a printed report. For example, you may have a worksheet that develops a loan amortization table and generates one line of output for each month of the loan; the Borders option could be used in this case to print column headings on each page. All you have to do is select the

Figure 4.13
Two ranges are required using the Borders option

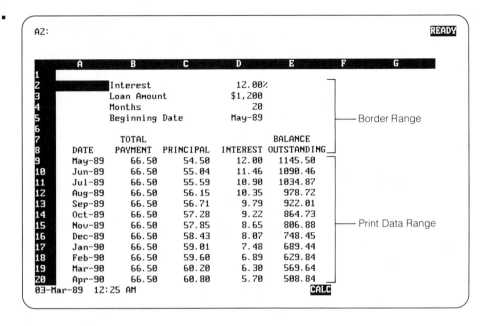

row or column (depending on where you want the labels) and then specify the range of cells containing the desired text. To clear the borders, you would enter the commands / PRINT PRINTER CLEAR BORDERS. The Borders option, to work properly, requires specifying the print range differently. When you use borders, do not specify any border cells in the print range; rather, specify them separately in the border range. Otherwise the border cells print twice on the first page. See Figure 4.13.

Setup This option tells your printer which escape code to use for printing the data. For example, for Epson FX or Epson-compatible printers, condensed printing (17.16 cpi) can be obtained by entering \015 as the setup string. In order to get back to pica (10 cpi) printing, you would have to enter \PRINT PRINTER OPTIONS SETUP, followed by \018. If you wished to print in elite (12 cpi), you would enter \077 to turn elite on; to turn it off, you would enter \080. Depending on the setup string, you can print in 10, 12, or 17.1 character pitch.

Page-Length This option, which allows you to tell 1-2-3 how many lines are on a page, becomes important when you use paper other than 11-inch paper.

Other This option displays the following menu:

As-Displayed Cell-Formulas Formatted Unformatted

As-Displayed. This option prints the output exactly as it appears on the screen.

Cell-Formulas. This option prints one cell per line and displays the cell contents (text or formula).

Formatted. This option restores any footings, headings, or page breaks that might have been suppressed.

Unformatted. This option overrides any footings, headings, or page breaks, printing the output without any of these features.

Clear As print specifications are entered, 1-2-3 stores them in RAM and uses them for any printing operations; in addition, it stores them to your worksheet file when the file is saved onto disk. Occasionally, you may not want these various print settings to be stored in memory; by selecting the **Clear option,** you can return all print options to their default values. This option results in the following menu being displayed:

All Range Borders Format

All. Resets all print settings to the default values.

Range. Cancels the print range.

Borders. Cancels the border range.

Format. Cancels margins, page length, and setup string and returns them to their default values.

Align The **Align command** is used when 1-2-3 has lost track of where it is on a sheet of paper—for example, when a user turns the knob on the printer platen to roll the paper forward, rather than using the Line or Page options. When this happens, position the paper in the printer to the top of a new sheet and execute the Align command; 1-2-3 will immediately assume that it is at the top of a new page.

Go The **Go option** tells 1-2-3 to send the designated range as output to the printer or to the named disk file, after which control is returned to Print Menu. This allows you to print other parts of the worksheet if you desire. If the printer is not on-line, 1-2-3 will try to print and find that it can't; it will then beep and display an error message. You must depress the Esc key to continue. If you are storing data onto a disk file, the Go command tells 1-2-3 to put the information in the file.

What happens if you forget to enter the setup string or print the wrong range? To stop printing, depress both the Ctrl and the Break keys; this will interrupt the printer and return control to the Print Menu. Use the Page command to go to the top of the next page, or position the paper to the top of the next page manually and enter the Align command.

Quit The **Quit option** tells 1-2-3 to terminate the print session and returns you to READY mode in the worksheet. When you are storing output data onto a disk file, you must use this command to close the file properly. If you do not, no data will be in the file when you try to access it later. When storing data onto a disk file, you must go through the following steps:

1. Name the file.
2. Establish the range and any options.
3. Enter the Go command to store data onto the disk file.
4. Enter the Quit command to close the disk file.

PRINT DEFAULT SETTINGS

Lotus 1-2-3 has a number of defaults for printing. Depending on the type of printer you have, some defaults may differ from those listed below. When a blank worksheet is started or when the Clear option is selected, 1-2-3 institutes or restores these default settings:

> Left margin is 4.
> Right margin is 76.
> Top margin is 2 lines from the top of the page.
> Bottom margin is 2 lines from the bottom of the page.
> Page length is 66 lines per page.
> Auto-line feed is No.
> Wait to insert a sheet of paper is No.
> Interface is parallel.
> Setup string is No.

1-2-3 AND THE PRINT LINE COUNTER

The 1-2-3 software package has an internal line counter for keeping track of the current printer position on a page. As it prints each line of a worksheet, 1-2-3 automatically adjusts this line counter. Three of the Print Menu commands—Line, Page, and Align—also affect this counter. The Line command not only issues a line feed for the printer but also increments the internal 1-2-3 line counter by a value of 1. The Page command tells the printer to go to the top of the next page and sets the line counter back to a beginning value. The Align command simply resets the line counter back to its beginning value.

It follows from the above discussion that you should not manually adjust the position of the paper within the printer, since 1-2-3 has no way of knowing that you have moved the paper. It remembers only the current line counter value. If you manually position the paper at the top of the next page and try to print another worksheet, you will have a ten-line gap wherever 1-2-3 "remembers" to issue a page break command to the printer. To solve this problem, issue a Ctrl-Break command and return to the Print Menu. Then manually move the paper to the top of the next page and issue an Align command. The line counter will be reset, and you will be ready to start printing.

FORCED PAGE BREAKS

One problem that faced many 1-2-3 users of Release 1A was how to get the spreadsheet to force a **page break,** that is, to force an end of page and start printing the next line at the top of the next page, in a long worksheet. This problem has been remedied in Release 2.x of 1-2-3 via the / Worksheet Page command. This command automatically forces a page break at the location in the worksheet in which it is entered. For example, if you wished to force a page break after the Liquor department line in the COMPSALS worksheet, you would first position the cursor to the Grocery line and enter the / Worksheet Page command (see Figure 4.14). Once this command has been entered, a blank line appears within the worksheet with a **::** entry. The **::** entry tells 1-2-3 that when it reaches this line in the worksheet it should issue a page break and begin the next line at the top of a new sheet of paper.

Figure 4.14

The COMPSALS worksheet with a hard page break (::) created with the pointer on the Grocery label

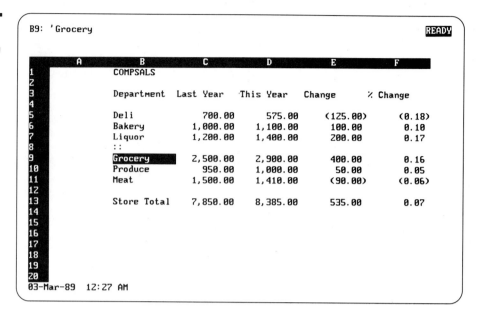

HINTS/HAZARDS

When you issue a page break command with the / Worksheet Page command, 1-2-3 inserts a new row into your worksheet and then places the page break symbol :: in the cell at which the pointer resided when the command was issued. This means that any portion of your worksheet off the screen also has this blank row added. You should, therefore, use this command carefully, since parts of your worksheet that are not currently viewed on your screen can be affected. To get rid of an undesired page break, use the / Worksheet Delete Row command if you have just entered the Page Break command. If you have had this command embedded in your worksheet for some time, make certain that no worksheet entries are currently on this row. If text, numbers, or formulas reside there, use the Move command or possibly the Range Erase command.

USING MULTIPLE PRINTERS WITH 1-2-3

You may have a copy of 1-2-3 that has been configured to allow you to use more than one printer for printing out worksheets. This means that if the default printer is different from the printer that you are trying to use, your printer output may not appear properly. For instance, all of the output may be printed on one line of the paper. Provided that drivers (sets of instructions) for other printers have been defined to your copy of 1-2-3, you can tell it to use another set of drivers by using the / Worksheet Global Default Printer Name command. After this command has been issued, a listing of printer driver numbers appears in the form of a menu at the top of your screen. Use the pointer to highlight the desired printer driver and press the Enter key. At this time 1-2-3 displays the name of the printer that corresponds with this number. If you wish to make this printer the default printer that will always be used by 1-2-3, issue the Update command to change the configuration file and then issue the Quit command to leave the menu. Usually you will want this change to be in effect only during a particular session with 1-2-3 and will only issue the Quit command after the new printer driver has been selected, which leaves the configuration file unchanged.

PASSING PRINT FILES TO OTHER SOFTWARE PACKAGES

Lotus 1-2-3 allows you to easily create print files that can be used as input to applications like word processing software. This is accomplished by entering the / Print File command. Once this command has been entered, 1-2-3 prompts you for the name of the file to be created. Enter the name of the file to be created, without specifying an extension, using regular DOS naming conventions. When you press the Enter key, an empty file with the specified name will be created on disk and 1-2-3 will automatically place a .PRN file extension on the file. You are now placed in the Print Menu; you can specify any options that you want the report to contain, such as headers, footers, margin changes, borders, and so on. After you have made all of the required entries, issue the Go command. You will note some disk activity as 1-2-3 saves the indicated range to disk. You must now enter the Quit command to tell 1-2-3 to close the file on disk. You will again see some disk activity.

The steps involved in generating a .PRN file on disk that can then be accessed by another application program are as follows:

1. Tell 1-2-3 to store data to disk (/ Print File)
2. Tell 1-2-3 the name of the file and press Enter
3. Make any changes using print commands in the Print Menu
4. Issue a Go command to save the print range to disk
5. Issue a Quit command to close the file

Steps 2, 4, and 5 are absolutely required any time you wish to create a .PRN file. If the Quit command is omitted, the File Allocation Table has not been updated and the file will be empty when it is accessed by another application program. Since the Quit command returns you to READY mode and is not used when multiple prints are sent to the printer instead of to a file, this portion of the command sequence is most frequently omitted. Remember that you must always end the process of creating a .PRN file by issuing the Quit command from the Print Menu and returning to READY mode.

If you have already covered WordStar, you have noted that it can directly access a worksheet file that has been created by Lotus 1-2-3 or work-a-like spreadsheet packages. Why, then, when WordStar has this ability, would you want to create a .PRN file? The reason is that the .PRN file provides more control over exactly how a print file is to be generated. For example, it allows the user to specify borders and to access the report containing those borders. It also frees the user from having to remember the cell addresses of the upper left-hand and lower right-hand corners of the worksheet containing the desired reports.

It doesn't matter whether you are using the ^KR command to load the worksheet directly into a WordStar document or to load a .PRN file. Remember, however, that you must include the file extension of the file being accessed by the ^KR command. You must, therefore, include the .WKS extension for a worksheet and the .PRN extension for a .PRN file.

Remember also that only the information that appears on the screen (the results generated by formulas), and not the formulas themselves, is accessed by your application program. If you make any changes to the data from a worksheet in your application program, the rest of the data will not automatically recalculate to reflect the change. You are dealing only with text data.

1-2-3 FUNCTIONS

You have already used the 1-2-3 function @SUM to take the place of a number of other, longer instructions. Functions save time and increase accuracy because they reduce the number of keystrokes and the chance for error. A function contains a preprogrammed set of instructions that you issue by using what 1-2-3 refers to as a **function call** (which involves naming the function) and then telling 1-2-3 where to find the data to act on.

A typical 1-2-3 function consists of the following parts:

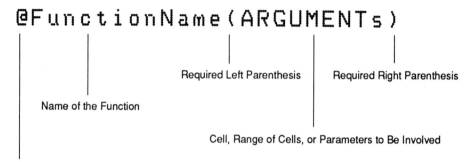

Some 1-2-3 functions used frequently in business and education are listed below. Other 1-2-3 functions can be found in Appendix A.

Date Functions:

@DATE (year, month, day)	Places the date for any day since 1/1/1900
@DAY (date)	Gets the day number from this date
@MONTH (date)	Gets the month number from this date
@YEAR (date)	Gets the year number from this date
@NOW	Gets the date from the DOS date register

Statistical Functions:

@COUNT (list)	Counts the number of entries in the specified list (range)
@SUM (list)	Sums the values of all cell contents in the list (range)
@AVG (list)	Averages the values of all cell contents in the list (range)
@MIN (list)	Finds the smallest value from the cells listed in the range
@MAX (list)	Finds the largest value from the cells listed in the range
@STD (list)	Finds the standard deviation from the values of the cells listed in the range

Figure 4.15
The black box approach to using functions

@VAR (list)   Finds the variance from the values of the cells listed in the range

Miscellaneous Functions:

@IF (cond,x,y)   Indicates that if the condition is true the value or formula in x will be used; otherwise, the value or formula in y will be used

@ROUND (x,n)   Indicates that number x will be rounded to n decimal positions. If the next position has a value of 5 or greater, the digit n will be rounded up; if that position has a value of 4 or less, the digit n will remain unchanged

The value of functions is best appreciated if you view them as "black boxes" that accept input and produce the output (correct answer) in the designated cell (see Figure 4.15). The input to a function consists of the arguments (if any) contained between parentheses. The meaning of these arguments varies from function to function. If multiple arguments appear, they are separated by commas. Sometimes arguments may consist of a range of cells; at other times they can have completely different roles. The point to keep in mind is that the function itself has all of the built-in routines required for producing the correct answer.

Functions can be **nested,** meaning that one function references another function. Suppose, for example, that you want to get the number of the month from the system date (DOS). You could do this by using the nested function statement @MONTH (@NOW), which uses the output of the @NOW function as input to the @MONTH function.

Another example of nesting would be the statement @ROUND (@AVG(F3..F6),1), which averages the numbers in the range F3 to F6 and then rounds the results to one decimal place. When you use nested functions, you must make certain that the number of left-hand parentheses equals the number of right-hand parentheses. If the numbers don't match, 1-2-3 will cause the computer to beep, indicating an error.

MORE ON DATA ENTRY

CHANGING A COLUMN WIDTH

When you are entering numeric data into a cell and receive asterisks (**********) in the cell, 1-2-3 is telling you that the column is not wide enough to display the number properly. You may also want to expand a column to provide sufficient room to display row labels properly. A column can be expanded via the **Column Width command:**

/	Gets the Main Menu
W	Selects the Worksheet option
C	Selects the Column Width command
S	Selects the Set command
_	Enters the desired column width
Enter	Executes the command

When you are entering the new column width, you can either enter a number or adjust the column width a character at a time by pressing the Arrow keys. The Right Arrow increases the column width by one position each time it is pressed, and the Left Arrow decreases the column width by one position each time it is pressed. The new column width appears on the status line between brackets ([ ]). For example, a cell in a column set to a width of 15 would contain a [1 5] on the status line of the control panel.

HINTS/HAZARDS For a numeric cell, 1-2-3 always reserves the rightmost character position to hold a right-hand parenthesis [)] or a percent sign (%).

CHANGING THE WIDTH OF SEVERAL COLUMNS

Many times, after you have set a global column width size, you may have a number of adjacent columns that you wish to set to a common column width other than the original width. For example, in the worksheet in Figure 4.16 (you'll build this worksheet later in this chapter), you may wish to change the column width of all the columns containing numbers from 5 to 10. Rather than using the / Worksheet Column Width command, it is easier to use the / Worksheet Column Column-Range command. This means that instead of entering four different commands, you only have to enter a single series of commands.

After positioning the pointer to cell B7, the command sequence for accomplishing this task is as follows:

/	Gets the Main Menu
W	Selects the Worksheet option
C	Selects the Column Width command
C	Selects the Column-Range option
S	Selects the Set option
E7 [by manual pointer movement]	Positions the pointer at cell E7
Enter	Establishes the range
10	Establishes the column width
Enter	Executes the command

The changed worksheet can now be seen in Figure 4.17.

Figure 4.16

A worksheet requiring column width change in columns B through E

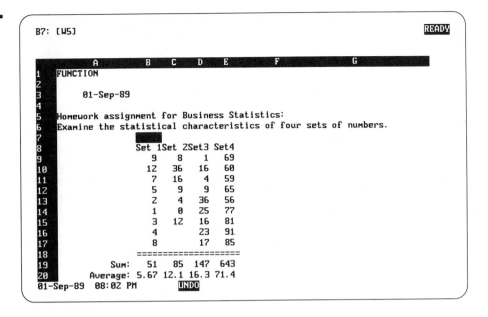

Figure 4.17

The worksheet after execution of the Column-Range command

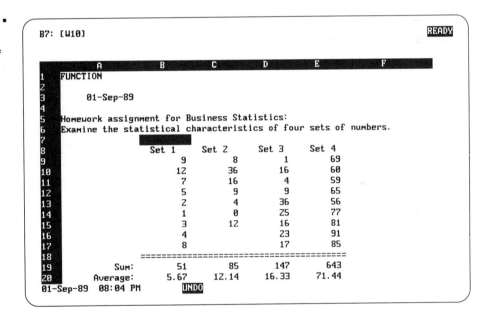

DATES

The 1-2-3 package gives you tremendous flexibility when it comes to entering numeric or text data in a cell. One of the features of 1-2-3 is its handling of dates as a numeric value. Since a date is really a numeric entry for 1-2-3, there can be no overflow to the next cell as with text data. The number generated by any date function represents the number of elapsed days since January 1, 1900. This number is meaningless until it is converted to a usable form via the / Range Format Date command. This means that the column width is extremely important no matter what date format has been selected. If the column is not wide enough to accept the text translation of the numeric date entry, 1-2-3 displays asterisks (*******) in the affected cell.

TEXT

When you enter text data within a worksheet cell, 1-2-3 automatically assumes that the text is to be left-justified within the cell and embeds a single quote (') to accomplish this task. If you want text right-justified or centered within a cell, you must instruct 1-2-3 via a label prefix character how the data should be presented. The label prefix characters are as follows:

'	Left-justify text
"	Right-justify text
^	Center text

While 1-2-3 automatically places the single quote in a cell for left-justifying text, you must manually enter a double quote (") or caret (^) as the first character within a cell when you want to right-justify or center text, respectively. Also keep in mind that the column has to be wide enough to properly display the text within the cell. For example, if you wish to right-justify the text Last Year within a cell, it would not appear properly justified if the column width were nine. In order for text to appear properly justified, the column width has to be greater than the text width.

HINTS/HAZARDS

You must never use a label prefix for a number that is to be involved in a calculation. When 1-2-3 sees a label prefix of ', ", or ^, it assumes that this is text data exactly as you have indicated and as a result assigns a number value of zero to the cell. If you sum a column of numbers that all have a label prefix, a value of zero will appear.

REPEATING TEXT

When you want to enter a repeating character or string of characters within a cell, 1-2-3 requires you to use the backslash (\) as a shorthand notation to tell it to repeat the character. Any character or characters following this **repeat symbol** will then be repeated until the cell is filled. The following examples assume that a column width of nine has been used.

Cell Entry	Cell Display
_	_ _ _ _ _ _ _ _ _
\ABC	ABCABCABC
\DOG	DOGDOGDOG
\=	=========

This shorthand method is frequently used to create subtotal lines (_ _ _ _ _ _ _ _ _) and total lines (= = = = = = = = =) within business reports.

1-2-3 SAMPLE FUNCTION WORKSHEET

Suppose you are taking an introductory class in statistics and early in the semester the teacher asks that you examine the characteristics of four sets of numbers. For each set of numbers, you are to calculate the average, the standard deviation, and the variance; you are also to give the high, the low, the sum, and the number of entries for each set of numbers. You are aware that 1-2-3 would be an ideal aid in performing this homework assignment. The sets of numbers are as follows:

1. 9, 12, 7, 5, 2, 1, 3, 4, and 8
2. 8, 36, 16, 9, 4, 0, and 12
3. 1, 16, 4, 9, 36, 25, 16, 23, and 17
4. 69, 60, 59, 65, 56, 77, 81, 91, and 85

After careful analysis, you conclude that the following worksheet will solve the problem:

```
FUNCTION
10-Jan-90
Homework assignment for Business Statistics:
Examine the statistical characteristics of four sets
of numbers.

              Set 1     Set 2     Set 3     Set 4
                  9         8         1        69
                 12        36        16        60
                  7        16         4        59
                  5         9         9        65
                  2         4        36        56
                  1         0        25        77
                  3        12        16        81
                  4                  23        91
                  8                  17        85
===========================================================
       Sum:      51        85       147       643
   Average:    5.67     12.14     16.33     71.44
Stand. Dev.:    3.4     10.86     10.26     11.83
  Variance:   11.56    117.84    105.33    140.02
   Maximum:      12        36        36        91
   Minimum:       1         0         1        56
     Count:       9         7         9         9
```

In doing this project, you will practice the following skills:

1. Using the @NOW and @DATE date functions
2. Changing the column width of one column
3. Using the F2 Edit function for correcting errors
4. Using statistical functions
5. Using the @ROUND function
6. Using nested functions
7. Copying a single-column range to multiple columns
8. Handling blank cells and cells with a blank on functions

Be sure that you enter the date before you start Lotus 1-2-3. It will become important later on. If you have already entered the date and there is material on the worksheet screen, you can erase it by typing

/

W Worksheet

E Erase

Y Yes

1-2-3 SAMPLE FUNCTION SPREADSHEET

1. Enter the name of the worksheet.

    A1   FUNCTION

2. "Stamp" the worksheet with today's date at cell A3, using the @NOW function.

    A3   @NOW

    ENTER

    In this sample worksheet, the @NOW function caused 33360 to be placed in the cell, signifying that 33,360 days have elapsed since December 31, 1899. That number must now be converted to a more useful format.

    You could also enter today's date manually, using the @DATE (yy,mm,dd) function. In this example, you would enter @DATE (91,5,2). You would receive the same result of 33360 in cell A3, however, and you would still need to format that cell in order for the information to become useful.

3. Change the number in cell A3 to a standard business format.

    | / | Gets the Main Menu |
    | R | Selects the Range option |
    | F | Selects the Format option |
    | D | Selects the Date command from Format |
    | Enter | Selects the first option of Date (DD-MMM-YY) |
    | Enter | Executes the command |

4. You will notice that ********* (1-2-3's overflow indication) now appears in cell A3, indicating that the cell is not wide enough to display the data. This generally happens after some type of data manipulation; it does not happen with standard text data. In order to get rid of this error, you must change the width of column A to 15—a size large enough for labels that are to be entered later.

    | / | Gets the Main Menu |
    | W | Selects the Worksheet option |
    | C | Selects the Column Width command |
    | S | Selects the Set command |
    | 15 | Enters the new desired column width for this column |
    | Enter | Executes the instruction |

5. Enter the text data exactly as they appear below (you'll correct any errors later).

A5	Homework assignment for Business Statistics:
A6	Examine the statistical characteristics of fours sets of numbers.
B8	^Set 1
C8	^Set 2
D8	^Set 3
E8	^Set 4
A19	"Sum:
A20	"Average:
A21	"Stand. Dev.:
A22	"Variance
A23	Maximum
A24	"Minimum:
A25	"Count:

The ^ character is found above the 6 key and is used to tell 1-2-3 to center the data within the cell. It is one of three commands that tell 1-2-3 how to position data within a cell. The three are

'	Left-justify text within the cell
"	Right-justify text within the cell
^	Center text within the cell

Notice that text data and manipulated data are handled differently by 1-2-3. Text data are allowed to overflow cell boundaries. For example, if you went to cell B6 and entered "new text," the words would appear in the middle of the text that was entered in A6.

6. You probably noticed that the text you entered above contains three errors: Cell A6 says *fours* instead of *four*; cell A22 does not have a : mark after *Variance*; and cell A23 is not right-justified and lacks a : mark. You could correct these errors by reentering all of the data, but to be more efficient you could use the Edit function (invoked by the F2 key) as part of the following procedure:

A6 [by manual pointer movement]	Positions the pointer to cell A6
F2	Displays the contents of cell A6 on both the status line and the entry line, and positions the pointer at the end of the line. (The text is now available to the user for manipulation.)
Back Arrow to *s* of *fours*	Moves the pointer to the *s* of *fours*
Del	Erases the *s*
Enter	Exits the Edit mode
A22 [by manual pointer movement]	Positions the pointer at cell A22
F2	Displays the contents of cell A22 for editing, with the pointer at the end of the line

:	Enters the : at the end of the line
Enter	Tells 1-2-3 to change the data within the cell
A23 [by manual pointer movement]	Positions the pointer at cell A23
F2	Displays the contents of cell A23 for editing, with the pointer at the end of the line
Home	Moves the pointer to the beginning of the line, under the ' mark
Del	Deletes the single quote (')
"	Tells 1-2-3 to right-justify the contents of the cell
End	Moves the pointer to the end of the text within the cell
:	Enters the : mark at the end of the line
Enter	Tells 1-2-3 to change the data within the cell

7. Enter the four sets of numbers.

B9	9	C9	8	D9	1	E9	69
B10	12	C10	36	D10	16	E10	60
B11	7	C11	16	D11	4	E11	59
B12	5	C12	9	D12	9	E12	65
B13	2	C13	4	D13	36	E13	56
B14	1	C14	0	D14	25	E14	77
B15	3	C15	12	D15	16	E15	81
B16	4			D16	23	E16	91
B17	8			D17	17	E17	85

8. Enter the total line for cell B18.

\=	Repeats the equal sign throughout the cell
Enter	Tells 1-2-3 to enter the data in the cell

The backslash (\), located above the Alt key, is used by 1-2-3 as the repeat indicator. Any character or characters that appear after the backslash will be repeated throughout the cell. For example, \ABC would place ABCABCABC in the cell.

9. Copy the Total line to the cell locations of C18, D18, and E18. Leave the pointer at cell B18.

/	Gets the Main Menu
C	Selects the Copy command
Enter	Establishes cell B18 as the only cell in the "From" range
C18 [by manual pointer movement]	Positions the pointer at cell C18 (the beginning of the "To" range)
.	Nails down the beginning of the range
E18 [by manual pointer movement]	Positions the pointer at the last cell in the "To" range
Enter	Tells 1-2-3 to execute the copy instruction

10. Enter the statistical functions for column B.
    a. Enter the @SUM function at B19.

@SUM(	Enters the first part of the @SUM function
B9 [by manual pointer movement]	Positions the pointer at cell B9 (the beginning of the range)
.	Nails down the beginning of the range
B17 [by manual pointer movement]	Positions the pointer at the last cell in the "To" range
)	Enters the right parenthesis
Enter	Tells 1-2-3 to execute the command and places the result in cell B19

    This method demonstrates using the pointer to point addresses to a 1-2-3 function. In addition to entering the locations via pointing, you can also give the locations directly to 1-2-3.

    b. Enter the @AVG function at B20 by directly entering the cell addresses of the cells involved.

    @AVG (B9.B17)   Enter

    Since you already know the cell locations from having pointed out the @SUM locations, you now need enter only the cell location at the beginning of the range and the cell location at the end of the range. To execute the command, just depress the Enter key.

    c. Enter the remaining functions, either by pointing or by entering the cell addresses directly. Remember, enter the formulas only for column B; you'll be copying them to the other columns later.

@STD	Standard Deviation
@Var	Variance
@MAX	Maximum
@MIN	Minimum
@COUNT	Count

11. You can now see that the average, standard deviation, and variance entries all have several decimal positions; having this many positions to the right of the decimal point can be distracting to anyone wishing to use the information in report form. You could use the / Range Format command to change the output format of these three cells, but this situation provides an excellent opportunity to use nested functions. You will use the Edit feature of 1-2-3 and add the @ROUND function to the three cells containing average, standard deviation, and variance entries. First, position the pointer at cell B20.

F2	Invokes 1-2-3's EDIT mode
Home	Positions the pointer at the beginning of the line
@ROUND(	Inserts @ROUND(at the beginning of the existing line
End	Positions the pointer at the end of the line
,2)	Tells 1-2-3 that you want only two positions to the right of the decimal
Enter	Tells 1-2-3 to enter the data in the cell

    Instead of seeing 5.6666666 in cell B20, you should now see 5.67.

12. Repeat the steps in task 11 to change the entries in cells B20 and B22.
13. Copy the formulas for the calculations from column B to columns C, D, and E. Position the pointer at B19.

/	Invokes the Main Menu
C	Selects the Copy command
B25 [by manual pointer movement]	Positions the pointer at the end of the "From" range
Enter	Tells 1-2-3 that the "From" range has been completely defined
C19 [by manual pointer movement]	Positions the pointer at the first cell in the "To" range
.	Marks the beginning of the "To" range
E19 [by manual pointer movement]	Positions the pointer at the last cell in the "To" range
Enter	Tells 1-2-3 that the "To" range has been completely defined and tells it to execute the command

The reason you didn't have to give cell E25 as the last address has to do with how 1-2-3 remembers your definition of the "From" range. You defined the range as one column wide and as going from cell B19 to cell B25. 1-2-3 is thus informed that the "From" range consists of seven rows of cells. Once you tell 1-2-3 in a Copy command where to put the first cell of the "From" range column, it will assume that you also wish to copy the rest of the cells in that column.

You indicated three cells as the columns to receive the range. Since each of these cells was in a different column, 1-2-3 assumed that you wanted three copies of the "From" range—one for each column.

14. Examine the results of the calculations on the screen. Notice that column C has two blank entries and that the count is indeed equal to 7. Lotus 1-2-3 is capable of determining when to include a cell in a calculation, and when not to, based on its contents or lack of them. Now what will happen if you make a change in cell C16? Position your pointer at C16.

Space	Adds a character space
Enter	Tells 1-2-3 to enter the data in the cell

Notice that, even though there is no value in C16, the results of the calculations on the screen have been altered dramatically. Notice also that a single quote (') appears in cell C16. Go back to cell C16 and enter the command / Range Erase. The results of the various statistical evaluations immediately return to their original values.

When using ranges that contain so-called "blank" cells, you should make certain that they really are blank. The single quote (') warns you that the contents of this cell will not work properly in any type of numeric calculation.

15. Save the worksheet using the filename FUNCTION.

/	Gets the Main Menu
F	Takes the File option
S	Takes the Save command
FUNCTION	Enters the name FUNCTION as the filename

16. Print the file and put the date, page, and name of the file in a footing.

/	Invokes the Main Menu
P	Selects the Print option
P	Directs the output to the printer
R	Selects the Range command
A1 [by manual pointer movement]	Positions the pointer at A1
.	Nails down the beginning of the print range
G25 [by manual pointer movement]	Positions the pointer at G25 (the end of the range), allowing all text to print
Enter	Indicates to 1-2-3 that the range has been established
O	Selects the Options Menu entry from the Print Menu
F	Selects the Footer command from the Options Menu
Page # ¦FUNCTIONS¦@	Tells 1-2-3 to divide the footing into three parts, as follows: the page number left-justified in the left-hand part; the name of the file, FUNCTION, centered in the middle part; today's date right-justified in the right-hand part
Enter	Submits the footing to 1-2-3
Q	Terminates the Options Menu and returns to the Print Menu
G	Prints the worksheet
P	Prints the footing while going to the top of the next page
Q	Quits and returns to the worksheet

Your worksheet should now appear exactly like the one at the beginning of this Sample Worksheet section. If it doesn't, compare your cell contents to those in the following list:

```
    FUNCTION Cell Contents
A1: 'FUNCTION
A3: (D1) @NOW
A5: 'Homework assignment for Business Statistics:
A6: 'Examine the statistical characteristics of four
    sets of numbers.
B8: ^Set 1
C8: ^Set 2
D8: ^Set 3
E8: ^Set 4
B9: 9
C9: 8
D9: 1
```

```
E9:  69
B10: 12
C10: 36
D10: 16
E10: 60
B11: 7
C11: 16
D11: 4
E11: 59
B12: 5
C12: 9
D12: 9
E12: 65
B13: 2
C13: 4
D13: 36
E13: 56
B14: 1
C14: 0
D14: 25
E14: 77
B15: 3
C15: 12
D15: 16
E15: 81
B16: 4
D16: 23
E16: 91
B17: 8
D17: 17
E17: 85
B18: \=
C18: \=
D18: \=
E18: \=
A19: "Sum:
B19: @SUM(B9..B17)
C19: @SUM(C9..C17)
D19: @SUM(D9..D17)
E19: @SUM(E9..E17)
A20: "Average:
B20: @ROUND(@AVG(B9..B17),2)
C20: @ROUND(@AVG(C9..C17),2)
D20: @ROUND(@AVG(D9..D17),2)
E20: @ROUND(@AVG(E9..E17),2)
A21: "Stand.Dev.:
B21: @ROUND(@STD(B9..B17),2)
C21: @ROUND(@STD(C9..C17),2)
D21: @ROUND(@STD(D9..D17),2)
E21: @ROUND(@STD(E9..E17),2)
A22: "Variance:
B22: @ROUND(@VAR(B9..B17),2)
C22: @ROUND(@VAR(C9..C17),2)
D22: @ROUND(@VAR(D9..D17),2)
E22: @ROUND(@VAR(E9..E17),2)
A23: "Maximum:
```

```
B23:  @MAX(B9..B17)
C23:  @MAX(C9..C17)
D23:  @MAX(D9..D17)
E23:  @MAX(E9..E17)
A24:  "Minimum:
B24:  @MIN(B9..B17)
C24:  @MIN(C9..C17)
D24:  @MIN(D9..D17)
E24:  @MIN(E9..E17)
A25:  "Count:
B25:  @COUNT(B9..B17)
C25:  @COUNT(C9..C17)
D25:  @COUNT(D9..D17)
E25:  @COUNT(E9..E17)
```

CHAPTER REVIEW

A range is any "box" of data cells that has four 90° angles. Various commands allow you either to point out a range of cells to be affected by a later command or to specify addresses of two opposite corners of the range, thereby identifying it.

The Copy command is used to copy the contents of one or more cells (the sending area) and place these contents in a receiving area of one or more other cells. The Copy command has two parts: specifying the sending area (the "From" range) and specifying the receiving area (the "To" range). Both areas are ranges that you can denote either by giving the cell addresses or by using the pointer to point them out.

The Format command can be used in either a range or a global manner. The Range option formats only a portion of the worksheet, whereas the Global option formats the entire worksheet not currently under a Range command format. A number of format options are available, including Fixed, Currency, Date, Percent, or Scientific.

The Print command allows you to specify exactly how you wish to print all or part of your worksheet—the range to be printed and any options that you desire, such as margins, headings, or footings—and then lets you tell 1-2-3 to print.

The built-in functions of 1-2-3 may be simple or compound (the so-called nested functions, produced when one function is used as input to another function). A worksheet using a number of statistical functions can accommodate many of the spreadsheet concepts involved in these various commands.

1-2-3 allows you to perform a number of special-purpose tasks to make certain that data are presented properly. It allows you to add and delete rows and columns, move text from one position in a worksheet to another, and issue page breaks within the worksheet for later printing.

1-2-3 also allows you to control how data appear within a cell. For example, it allows you to change the column width, right-justify text, center text, and repeat text within a cell.

KEY TERMS AND CONCEPTS

Align command
Borders option
Clear option
Column Width command
Copy command
Footer option
format
Format Currency option

Format Date option
Format Fixed option
Format General option
Format Percent option
Format Scientific option
Format Text option
Format , option
Format +/− option
function call
Go option
Header option
Line option
Margins option
Move feature
nailing down
nested functions
Options Menu

Other option
page break
Page-Length option
Page option
Print command
Print Menu
Print Range option
Quit option
range
Range Format option
receiving ("To" range)
repeat symbol
sending ("From" range)
settings sheet
Setup option
Worksheet Global Format option

CHAPTER QUIZ

Multiple Choice

1. Which of the following statements about ranges is false?
   a. A range must be either a rectangle or a square.
   b. A range can be defined by "pointing."
   c. A range can be defined by giving the cell addresses of two opposite corners.
   d. A range can be defined by pointing to the first cell and entering the address of the second cell.
   e. All of the above methods can be used to define a range to 1-2-3.

2. Which of the following statements about the Copy command is false?
   a. The first item to be defined is the sending cell/range.
   b. The second item to be defined is the receiving cell/range.
   c. The receiving range can overlap with the sending range without data being lost.
   d. The receiving range can be larger than the sending range.
   e. All of the above statements are true.

3. Which of the following steps is not involved in printing a worksheet to a file?
   a. Name the file.
   b. Establish the range and any options.
   c. Issue the Go command.
   d. Take the Quit command to close the file.
   e. All of the above are necessary.

4. Which of the following is not available using the Print Menu?
   a. Specify the right margin.
   b. Specify the page length.
   c. Specify the subtotal point.
   d. Specify the heading and/or footing for each page.
   e. Specify the setup string for printing.
   f. All of the above are print commands.

5. Which of the following statements is true for functions?
   a. It is difficult to nest functions.
   b. The character used to denote a function is *.
   c. The date functions are of relatively little use.
   d. The function @MONTH (@NOW) is used to get the month of the year when the date was entered after the boot process.

True/False

6. Functions can save you, the user, a tremendous amount of time.

7. Ranges are typically entered by using three cell addresses.

8. You can print a worksheet without specifying the print range.

9. The setup string allows you to print in 10, 12, or 17.1 cpi.

10. Print footings allow you to print out the page number, today's date, and some text data.

Answers

1. d   2. c   3. e   4. c   5. d   6. t   7. f   8. f   9. t   10. t

Exercises

1. Define or describe each of the following:
   a. range
   b. Range Format
   c. Global Format
   d. Setup string
   e. footing
   f. Align command
   g. Line option
   h. Page option
   i. nested function

2. When using the Copy command, you must first define the _____ range and then define the _____ range.

3. When the receiving range overlaps the sending range, some data will be _____.

4. A(n) _____ format affects the entire worksheet, while a(n) _____ format affects only an area of the worksheet.

5. The _____ places a $ and any needed commas in a number.

6. Before the worksheet or a part of the worksheet can be printed out, the print _____ must be defined to 1-2-3.

7. In addition to dumping output to a printer, 1-2-3 can also place it in a(n) _____.

8. The _____ selection under the Options Menu allows you to change the print pitch.

9. The _____ command allows you to define *top of page* to 1-2-3.

10. The _____ command moves the paper a small increment, while the _____ command moves the paper to the top of the next page.

11. How does the role of the Quit command in creating printer output differ from its role in creating disk output?

12. What is the advantage of nesting functions?

13. List the functions you consider to be useful at this time.

14. When a number will not fit in a cell, 1-2-3 fills that cell with _____.

15. The _____ character tells 1-2-3 to repeat the text across the cell.

16. If you delete a row or a column, all of the _____ in that row or column will be deleted.

17. The _____ command is used to increase the width of a column.

18. The @NOW function results in _____ appearing in the cell in which it resides.

19. The label prefix _____ is used to center text.

20. The "repeat the following characters" command in 1-2-3 is the _____.

21. The screen that provides information about the options that you have selected as well as the defaults of command options is called a(n) _____ sheet.

22. If you wish to set the width of several columns at one time, the _____ command must be used.

23. A settings screen can be made to disappear by using the _____ command.

24. The _____ of the Margins command resets all margins except the right-hand margin to zero.

25. The command sequence _____ is used to select a printer other than the default.

Figure 4.18
Payroll register worksheet

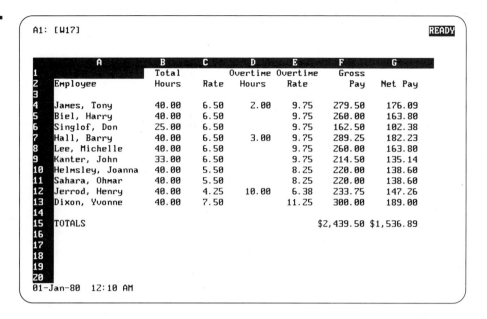

COMPUTER EXERCISES

1. In this exercise, you are to prepare a payroll register. Enter the formulas that would be necessary to prepare the register shown in Figure 4.18. The Net Pay figure is calculated by subtracting the appropriate deductions and taxes from the Gross Pay figure that has been previously calculated. The deductions and taxes, for the sake of simplicity, are assumed to be 37%. The overtime rate is computed by rate * 1.5. Set column A to a width of 20. Set the remaining columns to a width of 11. Your worksheet will not appear so crowded.
   Save your worksheet file using the name CH4EX1.

2. A teacher friend has asked your assistance in developing a worksheet for calculating grades (see Figure 4.19). Your friend has developed the following criteria for the worksheet:
   a. It is important to have the worksheet stamped with today's date.
   b. The total possible points are to appear at the top of each column.
   c. The average, high grade, low grade, standard deviation, and variance statistics are to be calculated using 1-2-3 functions.
   d. The % of Total Points entry is to be calculated by dividing the average by total possible points.

   The following information contains the format for the worksheet:
   a. You must set column A to a width of 15.
   b. Set the rest of the columns to a width of 11.
   c. You must also use the @NOW function to "date-stamp" the worksheet in cell A1.
   d. The ¦ character is found above the Alt key.

   Save this worksheet file using the CH4EX2 filename.

Figure 4.19
Worksheet for calculating grades

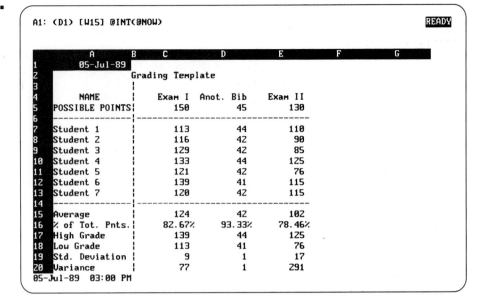

3. Print out your CH4EX2 worksheet file. Specify a heading that has "Introduction to Microcomputers" as the text to appear at the top of the page. Specify a footing that has the page number, the name of the worksheet file, and the date at the bottom of the page. Refer to the Print command structure in Appendix A if you have questions about how to get to a command.

4. Print out your CH4EX1 worksheet file. Specify a condensed print setup so that the worksheet will print on one page of paper. Refer to the print structure chart in Appendix A. You will also have to expand the right-hand column to a width of 120.

5. Print out your CH4EX2 worksheet to a disk file called TEST. Leave 1-2-3 and access the TEST.PRN file with your word processing software, or use the DOS TYPE command to make sure that you created the file properly. Remember that 1-2-3 has placed the .PRN extension on the file.

6. Retrieve the worksheet CH4EX2. You have just received word that your teacher friend forgot to include a student named Student5a in the list. This individual's scores are 100 for Exam I, 41 for Anot. Bib., and 113 for Exam II. Add this individual to the existing grading worksheet, making any necessary changes. Store the changed worksheet to a file named CH4EX6.

7. You are now to add a column to replace the existing column A in the CH3EX5 file. This column should have a heading of "Dept." The two different sales forces in the business are the new-car sales staff (1) and the preowned-car sales staff (2). Ralph, Louise, and Caroline are in the Dept. 1 cells, while the others are in Dept. 2. Place the result in a file called CH4EX7.

Figure 4.20
Golf score worksheet

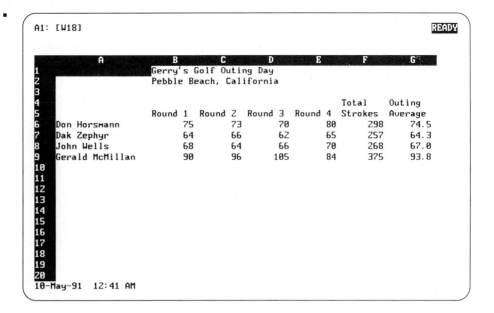

 8. Prepare a worksheet that Gerry can use for his golf outing day. Gerry is interested in tracking scores for golfers over four rounds. He is interested not only in calculating the total strokes over the four rounds of golf but also in finding the average number of strokes for each golfer during the outing. Give the average score column a range format of fixed with one position to the right of the decimal. (See Figure 4.20.) Save as CH4EX8.

CHAPTER 5

MAINTAINING AND ENHANCING YOUR WORKSHEETS

CHAPTER OBJECTIVES

After completing this chapter, you should be able to:

- **Discuss commands that allow you more control over your environment**
- **Use range names**
- **Use dummy rows and columns in ranges**
- **Use the Sort command**
- **Use the Titles option**
- **Know when to use relative and absolute addressing**
- **Use mixed cell addresses**
- **Use absolute range names**
- **Use automatic worksheet recalculation**
- **Use the @PMT, @ROUND, and @IF functions**
- **Use the @DATE function**

After you have initially built a worksheet, you are usually still not finished with it. You may wish to correct minor errors or add enhancements to your worksheet to give it a more professional appearance.

This chapter will cover the following topics: controlling your worksheet environment; range names; sorting; titles; absolute versus relative addressing; automatic recalculation; and more on the functions @PMT, @IF, and @DATE.

CONTROLLING YOUR WORKSHEET ENVIRONMENT

The Lotus 1-2-3 package provides you with a number of options you can use to obtain more control over your worksheet environment. Some of these commands make it easier to generate reports with the exact columns desired and to present numeric information in the manner desired. Others allow you to change directories on a fixed disk, rearrange column and row data, and save files with password protection.

WORKSHEET ZERO COMMAND

The Worksheet **Zero command** allows you to suppress any zeros that occur within numeric cells. These zeros can be either the answer generated by a formula or a zero that has been entered. The command / Worksheet Global Zero Yes tells 1-2-3 that no zeros are to be displayed in cells. The command / Worksheet Global Zero No tells 1-2-3 that zeros are again to be displayed in a cell.

The Label option of the Zero command allows you to tell 1-2-3 to place a character string in any cell that contains a zero value. When this option is selected, the prompt below appears at the top of your screen:

```
Enter label (can include label prefix):
```

You now enter the desired characters; for instance, you could enter the text N/A. Now, whenever any cell contains a zero value, the N/A character string appears in that cell.

GOTO COMMAND

Up to this point, you have positioned the pointer to a location in your worksheet via pointer movement commands. 1-2-3 provides a faster way to go directly to the address of a cell via the **GoTo command,** invoked by pressing the function key F5. Once the GoTo command has been issued, the prompt `Enter address to go to: E14` is displayed. The cell address displayed after the command has been issued is the current pointer address. You can now enter the new cell location and press the Enter key. The pointer then moves to the new cell address. The GoTo command (F5) can save you many keystrokes when you are working on a large worksheet application.

SYSTEM COMMAND

1-2-3 allows you to temporarily exit 1-2-3 and enter DOS via the **System command** of the Main Menu. The System command allows you to run a program or execute a DOS command. For example, many people routinely forget to enter the date and time when they boot the system. Using the System command, you can drop to DOS and use the DOS DATE and TIME commands to

Figure 5.1

Your screen after you execute the 1-2-3 System command

```
(Type EXIT and press ENTER to return to 1-2-3)

Microsoft(R) MS-DOS(R)  Version 3.20
          (C)Copyright Microsoft Corp 1981-1986

C>date 9-4-89

C>time 13:45

C>
```

enter this information (see Figure 5.1). Once you have finished with your tasks at the DOS level, enter the EXIT command; you will return to your worksheet in READY mode.

CHANGING THE DIRECTORY

Directory Command in Default Submenu When you use 1-2-3 on a fixed disk, 1-2-3 usually assumes that worksheet files are to be saved to the directory in which your 1-2-3 program files reside. You may, however, wish to save worksheet files to another directory or even to a diskette in a disk drive (for example, drive B). To accomplish this, you must use the / Worksheet Global Default **Directory command** and then enter either the new directory path (for example, C:\wksfiles \ school) or the disk drive followed by a backslash (for example, B:\).

Once you have entered the appropriate information, 1-2-3 returns you to the Default submenu. To make this change permanent so that 1-2-3 always uses the entity you have just described for storing any worksheet, issue the Update command. Most of the time, however, this change is temporary. In that case, issue the Quit command and you will be returned to READY mode.

Note that when you issue the Quit command after changing the directory, the change has been made only for this worksheet session. If you use the Update command before you quit from the Default submenu, the change becomes permanent. This means that when you now leave 1-2-3 and start it at a different date, it will default to the directory/disk that it currently finds in its default information file.

Directory Command in File Submenu A second way to change the default directory involves using the **Directory command** found in the File submenu. This Directory command allows you to change the default directory for this 1-2-3 session only but does not permit you to change this default in the configuration file. Executing this command involves entering the command / File Directory and then entering the drive identifier/path. Changing the default drive to the A drive entails entering A:.

Figure 5.2
COMPSALS worksheet

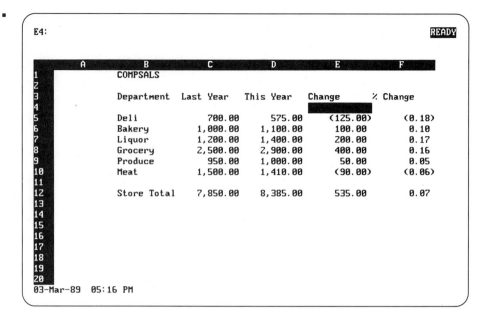

COLUMN HIDE

You may run into a situation where it is advantageous to print certain columns of a worksheet without printing certain other embedded columns. This is accomplished via the / Worksheet Column **Hide command**. For example, suppose that you wished to print, as well as display, your COMPSALS worksheet (see Figure 5.2) without the Change column (column E). You must first position your pointer anywhere in column E and then issue the following command:

/	Gets the Main Menu
W	Selects the Worksheet option
C	Selects the Column option
H	Selects the Hide option
Enter	Tells 1-2-3 that this is the only column to be hidden (To hide multiple columns, expand the range.)

The worksheet depicted in Figure 5.3 is now displayed on your screen. Even though column F's entries are dependent on the hidden column E, the data still are calculated properly. The only way that you can tell that column E has been hidden is to examine the row border labels. The hidden column has no detrimental impact on the rest of the worksheet. To make the hidden column reappear, issue the above command, but replace the Hide option with the Display option. Columns previously hidden reappear on the screen with an asterisk to the right of the column identifier in the column border (see Figure 5.4). To "unhide" the column, place the pointer in the column marked with the asterisk (column E) and press the Enter key. The column has now been restored.

The real advantage of hiding columns is that you can hide columns containing intermediate results when it comes time to print a report. Only the columns that contain data meaningful for a specific report need be displayed on the screen and printed. This feature allows you to prepare reports that are more easily understood by their users.

Figure 5.3
Worksheet with column E hidden

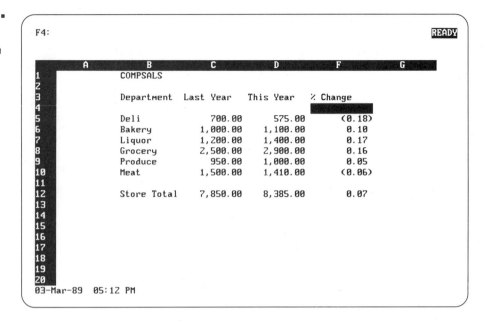

Figure 5.4
Worksheet hidden column marked with * using Display command

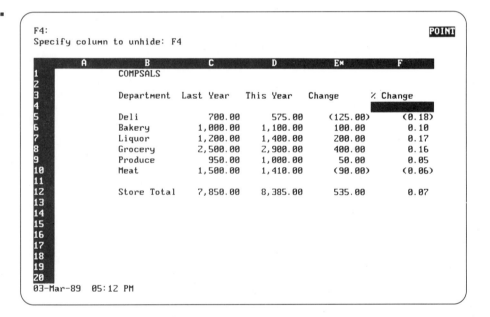

FINDING CIRCULAR REFERENCES AND STATUS COMMANDS

Suppose that you are working on an application like the COMPSALS worksheet and suddenly a **circular reference** (CIRC) is indicated in your worksheet (see Figure 5.5). You have no idea what has caused this to occur. You don't even have any idea how long ago the CIRC reference indicator appeared on

Figure 5.5

Worksheet with a circular reference

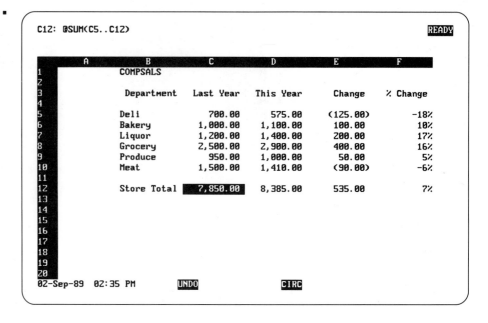

Figure 5.6

Status screen for COMPSALS worksheet

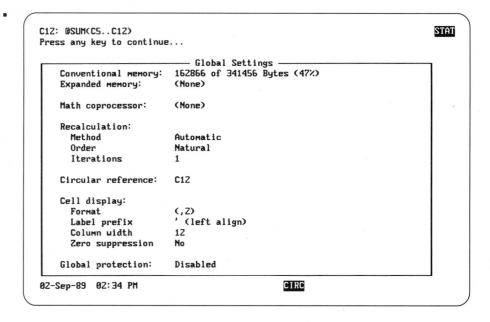

your screen, because you were not looking at the indicators area of the worksheet. Finding the location of the circular reference with the least amount of difficulty involves using the / Worksheet Status command. This information can also be seen in the Global settings screen.

Once that command is issued to 1-2-3, a screen similar to the screen in Figure 5.6 appears. You see that 1-2-3 indicates that a circular reference exists in cell C12. You press the Enter key to return to READY mode and find that the formula @SUM(C5..C12) is in cell C12 (see Figure 5.5). The problem is that cell C12 has been told not only to hold the answer but also to participate

Figure 5.7

The Default Status screen for COMPSALS

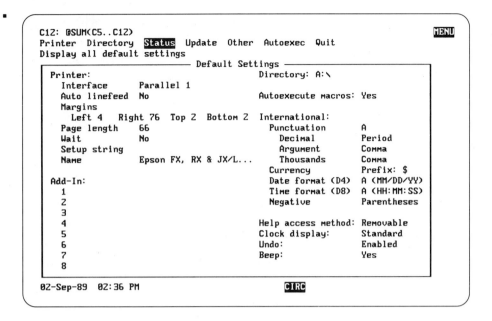

in the calculation. After you use the Edit command and change the 12 in the formula to 10, the circular reference disappears from the screen.

If multiple circular references occur within a worksheet, 1-2-3 finds only one at a time. Therefore, you must correct each as it is found and then issue another / Worksheet Status command to find the next.

Besides finding circular references, the / Worksheet Status command provides other valuable pieces of information. For example, it indicates the amount of memory available for a worksheet as well as the amount of memory used by your worksheet. It also contains information about methods of recalculation, global format use, the current global column width, and whether or not zero suppression is in effect.

Another important settings screen can be invoked via the / Worksheet Global Default command. The report generated by this command (see Figure 5.7) contains information about the defaults currently in effect in your worksheet. For example, it contains information about the printer interface used, margins, page characteristics, directory in use, and various formats that are in effect for punctuation, currency, and date and time presentation.

PASSWORD-PROTECTING YOUR WORKSHEETS

Release 2 provides you with the ability to password-protect your worksheet files.

HINTS/HAZARDS

If you have a bad memory, you should not use passwords. Once you save a file with a **password,** you will always be prompted for the password before 1-2-3 will allow you to access the file. If you forget your password, 1-2-3 will deny you access to the worksheet.

The following example shows how to save the worksheet YEAREND with the password FINLCOPY.

/	Invokes the Main Menu.
F	Selects the File option.
S	Tells 1-2-3 to save the worksheet file.
YEAREND P	Enter the name of the file, press the Space Bar, and enter a P. The P indicates to 1-2-3 that a password is to be assigned to this file.
FINLCOPY	Enter the password, using up to 15 characters. (It does not appear on your screen, so be careful to enter it correctly.)
FINLCOPY	1-2-3 now asks you to verify the password. To do so, you must reenter the original password and press the Enter key. In this example, the FINLCOPY password is now operational.

To change or cancel a password, you must enter the / File Retrieve command and enter the appropriate filename. 1-2-3 now prompts you for the password. You must enter the appropriate password before you can cancel it or enter a new one. To cancel a password, save the worksheet and press Esc or Backspace when you are prompted for the password. The worksheet will now be saved to disk without a password.

RANGE TRANSPOSE

The **/ Range Transpose** command allows you to rearrange the rows and columns within a range in your worksheet. Any alphanumeric or numeric label can be rearranged; however, you are not allowed to arrange any relative address formulas. Trying to do so will result in ERR messages in any cells that have formulas. If formulas are desired, rearrange the labels and then add the formulas.

Assume that you wish to rearrange the rows and columns of the worksheet shown in Figure 5.8 so that the columns are rows (and vice versa). You would need to enter the following commands:

/	Gets the Main Menu
R	Selects the Range option
T	Selects the Transpose option
B3.D10 Enter	Enters the Copy From Range (Transpose Range) either by entering the actual cell addresses or by manual pointer movement "painting" the affected area
B16 Enter	Tells 1-2-3 where to place the transposed range

Your screen will now look like the screen in Figure 5.9. Remember, only text can be moved using the Transpose command. Any formulas will move improperly, causing ERR messages to appear in the affected cells.

RANGE VALUE

The **/ Range Value** command allows you to take the result of a formula (the number that appears in the cell containing the formula) and place that number in the same or another cell. This means that the formula is replaced with a

Figure 5.8
COMPSALS worksheet

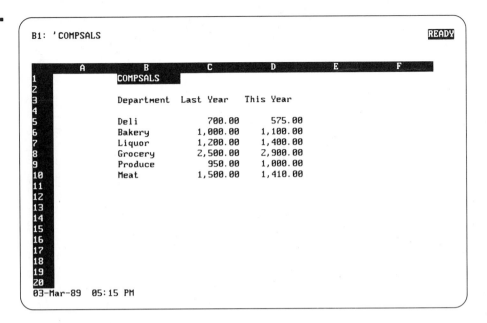

Figure 5.9
COMPSALS worksheet with rows and columns rearranged

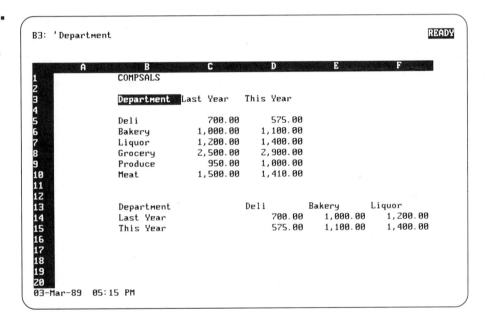

numeric constant. If, for example, a cell contains the formula +E5/C5, which results in value −.18, the / Range Value command copies the −.18 rather than the formula +E5/C5.

HINTS/HAZARDS If the CALC indicator appears at the bottom of the screen, execute the CALC command (F9) before you issue the / Range Transpose command. This command is discussed in detail later in this chapter.

RANGE SEARCH

The / **Range Search** command allows you to locate a character string consisting of letters or numbers in cells containing labels and/or formulas within a specified range. The Range Search command does not locate numbers that are not part of a label or formula. Once the command starts to execute, 1-2-3 searches the first column in the range and then proceeds to the right to the next column.

When you are telling 1-2-3 the character string to search for, it does not matter which case you use for the characters. If, for example, you specify B as the search string, 1-2-3 searches for both the uppercase B and lowercase b. The replacement string, on the other hand, is case sensitive. If you specify the replacement string as Year-To-Date, 1-2-3 uses that exact combination of upper- and lowercase letters in executing the Replace command.

Once you issue the / Range Search command, 1-2-3 prompts you for the range of cells to be included in this command. You must now either enter the corner cell addresses of the cells to be included or highlight the cells by placing the pointer at one of the corner cells, entering a period, and highlighting the remaining cells. Once you have specified the cells to be searched, 1-2-3 prompts you to enter the character string that you are looking for. If the contents of a prior search appear, you can cancel this character string by pressing the Backspace key or the Esc key. Be sure to press the Enter key when you are finished. Once this is accomplished, 1-2-3 displays the following menu:

```
Formulas Labels Both
```

The selection made from this submenu tells 1-2-3 which type of cells to search: The Formulas option results in 1-2-3 searching only those cells with formulas; the Labels option tells 1-2-3 to search only cells containing a label prefix; the Both option results in both types of cells being searched.

After you have made the appropriate selection, the menu options contained below appear on your screen.

```
Find Replace
```

The **Find** option positions the pointer to the first cell in the search range that meets the characteristics of the search string. A menu with the options Next and Quit appears at the top of the screen. When the last cell that meets the search criteria is located in the search range using the Next command, the message `No more matching strings` appears at the bottom of the screen along with the ERROR mode indicator. Press either the Enter or Esc key to continue.

If you select the **Replace** option, you receive the prompt for the replacement string `Enter replacement string:`. If another character string is present from a prior / Range Search command, you can clear these characters by pressing the Backspace or Esc key. Be sure to press the Enter key when you have finished. The pointer now positions to the first cell that meets the search criteria, and the menu below appears on your screen.

```
Replace All Next Quit
```

The **Replace** option results in the contents of the highlighted cell being replaced, after which 1-2-3 positions the pointer to the next cell that meets the search criteria. The **All** option replaces any cells in the range that meet the search criteria with the replacement string. The **Next** option finds the next cell

Figure 5.10

The worksheet in which the column heading Yr. is to be changed to Year via the / Range Search command

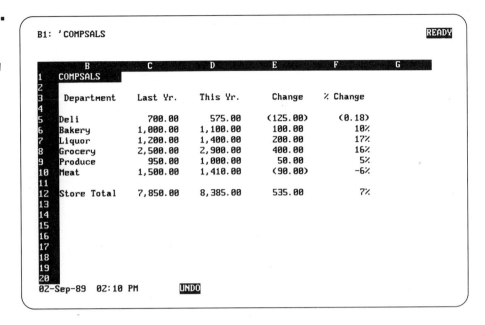

that meets the search criteria and leaves the current cell unchanged. The **Quit** option stops the search and returns you to READY mode.

Once the search is finished using the Next option (unless the Quit command was issued), the message No more matching strings, along with an ERROR mode indicator, appears on your screen. Press either the Enter key or the Esc key to continue.

Assume that you have a worksheet like that depicted in Figure 5.10. After the worksheet has been built, you decide that instead of having the column heading Yr. you want the entire word Year. In this situation, you can use the / Range Search command by issuing the following commands:

/	Gets the Main Menu
R	Selects the Range option
S	Selects the Search option
C3 [by manual pointer movement]	Positions the pointer to cell C3
.	Nails down the pointer
D3 [by manual pointer movement 3]	Positions the pointer to cell D3
Enter	Establishes the range
Yr.	Enters the search string of the characters to be located
Enter	Finishes the command
L	Tells 1-2-3 to search only label cells
R	Tells 1-2-3 to execute the Replace command
Year	Tells 1-2-3 to use these characters as the replacement string
Enter	Finishes the command
A	Tells 1-2-3 to execute the command against any cell that meets the search criteria

The changed worksheet now appears like that in Figure 5.11.

Figure 5.11
The worksheet after execution of the / Range Search command

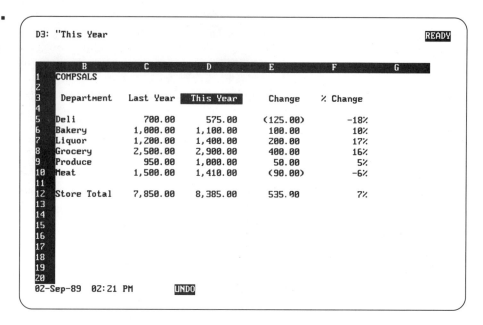

RANGE NAMES

By now, you have used ranges extensively in formatting, copying, and printing information from worksheets. One problem with using ranges is that you must always keep track of the cell addresses of two opposite corner cells in each range; to help avoid this problem, Lotus 1-2-3 has a feature that allows you to give a **range name** to a range of cells and thereafter refer to that range by the given name.

Let's reexamine the procedure involved in setting up function formulas for the FUNCTION worksheet you practiced on in Chapter 4. Every time you wanted to add a function in column B of the worksheet, you had to either point to the cell locations in the range or enter the previously recorded cell locations. Another alternative is to give the cell range a name like COLB (short for column B); then every time 1-2-3 requests a range, you can simply use COLB.

Another advantage of using range names is that they make a worksheet self-documenting and, therefore, more readable. Setting up formulas to refer to a range name rather than merely a cell location, for example, can be very helpful. If you come back to a worksheet later, a formula using range names will make much more sense.

NAME MENU

To give a range a name, you must invoke the Range option from the Main Menu and select the Name option from the Range Menu. You then receive a menu that looks like the following:

```
Create   Delete   Labels   Reset   Table
```

Create The **Create option** is used either to give a name to a range of cells or to redefine the location of the named range. The range name can be 1 to 14 characters in length (including special characters and spaces); Lotus recommends that you use only A–Z, 0–9, and the dash (–), without using spaces.

After you select the Create option, you are prompted for the name you wish to give the range. You are then prompted to define the range to 1-2-3 by pointing or by typing in the actual addresses.

At this point, you can use the F5 (GoTo) key to reference a range name or a cell address. You are not restricted in the number of times that you can include a cell in different named ranges. When the worksheet is saved, the range names are also saved.

Delete The **Delete option** of the Name submenu is used to allow 1-2-3 to drop a named range from memory. The contents of the individual cells involved remain unchanged. After you select this option, you are prompted to enter the name of the range to be deleted or to point to the range to be deleted on the prompt line.

Each entry is treated as a separate range name. You cannot delete all range names in one step, as you can create them; instead, you have to delete them individually or use the Reset option.

Labels The **Labels option** is very similar to the Create option, except that the name for the range is taken directly from an adjacent label entry. You must make certain that the label to be used as the range name does not contain more than 14 characters.

For example, assume that you have two adjacent entries like those shown below. Position your pointer at cell D3 and enter the command / Range Name Labels. Press the Enter key (or, if there are multiple cells involved, indicate the end of the range). You must now tell 1-2-3 whether the named cells are right, down, left, or up with respect to the labels.

```
  D3            E3
|Sales |    $100.00|
```

Reset The **Reset option** makes 1-2-3 drop from its memory all range names that have been assigned.

Table The **Table option** of the Name submenu allows you to construct a report containing all range names and their appropriate cell addresses in your worksheet. The pointer location is used as the upper left-hand corner of the report. Since the report actually takes up space within the worksheet, make certain that you are in an unused area; otherwise, a valuable portion of your worksheet model may be lost.

NAMING INSTRUCTIONS

The steps needed to give the numbers in column B of the FUNCTION worksheet the range name COLB are as follows:

/	Gets the Main Menu
R	Takes the Range option and displays the Range Menu
N	Takes the Name option of the Range Menu and displays the Name Menu
C	Takes the Create option of the Name Menu
COLB	Specifies the range name to be used
B9 [by manual pointer movement]	Points to the first cell in the COLB range

.	Nails down the beginning of the range
B17 [by manual pointer movement]	Points to the last cell in the COLB range
Enter	Tells 1-2-3 to execute the command

You can now enter functions simply by referring to the range name, COLB. For example, you could enter the @SUM function as @SUM (COLB), without entering the cell addresses or pointing. You can also copy this formula to the other columns, in which case 1-2-3 keeps track of the range but not the range name.

MORE RANGE NAME EXAMPLES

Load the COMPSALS worksheet and create the range names indicated in Figure 5.12. When you are finished, you should have the following range names: Header, Dept, Sales, and Print. Notice that as you are creating the range names 1-2-3 displays them in alphabetical order on the prompt line (see Figure 5.13). Once you have created the named ranges, you can verify that, for instance, the Sales named range was created properly by going through the keystrokes required to create it.

Verifying Named Ranges Once you have indicated a range name on the prompt line (via highlighting the Sales range name, for example, and pressing the Enter key), the cells contained in the Sales named range will be highlighted on your screen (see Figure 5.14). This method works well if you wish to verify only one named range, but if you wish to verify all your named ranges, the best technique is to use the Table command of the Range Name submenu. Position your pointer to cell B16 (this will become the upper left-hand corner of the report) and enter the following commands:

/	Gets the Main Menu
R	Takes the Range option
N	Takes the Name option
T	Takes the Table option
Enter	Tells 1-2-3 to create the report

Your worksheet should now appear like the one depicted in Figure 5.15. Notice that each range name appears on a separate line in the report. Also notice that the beginning and ending cell addresses are included in the report. The beginning cell is always viewed as the upper left-hand cell by 1-2-3, and the ending cell is always viewed as the lower right-hand cell. Therefore, for a named range composed of a single row, the first cell is really the upper left-hand corner of the range. Notice also that the entries generated by the Table command have actually become part of the worksheet and have been treated as labels by 1-2-3 (notice the 'DEPT entry in Figure 5.15).

Using Named Ranges Once you have created named ranges in your worksheet, you can use them in any command that requires a cell address or a range of cells before it will work. For example, you can use named ranges with the GoTo (F5) command. After pressing the F5 key, enter the named range Dept, and your pointer will move to cell B5 (your pointer always positions to the upper left-hand cell of a named range when the GoTo command is invoked).

Instead of actually entering the characters contained in a named range, you can also use the Names (F3) function key. If you are in a command that requires you to enter a cell address or a cell range and you want to use a

Figure 5.12
Cells included in the specified named ranges

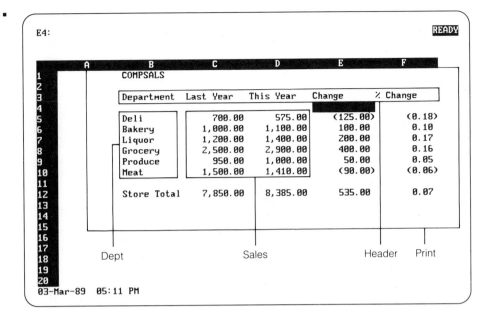

Figure 5.13
Named ranges in COMPSALS listed via the / Range Name Create command

named range, you can press the F3 key and highlight the named range to be included in the instruction. For example, the Names (F3) key can be used in conjunction with the Copy command. The following example will copy the Dept named range to cell E15 without extensive pointer movement. Position your pointer to cell E15.

/	Gets the Main Menu
C	Takes the Copy command
F3	Press the Names (F3) function key
Dept	Highlight the Dept named range
Enter	Specifies the Dept named range as the "From" cells
Enter	Specifies cell E15 as the "To" range

Figure 5.14

Verifying the named range Sales via the Create command

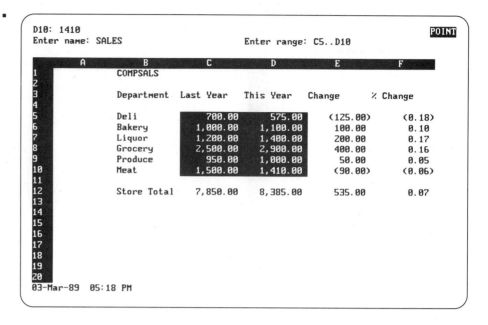

Figure 5.15

The output of the / Range Name Table command

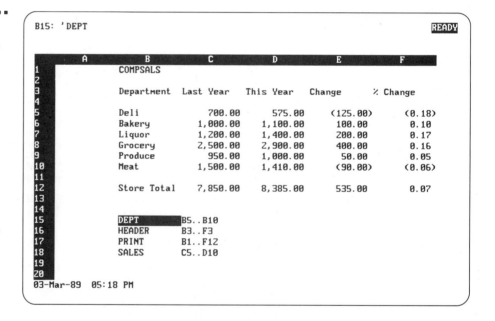

Notice that the cells contained in the Dept named range (see Figure 5.16) have been copied without your positioning the cursor to cell B3, highlighting cells B3..F3, and then indicating that cell E15 is the destination cell. The Names function key technique is extremely useful when you have common text (such as lines of dashes used to indicate subtotals in a business report) required at multiple locations in a document.

Now use a named range to calculate the grand total for the This Year and Last Year columns. This calculation could be accomplished by the formula +C12+D12, but this method would not allow us to use a named range. Instead, enter the formula @SUM(SALES) in cell C13. Once this formula has been entered, the result, 16,235.00, is displayed in the cell. Notice that the entry in the status line shows C13: @SUM(SALES). Now delete the named range called Sales using the following commands:

Figure 5.16

Result of a Copy command using the Names (F3) function key

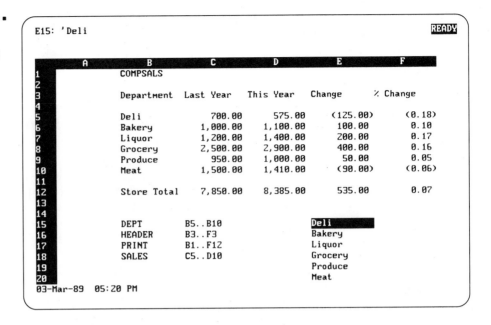

Figure 5.17

Example of a formula after a named range is deleted

/	Gets the Main Menu
R	Takes the Range option
N	Takes the Name option
D	Takes the Delete option
Sales	Highlight the Sales named range using pointer movement commands
Enter	Tells 1-2-3 to execute the command

Notice that the @SUM function entry in the status line no longer contains the Sales named range but, instead, contains the cell address C5..D10 (see Figure 5.17). After you have created a named range, 1-2-3 still keeps track of that range via the cell addresses that were entered when the named range was created. Instead of requiring you to refer to a range via the addresses, 1-2-3 allows you to substitute a variable name. If you delete the variable name via the /Range Name Delete command, 1-2-3 simply substitutes the cell addresses that you initially used in creating the named range.

USE OF DUMMY COLUMNS OR ROWS IN EXPANDING RANGES

Dummy Columns Load the file called COLSALES. Many times you will have an application in which you wish to create year-to-date sales totals for each department. You may also want to set up the report so that it automatically expands as you insert a column to enter the sales for a new month. Such a report requires a format similar to that in Figure 5.18. If you use the @SUM command as shown in Figure 5.18, you immediately have problems when you insert a new column for the figures for March. In order to generate the correct store totals, you must change the @SUM function each time you add a new month. Requiring this kind of change each month not only results in an inflexible worksheet but also produces a worksheet that sooner or later is going to contain incorrect answers when someone forgets to change the @SUM function.

The solution to this problem is to use a **dummy column.** When you want to add and delete rows and columns and have this change reflected in any calculation that references a range, such as the @SUM function, your range must be set up so that any additions or deletions occur after the beginning cell in the range and before the ending cell in the range. To incorporate this flexibility into the worksheet depicted in Figure 5.18 requires a number of changes:

1. A blank column (the dummy column to be referenced later) must be inserted to the left of the grand total column (column D).
2. The new column D is set to a width of 1.
3. The @SUM function must be edited so that the ending cell in the range is D5 [the function should now be @SUM(B5..D5)].

Your worksheet should now look like the worksheet in Figure 5.19.

Now when you want to add a new month and have the sales figures for that month automatically included in the Store Total, position the pointer to the dummy column, insert a new column, and enter the sales figures. Since the new column gets inserted to the left of the dummy column and, therefore, before the last cell in the @SUM function range, the new data are automatically included in the store total. You can now copy this new sum formula down column F.

Dummy Rows Load the file COMPSALS. If you want to incorporate the concepts just covered to allow you to add new departments so that they are automatically included in the yearly total, you have to change the @SUM functions to include the blank row entry after the Meat department. Your Last Year sum function in cell C12 now appears as `@SUM(C5..C11)`. Of course, you must make the same change to the This Year column @SUM function. To add a new department (leaving the order of the others unchanged) so that it can be included in the total now requires you to position your pointer to row 11, insert a new row, and enter the new sales figures. The newly entered sales figures are now included within the total for that year.

Figure 5.18
A typical worksheet tracking year-to-date totals

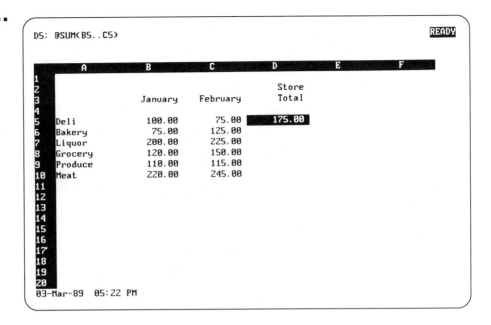

Figure 5.19
Worksheet with a dummy column D

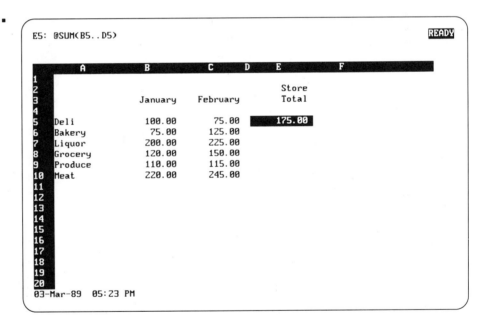

Expanding the range of the @SUM function for the COMPSALS worksheet was a straightforward task, since a blank row existed that could be used as the dummy row. What happens, however, when you have an application like that depicted in Figure 5.20 that requires you to indicate subtotal lines with a cell of dashes (———) and a total line with a cell of equal signs (= = = = = = =)? If you remember back to the previous chapter, text entries are given the value of zero by 1-2-3. Since a value of zero does not affect the summation of a column of numbers, the dummy row can be the row containing the total or subtotal text indicators. You must, however, never use such a dummy row for statistical functions like @AVG, @MIN, @STD, and @VAR, since a cell with a zero value is included in these calculations. For example, an @AVG function that includes a text cell with a zero value has a deflated average.

Figure 5.20
Worksheet with a dummy row containing equal signs (=)

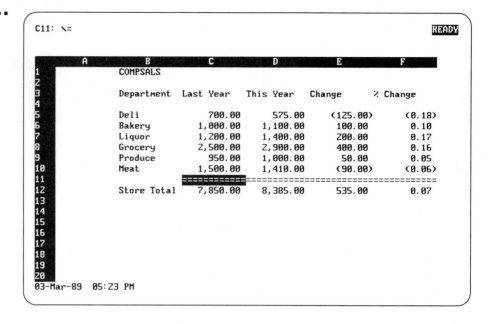

Any time an application requires you to add several numbers together, you should use the @SUM function with a dummy ending cell. Later on, when you add numbers to that list, you won't have to change any formulas in order to include the new items in the list. Any range or named range including a dummy column or row will automatically expand and contract as columns are added to the left of a dummy column or above a dummy row. When the dummy row or column contains text data, make certain that you do not use functions that will be affected by a zero value.

HINTS/HAZARDS

When you are using lines of dashes (-) or equal signs (=) or a column of broken bars (|) for a dummy entity, make certain that you are using only the @SUM function for mathematical manipulation. If you are using any other statistical function, this cell will have the value of zero and will result in functions such as @AVG, @MIN, @MAX, and so on generating incorrect results.

SORTING

From time to time, you may want to rearrange data in a particular order. Some spreadsheets allow you to perform such a task via the Move statement; 1-2-3, however, contains a **Sort command.** This feature allows a worksheet to be constructed in a way that is logical for the individual building it and then to be accessed by another user and rearranged in a manner that is logical for that person's application.

SORT MENU

The Sort command has its own settings screen and is found in the Data Menu, which is invoked from the Main Menu. When the Sort option is selected, the following menu is displayed:

```
Data Range   Primary Key   Secondary Key   Reset   Go   Quit
```

Data Range   The **Data Range option** allows you to mark the area to be sorted; this operation must occur before a sort can take place. Column headings and total lines are not included in the data range. It is wise to save a worksheet before you perform a sort; then if you really mess things up, you can just reload the worksheet from disk.

Primary Key   The **Primary Key option** allows you to select the column by which you want the data range to be sorted. Since the entire range has been described to 1-2-3, all you have to do is point to a cell in the column; 1-2-3 will then prompt you to select the sort order, in either ascending or descending order.

Secondary Key   The **Secondary Key option** allows you to arrange data within the primary key when the sort is executed. For example, in a sort of name and address data, you could establish City as the primary key and Last Name as the secondary key; the data would then be sorted by city, and within each city the data would be sorted by last name.

Reset   The **Reset option** is selected to make 1-2-3 drop from its memory all the sort parameters you have given it.

Go   The **Go option** is the command that tells 1-2-3 to execute the sort.

Quit   The **Quit option** returns you to your worksheet and READY mode.

HINTS/HAZARDS   When you have a large worksheet, you may want to set up a number of sorts for different data ranges. In such an application, it is advisable to use the Reset before the next sort, especially when you are going from an application that has both primary and secondary sort keys to an application that has only a primary sort. Unless you tell 1-2-3 to reset the sort parameters, it still remembers the secondary key. In this type of situation, you would receive a `Key column outside of sort range` error message.

WORKSHEET PRACTICE WITH THE SORT COMMAND

Load the CH4EX1 worksheet you created in Chapter 4 and try some experiments with the Sort command. The loading process is accomplished via the following commands:

/	Gets the Main Menu
F	Selects the File option
R	Selects the Retrieve option
CH4EX1	Identifies the name of the worksheet
Enter	Tells 1-2-3 to get the worksheet

You should now have the worksheet shown in Figure 5.21 loaded (since the entire worksheet will not normally fit on one page, spaces have been deleted to make it fit here).

Figure 5.21
Payroll worksheet

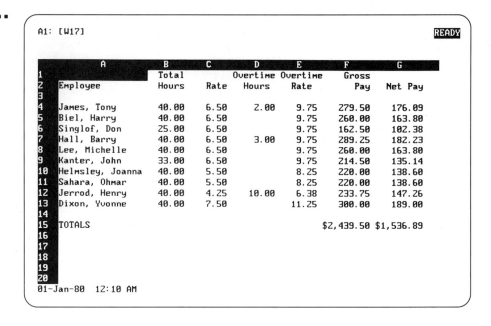

Once the worksheet has been loaded, you must tell 1-2-3 how to sort the information by invoking the Main Menu and selecting the Data option. The following steps should now be taken:

S	Takes the Sort option from the Data Menu
D	Selects the Data Range option to define the area of the worksheet to be sorted
A4 [by manual pointer movement]	Positions the pointer at A4 (the cell with the contents "Tony James")
.	Nails down the beginning of the range
G13 [by manual pointer movement]	Positions the pointer at cell G13 (the cell with the contents "189.00")
Enter	Tells 1-2-3 that the data range is defined
P	Selects the Primary Key option
A4 [by manual pointer movement]	Positions the pointer at A4 (the cell with the contents "Tony James") (Actually, the pointer could just as well be placed anywhere in column A inside the data range.)
Enter	Tells 1-2-3 to accept this information
A	Tells 1-2-3 to perform the sort in ascending order
Enter	Indicates to 1-2-3 that the sort order has been completed
G	Tells 1-2-3 to perform the sort

Your worksheet should now look like the one shown in Figure 5.22. This format is ideal if you're looking for a payroll listing of employees in the company. What happens, though, if you want to group individuals in alphabetic order by department? On this worksheet, such grouping would involve adding a column (Dpt.) to the left of the Employee column to contain the department number, setting the Dpt. column to a width of four positions, and changing the format to zero decimal positions.

Figure 5.22

Sorted payroll worksheet

```
A1: [W17]                                                              READY

            A              B       C        D        E       F        G
                         Total          Overtime Overtime  Gross
 1
 2       Employee        Hours    Rate    Hours    Rate     Pay     Net Pay
 3
 4    Biel, Harry        40.00    6.50             9.75    260.00   163.80
 5    Dixon, Yvonne      40.00    7.50             11.25   300.00   189.00
 6    Hall, Barry        40.00    6.50    3.00     9.75    289.25   182.23
 7    Helmsley, Joanna   40.00    5.50             8.25    220.00   138.60
 8    James, Tony        40.00    6.50    2.00     9.75    279.50   176.09
 9    Jerrod, Henry      40.00    4.25    10.00    6.38    233.75   147.26
10    Kanter, John       33.00    6.50             9.75    214.50   135.14
11    Lee, Michelle      40.00    6.50             9.75    260.00   163.80
12    Sahara, Ohmar      40.00    5.50             8.25    220.00   138.60
13    Singlof, Don       25.00    6.50             9.75    162.50   102.38
14
15    TOTALS                                              $2,439.50 $1,536.89
16
17
18
19
20
01-Jan-80  12:11 AM
```

First, position the pointer anywhere in column A and add a column as follows:

/	Invokes the Main Menu
W	Selects the Worksheet option
I	Selects the Insert option
C	Selects the Column option
Enter	Executes the Insert command

Next, position the pointer in new column A and change it to a width of four.

/	Invokes the Main Menu
W	Selects the Worksheet option
C	Selects the Column Width option
S	Selects the Set option
4	Specifies the new width
Enter	Executes the command

Next, position the cursor to cell A4 (the one to the left of "Harry Biel"). Change the format to zero positions to the right of the decimal.

/	Invokes the Main Menu
R	Selects the Range option
F	Selects the Format option
F	Selects the Fixed option
0	Identifies the number of decimal positions
Enter	Executes the command
A13 [by manual pointer movement]	Positions the pointer at the end of the range
Enter	Tells 1-2-3 to execute the command

Enter the Dpt. heading and department numbers to your worksheet as shown in Figure 5.23. More sort instructions must now be issued to tell 1-2-3 exactly how to sort information in the data range, including giving a new sort range to 1-2-3 (remember, a field outside the old range has been added),

Figure 5.23
Payroll worksheet with department numbers added

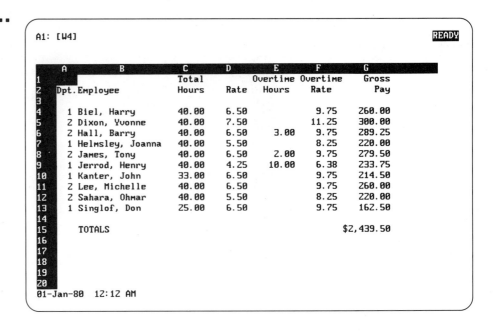

specifying a new primary key, and specifying a secondary key. (Since the data range has not changed dramatically and both a primary and a secondary key sort will be executed, the Reset command does not have to be executed.) These tasks require the following steps:

/	Invokes the Main Menu
D	Selects the Data option
S	Selects the Sort option from the Data Menu
D	Selects the Data Range option
Backspace	Cancels the existing range
A4 [by manual pointer movement]	Positions the pointer at the left of the cell with "Harry Biel" in it
.	Nails down the beginning of the range
H13 [by manual pointer movement]	Positions the pointer at the end of the range
Enter	Tells 1-2-3 that the range has been established
P	Selects the Primary Key option
Backspace	Cancels the existing range
A4 [by manual pointer movement]	Positions the pointer at cell A4 (Any other cell in column A inside the data range would do just as well.)
Enter	Tells 1-2-3 that the primary key range has been established
Enter	Tells 1-2-3 to sort in ascending order (default)
S	Selects the Secondary Key option
B4 [by manual pointer movement]	Positions the pointer at cell B4 (Any other cell in column B within the data range would do just as well.)
Enter	Tells 1-2-3 that the secondary key range has been established

Figure 5.24
Payroll worksheet showing both primary and secondary sort

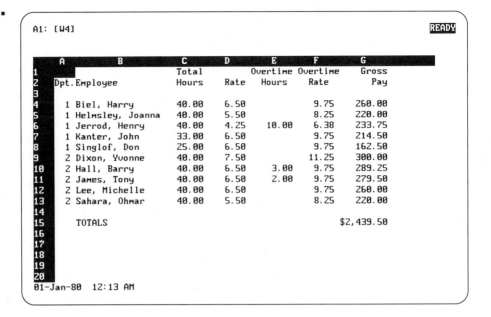

A		Tells 1-2-3 to sort in ascending order
Enter		Tells 1-2-3 that the order of the sort is specified
G		Tells 1-2-3 to sort the worksheet

Your worksheet should now look like the worksheet shown in Figure 5.24. Save this worksheet to a file called PAYSORT by issuing the following commands:

/	Invokes the Main Menu
F	Selects the File option from the Main Menu
S	Selects the Save option
PAYSORT	Keys in the new worksheet name
Enter	Saves the file to disk

TITLES

By this time, you have surely noticed that it is inconvenient to work with large spreadsheets, like PAYROLL, whose width exceeds the display on the screen—especially when you are interested in gross pay and net pay information for an employee. You can see the net or gross pay numbers on the screen, but you can't see the employee names. You may have wished you could freeze a column of data or a row of text to act as labels for an off-screen row or column. Lotus, like many spreadsheet packages, has a feature that provides this capability; it is referred to as the **Titles option**.

When you are using the Titles option, the pointer plays an important role. Any columns to the left of the pointer or any rows above the pointer that appear on the screen can be frozen to act as labels. You cannot move the pointer into a title area by using the Arrow keys. In order to get the pointer into the titles area, you must press the F5 key and then enter the address of the cell. This causes two copies of the title cells to be displayed on the screen.

TITLES MENU

The Titles command is invoked from the Worksheet Menu. It presents a menu consisting of the following options:

```
Both    Horizontal    Vertical    Clear
```

Both The Both option freezes the rows above the pointer and the columns to the left of the pointer, creating a fixed border of headings for vertical and horizontal scrolling through the worksheet.

Horizontal The Horizontal option freezes the rows above the pointer, creating fixed headings for vertical scrolling through the worksheet.

Vertical The Vertical option freezes the columns to the left of the pointer, creating fixed line labels for horizontal scrolling through the worksheet.

Clear The Clear option causes any rows or columns that have been frozen to return to unfrozen status. (Note that in order for a cell to be frozen on the screen it must appear on the screen at the time that the Titles option of the Worksheet Menu is selected. If a cell does not physically appear on the screen, it cannot be frozen on the screen.)

TITLES INSTRUCTIONS

Using the Titles command to freeze the employee names would require the following steps:

Home	Positions the pointer at cell A1
C1 [by manual pointer movement]	Positions the pointer at cell C1
/	Gets the Main Menu
W	Selects the Worksheet option
T	Selects the Titles option
V	Selects the Vertical titles option

When you move the pointer to the Net Pay column, the Employee column will remain on the screen and your display will look like that in Figure 5.25.

RELATIVE AND ABSOLUTE ADDRESSING

As you have already seen, a formula can be copied across a row or down a column, and 1-2-3 will automatically adjust the formula placed in each cell to reflect its new location and the location of any participating cells. This is the concept behind **relative addressing**. But what happens if you don't want 1-2-3 to change a formula automatically to reflect a new cell location? How do you tell 1-2-3, without directly entering a different formula in each cell, to refer to only one cell in a series of calculations?

Let's examine a concrete application of this question. How would you find out what percentage each individual's gross pay was of the total gross pay in the CH4EX1 worksheet? You could insert a column between the Gross Pay and Net Pay columns, but how could you enter a formula and copy it to the other cells in the column in such a way that it would always refer to the contents of the total gross pay cell in calculating the percentage?

Figure 5.25
Payroll worksheet showing Net Pay column

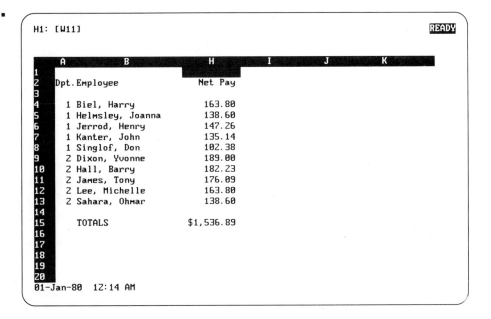

The first possibility, manually entering the required formula for each row in the column, is feasible with the few employees currently in the worksheet, but it would require a tremendous amount of work if you were dealing with 100 employees. The easiest way to solve the problem is to use a technique referred to as **absolute addressing.**

An absolute cell reference is easy to distinguish from a relative cell reference because it appears with one or more dollar signs ($) in the cell reference—for example, A1, $A1, or A$1.

Let's begin by examining why the relative addressing feature of 1-2-3 is inappropriate for this application.

 Load the worksheet file PAYSORT, if it is not already on your screen.

1. Position the pointer anywhere in column H (Net Pay) and insert the new column, using the following instructions:

/	Gets the Main Menu
W	Selects the Worksheet option
I	Selects the Insert option from the Worksheet Menu
C	Selects the Column option
Enter	Executes the Insert command

2. Enter the column headings.

   H1   % of Total
   H2   ^Gross

   Center (^) the second line of the heading.

3. At cell H4, enter the formula for calculating the percentage of total gross pay, using the relative addressing convention.

   H4   +G4/G15

   When you depress Enter, you should see 0.10 as the cell contents.

4. Set the column to a percentage format with one decimal position.

   | / | Invokes the Main Menu |
   | R | Selects the Range option |

F	Selects the Format option from the Range Menu
P	Selects the Percent format
1	Sets the number of decimal positions to one
Enter	Tells 1-2-3 that this part of the command is finished
H13 [by manual pointer movement]	Positions the pointer at the last cell in the range
Enter	Tells 1-2-3 that the range has been defined and that the command is to be executed

5. Copy this formula to the rest of the cells in the column.

H4 [by manual pointer movement]	Positions the pointer at cell H4
/	Invokes the Main Menu
C	Selects the Copy command option
Enter	Indicates to 1-2-3 that cell H4 is the only "From" cell
H5 [by manual pointer movement]	Positions the pointer at cell H5, the beginning of the "To" range
.	Nails down the beginning of the "To" range
H13 [by manual pointer movement]	Positions the pointer at the last cell in the "To" range
Enter	Tells 1-2-3 to execute the Copy command

You should now see the worksheet shown in Figure 5.26 on your screen. Obviously, something is drastically wrong with this worksheet. What happened? When 1-2-3 copied the formula +G4/G15 to the other cells in the column, it automatically changed the formula for each cell as it proceeded down the column; as a result, cell H5 contains the formula +G5/G16, and cell H6 has the formula +G6/G17. But cells G16 and G17 do not contain any numeric values—hence the error message ERR.

1-2-3 did not use the contents of the total gross pay cell for each of the calculations after the Copy command was used because no absolute cell references were contained in the original formula entered in H4.

Go to cell H4 and enter the formula +G4/G15. Then use the instructions contained in step 5 above to copy the formula to the other cells in the column. Afterward, your screen should have a display like that in Figure 5.27. The dollar signs in the amended formula tell 1-2-3 that it is to leave this part of the formula exactly the same as it copies it from one cell to another. Relative addressing will not affect any part of the formula containing dollar signs.

In the above example, the formula containing the absolute cell reference had a cell address of G15. As was noted earlier, you can also use addresses like $A1 or A$1. This type of cell reference has elements of both absolute addressing and relative addressing and is referred to as a **mixed cell address.** The relative part of a mixed cell address will change, and the absolute part will remain the same, as described below:

- $A1 (**$columnrow**). The absolute address portion of this reference is the column portion of the reference, so the row can change within the

Figure 5.26
PAYSORT worksheet changed using relative addressing

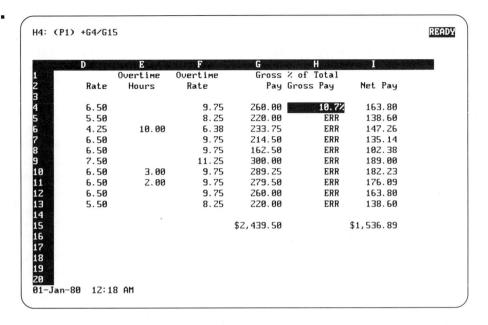

Figure 5.27
PAYSORT worksheet changed using absolute addressing

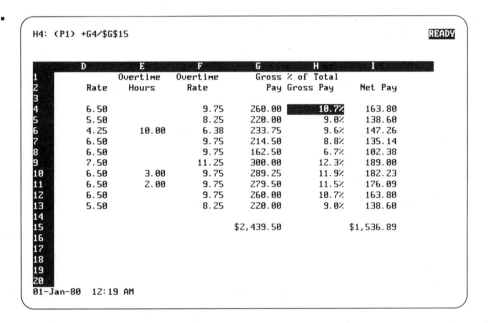

address, but the column must remain as A. This formula could be read as "any row in column A."

- A$1 (**column$row**). The absolute address portion of this reference is the row portion of the reference, so the column can change within the address, but the row must remain as 1. This formula could be read as "any column in row 1."

It is important to be aware that mixed cell addresses cannot be used with range names. If absolute addresses are indicated for range names (for example, $COLB), the range name will be treated as though both the column and the row portions of the address are absolute—that is, it will be wholly an **absolute range name.**

AUTOMATIC WORKSHEET RECALCULATION

Beginning with Release 2.2 of Lotus 1-2-3, you no longer have much delay in the time it takes to recalculate your worksheet. Previous to Release 2.2, any time that you changed the contents of a single cell, the entire worksheet had to be recalculated. Now, with **minimal recalculation,** however, any time a change is made to a cell in the worksheet, only those cells actually affected have to be recalculated.

The recalculation defaults of 1-2-3 are automatic and natural. The natural recalculation option allows 1-2-3, before it recalculates a particular formula, to recalculate any other formulas on which that formula depends. This means that if the formula in cell C23 depends on the formula in cell B23, 1-2-3 recalculates the formula in B23 before it calculates the one in C23.

The automatic recalculation method means that each time you change the contents of a cell, 1-2-3 recalculates any formulas affected by the change. With the default setting on natural, 1-2-3 recalculates only those cells that have changed since the worksheet was last recalculated, along with the cells that depend on them. This minimal recalculation feature optimizes the recalculation of cells in a worksheet and decreases recalculation time. There is no way to turn minimal recalculation on or off when the recalculation order is specified as natural.

If you specify either rowwise or columnwise calculation (neither of these is needed for any examples in this text—you may, however, need to do this for some other project, in which case the following discussion might be useful), 1-2-3 recalculates every cell in your worksheet. It cannot use minimal recalculation. This necessitates the need for manual recalculation, which is accomplished by entering the following command sequence:

/	Invokes the Main Menu
W	Selects the Worksheet option
G	Selects the Global option from the Worksheet Menu
R	Selects the Recalculation option from the Global Menu
M	Executes the Manual command

If you make changes to any cell after this **manual recalculation** option has been selected, 1-2-3 tells you by displaying a CALC message at the bottom of your screen next to the indicators area. To get 1-2-3 to recalculate the worksheet, you must depress the F9 function key.

If you save the worksheet file onto disk, the manual recalculation setting is saved in the worksheet file. If you wish to reset the spreadsheet to automatic, all you need to do is enter the above commands, replacing the M with an A (for automatic).

MORE ON FUNCTIONS

@PMT

Lotus has incorporated a financial function that is a true time-saver. The **@PMT** (principal, interest, periods)—payment per period—function calculates the payment of a loan or mortgage based on the three available pieces of information: principal, interest, and number of periods. Using this function allows you to avoid entering the following formula:

```
Prin*Inter/12/(1-1/(1+Inter/12)^Periods)
```

@IF AND LOGICAL OPERATORS

The @IF function allows Lotus 1-2-3 to check for certain conditions and then take actions based on the results of the check. The format of the @IF function is @IF (condition, true, false). The condition portion of the function allows you to set up an equation to check for specific results or cell contents; the true portion contains instructions that will be executed if the condition is true; the false portion contains instructions that will be executed if the condition is false.

The operators allowed in a 1-2-3 @IF function are as follows:

Relational:

=	Equal to
<	Less than
<=	Less than or equal to
>	Greater than
>=	Greater than or equal to
<>	Not equal to

Logical:

#NOT#	Not (the opposite of any equation or relation must be the case before the true option is executed)
#AND#	And (both conditions must be true before the true option is executed)
#OR#	Or (either action can be true for the true option to be executed)

These operators can be used to set up a number of different conditions:

+B13=60#OR#D17<20   The value contained in cell B13 is equal to 60, or the value contained in cell D17 is less than 20.

+H14>0#AND#D19>1985   The value contained in cell H14 is greater than zero, and the value in cell D19 is greater than 1985.

#NOT#(YEAR=1985)   The value stored in the cell named YEAR is not 1985.

(B15−C10)=D3#AND#C5>D7   The value of cell B15 minus the value of cell C10 is equal to the value contained in cell D3, *and* the value contained in cell C5 is larger than the value contained in cell D7.

These new conditions also have places in the order of precedence discussed earlier. The complete listing of this order is given in Table 5.1.

Applications of the @IF Function   Assume that you have a worksheet that calculates the sales commission for the sales representatives of a manufacturing company. The extension (calculated by multiplying the units sold times the price) is contained in cell H4. Sales commissions are calculated based on the extension amount. If the extension is greater than $1,000, the sales commission is 10% of the extension; otherwise, the commission amount is zero. This type of application requires the use of the @IF function of 1-2-3. The @IF function that would be placed in cell I4 is

```
@IF(H4>1000,H4*.1,0)
```

Table 5.1: The Operator Order of Precedence

Operator	Meaning	Level
^	Exponentiation	7
−	Negative	6
+	Positive	6
*	Multiplication	5
/	Division	5
+	Addition	4
−	Subtraction	4
=	Equal	3
<	Less than	3
<=	Less than or equal	3
>	Greater than	3
>=	Greater than or equal	3
<>	Not equal	3
#NOT#	Logical not	2
#AND#	Logical and	1
#OR#	Logical or	1

This function could be translated as follows:

If the sales extension (H4) is greater than 1,000
    compute the sales commission as 10% of the extension
else
    enter 0 for the sales commission value
Endif

You could also set two levels of sales commissions. For example, in the situation above, you might have one commission of 10% for sales over $1,000, a sales commission of 5% for sales equal to or less than $1,000 but greater than $500, and a sales commission of zero for sales equal to or less than $500. This situation requires the use of a nested function. When you are using nested @IF functions, always start with the most inclusive entry and work downward (in this case, first check for a commission greater than $1,000 and then check for a commission of greater than $500).

```
@IF(H4>1000,H4*.1,@IF(H4>500,H4*.05,0))
```

This function could be translated as follows:

If the sales extension (H4) is greater than 1,000
    compute the sales commission as 10% of the extension
else
    If the sales extension (H4) is greater than 500
        compute the sales commission as 5% of the extension
    else
        enter a commission rate of zero
    Endif
Endif

The @IF function also allows you to perform string tests on data in a worksheet and then take actions based on the results of the comparison. If, for example, you wished to generate a Pass/Fail message in a grade book application with the message Pass displaying for a grade equal to or greater than 65 and a `Fail` message displaying for a grade less than 65, the @IF function depicted below would be used.

```
@IF(D27<=65,"Fail","Pass")
```

Any text that is to be entered in the cell must be included within double quotes.

The next example checks the value of a cell to see if it is equal to Il. Since sales taxes for the state of Illinois do not have to be collected on mail orders outside Illinois, you are interested in calculating tax only if the state is equal to IL or Il.

```
@IF(D7="IL"#or#D7="Il",D15*.0625,"No Tax")
```

This @IF function first checks to see if the state has been entered as IL or Il. If the state entry is equal to either of these values, the sales tax is computed; otherwise, the message "No Tax" is entered in the cell.

@DATE AND ARITHMETIC

You were introduced to some aspects of the **@DATE** function when you entered the FUNCTION worksheet. The information returned by the @NOW and @DATE functions is numeric and represents the number of elapsed days since December 31, 1899. Thus, when 1-2-3 displays a date via one of the three formats listed below, it is merely formatting numeric information for display. If you loaded the FUNCTION worksheet and looked in cell A3, you would see a number that corresponds to today's date. 1-2-3 displays date information in one of the following formats:

    (D1) 1(DD-MMM-YY) 29-Jan-88
    (D2) 2(DD-MMM)   29-Jan
    (D3) 3(MMM-YY)   Jan-88

Displaying a date is a two-step process: First, you get the date via the @DATE or @NOW function, causing a number to appear on the screen and in the cell; second, you use the Range Format commands on the cell to hold one of the above formats, causing a date display to appear on the screen.

The numeric method that 1-2-3 uses to display dates can be very beneficial in manipulating dates. Since the date is really numeric, any arithmetic operations can be performed on it. To get the date for a week from today, for example, you simply add 7 to the existing numeric date. Or, if you want to find out how many weeks there are between two dates, you can subtract the ending date from the beginning date, divide by 7, and round the result using the @ROUND or @INT functions.

With date arithmetic involving months, you must be careful. You can't simply convert a month to 30 days and expect it to work. Adding a number like 30.5 doesn't work well either, unless the period covered is small. The following method assumes that payment will occur on or before the twenty-eighth day of the month:

1. Add 31 to the previous date.
2. Subtract the current @DAY from the present number to bring you back to the present day of the prior month.

3. Add @DAY to the original number to move you forward to the proper day in the next month.

This method allows you to advance from one month to the next if the day of the month is 1 through 28.

You can also compare the value of the @NOW function with another date already entered on the worksheet or with a date in a formula. To do this requires using the command @IF(@NOW>@DATE(88,2,1),x,y). The x represents the action to be taken if the condition is true, and the y represents the action to be taken if the condition is false. More information on 1-2-3 functions appears in Appendix A.

WORKSHEET PRACTICE

Many of the topics discussed in this chapter are used in the next few pages to prepare two worksheets. The first worksheet involves generating a loan amortization table; the second serves as the basis for evaluating various automobile loan alternatives.

LOAN AMORTIZATION WORKSHEET

The following loan amortization table requires you to enter the loan amount, the interest on the loan, the length of the loan in months, and the starting date of the loan. It will then generate a table that includes the amount of the payment, the month of the payment, the portion applied toward the principal, the portion applied to the interest, and the outstanding balance.

In doing this project, you will practice the following skills:

1. Using the @PMT function
2. Using the @IF function
3. Using date arithmetic
4. Using absolute addressing

The worksheet is as shown in Figure 5.28. To present the information in the format shown, you'll obviously have to use absolute addressing to allow each line of formulas to refer to the data at the top of the worksheet. In addition, you'll have to use date arithmetic to advance the date month-by-month from one line to the next; you'll have to use the @PMT function for easy calculation of the payment (you could place this piece of information at the top also); and later you'll have to use the @IF function to properly generate the worksheet.

The various column amounts are calculated as follows:

- The payment is calculated via the @PMT function.
- The interest is calculated by multiplying the outstanding balance by the interest rate and dividing that result by 12 (interest for one month).
- The principal is calculated by subtracting the interest amount from the payment amount.
- The new outstanding balance is calculated by subtracting the amount of the payment applied toward the principal from the old outstanding balance.

Now let's go through the individual tasks involved in creating this worksheet.

Figure 5.28

Loan amortization worksheet

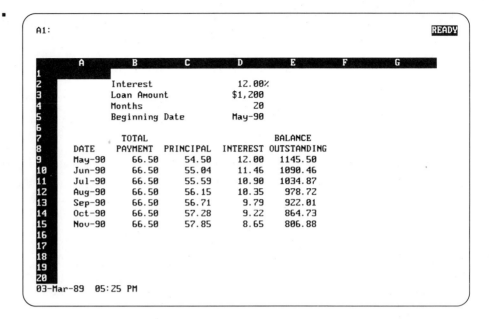

1. Set the global column width to 10.

/	Invokes the Main Menu
W	Selects the Worksheet option of the Main Menu
G	Selects the Global option of the Worksheet Menu
C	Selects the Column Width option
10	Specifies the new column width
Enter	Tells 1-2-3 to execute the command

2. Enter label information in the appropriate cells.

A2	Interest
A3	Loan Amount
A4	Months
A5	Beginning Date
A8	^DATE
B7	^TOTAL
B8	^PAYMENT
C8	^PRINCIPAL
D8	^INTEREST
E7	^BALANCE
E8	^OUTSTANDING

3. Enter the loan information.

C2	.12
C3	1200
C4	20
C5	@DATE(90,5,1)

4. Format cell C2 for percentage, with two decimal positions.

C2 [by manual pointer movement]	Positions the pointer at cell C2
/	Invokes the Main Menu
R	Selects the Range option
F	Selects the Format option from the Range Menu

	P	Selects the Percent option
	Enter	Takes the default of two decimal positions
	Enter	Tells 1-2-3 to format only this cell

5. Format cell C3 for currency, with zero decimal positions.

	C3 [by manual pointer movement]	Positions the pointer at cell C3
	/	Invokes the Main Menu
	R	Selects the Range option
	F	Selects the Format option from the Range Menu
	C	Selects the Currency option
	0	Tells 1-2-3 the number of decimal positions
	Enter	Tells 1-2-3 to accept the decimal position information
	Enter	Tells 1-2-3 to format only this cell

6. Format cell C4 for whole months.

	C4 [by manual pointer movement]	Positions the pointer at cell C4
	/	Invokes the Main Menu
	R	Selects the Range option
	F	Selects the Format option from the Range Menu
	F	Selects the Fixed Format option
	0	Specifies the number of decimal positions
	Enter	Tells 1-2-3 to accept the decimal position information
	Enter	Tells 1-2-3 to format only this cell

7. Format cell C5 for the date.

	C5 [by manual pointer movement]	Positions the pointer at cell C5
	/	Invokes the Main Menu
	R	Selects the Range option
	F	Selects the Format option from the Range Menu
	D	Selects the Date option
	3	Selects the (MMM-YY) option
	Enter	Tells 1-2-3 to format only this cell

Since the information on the first line of the schedule also represents the first payment, the formulas in this row will be a little bit different from those in subsequent rows.

8. Copy the beginning date onto the schedule.

	A9 [by manual pointer movement]	Positions the pointer at cell A9
	+C5	Tells 1-2-3 to refer to the contents of cell C5 and place them here also (If the contents of cell C5 change, the contents of this cell will also change.)
	Enter	Tells 1-2-3 to execute the command

9. Format cells A9 and A10 for the date.

A9 [by manual pointer movement]	Positions the pointer at cell A9
/	Invokes the Main Menu
R	Selects the Range option
F	Selects the Format option from the Range Menu
D	Selects the Date option
3	Selects the (MMM:YY) option
Down Arrow	Includes cell A10
Enter	Tells 1-2-3 to execute the command

10. Enter the formula to calculate the monthly payment in cell B9.

    @PMT(C$3,C$2/12,C$4)

    The first parameter in the formula above provides the address of the cell containing the principal; the second parameter provides the address of the cell containing the interest; the third parameter provides the address of the cell containing the number of periods. Since each of these pieces of information must be referenced in each row, absolute addressing is required; the absolute portion of each parameter freezes the location to a particular row. The formula can now be copied correctly.

11. Enter the formula to calculate the interest portion of this payment in cell D9.

    +C$3*C$2/12

    The amount must be divided by 12 to provide the amount of interest for this particular month rather than for the whole year.

12. Enter the formula to calculate the amount of the payment applied toward the principal in cell C9.

    +B9-D9

13. Enter the formula to calculate the outstanding balance in cell E9.

    +C3-C9

14. Format the entire worksheet for two decimal positions.

/	Invokes the Main Menu
W	Selects the Worksheet option
G	Selects the Global option from the Worksheet Menu
F	Selects the Format option from the Global Menu
F	Selects the Fixed command
Enter	Takes the default and reformats the worksheet

15. Copy the payment and principal formulas (which will stay the same) to the next line. (The cells will contain the correct results after the next steps are finished.)

B9 [by manual pointer movement]	Positions the pointer at cell B9
/	Invokes the Main Menu

C	Selects the Copy command
C9 [by manual pointer movement]	Positions the pointer at the last cell in the "From" range
Enter	Tells 1-2-3 that the "From" range has been established
B10 [by manual pointer movement]	Positions the pointer at the beginning of the "To" range
Enter	Tells 1-2-3 to copy the formulas

16. Enter the formula to advance the date incrementally in cell A10.

   `+A9+31-@DAY(A9+31)+@DAY(A9)`

   This command provides you with the ability to advance the date by the proper increment from one month to the next, as long as the loan begins on day 1 through 28. This formula can now be copied to the rest of the rows.

17. Enter the new formula for calculating the interest in cell D10.

   `+E9*C$2/12`

   You now have a formula that can be easily copied to other rows.

18. Enter the new formula for calculating the outstanding balance in cell E10.

   `+E9-C10`

   You now have a formula that can be easily copied to other rows.

19. Copy the formulas contained in row 10 down enough rows. (The number of rows depends on the maximum number of periods that you wish to allow in a loan; you'll copy this one down 40 rows. Remember, the more rows you have, the longer your worksheet will take to recalculate.)

A10 [by manual pointer movement]	Positions the pointer at cell A10
/	Invokes the Main Menu
C	Selects the Copy option command
E10 [by manual pointer movement]	Positions the pointer at the last cell in the "From" range
Enter	Tells 1-2-3 that the "From" range has been defined
A11 [by manual pointer movement]	Positions the pointer to cell A11, the first cell in the "To" range
.	Nails down the beginning of the "To" range
Pg Dn [twice]	Moves the pointer down the worksheet 40 rows
Enter	Tells 1-2-3 to copy the formulas and recalculate the worksheet

Now sit back and watch 1-2-3 do all the work! When you look at your worksheet, everything seems to have worked until about row 29—when negative numbers suddenly begin popping up in the worksheet. What happened? The loan was completely paid, but 1-2-3 wasn't aware of it, so the balance went from positive to negative.

Somehow you have to indicate to 1-2-3 to take appropriate action when the balance is completely paid to get rid of the negative numbers. Let's review the logic and determine which are the critical formulas.

On examination, the two most important calculations seem to be the outstanding balance and the payment. When the outstanding balance equals a few cents or less, it means that the loan is paid off. (The outstanding balance never comes out to exactly zero because of rounding errors.) All other calculations are based on the contents of either the outstanding balance or the payment entry; if you can get these fields to zero out, the other fields will also contain zeros.

To examine the contents of a cell and check for a value, you must use the @IF function.

20. Position your pointer at cell E10 and either reenter the formula or use the Edit feature to enter changes. Your new formula should now look like the following:

    `@IF(E9<=1,0,@ROUND(+E9-C10,2))`

    This formula can be translated as follows: If the result of the old balance is just a few cents, put a zero in this cell; otherwise, calculate the new rounded outstanding balance.

21. You also have to do something to make the payment column stop printing. Position your pointer at cell B10 and either enter the new formula or use the Edit feature to enter changes.

    `@IF(E9<=1,0,@PMT(C$3,C$2/12,C$4))`

    This formula can be translated as follows: If the contents of the outstanding balance cell are just a few cents, place a zero in the payment cell; otherwise, execute the payment function.

22. Copy these new formulas onto the rest of the worksheet, using the commands from step 19 above.

23. Center the information at the top of the spreadsheet to give it a more balanced appearance.

A2 [by manual pointer movement]	Positions the pointer at cell A2
/	Invokes the Main Menu
M	Selects the Move command
C5 [by manual pointer movement]	Positions the pointer at cell C5, to establish the "From" range
Enter	Tells 1-2-3 that the "From" range is defined
B2 [by manual pointer movement]	Positions the pointer at the beginning of the "To" range
Enter	Executes the Move instruction

24. Save the worksheet under the name LOANAMOR. You should now have a worksheet that looks like the one shown in Figure 5.29.

Figure 5.29
LOANAMOR worksheet

```
D31: +E30*D$2/12                                          READY

     A       B      C      D       E       F      G
12  Aug-90  66.50  56.15  10.35  978.72
13  Sep-90  66.50  56.71   9.79  922.01
14  Oct-90  66.50  57.28   9.22  864.73
15  Nov-90  66.50  57.85   8.65  806.88
16  Dec-90  66.50  58.43   8.07  748.45
17  Jan-91  66.50  59.01   7.48  689.44
18  Feb-91  66.50  59.60   6.89  629.84
19  Mar-91  66.50  60.20   6.30  569.64
20  Apr-91  66.50  60.80   5.70  508.84
21  May-91  66.50  61.41   5.09  447.43
22  Jun-91  66.50  62.02   4.47  385.41
23  Jul-91  66.50  62.64   3.85  322.77
24  Aug-91  66.50  63.27   3.23  259.50
25  Sep-91  66.50  63.90   2.59  195.60
26  Oct-91  66.50  64.54   1.96  131.06
27  Nov-91  66.50  65.19   1.31   65.87
28  Dec-91  66.50  65.84   0.66    0.03
29  Jan-92   0.00  -0.00   0.00    0.00
30  Feb-92   0.00   0.00   0.00    0.00
31  Mar-92   0.00   0.00   0.00    0.00
03-Mar-89  05:36 PM
```

CAR LOAN EVALUATION WORKSHEET

In doing this project, you will practice the following skills:

1. Using mixed cell addressing
2. Observing the effects of copying mixed cell addresses

A friend of yours, Sandy, is trying to decide which vehicle to purchase, and a major part of the decision-making process involves the size of the monthly payment. Sandy wishes to finance the purchase over four years, but she also wants to easily change the loan length. The vehicles being considered, along with the amount to be financed, are as follows:

Conversion van	$18,000
Toyota pickup	8,000
Chrysler LeBaron	10,000
Ford Thunderbird	11,000

Sandy has also visited a number of financial institutions to find the interest rate offered. They are as follows:

Credit union	11%
Car manufacturer	15.5%
Bank 1	12.5%
Bank 2	13%

The spreadsheet shown in Figure 5.30 allows you to present the above information in a tabular format to assist your friend's decision-making process.

The @PMT function is perfect for this application. Mixed cell addressing, combining absolute and relative addressing, will also be useful.

Entering the spreadsheet involves a number of steps.

Figure 5.30
Car loan spreadsheet

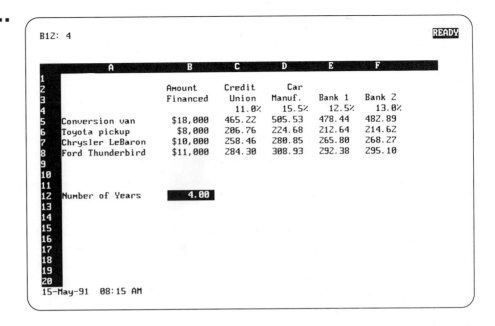

1. Position the pointer in column A and change the width of column A to 20.

/	Invokes the Main Menu
W	Selects the Worksheet option
C	Selects the Column Width command from the Worksheet Menu
S	Sets the column width
20	Specifies the new width
Enter	Executes the command

2. Enter the label data.

C1	Sandy's Loan Evaluation
B2	Amount
C2	"Credit
D2	"Car
B3	Financed
C3	"Union
D3	"Manuf.
E3	"Bank 1
F3	"Bank 2
C4	.11
D4	.155
E4	.125
F4	.13
A5	Conversion van
A6	Toyota pickup
A7	Chrysler LeBaron
A8	Ford Thunderbird
B5	18000
B6	8000
B7	10000

B8   11000
A12 Number of Years
B12 4

3. Format the percentages. Begin by positioning the pointer at cell C4.

/	Invokes the Main Menu
R	Selects the Range option
F	Selects the Format option from the Range Menu
P	Selects the Percent format
1	Specifies the number of desired decimal positions
Enter	Submits the decimal positions to 1-2-3
F4 [by manual pointer movement]	Extends the range to cell F4
Enter	Executes the format change

4. Format the amount financed to currency. Begin by positioning the pointer at cell B5.

/	Invokes the Main Menu
R	Selects the Range option
F	Selects the Format option from the Range Menu
C	Selects the Currency format
0	Specifies the number of desired decimal positions
Enter	Submits the decimal positions to 1-2-3
B8 [by manual pointer movement]	Extends the range to cell B8
Enter	Executes the format change

5. Set the worksheet format to two decimal positions.

/	Invokes the Main Menu
W	Selects the Worksheet option
G	Selects the Global option
F	Selects the Format option from the Global Menu
F	Selects the Fixed option
Enter	Changes the worksheet format

6. Format the length of loan cell to fixed with zero decimal positions. Begin by positioning the pointer to cell B12.

/	Invokes the Main Menu
R	Selects the Range option
F	Selects the Format option from the Range Menu
F	Selects the Fixed option
0	Specifies the number of desired decimal positions
Enter	Submits the decimal positions to 1-2-3
Enter	Executes the format change

7. Enter the @PMT function for cell C5.

```
@PMT($B5,C$4/12,$B$12*12)
```

The principal entry, $B5, keeps 1-2-3 returning to column B of "this" row. The interest entry, C$4, keeps 1-2-3 returning to "this" column of row 4. It is divided by the 12 months of the year.

The periods entry, B12, keeps 1-2-3 returning to cell B12. It is multiplied by the 12 monthly payments.

8. Copy this formula to the rest of the spreadsheet. Begin by positioning the pointer to cell C5.

/	Invokes the Main Menu
C	Selects the Copy command
Enter	Establishes the "From" range
.	Nails down the beginning of the "To" range
F8 [by manual pointer movement]	Moves the pointer to the end of the "To" range
Enter	Executes the Copy command

9. Save this worksheet to the file CARLOANS.

CELL CONTENTS LISTING FOR AMORTIZATION WORKSHEET

```
B2:     'Interest
D2:     (P2) 0.12
B3:     'Loan Amount
D3:     (C0) 1200
B4:     'Months
D4:     (F0) 20
B5:     'Beginning Date
D5:     (D3) @DATE(90,5,1)
B7:     ^TOTAL
E7:     ^BALANCE
A8:     ^DATE
B8:     ^PAYMENT
C8:     ^PRINCIPAL
D8:     ^INTEREST
E8:     ^OUTSTANDING
A9:     (D3) +D5
B9:     (F2) @PMT(D$3,D$2/12,D$4)
C9:     (F2) +B9-D9
D9:     (F2) @ROUND(+D$3*D$2/12,2)
E9:     (F2) @ROUND(+D3-C9,2)
A10:    (D3) +A9+31@DAY(A9+31)+@DAY(A9)
B10:    (F2) @IF(E9<=1,0,@PMT(D$3,D$2/12,D$4))
C10:    (F2) +B10-D10
D10:    (F2) +E9*D$2/12
E10:    (F2) @IF(E9<=1,0,@ROUND(+E9-C10,2))
A11:    (D3) +A9+31@DAY(A9+31)+@DAY(A9)
B11:    (F2) @IF(E10<=1,0,@PMT(D$3,D$2/12,D$4))
C11:    (F2) +B11-D11
D11:    (F2) +E10*D$2/12
E11:    (F2) @IF(E10<=1,0,@ROUND(+E10-C11,2))
A12:    (D3) +A9+31@DAY(A9+31)+@DAY(A9)
B12:    (F2) @IF(E11<=1,0,@PMT(D$3,D$2/12,D$4))
```

```
C12:   (F2)   +B12-D12
D12:   (F2)   +E11*D$2/12
E12:   (F2)   @IF(E11<=1,0,@ROUND(+E11-C12,2))
```

 CELL CONTENTS LISTING FOR CAR LOAN WORKSHEET

```
C1:    'Sandy's Loan Evaluation
B2:    'Amount
C2:    "Credit
D2:    "Car
B3:    'Financed
C3:    "Union
D3:    "Manuf.
E3:    "Bank 1
F3:    "Bank 2
C4:    (P1) 0.11
D4:    (P1) 0.155
E4:    (P1) 0.125
F4:    (P1) 0.13
A5:    'Conversion van
B5:    (C0) 18000
C5:    @PMT($B5,C$4/12,4$B$12*12)
D5:    @PMT($B5,D$4/12,4$B$12*12)
E5:    @PMT($B5,E$4/12,4$B$12*12)
F5:    @PMT($B5,F$4/12,4$B$12*12)
A6:    'Toyota pickup
B6:    (C0) 8000
C6:    @PMT($B6,C$4/12,4$B$12*12)
D6:    @PMT($B6,D$4/12,4$B$12*12)
E6:    @PMT($B6,E$4/12,4$B$12*12)
F6:    @PMT($B6,F$4/12,4$B$12*12)
A7:    'Chrysler LeBaron
B7:    (C0) 10000
C7:    @PMT($B7,C$4/12,4$B$12*12)
D7:    @PMT($B7,D$4/12,4$B$12*12)
E7:    @PMT($B7,E$4/12,4$B$12*12)
F7:    @PMT($B7,F$4/12,4$B$12*12)
A8:    'Ford Thunderbird
B8:    (C0) 11000
C8:    @PMT($B8,C$4/12,4$B$12*12)
D8:    @PMT($B8,D$4/12,4$B$12*12)
E8:    @PMT($B8,E$4/12,4$B$12*12)
F8:    @PMT($B8,F$4/12,4$B$12*12)
A12:   Number of Years
B12:   4
```

CHAPTER REVIEW   Lotus 1-2-3 provides several commands that allow you to control your worksheet environment. The Worksheet Zero command allows you to suppress any cell that has a zero. The GoTo (F5) command allows you to quickly position the pointer to a specific cell. The System command allows you to temporarily leave 1-2-3 and issue commands at the system (DOS) level. You are allowed to hide columns so that they appear neither on the screen nor in print. You can use the Worksheet Status command to find circular references. You can password-protect your worksheet. And you can use the Range Transpose command to rearrange text within a worksheet.

After a worksheet has been created, you will probably want to make a number of improvements to it. One of these, making cell formulas self-documenting and easier to read, can be accomplished easily by the use of range names. A single cell or a range of cells can be given a name and accessed under that name in such applications as calculations, uses of the Copy command, and printing a portion of your worksheet.

The Sort feature included with 1-2-3 enables you to arrange data in an order that is logical for any given application. Another handy (and more common) feature is the Titles feature, which allows you to freeze column or row headings on the screen so that they are visible no matter where you are in the worksheet. This feature makes it much easier to track information in large spreadsheets.

The ability to reference a single cell over and over, even when the formula is copied down a column, is often useful. In 1-2-3, this technique is called absolute addressing. An entire address can be absolute, or only the row or column can be; the latter situation is referred to as a mixed cell address.

The @IF function allows you to embed logic within the worksheet that enables the function to perform one action if the logic is satisfied and perform another action if it is not.

KEY TERMS AND CONCEPTS

absolute addressing
absolute range name
#AND#
automatic recalculation
circular reference
$columnrow
column$row
Create option
Data Range option
@DATE
Delete option
Directory command
dummy column
dummy row
Go option
GoTo command
Hide command
@IF
Labels option
manual recalculation
minimal recalculation

mixed cell address
Name Reset option
#NOT#
#OR#
password
@PMT
Primary Key option
Quit option
range name
Range Search command
Range Transpose command
Range Value command
relative addressing
@ROUND
Secondary Key option
Sort command
Sort Reset option
System command
Table option
Titles option
Zero command

CHAPTER QUIZ

Multiple Choice

1. Which of the following statements is false about range names?
    a. Range names can be used to enhance readability.
    b. Range names make cell formulas self-documenting.

c. Using range names in formulas is better than using cell addresses.
d. A range name created via the Labels option takes its name from the contents of an adjacent cell.
e. All of the above statements are true.
f. All of the above statements are true except d.

2. Which of the following statements is false about the Sort command?
   a. It is safest to save your worksheet before you do any sorting.
   b. Three levels of sorts or keys can be specified.
   c. All or part of a worksheet can be sorted.
   d. The Sort command allows you to rearrange data quickly within the worksheet.
   e. None of the above statements is false.

3. Which of the following statements is false about an absolute address?
   a. It can have both the column and row absolute—CR.
   b. It can have only the column portion absolute—$CR.
   c. It can have only the row portion absolute—C$R.
   d. It can actually be a range name—$EXPENSES.
   e. All of the above responses are correct.

4. Which of the commands below allows you to freeze portions of the worksheet so that they can be used as column or row headings on the screen?
   a. Titles
   b. Labels
   c. Borders
   d. Legend
   e. None of the above responses is correct.

5. Which command allows you to detect circular references within your worksheet?
   a. Worksheet Hide
   b. Directory Status
   c. Worksheet Status
   d. Worksheet Reference Hide
   e. None of the above

True/False

6. Using manual recalculation slows down the operation of the spreadsheet.

7. The Titles command allows only horizontal text to be frozen on the screen.

8. Relative addressing is used whenever you want a formula that is to be copied down a column or across a row to refer to the identical cell.

9. It is impossible to create a mixed range name by using a mixed cell address.

10. The function @IF allows you to embed sophisticated logic within your worksheet quickly.

Answers

1. e   2. b   3. e   4. a   5. c   6. t   7. f   8. f   9. t   10. t

Exercises

1. Define or describe each of the following:
   a. range name
   b. titles
   c. manual recalculation
   d. absolute address
   e. mixed cell address
   f. date arithmetic

2. One of the greatest benefits of range names is that they allow a cell formula to be self-_____.

3. Positioning the pointer at a word (cell) and then making that word the range name is accomplished via the _____ option of the Range Name Menu.

4. The Create and Delete commands reside in the _____ Menu.

5. A hidden column is so indicated by a(n) _____ when the / Worksheet Column Display command is issued.

6. The option of the Range Name submenu that is used to create a report of the various named ranges created within the worksheet is _____.

7. The _____ command can be used to reset the date or time without leaving 1-2-3.

8. A(n) _____ key will have information sorted in order inside a(n) _____ key.

9. The Sort option is found in the _____ Menu.

10. Before you use the Sort command, it is probably wise to _____ _____ your worksheet file.

11. The _____ command allows you to freeze rows and/or columns on the screen for use as headings.

12. _____ addressing allows cell references to change as they are copied; _____ addressing maintains all or part of the cell address from one cell to the next.

13. _____ cell addressing allows one part of the cell address to change while keeping the other part intact.

14. _____ recalculation may cause you to wait for long spreadsheets to recalculate each time a cell is changed or a new cell is entered.

15. The function key _____ is pressed when you wish 1-2-3 to recalculate a worksheet while you are in manual recalculation mode.

16. The message _____ appears at the bottom of the screen when a change has been made to the contents of some cell during manual recalculation mode.

17. The _____ function allows you to embed logic in your worksheet.

18. The logical operators _____, _____, and _____ allow you to specify how comparisons are to interact.

19. The operators <, >, and <= are referred to as _____ operators.

20. The @DATE function is extremely useful because it allows you to perform _____ to advance the date from one month to the next.

21. The _____ allows 1-2-3 to optimize how cells are recalculated.

22. The _____ command can be used to change the text content of cells.

23. The minimal recalculation method of 1-2-3 is disabled if either the _____ or _____ recalculation method is selected.

24. The _____ command can convert a formula to a numeric constant that depicts the result of a formula.

25. The / Range Search command can either _____ or _____ text in a specified range.

COMPUTER EXERCISES

1. Ed has been approached to invest in a microcomputer store that will specialize in selling relatively low-cost microcomputers. Ed has done an excellent job of collecting information about this proposed business venture. He is interested in modeling the next four years of business activity. He wants a worksheet built to present information in two basic areas—an input area and an income statement area—as appears on the next page.*

    The following criteria must be applied to the worksheet:

    a. The input area will start in column A. Column A should be set to a width of 25.
    b. The income statement will start in column F.
    c. Sales are expected to be 300 units the first year.

*Adapted from Arthur Andersen & Co. materials.

d. Rent for each year is $7,500 per year.
e. Salaries are equal to 10% of sales (commission sales).
f. Supplies are 1.5% of sales.
g. Clerical costs are $4,000 the first year and 6% more each additional year.
h. Advertising costs are $50,000 plus 7% of sales the first year, $25,000 plus 7% of sales the second year, and 5% of sales in subsequent years.

```
INPUT AREA
UNITS SOLD (YEAR 1)        300
COST PER UNIT             $650
ANNUAL SALES GROWTH      15.00%
ANNUAL PRICE REDUCTION    7.00%
PRODUCT MARGIN           40.00%
```

```
                        ED'S MICROCOMPUTER SHOP
                        Projected Financial Statements
                            1        2        3        4
                        -------- -------- -------- --------
Sales                    325,000  347,588  371,745  397,581
Cost                     195,000  208,553  223,047  238,549
                        -------- -------- -------- --------
Margin                   130,000  139,035  148,698  159,032
Expenses:
  Advertising             72,750   49,331   18,587   19,879
  Salaries                32,500   34,759   37,174   39,758
  Rent                     7,500    7,500    7,500    7,500
  Supplies                 4,875    5,214    5,576    5,964
  Clerical                 4,000    4,240    4,494    4,764
  Other Costs             10,000   10,500   11,025   11,576
                        -------- -------- -------- --------
Total Expenses          131,625  111,544   84,357   89,441
                        -------- -------- -------- --------
Income b/f Taxes         (1,625)  27,491   64,341   69,591
Income Taxes                  0   13,746   32,170   34,796
                        -------- -------- -------- --------
Net Income               (1,625)  13,746   32,170   34,796
```

i. There is a 50% tax rate.
j. Other costs are $10,000 the first year and 5% more each additional year.
k. An @IF statement must be set up to check for a positive income before taxes.
l. The following range names will be used:

Units sold	Units
Costs per unit	Cost
Annual growth	Growth
Annual price reduction	Ann.red
Profit margin	Margin
First year sales	Sales

Year 1 net income	Year 1
Year 2 net income	Year2
Year 3 net income	Year3
Year 4 net income	Year4

    m. Column F will be set to a width of 16.
    n. The global column will be set to a width of 11.
    o. For year 1, the following sales formula will be used:

```
$UNITS*($COST/(1-$MARGIN))
```

    p. For years 2–4, the following sales formula will be used:

```
+SALES*(1+$GROWTH)*(1-$ANN.RED)
```

    q. The following is the cost formula for year 1:

```
$SALES*(1-$MARGIN)
```

    r. Generate a report of named ranges and print it out. Save this worksheet to a file called CH5EX1.

2. Retrieve the worksheet CH5EX2. Locate and correct all circular references contained in the worksheet. Be sure to use the GoTo command to position the pointer directly to each circular reference once you have located it.

3. Retrieve the CH3EX5 file. Use the 1-2-3 Sort command to place the rows of the worksheet in order by the names of the sales representatives. Don't include any total or heading lines in the sort. Save the sorted worksheet to a file called CH5EX3.

4. Load the worksheet CH3EX8. Set up the worksheet so that any additional monthly sales data are automatically included in the total for each region. Also set up the vertical totals such that a new region can be added at the bottom of the column. Enter sales for April and May. (You supply them.) A new region, F, is added in March. The sales figures are $4,500 for March and $3,700 for April for the new region.

5. Retrieve the CH4EX2 worksheet. To the right of the worksheet, enter a Final % column as depicted in Figure 5.31. Take the students' total earned points and divide them by the total possible points to calculate the current percentage grade. Save this worksheet using the name CH5EX5.

6. Develop a loan amortization schedule for a 15-year mortgage. The principal is $20,000. The interest rate is 13.5%. You select the beginning date. Each line in the amortization schedule should have the month, payment amount, principal reduction amount, amount applied toward interest, and remaining outstanding balance. [Remember that you must multiply the periods (years) by 12 when dealing with months.]
    In solving this problem and looking at the worksheet, you must use the Horizontal Titles option to keep the column headings on the

Figure 5.31
Student grade worksheet

```
A1: (D1) [W15] @INT(@NOW)                                    READY

         A         B      C         D        E      F      G         H
    1  05-Oct-91
    2              Grading Template
    3
    4     NAME          Exam I  Anot. Bib  Exam II  Final %
    5  POSSIBLE POINTS    150       45       130       325
    6  ---------------------------------------------------------
    7  Student 1          113       44       110       82.15%
    8  Student 2          116       42        90       76.31%
    9  Student 3          129       42        85       78.77%
   10  Student 4          133       44       125       92.92%
   11  Student 5          121       42        76       73.54%
   12  Student 6          127       42        95       81.23%
   13  Student 7          120       42       115       85.23%
   14  ---------------------------------------------------------
   15  Average            123       43        99
   16  % of Tot. Pnts.  82.00%   95.56%    76.15%
   17  High Grade         133       44       125
   18  Low Grade          113       42        76
   19  Std. Deviation       7        1        16
   20  Variance            45        1       268
   05-Oct-91  12:10 AM
```

screen. You must also design the worksheet so that it quits calculating and outputting negative numbers when the principal is completely paid.

Print this worksheet using the Borders option. This option will print the column headings at the top of each page of the printout, making the output more readable. Save this worksheet under the name CH5EX6.

7. Develop a worksheet that allows users to investigate a number of different principal amounts plotted against a number of different interest rates for home mortgages. Start with principal amounts of $20,000, $40,000, $60,000, $80,000, $100,000, and $120,000. Use interest rates of 11.5%, 12.5%, 13%, 14%, 14.5%, 15%, and 15.5%. Refer to the Car Loan Evaluation Worksheet for ideas. The loans are all for 25 years. Save this file using the name CH5EX7.

8. Load the CH4EX1 worksheet containing the payroll information. Sort it alphabetically by rate of pay—that is, so that rate of pay is the primary key and last name is the secondary key. Save this file using the name CH5EX8.

9. Load the CH5EX6 worksheet. Move the input labels to column A. Hide the Total Payment column. Print the first three years of payments.

10. Create a worksheet like that depicted in Figure 5.32. Save the worksheet to the file CH5EX10. Set column B to a width of 20. The extension is calculated by multiplying the units cells times the price cells. The commission is calculated as follows: Sales equal to or greater than $2,000 receive a 12% commission; sales equal to or greater than $1,000 and less than $2,000 receive an 8% commission; all other sales receive a 4% commission.

Figure 5.32

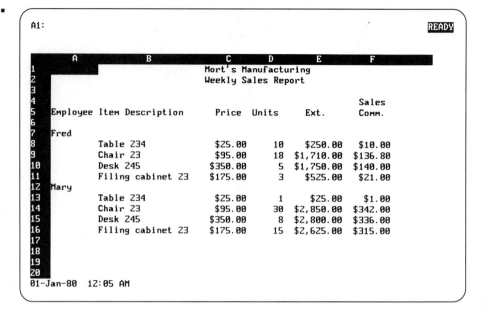

Figure 5.33

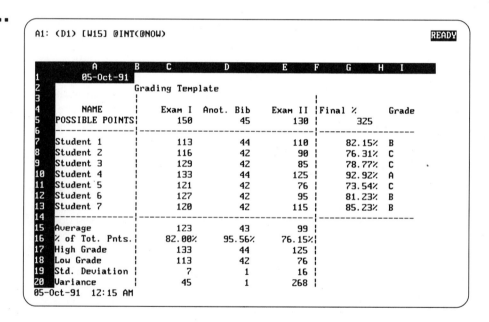

11. Retrieve the CH5EX5 worksheet. Change it so that the letter grade is automatically entered, via a nested @IF function, based on the final percentage figure. (See Figure 5.33.) Use the table below for generating the letter grade. Save the worksheet to the file CH5EX11.

90% and above	A
80%–89%	B
70%–79%	C
60%–69%	D
Less than 69%	F

12. Enter the following salary negotiation worksheet and save it to a file called CH5EX12.

    One of the most difficult areas for both school boards and teachers unions to deal with is contract negotiation. The union and the school board must sit down and try to negotiate a new contract for teachers. Depending on the school district, this process must be performed every one to five years.

    This process becomes complex because it is extremely difficult for both the school board and the union to quickly determine the economic impact of a proposal or counterproposal. Because of the different types of job steps and educational categories often found in education, this is an ideal application for Lotus 1-2-3. After a proposal or counterproposal has been presented, it can be quickly modeled using 1-2-3.

    This particular exercise attempts, as much as possible, to keep the negotiation model simple and easy to use. The model itself has five different parts: input/impact areas, salary schedule, individuals in each category, salary subtotals for each category, and a financial statement.

    The input/impact areas of the worksheet can be seen following this discussion. The input area allows you to change three pieces of data. The beginning salary is the salary received by anyone hired directly from college with a bachelor's degree. The job step increment is the amount that is added to an individual's salary for each year worked. The educational increment is the amount that is added to a teacher's salary for additional education obtained.

    The impact area shows the current total amount paid for salaries, as well as other information. The results of any changes made to the input area are reflected in these entries. For instance, once a change has been entered in the base salary, job step increment, or educational increment entries, the change is reflected in the impact area.

    The impact area is also affected by changes in projections for next year's revenues and expenditures in the financial statement. You are allowed to change the Estimated % Increase column of the financial statement. The projected expenditures are subtracted from the expected revenues to arrive at the Present Available Monies entry. The Total Differential Cost is now subtracted from the Present Available Monies to arrive at the Difference with Proposal.

    Let's now examine each of the other different areas of the negotiation model. First, let's take a look at the information contained in Table 5.2, which shows the salary for each job category. The job step (vertical) entries represent the salary based on longevity or length of service with the school district. The educational increment (horizontal) entries represent the salary increments that accrue to teachers based on additional education that a teacher receives.

    Table 5.3 shows how many people are in each separate job category. A check figure indicating the total number of teachers in the table is used to guard against data entry errors.

    Table 5.4, salary totals of each job category, is calculated by multiplying each entry in the salary schedule by the corresponding number of individuals in that entry. A grand total of all subtotals in this table is generated and used in the impact area of the worksheet.

    Table 5.5, the financial statement, contains this year's revenue and expenditures. It also contains a projected percent increase column used for generating each category of next year's projected revenue and

Table 5.2: Salary Schedule

Your School District for the Year 19xx
Education and Job Steps

Step	B.S.	B.S. +8	B.S. +16	B.S. +24	M.A.	M.A. +8	M.A. +16
1	15,700	16,075	16,450	16,825	17,200	17,575	17,950
2	16,200	16,575	16,950	17,325	17,700	18,075	18,450
3	16,700	17,075	17,450	17,825	18,200	18,575	18,950
4	17,200	17,575	17,950	18,325	18,700	19,075	19,450
5	17,700	18,075	18,450	18,825	19,200	19,575	19,950
6	18,200	18,575	18,950	19,325	19,700	20,075	20,450
7	18,700	19,075	19,450	19,825	20,200	20,575	20,950
8	19,200	19,575	19,950	20,325	20,700	21,075	21,450
9	19,700	20,075	20,450	20,825	21,200	21,575	21,950
10	20,200	20,575	20,950	21,325	21,700	22,075	22,450
11	20,700	21,075	21,450	21,825	22,200	22,575	22,950
12	21,200	21,575	21,950	22,325	22,700	23,075	23,450
13	21,700	22,075	22,450	22,825	23,200	23,575	23,950
14	22,200	22,575	22,950	23,325	23,700	24,075	24,450
15	22,700	23,075	23,450	23,825	24,200	24,575	24,950
16		23,575	23,950	24,325	24,700	25,075	25,450
17		24,075	24,450	24,825	25,200	25,575	25,950
18		24,575	24,950	25,325	25,700	26,075	26,450
19		25,075	25,450	25,825	26,200	26,575	26,950
20			25,950	26,325	26,700	27,075	27,450
21				26,825	27,200	27,575	27,950
22				27,325	27,700	28,075	28,450
23					28,200	28,575	28,950
24							29,450

expenditures. Subtracting projected expenditures from projected revenues generates the available monies entry in the impact area.

Most of the entries in the financial statement are self-explanatory, but a few merit some explanation. Let's examine the revenue portion of the financial statement first.

a. The Governmental Divisions entry is composed of revenue received from a number of state and federal programs, such as general state aid, driver education, special education, vocational education, gifted education, and federal subsidies.

b. The Student and Community Services entry is composed of revenue received from tuition from regular or adult education programs, as well as revenue from textbooks, lunch programs, and snack bars.

c. The Anticipation Warrants Receivable entry represents a source of short-term financing. These warrants are securities issued in anticipation of the receipt of the tax levy and are repaid when the tax levy is distributed.

Now let's look more closely at the expenditures portion of the financial statement.

a. The Administration category includes monies expended for administrators and their support personnel, as well as contractual entries for legal services.

Table 5.3: Teachers by Job Step and Education

Your School District for the Year 19xx
Individuals in Education and Job Steps

Step	B.S.	B.S. +8	B.S. +16	B.S. +24	M.A.	M.A. +8	M.A. +16
1	1		1	1	1	1	
2	1						
3		1					
4		1					
5			4			1	3
6	1	2			1		
7	1			1			
8	1		2				
9					3		1
10	2					1	
11		3	1	2			
12	1						
13			3	1	2		2
14	1						
15						4	
16		1		1			
17							
18							
19		1		2		2	1
20			1			3	
21							
22					2	1	
23							3
24							
Total Teachers		70					

b. The Fixed Charges category includes monies expended for the employer's share of retirement systems payments, various insurance policies provided for employees, and interest on anticipation warrants.

c. The Capital Outlay category includes new equipment for educational programs, as well as for replacement equipment.

d. The Debt Service category includes the total for anticipation warrants payable.

Hints for Building the 1-2-3 Model:

a. Design the input and impact areas so that they appear on different screens. Reach them by pressing the Pg Dn and Pg Up keys.

b. Arrange each of the schedules so that they can be reached by pressing the Tab key.

c. Set column A to a width of 22 and the first column of your financial statement to a width of 32.

d. Enter the Current Salary Base total as a numeric constant so changes can be tracked. This figure is the only figure, besides the financial statement figures, that has to be manually changed.

e. The beginning salary figure in Table 5.2 (15,700) must appear via a cell reference to the input area. If that figure subsequently changes, the change will automatically be reflected in the table.

Table 5.4: Salaries by Job Step and Education

Your School District for the Year 19xx
Salary Totals of Individuals in Education and Job Steps

Step	B.S.	B.S. +8	B.S. +16	B.S. +24	M.A.	M.A. +8	M.A. +16
1	15,700	0	16,450	16,825	17,200	17,575	0
2	16,200	0	0	0	0	0	0
3	0	17,075	0	0	0	0	0
4	0	17,575	0	0	0	0	0
5	0	0	73,800	0	0	19,575	59,850
6	18,200	37,150	0	0	19,700	0	0
7	18,700	0	0	19,825	0	0	0
8	19,200	0	39,900	0	0	0	0
9	0	0	0	0	63,600	0	21,950
10	40,400	0	0	0	0	22,075	0
11	0	63,225	21,450	43,650	0	0	0
12	21,200	0	0	0	0	0	0
13	0	0	67,350	22,825	46,400	0	47,900
14	22,200	0	0	0	0	0	0
15	0	0	0	0	0	98,300	0
16	0	23,575	0	24,325	0	0	0
17	0	0	0	0	0	0	0
18	0	0	0	0	0	0	0
19	0	25,075	0	51,650	0	53,150	26,950
20	0	0	25,950	0	0	81,225	0
21	0	0	0	0	0	0	0
22	0	0	0	0	55,400	28,075	0
23	0	0	0	0	0	0	86,850
24	0	0	0	0	0	0	0

      The same holds true for the vertical and horizontal increments. They must also be accessed via cell references. Some form of absolute addressing is required.

f. Make certain that you sum the number of teachers in the various categories in Table 5.3. This provides you with a check figure that indicates whether or not you have all of the teachers entered. It does not, however, indicate whether the teachers have been entered in the appropriate categories.

g. The grand total of Table 5.4 provides you with the total cost of any changes made in the input area. Use the @SUM function to sum each category subtotal.

h. The impact area entries are calculated as follows:
  1. The Current Salary Base total is derived via a cell reference to the Instruction expenditure entry in the Financial Statement of Table 5.5. This figure does not change.
  2. Total Cost of Change is derived by summing the entries contained in Table 5.4.
  3. Total Differential Cost is derived by subtracting Current Salary Base from Total Cost of Change.
  4. Percentage Change is derived by dividing Total Differential Cost by Total Cost of Change.

Table 5.5: School Income Statement with Next Year's Projections

Your School District Financial Statement for the Year 19xx
Educational Fund

	This Year	Est. % Inc.	
Revenue			
Beginning Balance	$ 6,704.63		$ 6,704.63
Local Taxes	1,156,300.00	2.00%	1,179,426.00
Governmental Divisions	592,870.00	1.50%	601,763.05
Student and Community Services	237,640.00	2.50%	243,581.00
Other Revenue	1,300.00	2.00%	1,326.00
Anticipation Warrants Rec.	435,170.37	2.50%	446,049.63
Total Estimated Revenue	$2,429,985.00		$2,478,850.31
Expenditures			
Administration	$ 174,825.00	3.00%	$ 180,069.75
Instruction	1,545,250.00		1,545,250.00
Health	7,650.00	1.50%	7,764.75
Maintenance	7,200.00	1.50%	7,308.00
Fixed Charges	65,150.00	1.50%	66,127.25
Student and Community Services	319,810.00	2.00%	326,206.20
Capital Outlay	50,000.00		50,000.00
Debt Service	240,000.00	1.80%	244,320.00
Contingency	20,000.00		20,000.00
Total Proposed Expenditures	$2,429,885.00		$2,447,045.95

5. Average Salary Increase is derived by dividing Total Differential Cost by the number of teachers.
6. Present Available Monies is derived by subtracting the total expenses from the total revenues of Table 5.5.
7. Difference with Proposal is derived by subtracting Present Available Monies from Total Differential Cost.

Input Area

Beginning Salary:	15,700
Job Step Increment (Vert):	500
Educational Increment (Horiz):	375

Impact Area

Current Salary Base	1,545,250 Before Change
Total Cost of Change	1,545,250
Total Differential Cost	0
Percentage Change	0.0%
Average Salary Increase	0
Present Available Monies	31,804
Difference with Proposal	31,804

13. *Part I—General Instructions*
   a. Enter the following financial statements using Lotus 1-2-3 and store them to a file called CH5EX13.
   b. Prepare a financial analysis of the Treadstone 21 Company based on information contained in the various financial schedules as they currently appear. If there is sufficient information available, explain how the various increases/decreases within the statements occurred.
   c. In addition to examining the various financial statements, you are also to prepare the other financial analysis measures contained in the worksheets at the end of this exercise and include these in your paper.
   d. You are responsible for gathering information concerning the formulas for the required ratios.
   e. What information not included would allow you to prepare a better analysis?
   f. Would you recommend investing in this company? Be sure to carefully state your rationale.
   g. Determine the impact on the Treadstone 21 Company and on your decision whether or not to purchase stock if the following changes occurred for 1991:
      1. Sales returns and allowances increased 10%.
      2. Accounts receivable increased by 15%.
      3. Long-term liabilities are $200,000.
      4. Sales increased 5% (gross profit percentage constant).

      Just enter the above changes and examine their impact on the worksheet. Do not try to make the debits balance the credits.
   h. You do not currently have any information about what type of business the Treadstone 21 Company is engaged in. Assume that the company could be in any one of the following five businesses. You are also given information about three of the ratios to be calculated. Based on the information from the ratios for each of the proposed businesses, would you invest in Treadstone 21? Give a rationale for each type of possible business.

	Retail	Electric	Machinery	Grocery	Clothing
Quick Ratio	1.3	0.9	1.8	0.8	1.1
Liability to Equity	60.2	210.0	57.4	34.2	43.7
Asset to Sales	74.0	173.0	65.0	16.3	39.2

Part II—Format Instructions

   a. Set the global column width to 12.
   b. Use the Copy feature of 1-2-3 as much as possible.
   c. Use WordStar or some other word processing package to write your paper.
   d. Save each of the schedules to disk as a print file (you may want to review this process from Chapter 4 and the discussion of the Quit command from the Print submenu), and use the WordStar ^KR command to include them in your report. You can use the ^KR command to load either a .PRN file or a named range from the worksheet. 1-2-3 may embed some strange-looking end-of-file indicators at the bottom of your .PRN file. You can get rid of them by issuing a delete to end of line (Ctrl + End) command. Also,

make certain that if you have double spacing in effect you change it to single spacing when you load in the schedules. You may also have to reset your pitch and/or margins to get the schedules to print properly.

e. Design your 1-2-3 worksheets so that data need be changed in only one location to affect the other financial statements and ratios. This means that one income statement's figures will refer to the other's and will change as the other changes. You accomplish this cross-reference by first deciding which income statement is to be changed and which is to reflect the changes entered on the other. For example, assume that you decide that the horizontal analysis income statement is to be the part of the worksheet that will receive any changes and that the vertical analysis income statement will reflect the changes made to the horizontal worksheet. To accomplish this, you must first build the horizontal analysis income statement. After you have done this, copy the various row and column headings from that area of the worksheet to the area that will hold the vertical analysis income statement. All that now remains to be done is to direct 1-2-3 to load the information into the vertical analysis cells by referencing the first cell in the other worksheet (for example, +V11). You can now copy this reference down this column. You will have to replace any zero entries with the appropriate rows of dashes.

f. Within the body of your spreadsheet, you are to give the various reports the following range names:

Comparative Balance Sheet	Balance1
Comparative Schedule of Current Assets	Balance2
Horizontal Analysis Income Statement	Income1
Vertical Analysis Income Statement	Income2
Retained Earnings Statement	Retained
Ratio Analysis Data and Ratios	Ratio

You can now give the range name to 1-2-3, instead of pointing out the range, when printing.

g. Turn in your report along with the diskette containing your WordStar and 1-2-3 files. The worksheet should reflect the changes from item g of Part I. The worksheets of the financial statements in the body of your report should have the same format as those on the following pages.

Treadstone 21 Company
Comparative Balance Sheet
December 31, 1991 and 1990
Horizontal Analysis

	1991	1990	Increase (Decrease) Amount	Percent
Assets				
Current assets	$635,713	$591,883	$43,830	7.4%
Long-term investments	106,000	183,000	(77,000)	−42.1%
Plant assets (net)	485,000	510,000	(25,000)	−4.9%
Intangible assets	35,000	35,000	0	0.0%
Total assets	$1,261,713	$1,319,883	($58,170)	−4.4%
Liabilities				
Current liabilities	$200,000	$247,000	($47,000)	−19.0%
Long-term liabilities	150,000	225,000	(75,000)	−33.3%
Total liabilities	$350,000	$472,000	($122,000)	−25.8%
Stockholders' Equity				
Preferred 6% stock, $100 par	$160,000	$155,000	$5,000	3.2%
Common stock, $10 par	550,000	550,000	0	0.0%
Retained earnings	201,713	142,883	58,830	41.2%
Total stockholders' equity	$911,713	$847,883	$63,830	7.5%
Total liab. & stockholders' equity	$1,261,713	$1,319,883	($58,170)	−4.4%

Treadstone 21 Company
Comparative Schedule of Current Assets
December 31, 1991 and 1990

	1991	1990	Increase (Decrease) Amount	Percent
Cash	$116,780	$89,683	$27,097	30.2%
Marketable securities	105,000	85,000	20,000	23.5%
Accounts receivable (net)	132,233	125,000	7,233	5.8%
Merchandise inventory	275,000	287,000	(12,000)	−4.2%
Prepaid expenses	6,700	5,200	1,500	28.8%
Total Current Assets	$635,713	$591,883	$43,830	7.4%

Treadstone 21 Company
Income Statement
For Years Ended December 31, 1991 and 1990
Horizontal Analysis

	1991	1990	Increase (Decrease) Amount	Percent
Sales	$1,607,025	$1,234,000	$373,025	30.2%
Sales returns and allowances	35,750	34,000	1,750	5.1%
Net sales	$1,571,275	$1,200,000	$371,275	30.9%
Cost of merchandise sold	1,095,150	820,000	275,150	33.6%
Gross profit	$476,125	$380,000	$96,125	25.3%
Selling expenses	$185,000	$141,000	$44,000	31.2%
General expenses	100,000	93,400	6,600	7.1%
Total operating expenses	$285,000	$234,400	$50,600	21.6%
Operating income	$191,125	$145,600	$45,525	31.3%
Other income	8,500	11,000	(2,500)	−22.7%
	$199,625	$156,600	$43,025	27.5%
Other expenses	6,000	13,000	(7,000)	−53.8%
Income before income tax	$193,625	$143,600	$50,025	34.8%
Income tax	85,195	61,985	23,210	37.4%
Net income	$108,430	$81,615	$26,815	32.9%

Treadstone 21 Company
Comparative Income Statement
For Years Ended December 31, 1991 and 1990
Vertical Analysis

	1991 Amount	1991 Percent	1990 Amount	1990 Percent
Sales	$1,607,025	102.3%	$1,234,000	102.8%
Sales returns and allowances	$35,750	2.3%	$34,000	2.8%
Net sales	$1,571,275	100.0%	$1,200,000	100.0%
Cost of merchandise sold	$1,095,150	69.7%	$820,000	68.3%
Gross profit	$476,125	30.3%	$380,000	31.7%
Selling expenses	$185,000	11.8%	$141,000	11.8%
General expenses	$100,000	6.4%	$93,400	7.8%
Total operating expenses	$285,000	18.1%	$234,400	19.5%
Operating income	$191,125	12.2%	$145,600	12.1%
Other income	$8,500	0.5%	$11,000	0.9%
	$199,625	12.7%	$156,600	13.1%
Other expenses	$6,000	0.4%	$13,000	1.1%
Income before income tax	$193,625	12.3%	$143,600	12.0%
Income tax	$85,195	5.4%	$61,985	5.2%
Net income	$108,430	6.9%	$81,615	6.8%

Treadstone 21 Company
Comparative Retained Earnings Statement
For Years Ended December 31, 1991 and 1990

			Increase (Decrease)	
	1991	1990	Amount	Percent
Retained earnings, January 1	$142,883	$100,568	$42,315	42.1%
Net income for year	108,430	81,615	26,815	32.9%
Total	$251,313	$182,183	$69,130	37.9%
Dividends:				
On preferred stock	$9,600	$9,300	$300	3.2%
On common stock	40,000	30,000	10,000	33.3%
Total	$49,600	$39,300	$10,300	26.2%
Retained earnings, December 31	$201,713	$142,883	$58,830	41.2%

Additional Data Needed for Ratio Analysis

	1991	1990
A/R Beginning of Year Balance	125,000	140,000
Total Assets Beg. of Year	1,314,400	1,187,500
Tot. Ass.—Long-Term Invest.	1,131,400	1,010,000
Shares Outstanding Common	50,000	50,000
Price per Share of Common	$20.50	$13.50
Dividend/Share of Common	$ 0.80	$ 0.60

Financial Ratio Analysis

	1991	1990
Current Ratio		
Acid Test		
Accounts Receivable Turnover		
No. of Days' Sales in Recbles.		
Plant Assets to Long-Term Liab.		
Stockholders' Equity to Liab.		

PROFITABILITY ANALYSIS
Net Sales to Assets
EPS on Common Stock
Price Earnings Ratio
Dividend Yield

Figure 5.34
The CH5EX14 worksheet.

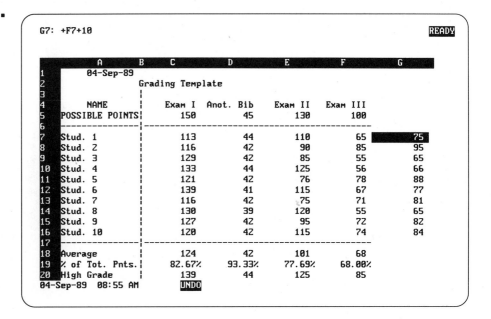

 14. Retrieve the worksheet named CH5EX14, which should appear like that depicted in Figure 5.34. Use the Range Search command to change each occurrence of Stud. in the worksheet to Student. The individual using this worksheet has also decided to adjust the grade for Exam III by adding 10 points to each score, which has been accomplished in column G. Notice that each grade adjustment has been made via a formula (refer to the status line in the control panel). Use the Range Value command to take the values in column G and place them in column F. When you are finished, delete column G. Save your worksheet to the file named CH5EX14A.

CHAPTER 6

PROFESSIONAL USE OF WORKSHEETS

CHAPTER OBJECTIVES

After completing this chapter, you should be able to:

- **Create a template and cover the steps involved in creating templates**
- **Use the 1-2-3 Window command**
- **Use worksheet and cell protection**
- **Use the Data Fill command**
- **Use sensitivity analysis via data tables with one or two variables**
- **Link files together**

This chapter will cover the following topics: template design, windows, cell protection, data fill, use of 1-2-3 tables in sensitivity analysis, and linking files.

TEMPLATES

After a worksheet has been designed, other people may also want to use it. When this happens, whoever originally designed the worksheet (or someone else in the firm) will have to spend some additional time on the worksheet converting it to a template. A **template** is a prewritten worksheet that guides a person step-by-step through a particular application.

The steps in designing a worksheet, which were covered in Chapter 3, apply to designing a template as well, but other factors are also important. In cases where the only person who uses a worksheet is the person who originally created it, the worksheet does not need to have a template's capacity to address concerns shared by many different users.

Another major difference between templates and worksheets is in the matter of documentation. The usual documentation supplied inside a worksheet is a memory-triggering device for the worksheet's author. The amount of documentation needed for a template is much greater, since someone with little understanding of the application and no understanding of spreadsheet software may be required to use it. In addition, written documentation is needed to augment documentation in the template itself.

Writing good spreadsheet templates is similar to generating third-party application programs. The person who develops a template is engaged in building a generalized set of instructions capable of solving various specific instances of a general type of problem. Not everyone can (or will want to) design and develop templates.

PLANNING

A template can be viewed as a system or application program with three functional parts: input, processing, and output. A good template should (1) require the user to input the data to be processed in a structured format, (2) process those data correctly, and (3) provide some way to get the results (output) to the user in an easy-to-use format.

The physical areas of the template should be divided to reflect these three functional parts. A good template will have one or more input screens that allow easy data entry. If a specific manual data form is used to capture information, it should also appear as part of the input screen so that users can simply fill in blanks that are familiar to them. An input area commonly has a lot of label entries to provide this formlike appearance. Making a good input screen is similar to designing a good form: Information is entered from the top downward and from left to right; numeric information and alphanumeric information are not indiscriminately mixed; and, as much as possible, information should be entered in rows or columns, but not both.

The processing area of the template should be in an area completely separate from the input and output screen(s). A good template locks the user out of making changes to template formulas by utilizing worksheet or cell-locking features provided by the spreadsheet software. Protecting cells makes it much more difficult for a user to change a formula erroneously.

Although any templates you build using this book will probably combine the processing and output areas into one area, many of the calculations referred to above utilize a special 1-2-3 feature called a macro, which will be covered in a later chapter.

The output or report area should also, as much as possible, be completely separate. The reports should have range names, which can then be used to quickly direct the spreadsheet to print reports needed by the user. Report and column headings should be descriptive of the use of their contents. The @NOW function should be used to date the various reports so a user can keep track of when various reports were run.

IMPLEMENTING TEMPLATE FUNCTIONS IN THE DESIGN

The three separate functions discussed above can be readily implemented in a rectangular format, making it easy to keep track of the various functional areas and allowing better utilization of RAM memory.

Each input area is designed as a screen for the user. The user can move easily from one input area to another either by depressing the Tab key or by depressing a paging key; each screen also has an instruction identifying the appropriate key to depress to continue from one page to the next. The number of columns that appear on a screen is, of course, determined by the width of the various columns. The user is prompted on how to move from one functional area (input, processing, or output) to another by screen prompts. If you lose your way on the worksheet of the template, you can also return to cell A1 by depressing the Home key.

On-line documentation providing instructions to the user often appears in the "home" position (cell A1). This documentation, called a **help screen,** can easily be created by giving column A the same width as the screen. Multiple help screens can then be stacked on top of one another, and the user can move from one to another by pressing the Pg Up or Pg Dn keys.

The first help screen typically contains identifying information about the template, such as the name of the template, what kind of processing is performed by it, who created it, and a telephone number to call if things go wrong in processing the data. Most important, it includes the revision number and date of the last update or revision. To ensure that this help screen appears as soon as the template is loaded into memory, you need only place the pointer in the "home" position before the template is saved. The pointer always appears in a worksheet at the same location that it was in when the Save operation was performed.

It is important that you not stack reports. Reports require different column widths to present various pieces of information attractively. When you vary column width, the width changes for the entire column within the worksheet. Since column widths cannot be one width in one part of a column and another width in another part of the same column, the best course is to place reports side by side.

DESIGNING THE LOGIC

Obtaining an in-depth understanding of the application to be modeled is the key to incorporating the correct logic. If the individual who builds the template does not have the proper understanding, the template will be of questionable value, at best.

The structured walk-through, a method used extensively in testing the logic of an application program, can be applied to the construction of templates. In a **structured walk-through,** the individual who designed the logic explains it to co-workers who are responsible for making certain that the logic is correct, straightforward, and easy to understand. In addition to using the structured walk-through approach, the template builder should sit down with potential users and go through the logic. This review will allow them to find any mistakes in logic and also to suggest changes for input screens or output reports. Active user involvement at this point can save expensive changes later; it is much easier to incorporate changes at the design step than to do so after all the logic is hard-coded within the template.

DEVELOPING THE TEMPLATE

This step is the one during which the logic that has been developed is implemented using the syntax of the spreadsheet package. Developing the template involves entering instructions by means of the spreadsheet software package. Error trapping at this step is critically important.

By this point, the individual entering the template should have an intimate knowledge of what the expected results are. A simple application is used to test the incorporation of the logic. This process of verifying the logic and results of a template, known as **testing,** allows you to verify that you've entered the formulas correctly and that the results generated by the template are reasonable. The term *reasonable* implies that you have some idea of what the results should look like.

You can also increase confidence in a template by building in redundancy features. For example, if you have to sum or "foot" several columns of numbers, you should also "crossfoot" the individual rows and sum those totals. The sum of the crossfooted totals should be the same as the sum of the footed totals.

For large template applications, the automatic recalculation feature should be switched to manual recalculation. This will save users a tremendous amount of time while using the template. Instructions must be included, however, to let template novices know how to make the template recalculate.

FINAL TESTING

Final testing should be a joint effort between the individual(s) who constructed the template and the people who will eventually be its day-to-day users. It is important to involve users who have an in-depth understanding of the application to which the template will be put in the final testing. They often detect minor errors that have escaped the developers or raise nuances of the application that the developers did not properly understand.

In addition to enlisting users to test templates, you might want to try one of a number of software packages on the market that are designed to examine the logic of a worksheet or template. Two such packages are Spreadsheet Auditor and Docucalc. These packages examine your worksheet and print formulas in the relative locations where they appear on the screen; they also keep track of the various range names used in a worksheet or template and are useful in locating a cell containing a circular reference.

FINAL DOCUMENTATION

The documentation manual that is to accompany the template must now be finished. The process of documentation is an ongoing task, *not* one of the last things done. Much of the documentation is identical to what appears inside the template itself. The final documentation should include the following:

1. Purpose of the template
2. Identifying characteristics
   a. Author(s)
   b. Revision number and date
   c. Phone number for assistance
3. Copies of the input screens and any explanations about what each data field represents
4. Copies of any reports that are generated by the system
5. Any explanatory text needed for clarifying how information is processed within the template
6. Formatted listings of all formulas

One extremely important piece of internal documentation is the prompt or prompts directing the user to save the completed worksheet built using the template. If the user were to save the worksheet back to the original template file, the template would be destroyed. To avoid having this happen, you must include very explicit instructions to the user to save the worksheet to a different file. Backing up a template is critical. Many harmful things can happen: It can be overwritten; it can inadvertently be erased; the diskette containing it can be lost. The steps required to back up a template, therefore, must be emphasized to the user.

One rule of thumb to keep in mind is that many users will not bother to read the written documentation. Consequently, as much documentation as possible should be placed in the template itself.

SUPPORT AND MAINTENANCE

When the template is "finished," it is not necessarily really finished. What happens if an error is found? Who provides the answers to any questions that arise from users? Who is responsible for making revisions to a template and sending them out to the user community? One or more people will have to be responsible for maintaining and supporting the templates. You can now begin to see why template preparation and support have been equated with programming—they require skill, effort, and lots of time.

WINDOWS

When you are using a large worksheet, regardless of whether or not it is a template, you will frequently want to be able to see two pieces of the worksheet at one time—for instance, the data input area and the data output area. This is accomplished in most spreadsheet packages via windows. **Windows** allow you to split the screen either vertically or horizontally, giving you two views of the same worksheet and allowing you to see the input area and the output area on the screen at the same time. When you make a change in one half of the screen, the result is automatically reflected in the other half. If the changes are not reflected in the other window immediately, they will appear as soon as you move the pointer to that window.

The pointer position determines where the screen is going to split. If you want a horizontal window, the screen will split above the pointer, and the

Figure 6.1

A screen with a horizontal window

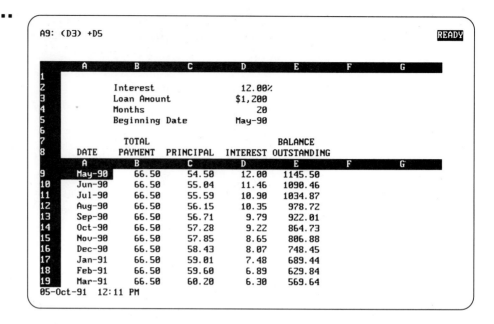

pointer will appear in the top window. If you want a vertical window, the screen will split to the left of the pointer, and the pointer will appear in the left-hand window. To jump from one window to the other requires depressing the F6 function key. The F6 key moves the pointer from the window where it is currently located to the other window.

 If you wish to follow along with a computer, for the following example load the worksheet file LOANAMOR, created in Chapter 5, and then position the pointer anywhere on row nine (9) of the worksheet.

To obtain a split screen or window, enter the following commands:

```
/   Invokes the Main Menu
W   Selects the Worksheet option
W   Selects the Window command from the Worksheet Menu
H   Selects the Horizontal option from the Window Menu
```

Your screen should now appear like the screen shown in Figure 6.1. When the Window option is selected, you see the following menu on the prompt line:

```
Horizontal   Vertical   Sync   Unsync   Clear
```

Horizontal This option creates a horizontal window above the present pointer position and causes the pointer to appear in the top window.

Vertical This option creates a vertical window to the left of the present pointer position and causes the pointer to appear in the left window.

Sync This option causes the contents of both windows to move synchronously, so that horizontal windows keep the same rows on the screen and vertical windows keep the same columns on the screen. This is the 1-2-3 default.

Unsync This option produces separate movement of the two visible parts of the worksheet within the two windows. The worksheet can be moved only when the pointer is in the appropriate window.

Clear This option is used to remove any windows and revert the display to a single screen. 1-2-3 returns you to the top or left-hand window settings, depending on which option you had selected.

> **HINTS/HAZARDS** It should be emphasized that only one worksheet resides in memory, and any changes made within a window will alter the worksheet currently in memory. All windows are saved with a file.

WORKSHEET AND CELL PROTECTION

After you've spent many hours building a template, you don't want to risk having someone inadvertently erase a critical formula while using the template. Such an action can totally destroy a template and may require you to spend many hours of effort trying to determine what went wrong.

PROTECTING THE WORKSHEET

The Lotus 1-2-3 spreadsheet package allows you to safeguard a template against this danger by using 1-2-3's protection feature. **Cell protection** guarantees that the contents of a cell cannot easily be changed by a user; if a change is attempted, the computer beeps and displays a `Protected cell` error message at the bottom of the screen.

Worksheet protection is obtained by giving the following commands to 1-2-3:

/	Invokes the Main Menu
W	Selects the Worksheet option
G	Selects the Global option from the Worksheet Menu
P	Selects the Protection command from the Global Menu
E	Selects the Enable option

The entire worksheet is now protected; it is impossible to change the contents of any cell. Although this protection is desirable for the template's calculation area, it is not at all desirable for the template's input areas. In order to allow data entry in the input areas, the protection must be disabled for those cells. What command can you use for this?

As you have probably already realized, any command you intend only for selected cells must go through the Range option of the Main Menu. Disabling protection is no exception.

/	Invokes the Main Menu
R	Selects the Range option
U	Selects the Unprotect option
-.- [by pointing or by entering the cell addresses]	Establishes the range
Enter	Tells 1-2-3 to execute the command

The newly unprotected cells appear on the screen in high-intensity video, indicating that you can now change them. The darker cell entries are protected

Figure 6.2

A protected worksheet, which does not allow you to make changes

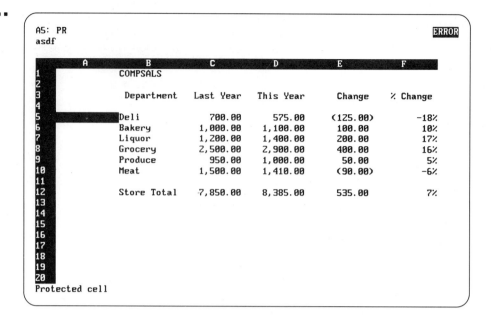

and do not allow changes. Only the areas of the spreadsheet against which the Range Unprotect command was executed now allow data entry or changes.

The unprotected cells can be differentiated from the protected cells in the following manner. When the pointer is on an unprotected cell, a U, along with the current cell contents, can be seen in the status line of the control panel. The U indicates that this is an unprotected cell. Any cell that is still protected will have a PR in the control panel.

To further illustrate the use of worksheet protection, load the file COMPSALS. Issue the appropriate commands from the example above to enable global protection. You can now no longer make any changes to the worksheet. When you try to press the Enter key, a Protected cell error message appears at the bottom of the screen (see Figure 6.2). To get rid of the error message, simply press the Esc key.

Now that the entire worksheet has been protected, any areas designated for change must be unprotected by using the Range Unprotect command. After examining the worksheet above, you decide to unprotect only the cells containing sales information for the This Year column. A user does not need access to any of the other cells: The headings don't have to be changed, sales for last year are history, formulas merely reflect changes in the designated cells, and the various department names do not have to be changed. Using the Unprotect command key sequence above, unprotect the indicated cells in column D (see Figure 6.3).

UNPROTECTING THE WORKSHEET

If someone finds an error that you want to correct, how do you reverse the above actions? First, you must remove the global protection by entering the following commands:

/ Invokes the Main Menu
W Selects the Worksheet option

Figure 6.3
A range of cells to be unprotected

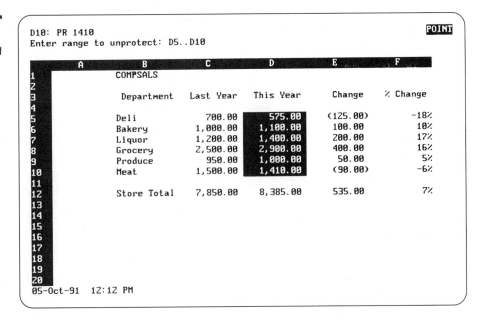

G   Selects the Global option from the Worksheet Menu
P   Selects the Protection command from the Global Menu
D   Selects the Disable option

You can now enter information in any cell on the spreadsheet, although the display of the cells in the input data areas may be misleading because the cells remain in high-intensity video. In order to get the appearance of the display back to normal, those cells have to be range-protected as follows:

/	Invokes the Main Menu
R	Selects the Range option
P	Selects the Protection option
–·– [by pointing or by entering the cell addresses]	Establishes the range
Enter	Tells 1-2-3 to execute the command

Once these cells have been unprotected, the unprotected cells appear in high-intensity video. Look at the contents of the status line, and you will notice that there is a U in the recently unprotected cells. Now change the sales of the Deli department from 575 to 1,410. Notice that even though other cells are still protected, and therefore unavailable to you, 1-2-3 uses the contents of the cell that you changed to generate a new worksheet.

UTILIZING THE DATA FILL FEATURE

Lotus 1-2-3 has a feature called the **Data Fill command** that allows a user to set up a range and then fill it with numbers. This feature is especially helpful if you wish to have a number of columns that will represent, for example, the years 1976 to 1990. Rather than manually entering each of these numbers, you can describe the range, start the initial cell with a value of 1976, specify an incremental value of 1 for each of the other cells in the range, and specify a maximum value (or ending value). Upon depressing the Enter key, you will see that the cells of the range are filled with the appropriate numbers. If you examine the contents of the cells, you will notice that there are numbers in each cell, meaning that you are able to left-justify or center the contents of these cells using the Label Prefix command. If centered or left-justified cells are desirable, all you have to do is convert them to labels rather than edit the contents of each cell you just filled.

The command steps for the above application are as follows (you want the years 1976 to 1990 in the cells B4 to P4):

/	Invokes the Main Menu
D	Selects the Data option
F	Selects the Fill command
B4.P4 [by pointing or address entering]	Establishes the beginning and ending of the range
Enter	Tells 1-2-3 to accept the range
1976	Enters 1976 as the beginning value in the range
Enter	Enters 1 (default) as the step or incremental amount from one cell to the next
Enter	Takes 8192 (default) as the ending value

The range now fills quickly with numbers. You are not limited to entering only whole numbers for the starting value or increment. The only real limitation is that the constant values cannot be greater than the default. If, for example, you wanted to fill a range starting with the value 9000, only the contents of the first cell containing the 9000 would print; since 9000 is greater than 8192, the other values will not appear within the range.

The maximum value of 8192 can be changed by entering another constant or formula; for example, the function @DATE (86,1,1) could be specified as the initial value and incremented with a step value of 5 and an ending value of 50,000. In this case, 1-2-3 does not stop when the original 8192 default has been reached.

The Data Fill feature has many labor-saving uses in building worksheets; it can be especially useful in conjunction with tables.

1-2-3 AND SENSITIVITY ANALYSIS

After a worksheet model has been created, most spreadsheet packages offer plenty of room for you to ask "what if" questions and to change one or more basic assumptions that were used in building the original worksheet. For example, you may have an application that used a rate of inflation of 4%; you can easily see what the effect of changing the rate of inflation to 5%, 6%, or 10% would be on the worksheet.

Sensitivity analysis is the process of asking these various "what if" questions with a view to determining the impact a change will have on a model. The process of sensitivity analysis is made much easier when the worksheet has been designed with basic assumptions as part of the input area. You can quickly change these entries and track the results simply by entering a single piece of information, rather than by changing a formula in a cell.

The only problem encountered with most spreadsheet packages in asking "what if" questions is the matter of keeping track of the changes generated by the worksheet. In order to compare results properly, you have to either keep track of the changes manually or print the worksheet after each important change. Although it remains relatively easy to ask the "what if" questions, the process can become so time-consuming that important alternatives are not examined.

MANUAL SENSITIVITY ANALYSIS EXAMPLE

Load the file PAYMENT for the following example. Suppose that you have been asked to calculate the monthly payment for a car loan of $10,000 for four years at various interest rates. For example, you might be interested in interest rates starting at 5% to 10% in increments of a half percent. To do this manually, you might create a report like the following:

*$10,000 Loan for Four Years at
the Following Interest Rates*

Interest	Monthly Payment
5.0%	
5.5%	
6.0%	
6.5%	
7.0%	
7.5%	
.	
.	
.	

To respond to these various "what if" questions via the PAYMENT worksheet, you must enter the characteristics of the loan (principal = 10000, loan years = 4) and then change the interest rate to reflect each "what if" value. Once you have finished, your report appears like the following:

Interest	Monthly Payment
5.0%	$230.29
5.5%	$232.56
6.0%	$234.85
6.5%	$237.15
7.0%	$239.46
7.5%	$241.79
.	
.	
.	

As you can see, the various "what if" questions about the impact of changes in the interest rate on the monthly payment were easy to ask. The real challenge lies in manually recording these changes. Also, what happens if you suddenly decide to ask the same "what if" questions for a loan length of 3 years, a principal of $12,500, or a principal of $11,500? Nobody wants to sit at a computer and enter the changes for this many "what if" questions.

TABLE COMMAND OF 1-2-3

Lotus solved the problem involved in asking multiple "what if" questions by incorporating the Table feature. **Table** allows either one or two inputs to be varied and then generates a table detailing the results. The Table feature allows you to examine many more "what if" questions than it is possible to do using other spreadsheets.

The table-generating process is similar to running a lot of different pieces of information through a worksheet and keeping track of the results. 1-2-3 takes a set of values that you have given it and substitutes them one at a time.

Figure 6.4

Parts of a one-assumption data table

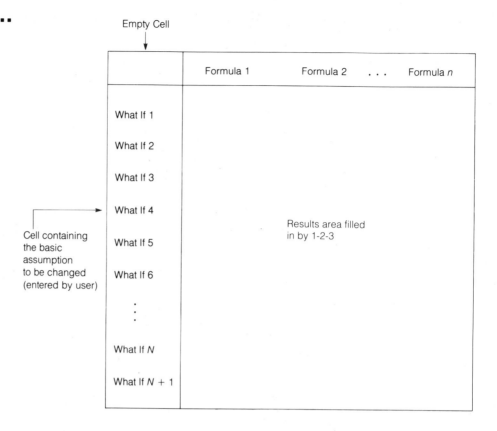

All you have to do is tell 1-2-3 where the "what if" values are in the worksheet for the one or two assumptions you want varied and where to put the results of these variations.

Several pieces of data must be supplied to 1-2-3 in building the table: the cell against which the "what if" questions are to be asked, the assumption(s) to be changed, the "what if" values to be used, and the extent or range of the table. Changes in the input to the formula or modeled cell can be made and new results generated by pressing the F8 Table function key—without redefining the table to 1-2-3 (see Figure 6.4).

HINTS/HAZARDS

No cell involved in a table can be protected, whether it be the modeled cell, the basic assumption cell, a cell containing a value to be substituted, or the receiving area for the "what if" results.

In the above example, the piece of data (cell) against which the various "what if" questions were asked was the monthly payment amount (calculated via the @PMT function). The various "what if" values used were changes in the interest rate. Where we filled in the various monthly payment amounts, 1-2-3 will calculate the values and enter them in their proper location.

SENSITIVITY ANALYSIS CHANGING ONE BASIC ASSUMPTION

Some of the concepts covered in this chapter can be illustrated by adapting the car loan worksheet from the previous chapter. In generating this worksheet, you will try to make it as flexible as possible and will follow good worksheet construction methods. The purpose of the worksheet is to evaluate the effect of a variety of interest rates on monthly payments of a car loan. You'll need three pieces of data as input: the principal of the loan, the interest rate, and the number of months of the loan.

In doing this project, you will practice the following skills:

1. Establishing an input area
2. Establishing an output/report area
3. Using the Data Fill command
4. Setting up a single-variable table
5. Using the Window command
6. Using the Text Format command

The input and output areas, which are to begin at cells A1 and F1, respectively, should appear as follows:

```
Cost of a Car Loan at a Variety
        of Interest Rates

Please enter the following
characteristics of the loan:

After you have entered the data,
press the [F8] key to generate the
new table.

Press the [F6] key to move to the
other window.

Be sure to enter the interest as a
decimal. Ex. 12% is entered as .12

Principal              $5,000
Interest                12.0%
Months                    40

                   INPUT AREA

Loan Principal        $5,000
Payment               152.28

           Payment
             +J2
           10.0%  147.50
           10.5%  148.69
           11.0%  149.88
           11.5%  151.08
           12.0%  152.28
```

```
12.5%  153.49
13.0%  154.70
13.5%  155.92
14.0%  157.14
14.5%  158.37
15.0%  159.61
15.5%  160.85
16.0%  162.09
16.5%  163.35
17.0%  164.60
17.5%  165.87
18.0%  167.14
18.5%  168.41
19.0%  169.69
19.5%  170.97
20.0%  172.26
```

OUTPUT AREA

The output area will eventually also contain the data table.

The cell +J2 references the cell of the worksheet against which you'll be performing the sensitivity analysis. That cell, of course, is the one containing the payment function, so you'll be asking "what if" questions about the effect of changes in interest rates on a car payment.

The basic assumption to be changed is the interest rate. Cell C18 contains this piece of information. The first column contains the 21 values of the basic assumption (interest rate) that are to be substituted into the worksheet one at a time. 1-2-3 will process the worksheet 21 times—one time for each different interest rate value.

The range of the table includes both columns. The top row of the range contains the +J2 entry; the bottom row contains the 20.0%. The second column contains the results of the various "what if" questions about each change in the interest rate.

A number of steps are involved in entering the worksheet, apart from enhancements.

1. Format the spreadsheet for fixed, with two decimal positions.
2. Enter label information.

```
A1   Cost of a Car Loan at a Variety
B2   of Interest Rates
A4   Please enter the following
A5   characteristics of the loan:
A7   After you have entered the data,
A8   press the F8 key to generate the
A9   new table.
A11  Press the F6 key to move to the
A12  other window.
A14  Be sure to enter the interest as a
A15  decimal. Ex. 12% is entered as .12
A17  Principal
A18  Interest
A19  Months
H1   Loan Principal
H2   Payment
```

3. Enter the principal amount of 5000 in cell C17. Format the cell for currency, with no decimal positions.
4. Enter the interest rate of .12 in cell C18. Format the cell for percent, with one decimal position.
5. Enter the number of months (40) of the loan in cell C19. Format the cell for no decimal positions.
6. At cell location J1, format the cell for currency with no decimal positions and display the contents of the principal entry by entering the following formula:

   +C17

7. Enter the following payment function at cell J2:

   @PMT(C17,C18/12,C19)

8. Prepare the interest/payment table.
   a. Enter the identifying text.

      I6 Payment

   b. Enter the cell that contains the information to be modeled (in this case, the payment formula).

      I7 +J2

      The result of the @PMT function is now copied onto cell I7. This is the part of the worksheet that will be modeled and undergo the various "what if" analyses.

   c. Change the number to a formula. This will avoid confusing the cell to be modeled with results in the table, and it will also quickly show the modeled cell location on the table. First, position the pointer at cell I7.

/	Invokes the Main Menu
R	Selects the Range option
F	Selects the Format option of the Range Menu
T	Selects the Text command from the Format Menu
Enter	Executes the command and displays the +J2 formula

   d. Use the Data Fill option to place in a single column the interest rates that are to be used in the various "what if" analyses by the @PMT function formula. Begin by positioning the pointer at cell H8.

/	Invokes the Main Menu
D	Selects the Data option
F	Selects the Fill option of the Data Menu
H8.H28 [by entering the cell addresses or by using the pointer]	Indicates the range to be filled
Enter	Establishes the range
.1	Identifies the beginning value (10%)
Enter	Tells 1-2-3 to accept the value
.005	Specifies the incremental value
Enter	Tells 1-2-3 to accept the incremental value

Enter	Accepts the default maximum size

e. Format the column for percent, with one decimal position.
f. Build the table.

/	Invokes the Main Menu
D	Takes the Data option
T	Selects the Table option from the Data Menu
1	Specifies the number of variables (basic assumptions) to be changed
H7.I28 [by pointing or by entering addresses]	Establishes the range of the table (Notice that the formula reference in cell I7 is part of the table range; this cell contains the basic assumption to be modeled.)
Enter	Establishes the range of the table
C18	Identifies the cell containing the basic assumption data (in this case, the interest data) that will be varied within the formula or part of the worksheet contained in cell I7
Enter	Causes a WAIT message to appear in the upper right-hand corner for a few seconds and then generates the table

9. Create the window. First, depress the Left Arrow key until column H is in the middle of the screen. Next, move the pointer back to column H. Next, enter the following instructions:

/	Invokes the Main Menu
W	Selects the Worksheet option
W	Selects the Window option from the Worksheet Menu
V	Creates a vertical window to the left of column H

10. Move the left window to cell A1 by depressing the Home key. The input area is now in the left part of the screen, and the payment table is now in the right part of the screen. You can jump from one screen to the other by pressing the F6 Window function key.

11. Position the pointer in the input area, and enter 10000 as the new principal amount.

12. Recalculate the table by depressing the F8 Table function key.

13. Jump back to the table part of the screen and examine the new table.

You now want to introduce one or two enhancements to the above template. Besides modeling the monthly payment, you must model the grand total paid and the total interest paid for each possible interest amount if you are to create the worksheet that appears on the next page.

The above changes require that you perform a number of additional tasks.

14. Enter label information.

   H3 Total Amount
   H4 Total Interest

15. Enter two new formulas.

J3 +J2*C19
   (payment amount × number of periods)
J4 +J3−C17
   (total amount paid − principal)

16. Add these two formulas to the table.
    a. Enter new labels

       J5 Grand
       K5 Total
       J6 Total
       K6 Interest

    b. Enter the formula or worksheet locations to be modeled, using the Table feature for sensitivity analysis.

       J7 +J3
       K7 +J4

    c. Format the formula locations to text, using the commands found in step 8c above.
    d. Redescribe the table to 1-2-3. The only part that will change is the width of the table, which can be expanded by pressing the Right Arrow key twice. All the other parameters stay the same. You do not have to re-create the Interest column.

/	Invokes the Main Menu
D	Takes the Data option
T	Takes the Table option of the Data Menu
1	Specifies that the table will have one variable
Right Arrow [twice]	Extends the range to the right two columns (The range is now H7..K28.)
Enter	Establishes the range
Enter	Accepts the input cell (interest) as the assumption to be varied

   After a few seconds, the table will have completed its recalculations and will show the two columns that have been added. This example illustrates that even though you are limited to using one variable as the basic assumption, you can model a number of areas on the worksheet that are affected by the changed variable.

17. Use the F6 key to switch screens and change the principal amount. Then use the F8 key to recalculate the table.

18. Save the worksheet using the name 1TABLE.

   With a principal amount of $5,000, the new table would look like Table 6.1. Since the information at the top runs into the body of the table, it might be desirable to move the table a number of rows down. This change would have no effect whatsoever on the table. 1-2-3 would adjust all of the information that you had previously given it to reflect the table's new location on the worksheet.

Table 6.1

Loan Principal	$5,000
Payment	152.28
Total Amount	6091.12
Total Interest	1091.12

	Payment +J2	Grand Total +J3	Total Interest +J4
10.0%	147.50	5900.16	900.16
10.5%	148.69	5947.56	947.56
11.0%	149.88	5995.19	995.19
11.5%	151.08	6043.04	1043.04
12.0%	152.28	6091.12	1091.12
12.5%	153.49	6139.42	1139.42
13.0%	154.70	6187.95	1187.95
13.5%	155.92	6236.70	1236.70
14.0%	157.14	6285.67	1285.67
14.5%	158.37	6334.87	1334.87
15.0%	159.61	6384.28	1384.28
15.5%	160.85	6433.92	1433.92
16.0%	162.09	6483.78	1483.78
16.5%	163.35	6533.86	1533.86
17.0%	164.60	6584.16	1584.16
17.5%	165.87	6634.68	1634.68
18.0%	167.14	6685.42	1685.42
18.5%	168.41	6736.38	1736.38
19.0%	169.69	6787.55	1787.55
19.5%	170.97	6838.94	1838.94
20.0%	172.26	6890.55	1890.55

SENSITIVITY ANALYSIS CHANGING TWO BASIC ASSUMPTIONS

Now that you've read about templates and the need for separate areas for input and output, you probably understand why some of the criteria used in building Ed's analysis worksheet were required in the last chapter. You are now going to use the previously assigned worksheet to create a table that allows two basic assumptions to be changed (see Figure 6.5).

Two of Ed's chief concerns are the effect of the number of units sold each year and the effect of annual sales growth on net income. He wants to be able to model net income based on these two assumptions. You are now going to create a table that will have the percentage-growth "what if" numbers along the left-hand column and the number-of-units-sold-each-year "what if" numbers along the top.

Your spreadsheet is divided into two parts: the input area and the balance sheet area. The input area starts at cell A1 and should currently look as follows:

```
INPUT AREA
UNITS SOLD (YEAR 1)            300
COST PER UNIT                 $650
ANNUAL SALES GROWTH         15.00%
ANNUAL PRICE REDUCTION       7.00%
PRODUCT MARGIN              40.00%
```

The income statement starts at cell H1 and should currently look as shown in Table 6.2. You are going to want the sensitivity analysis table beginning in column L to appear as shown in Table 6.3 (some spaces in the table have been omitted so that it will fit across one page).

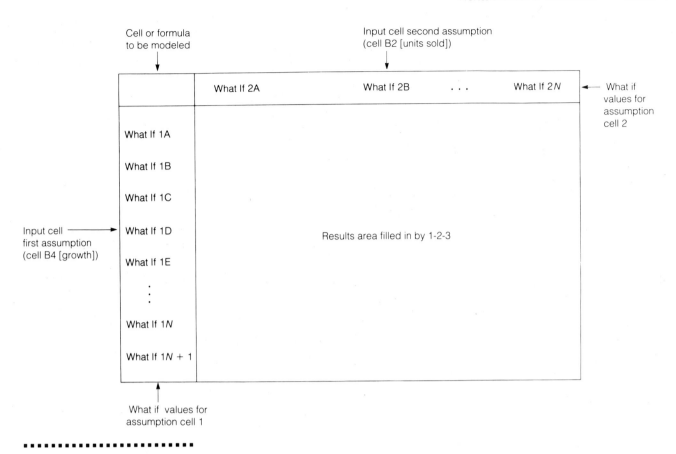

Figure 6.5
Parts of a two-assumption data table

Table 6.2

```
               ED'S MICROCOMPUTER SHOP
              Projected Financial Statements
                          1         2         3         4
                       -------   -------   -------   -------
          Sales        325,000   347,588   371,745   397,581
          Cost         195,000   208,553   223,047   238,549
                       -------   -------   -------   -------
          Margin       130,000   139,035   148,698   159,032
          Expenses:
            Advertising 72,750    49,331    18,587    19,879
            Salaries    32,500    34,759    37,174    39,758
            Rent         7,500     7,500     7,500     7,500
            Supplies     4,875     5,214     5,576     5,964
            Clerical     4,000     4,240     4,494     4,764
            Other Costs 10,000    10,500    11,025    11,576
                       -------   -------   -------   -------
          Total Expenses 131,625 111,544    84,357    89,441
                       -------   -------   -------   -------
          Income b/f Taxes (1,625) 27,491   64,341    69,591
            Income Taxes        0  13,746   32,170    34,796
                       -------   -------   -------   -------
          Net Income     (1,625)  13,746   32,170    34,796
                       =======   =======   =======   =======
```

Table 6.3

		UNITS SOLD (YEARx)					
+YEAR2		125	150	175	200	300	425
	10%	(17,456)	(11,499)	(5,542)	207	12,121	27,013
	15%	(16,102)	(9,874)	(3,647)	1,290	13,746	29,315
ANNUAL	20%	(14,748)	(8,250)	(1,751)	2,374	15,370	31,616
SALES	25%	(13,394)	(6,625)	72	3,457	16,995	33,918
GROWTH	30%	(12,040)	(5,001)	1,020	4,540	18,619	36,219
	35%	(10,687)	(3,376)	1,967	5,623	20,244	38,521

The following 10 steps are involved in creating and saving this table.

1. Load the spreadsheet containing the income statement and input area (CH5EX1).
2. Position the pointer at cell L1 using the Tab key.
3. Enter label information.

   L1 ED'S MICROCOMPUTER SHOP
   N2 Annual Sales Growth/Units Sold Analysis
   O5 UNITS SOLD (YEARX)
   L9 ANNUAL
   L10 SALES
   L11 GROWTH

4. Enter the part of the worksheet to be modeled (net income for year 2) at cell location M6. This marks the beginning of the table. For this action to work, you must have given the net income figures the range names specified in Chapter 5.

   +YEAR2

5. Change the contents of cell M6 to text to avoid confusion.
6. Enter the quantity-sold "what if" numbers.

   N6 125
   O6 150
   P6 175
   Q6 200
   R6 300
   S6 425

7. Enter the percent-growth "what if" numbers, using the Data Fill command.

/	Invokes the Main Menu
D	Selects the Data option
F	Selects the Fill command from the Data Menu
M7.M12 [by pointing or by giving the cell addresses]	Establishes the range
Enter	Tells 1-2-3 to accept the range
.10	Identifies the beginning value
Enter	Accepts the beginning value
.05	Specifies the step increment

Enter	Accepts the increment entered
Enter	Accepts the default and executes the command

8. Format the table for percent, with zero decimal positions. Begin by positioning the pointer at cell M7.

/	Invokes the Main Menu
R	Selects the Range option
F	Selects the Format option
P	Selects the Percent option
0	Indicates the number of positions to the right of the decimal
Enter	Tells 1-2-3 to accept the command
.	Nails down the pointer at cell M7
M12 [by manual pointer movement]	Positions the pointer at cell M12
Enter	Tells 1-2-3 to accept the range

9. Build the table.

/	Invokes the Main Menu
D	Selects the Data option
T	Selects the Table option from the Data Menu
2	Tells 1-2-3 that two basic assumptions will be used
M6.S12 [by pointing or by giving addresses]	Establishes the table range
Enter	Tells 1-2-3 to accept the range
GROWTH	Identifies the first assumption range name (or you may give B4 as the address) (The first assumption is always the vertical set of numbers.)
Enter	Tells 1-2-3 to accept the address of the first assumption
UNITS	Identifies the range name of the second assumption (or you may give cell B2 as the address)
Enter	Tells 1-2-3 to accept the second assumption and to complete the table with the results of the "what if" analyses that have been performed (This process, you will notice, takes much longer with two assumptions than with only one.)

10. Save the worksheet using the name 2TABLE.

You can model any of the Year2, Year3, or Year4 net incomes. All you have to do to recalculate the table is change the cell to be modeled in the upper left-hand corner of the table and depress the F8 Table function key. Year1 does not work well because it is the basis of the assumptions.

You can always test your table by checking inside it for the net income for the year modeled. If you can't find the net income for the modeled year inside the table, either you have used different net income or you have specified a wrong assumption cell.

Figure 6.6a
Worksheet for Bloomington
branch of Ed's Supermarket

Figure 6.6b
Worksheet for Normal branch of
Ed's Supermarket

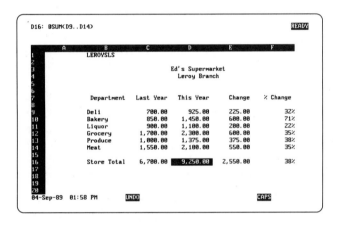

Figure 6.6c
Worksheet for Leroy branch of
Ed's Supermarket

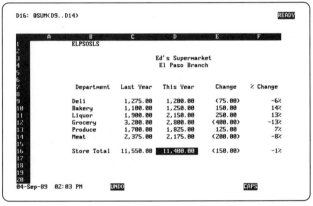

Figure 6.6d
Worksheet for El Paso branch of
Ed's Supermarket

LINKING FILES

Ed, the owner of Ed's Supermarket, has experienced a tremendous growth in sales over the last few years. The response to his type of supermarket has been overwhelming, and Ed has opened several branches to augment his original, Bloomington-based business. Ed now has stores in Normal, El Paso, Downs, and Leroy, all of which are affiliated with his Bloomington store. Ed has the sales for each of his branches contained in a separate worksheet (see Figures 6.6a through 6.6e). Although the sales data for each store have been placed in a worksheet, Ed has to spend additional time manually taking the sales totals from each worksheet to create a consolidated worksheet that combines the sales figures for all branches of his supermarket. Instead of performing this consolidation of sales figures manually, Ed would like to automate the process. To do so requires the use of 1-2-3's file linking capability.

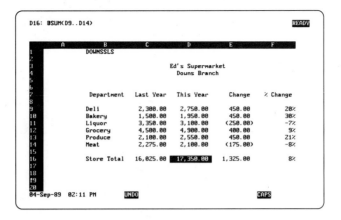

Figure 6.6e
Worksheet for Downs branch of
Ed's Supermarket

When you are using the file linking capability of 1-2-3, you are actually dealing with two types of files, the source file and the target file. The **target file** can also be viewed as the current file (the one on which you are working). You are able to create a link to the source file by entering a special linking formula that refers to a cell in another file. The file that the formula refers to is called the **source file** because it is the file that supplies the data.

Once a file linkage has been accomplished, 1-2-3 copies the value of the cell in the source file (sometimes referred to as the **source cell**) to the cell in the target file (the **target cell**). The value contained in this target cell is automatically updated whenever you retrieve the target file.

HINTS/HAZARDS

You can also update a file containing file links by issuing the command / File Admin Link-Refresh. This is an especially useful command when you are linking to files that can be accessed by other people on a network. This command allows other users to go ahead with their work without concern that changes they might make to a linked file will not be included in your worksheet.

In the example above, the total sales for the Last Year and This Year columns will be transferred to a consolidated worksheet. The sales total for this year is contained in cell C16 of each worksheet, and the sales total for last year is contained in cell D16. A graphic depiction of this process can be seen in Figure 6.7.

Once the linkage is established, any changes that have been made to any of the branch worksheets will automatically be reflected when you retrieve the consolidated worksheet. If, however, you had another lower set of worksheets like that depicted in Figure 6.8 and a change was made to one of the daily total worksheets, the DOWNSSLS worksheet would have to be retrieved and then saved before you could retrieve the consolidated sales worksheet. This is required because the links between the daily and DOWNSSLS must be refreshed before the links between DOWNSSLS and the consolidated sales worksheet can be refreshed.

Figure 6.7

The branch files to be linked to the consolidated worksheet

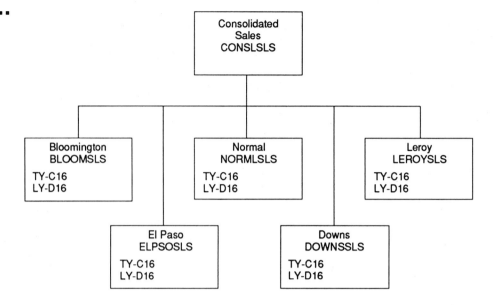

ESTABLISHING A LINK

A formula in a target cell (the cell at the pointer location) that you want to refer to a cell in another worksheet must have the following format:

```
+<<filename>>cell address
```

The following rules for a file linkage formula apply:

1. The reference (formula) must always start with a plus sign (+).
2. The filename and cell address can be entered in any combination of upper- and lowercase characters.
3. Angled brackets must be used to enclose the name of the source file containing the cell address. These brackets are the greater than (>) and less than (<) symbols on your keyboard.

    If the worksheet file that you are linking to has a .WK1 file extension, you are not required to include this extension in the filename. When you press the Enter key, 1-2-3 will automatically place the .WK1 extension on the file reference, find the source file on disk, and copy the data to the target cell.

    If the file to be linked has a .WKS file extension, you must include this extension with the filename reference.

    If the file resides on a different drive or in a different directory, all of this path information must be included in the filename reference of the source file. For example, if you are using a directory called 123-2 for your 123 files and have a subdirectory called BUSINESS, and you want to access a file called CONSLSLS using cell C16, your filename reference is:

    ```
    +<<C:\123-2\BUSINESS\CONSLSLS>>C16
    ```

4. The cell address can be either a specific cell address or a named range. If a named range is used that includes several cells, 1-2-3 uses only the value contained in the upper left-hand cell.

Figure 6.8
A third level to be linked to the consolidated worksheet

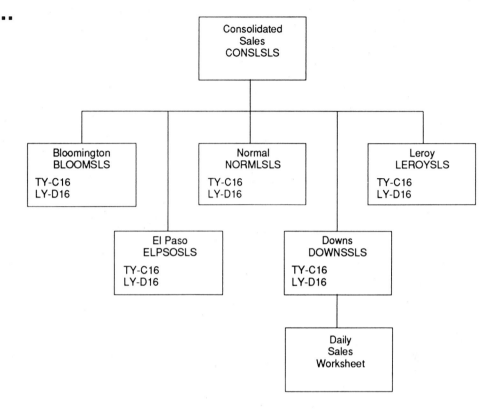

If any of the following conditions exist in trying to establish a file link, 1-2-3 displays an ERR message and does not establish the link.

The source file does not exist on the default disk or in the defined path, or the disk drive door was not closed.

The specified range was not correctly established in the source file.

The source file is password-protected.

You have shared files on a network and another user is in the process of saving or retrieving the source file.

LIMITATIONS OF FILE LINKING

Lotus 1-2-3 places the following limitations on link files:

You cannot include two linking references or a linking reference and a formula in a single cell. For example, +<<FILE1>>C23/<<FILE2>>D25 and @ABS(<<FILE3>>D25) are not valid formulas.

If the range name from the source file is erased or renamed, 1-2-3 displays an ERR message in the cell.

If a cell address is referenced in a linking formula and you later move the source cell to a different location in the source file, 1-2-3 does not change the linking formula. For example, if you originally reference cell <<FILE1>>C16 and then move the data in cell C16 to cell G16, the target cell still displays the result of C16 rather than G16. You can avoid this problem by using named ranges instead of cell addresses.

Figure 6.9
The skeleton CONSLSLS worksheet to be used in consolidating the information from the branch stores of Ed's Supermarket

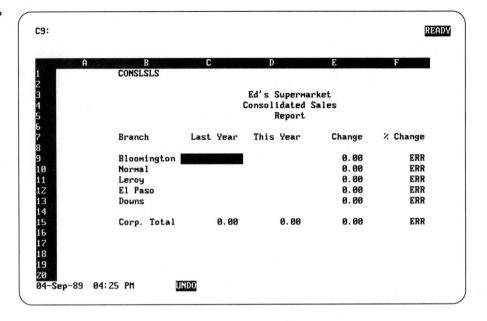

HINTS/HAZARDS	The more file link formulas a file contains, the longer it will take to retrieve the file because 1-2-3 must update each link that is referenced in the worksheet.

SAMPLE WORKSHEET FOR LINKING FILES

Assume that you have already built the skeleton CONSLSLS worksheet depicted in Figure 6.9. The labels and formulas have already been entered in preparation for establishing the links between the five branch worksheets depicted in Figures 6.6a through 6.6e. Remember, your data disk/directory must have these worksheet files before this sample worksheet can be completed.

1. Retrieve the CONSLSLS.WK1 worksheet.
2. Position the pointer to cell C9 and enter the following file link formula:

   +<<BLOOMSLS>>C16

   When you press the Enter key, you should notice some disk activity as 1-2-3 retrieves this information from the BLOOMSLS.WK1 file. You should now see 5650.00 in cell C9 as well as that 1-2-3 has added a .WK1 to your filename reference.

3. Position the pointer to cell D9 and enter the following file link formula:

   +<<BLOOMSLS>>D16

   When you press the Enter key, you should again notice some disk activity as 1-2-3 retrieves this information from the BLOOMSLS.WK1 file. You should now see 7170.00 in cell D9.

Figure 6.10a
The consolidated worksheet with links established to all of the branch worksheets

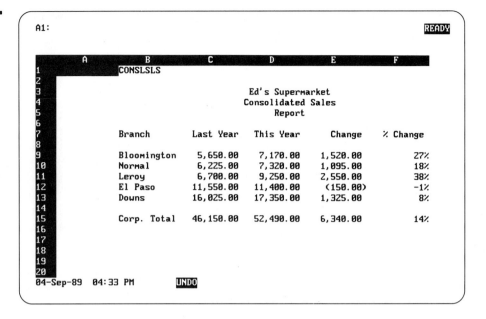

Figure 6.10b
A listing of files linked to the current worksheet

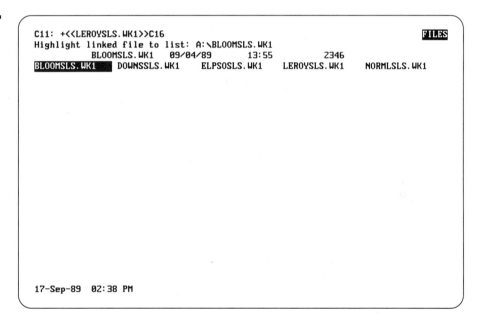

An alternative method of entering the formula is to use the Copy command to copy this file link formula from cell C9 to cell D9. Since the cells are beside each other in the source file, you can take advantage of 1-2-3's relative addressing.

4. Continue establishing the file links until they have been established for all five branches. Once you have finished, your worksheet should look like that depicted in Figure 6.10a.

Lotus 1-2-3 allows you to verify all of the linked files within a worksheet by using the / File List Linked command sequence. Once that command is executed, all the filenames of files linked to the current worksheet are displayed to the screen (see Figure 6.10b).

CELL CONTENTS OF CAR LOAN SENSITIVITY ANALYSIS

Input Screen:

```
A1:   'Cost of a Car Loan at a Variety
B2:   'of Interest Rates
A4:   'Please enter the following
A5:   'characteristics of the loan:
A7:   'After you have entered the data,
A8:   'press the [F8] key to generate the
A9:   'new table.
A11:  'Press the [F6] key to move to the
A12:  'other window.
A14:  'Be sure to enter the interest as a
A15:  'decimal. Ex 12% is entered as .12
A17:  'Principal
C17:  (C0) 5000
A18:  'Interest
C18:  (P1) 0.12
A19:  'Months
C19:  (F0) 40
```

Table for Sensitivity Analysis:

```
H1:   'Loan Principal
J1:   (C0) +C17
H2:   'Payment
J2:   (F2) @PMT(C17,C18/12,C19)
I6:   'Payment
I7:   (T) +J2
H8:   (P1) 0.1
I8:   147.50394651
H9:   (P1) 0.105
I9:   148.68900829
H10:  (P1) 0.11
I10:  149.87970957
H11:  (P1) 0.115
I11:  151.07604023
H12:  (P1) 0.12
I12:  152.27798989
H13:  (P1) 0.125
I13:  153.48554786
H14:  (P1) 0.13
I14:  154.69870319
H15:  (P1) 0.135
I15:  155.91744466
H16:  (P1) 0.14
I16:  157.14176077
H17:  (P1) 0.145
I17:  158.37163974
H18:  (P1) 0.15
I18:  159.60706954
H19:  (P1) 0.155
I19:  160.84803787
H20:  (P1) 0.16
I20:  162.09453215
H21:  (P1) 0.165
```

I21: 163.34653957
H22: (P1) 0.17
I22: 164.60404703
H23: (P1) 0.175
I23: 165.8670412
H24: (P1) 0.18
I24: 167.13550849
H25: (P1) 0.185
I25: 168.40943505
H26: (P1) 0.19
I26: 169.68880679
H27: (P1) 0.195
I27: 170.97360939
H28: (P1) 0.2
I28: 172.26382827

Input Screen:

A1: 'INPUT AREA
A2: 'UNITS SOLD (YEAR 1)
B2: 300
A3: 'COST PER UNIT
B3: (C0) 650
A4: 'ANNUAL SALES GROWTH
B4: (P2) 0.15
A5: 'ANNUAL PRICE REDUCTION
B5: (P2) 0.07
A6: 'PRODUCT MARGIN
B6: (P2) 0.4

Balance Sheet:

H1: 'ED'S MICROCOMPUTER SHOP
G2: 'Projected Financial Statements
G4: 1
H4: 2
I4: 3
J4: 4
G5: '--------
H5: '--------
I5: '--------
J5: '--------
F6: 'Sales
G6: +$UNITS*($COST/(1-$MARGIN))
H6: +G6*(1+$GROWTH)*(1-$ANN.RED)
I6: +H6*(1+$GROWTH)*(1-$ANN.RED)
J6: +I6*(1+$GROWTH)*(1-$ANN.RED)
F7: 'Cost
G7: +G6*(1-$MARGIN)
H7: +H6*(1-$MARGIN)
I7: +I6*(1-$MARGIN)
J7: +J6*(1-$MARGIN)
G8: '--------
H8: '--------
I8: '--------
J8: '--------
F9: 'Margin

```
G9:   +G6-G7
H9:   +H6-H7
I9:   +I6-I7
J9:   +J6-J7
F11:  'Expenses:
F12:  'Advertising
G12:  50000+G6*0.07
H12:  25000+H6*0.07
I12:  +I6*0.05
J12:  +J6*0.05
F13:  'Salaries
G13:  +G6*0.1
H13:  +H6*0.1
I13:  +I6+0.1
J13:  +J6*0.1
F14:  'Rent
G14:  7500
H14:  7500
I14:  7500
J14:  7500
F15:  'Supplies
G15:  +G6*0.015
H15:  +H6*0.015
I15:  +I6*0.015
J15:  +J6*0.015
F16:  'Clerical
G16:  4000
H16:  +G16*1.06
I16:  +H16*1.06
J16:  +I16*1.06
F17:  'Other Costs
G17:  10000
H17:  +G17*1.05
I17:  +H17*1.05
J17:  +I17*1.05
G18:  '--------
H18:  '--------
I18:  '--------
J18:  '--------
F19:  'Total Expenses
G19:  @SUM(G12..G17)
H19:  @SUM(H12..H17)
I19:  @SUM(I12..I17)
J19:  @SUM(J12..J17)
G20:  '--------
H20:  '--------
I20:  '--------
J20:  '--------
F22:  'Income b/f taxes
G22:  +G9-G19
H22:  +H9-H19
I22:  +I9-I19
J22:  +J9-J19
F23:  'Income Taxes
G23:  @IF(G22<0,0,G22*0.5)
```

H23: @IF(H22<0,0,H22*0.5)
I23: @IF(I22<0,0,I22*0.5)
J23: @IF(J22<0,0,J22*0.5)
G24: `--------
H24: `--------
I24: `--------
J24: `--------
F25: `Net Income
G25: +G22-G23
H25: +H22-H23
I25: +I22-I23
J25: +J22-J23
G26: `========
H26: `========
I26: `========
J26: `========

Sensitivity Table:

O1: `ED'S MICROCOMPUTER SHOP
N2: `Annual Sales Growth/Units Sold Analysis
O5: `UNITS SOLD (YEARx)
M6: (T) +YEAR2
N6: 125
O6: 150
P6: 175
Q6: 200
R6: 300
S6: 425
M7: (P0) 0.1
N7: -17455.78125
O7: -11498.9375
P7: -5542.09375
Q7: 207.375
R7: 12121.0625
S7: 27013.171875
M8: (P0) 0.15
N8: -16101.953125
O8: -9874.34375
P8: -3646.734375
Q8: 1290.4375
R8: 13745.65625
S8: 29314.679688
M9: (P0) 0.2
N9: -14748.125
O9: -8249.75
P9: -1751.375
Q9: -2373.5
R9: 15370.25
S9: 31616.1875
M10: (P0) 0.25
N10: -13394.296875
O10: -6625.15625
P10: -71.9921875
Q10: 3456.5625
R10: 16994.84375

```
S10:   33917.695313
M11:   (P0) 0.3
N11:   -12040.46875
O11:   -5000.5625
P11:   1019.671875
Q11:   4539.625
R11:   18619.4375
S11:   36219.203125
M12:   (P0) 0.35
N12:   -10686.640625
O12:   -3375.96875
P12:   1967.3515625
Q12:   5622.6875
R12:   20244.03125
S12:   38520.710938
```

CELL CONTENTS FOR THE FILE LINK SAMPLE WORKSHEET

```
B1:    'CONSLSLS
D3:    'Ed's Supermarket
KD4:   'Consolidated Sales
D5:        Report
B7:    'Branch
C7:    "Last Year
D7:    "This year
E7:    "Change
F7:    "% Change
B9:    'Bloomington
C9:    +<<BLOOMSLS.WK1>>C16
D9:    +<<BLOOMSLS.WK1>>D16
E9:    +D9-C9
F9:    (P0) +E9/C9
B10:   'Normal
C10:   +<<NORMLSLS.WK1>>C16
D10:   +<<NORMLSLS.WK1>>D16
E10:   +D10-C10
F10:   (P0) +E10/C10
B11:   'Leroy
C11:   +<<LEROYSLS.WK1>>C16
D11:   +<<LEROYSLS.WK1>>D16
E11:   +D11-C11
F11:   (P0) +E11/C11
B12:   'El Paso
C12:   +<<ELPSOSLS.WK1>>C16
D12:   +<<ELPSOSLS.WK1>>D16
E12:   +D12-C12
F12:   (P0) +E12/C12
B13:   'Downs
C13:   +<<DOWNSSLS.WK1>>C16
D13:   +<<DOWNSSLS.WK1>>D16
E13:   +D13-C13
```

```
F13:  (P0) +E13/C13
B15:  'Corp, Total
C15:  @SUM(C9..C13)
D15:  @SUM(D9..D13)
E15:  +D15-C15
F15:  (P0) +E15/C15
```

CHAPTER REVIEW

A template is used when a number of different people will want to make use of the same worksheet. Because many of these future users are likely to not know too much about either computers or spreadsheets, built-in directions and documentation are necessary.

The process of building a template is very similar to programming: The problem to be solved must be well defined, and the logical processes involved in solving the problem and the physical layout of the worksheet must be planned. The input, processing, and output portions of the template should be separated, and help screens with directions on how to use the worksheet must be included for the user. A structured walk-through should be conducted in order to catch any errors in logic or any items that the developer has overlooked. The template must be properly tested, and final documentation must be developed. When the template is released for use, someone must be assigned to provide support and maintenance in case of problems.

Windows split the display screen either vertically or horizontally, providing two different but simultaneous views of the same worksheet. Windows are frequently used with templates.

When you build a template, you do not want unknowledgeable users to destroy a part of the worksheet inadvertently. 1-2-3 allows you to protect the entire worksheet to prevent any changes being made to a cell; if a change is attempted, the computer merely beeps. Cells that are used as input cells can be returned to unprotected status, in which case they will appear in high-intensity video.

The Data Fill command is used to rapidly fill a range with numbers that change by some incremental value. This command can easily develop column headings for the years 1985–2000, for example, saving you a lot of data entry work.

Sensitivity analysis is the process of asking a number of "what if" questions. Various changes can be entered in a worksheet to see what effect they have on other values. For instance, if you are interested in what effect inflation has on a worksheet, you can enter a number of different values to determine the consequences of various rates of inflation. In order to do this, you have to enter the value and then note the effect of the change. The Data Table feature of 1-2-3 automates this process, allowing a table of values to be created and defined to 1-2-3; 1-2-3 can then be directed to note the impact of each change and to fill in the table with the data that result from changes in the targeted cell.

The file link feature of Lotus 1-2-3 provides the ability to link information from a source file to a target file. The filename must be contained between link brackets << >>. Only the value from the source cell appears in the target cell. The link is refreshed each time the file is retrieved or a / File Admin Link-Refresh command is executed.

KEY TERMS AND CONCEPTS

cell protection
Clear option
Data Fill command
file link
help screen
Horizontal option
sensitivity analysis
source file
structured walk-through

Sync option
Table option
target file
template
testing
Unsync option
Vertical option
windows
worksheet protection

CHAPTER QUIZ

Multiple Choice

1. Which of the following is not a separate part of a template?
   a. Input screen
   b. Processing area
   c. Output area
   d. Planning area
   e. All of the above are parts of a template.

2. Which of the following is *not* a step in developing a template?
   a. Planning
   b. Walk-through
   c. Designing logic
   d. Testing
   e. Documenting
   f. All of the above are steps in developing a template.

3. Which of the following statements about worksheet and cell protection is false?
   a. In building an input area, the designer first protects the worksheet and then "unprotects" the input area.
   b. It is possible to change the contents of a protected cell by holding down the Ctrl key.
   c. When a protected worksheet has been unprotected, the input area cells must be protected in order to make them look right.
   d. The worksheet is protected via an option off the Worksheet Menu, while the input area is unprotected via an option off the Range Menu.
   e. All of the above statements are true.

4. Which command is used to enter numeric information quickly into a range of cells when each subsequent cell is to be changed by a fixed, incremental value?
   a. Simple data entry
   b. Step Fill command
   c. Data Fill command
   d. Step Increment command
   e. None of the above

5. Sensitivity analysis involves
   a. asking a number of "what if" questions.
   b. entering each separate value to determine the impact.

c. using the Data Table feature of 1-2-3.
d. all of the above.
e. none of the above.

True/False

6. Template documentation will typically appear only in an instruction manual.

7. Column A is typically used for help screens.

8. The process of reviewing the logic of the template is called a walkabout.

9. Windows can be used to split the screen either vertically or horizontally.

10. Input cells in a protected template appear in high-intensity video.

Answers

1. d   2. f   3. b   4. c   5. d   6. f   7. t   8. f   9. t   10. t

Exercises

1. Define or describe each of the following:
   a. template
   b. help screen
   c. structured walk-through
   d. window
   e. worksheet protection
   f. sensitivity analysis

2. List the differences between a regular worksheet and a template.
   a.
   b.
   c.

3. List the three functional areas of a template.
   a.
   b.
   c.

4. The _____ data table is recalculated by pressing the F8 key.

5. The _____ involves the explanation of a template by the developer to potential users. This ensures that all design considerations have been addressed.

6. The process of verifying the logic and results of a template is known as _____.

7. One of the primary advantages of using the structured walk-through is to catch _____.

8. Two software packages used to verify the logic and results of a template are _____ and _____.

9. List the items that should be included in the final documentation.
   a.

   b.

   c.

   d.

   e.

10. _____ allow you to split the screen either vertically or horizontally, giving you two views of the same worksheet.

11. When newly created, a horizontal window appears _____ the pointer, and a vertical window appears to the _____ of the pointer.

12. In a synchronized window, both windows _____ at the same time.

13. The cell _____ allows you to prohibit a user from changing an important cell.

14. The _____ allows you to set up a range and then fill it with numbers.

15. The number _____ is the upper limit for the Data Fill command.

16. The process of asking a number of "what if" questions is known as _____.

17. The 1-2-3 _____ is used in sensitivity analysis.

18. After a worksheet has been protected, the input area must be _____.

19. The 1-2-3 table feature allows you to vary either _____ or _____ variables.

20. The number entered in response to the _____ prompt of the Data Fill command determines the increment from one cell to the next.

21. The _____ feature of 1-2-3 allows a value contained in one file to be accessed by another file.

22. The _____ contains information that is passed to the current file.

23. The current file is also referred to as the _____ file.

24. A file link formula always starts with a plus sign (+) and encloses the filename reference in _____.

25. If you are on a network, the command _____ allows you to refresh the file links in your worksheet.

COMPUTER EXERCISES

1. Develop a sensitivity analysis template for examining the impact of a number of interest rates on the principal of a house mortgage. Use the principles of good template design in developing your worksheet. There should be separate areas for the input and for the sensitivity table. Use the manual recalculation mode. Use a principal of $90,000. The interest rates should start at 8% and go to 17% by half-percent increments. There should be a 20-year mortgage. This means that you have to either enter the number of months in 20 years or enter 20*12 in the payment formula. Use the window feature so that you can see both the input and the sensitivity table on the screen at the same time. Save the template to a worksheet file called CH6EX1.

2. Develop an expanded mortgage sensitivity analysis table that will track not only the payment but also the grand total of loan payments and total interest payments at the various interest rates above. Also examine mortgage principals of $75,000, $60,000, $120,000, and $150,000. Save this template to a worksheet file called CH6EX2.

3. Perform a two-assumption sensitivity analysis on the CH5EX1 worksheet. Instead of varying units sold and sales growth, vary cost per unit and annual price reduction. Save this worksheet onto a file called CH6EX3.

4. Load the worksheet file PAYMENT. This worksheet already has all cells but the input cells protected. Try to change any cells other than the high-intensity cells. You will receive a Protected cell error message at the bottom of the screen. Unprotect the worksheet and do a range protect on the input cells. You can now make any desired changes to the worksheet. Now protect the worksheet and change the protection on the input cells so that new data can be entered.

5. You are to create an order-form template like that depicted on the next page, which allows an individual to take orders over the phone for the Basket Tree. The global column width should be set to 10 positions. Column A should be four positions wide, and column B should be 20 positions wide. Enable global protection. The following cells should be unprotected to allow for input: the name and address cells along with the credit card entry in column B, the cell containing the name of the order taker, and the quantity cells for the various merchandise items.

The cell containing the state tax should calculate the 6.5% tax only if the state entry on the order contains IL, Il, or il. Save the completed worksheet to a file called CH6EX5.

```
           A              B              C            D            E            F

 1                                    Basket Tree
 2                              Telephone Order Entry Form
 3
 4       For:Tim Duffy                          Prepared By:         Fred
 5            1413 S. Cottage Ave.              Preparation Date:    06-Mar-89
 6            Normal                            Subtotal:            $144.90
 7            Il                                State Tax:           $9.42
 8                           61761              Total Sale:          $144.90
 9       Visa
10       /MC
11         #:_____  Price    Quantity     Amount
12
13         Large Basket
14                          Blue:      $34.95       2         $69.90
15                          Mauve:     $34.95                  $.00
16                          Green:     $34.95                  $.00
17                          Pink:      $34.95                  $.00
18
19         Brooms
20                          Large:     $20.00       2         $40.00
21                          Medium:    $15.00       1         $15.00
22                          Small:     $10.00       2         $20.00
```

6. Use the information from the worksheet in CH6EX6A (depicted in Figure 6.11) to update the CH6EX6B worksheet (depicted in Figure 6.12). The grand total sales figure depicted in cell F13 of CH6EX6A is used to provide the initial sales figure cell B7 for the Projected Profit Report. Since the formulas for the profit report are already entered, once the file link is established the profit report will have appropriate numbers. When you are establishing the link to CH6EX6A, make certain that you use a named range (Grandtot, for example) for the grand total sales figure. Once the link is established, your worksheet should appear like that in Figure 6.13. Now retrieve the CH6EX6A worksheet; insert a column and enter new sales for the month of April. (Make certain that these new sales have been included in the grand total figure.) Save the file and then retrieve the CH6EX6B file. The new numbers for April should now be included in the file linked worksheet.

Figure 6.11
The CH6EX6A worksheet that contains the sales information and is to serve as the source worksheet for a file link

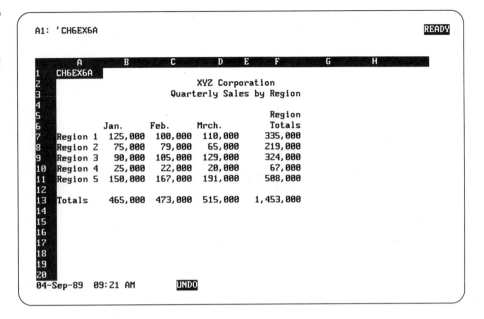

Figure 6.12
The CH6EX6B target worksheet to be linked to the region sales worksheet (CH6EX6A)

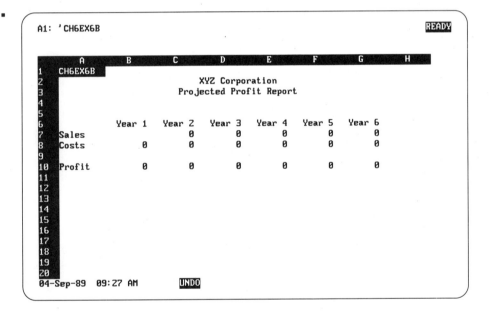

Figure 6.13
The CH6EX6B worksheet after the file link is established

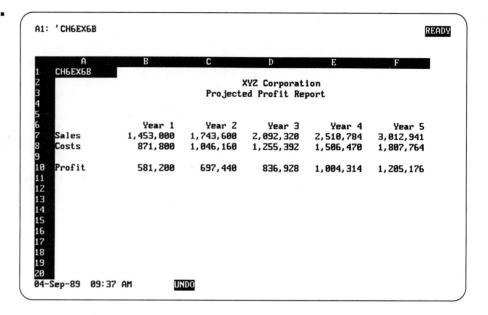

CHAPTER

7

GRAPHING
WITH 1-2-3

CHAPTER OBJECTIVES

After completing this chapter, you should be able to:

- **Use the various options contained in the Graph Menu**
- **Build a graph**
- **Generate various types of graphs using 1-2-3**
- **Save graph settings for later use**
- **Use additional items for graphs, such as Titles and Legends**
- **Generate a table of graph names**
- **Save a graph to disk for later printing**
- **Use the PrintGraph utility**

This chapter is divided into three parts: The first deals with the various options provided in the Graph Menu, the second deals with building graphs, and the third deals with printing graphs.

The information presented in the last four chapters demonstrates how 1-2-3 can be used to manipulate information arithmetically through the use of formulas for processing data that have been entered on the worksheet. The worksheet is automatically updated and completely recalculated whenever information is entered in a cell, allowing you to play a number of "what if" games to see how a change will affect the rest of the worksheet.

These characteristics alone may satisfy your needs when a worksheet containing small amounts of data is being used, but what happens when you have large amounts of data or when you cannot make sense of the small amount of data that is in the worksheet? The answer lies in the old maxim "a picture is worth a thousand words." 1-2-3 allows you, with only a little effort, to depict the data that have been entered in a worksheet on the screen in the form of a graph (see Figure 7.1).

If you want to use this feature, your computer must have either an EGA, VGA, or color graphics board and a color (or regular) monitor or a board that makes it possible to display graphics on a monochrome monitor. If you don't have this hardware, your computer will only beep when you try to display the graph; in this case, you must save the graph onto a file and then print the graph via the PrintGraph feature of the Lotus Access System.

If your computer has both a monochrome monitor and a color monitor attached to it, 1-2-3 will use the monochrome monitor to display the worksheet and the color monitor to display the graph.

STEPS IN BUILDING A GRAPH AND PRINTING THE GRAPH

The process of building a graph using 1-2-3 involves the following simple, easy-to-follow steps:

1. Selecting and loading in a worksheet file from disk, or using the current worksheet
2. Selecting the Graph Menu via the command sequence / Graph
3. Selecting the type of graph to be used (line, bar, XY, stacked bar, or pie)
4. Telling 1-2-3 which data ranges are involved in the graph (up to six ranges of data can be depicted in a graph)
5. Telling 1-2-3 to include any labels or extra information
6. Displaying the graph on the screen
7. Making any changes in the graph
8. Saving the graph onto disk for later printing, if desired (in which case 1-2-3 will place a .PIC extension on the graph file)
9. Printing the graph with PrintGraph

After you become accustomed to using the Graph option, you can go through this process easily in three to five minutes.

You can also enter "what if" changes in your data and automatically regraph the new information via the **F10 Graph key,** without going back through the Graph Menu.

Figure 7.1
(a) exploded pie graph; (b) side-by-side bar graph

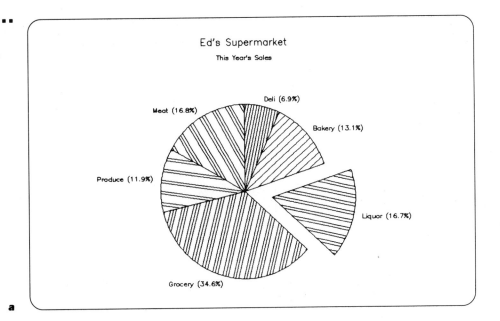

a

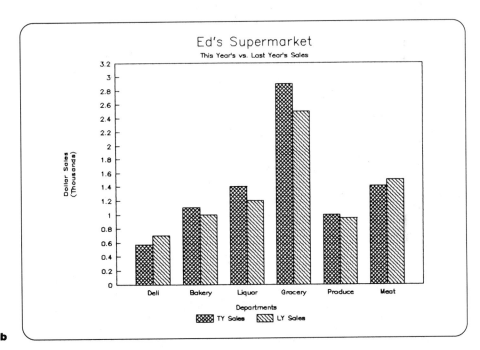

b

GRAPH MENU

The **Graph Menu** is invoked by entering a /Graph command sequence. Unless you wish to add information to a "naked" graph, you can build the entire graph from this menu, without entering any submenus; the submenus allow you to dress up a graph with meaningful, descriptive data. Appendix A includes a chart of the Graph command structure.

The Graph Menu that appears on your screen when you depress the command sequence / Graph is as follows:

```
Type  X  A B C D E F  Reset  View  Save  Options  Name  Group  Quit
```

Figure 7.2
The graph settings sheet

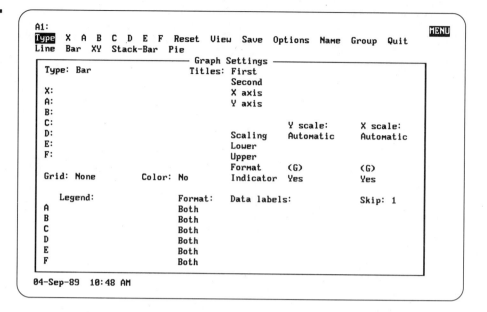

GRAPH SETTINGS SHEET

Whenever you enter the Graph Menu, a graph settings sheet like that depicted in Figure 7.2 appears on the screen. This settings sheet has data that have been generated from any commands in the Graph Menu that have been executed. It is an excellent summary of all the actions that you have taken in building a graph.

TYPE

The **Type option** of the Graph Menu allows you to select the type of graph you wish to display from the following menu:

```
Line   Bar   XY   Stacked Bar   Pie
```

Line The standard one-dimensional **line graph** presents the data on the **Y (vertical) axis** and the label of the data on the **X (horizontal) axis.** Up to six lines (sets of data) can be depicted. When graphing multiple sets of data, 1-2-3 automatically uses different data point symbols for each set of data.

Bar The standard one-dimensional **bar graph** (when multiple data ranges are used) places the bars for each data point from the data ranges side by side. Different shadings are used for each data range.

XY An **XY graph** is a two-dimensional graph with a set of data points referenced on both the X axis and the Y axis. For example, if you wanted to graph a company's profits compared to inflation over a period of years, you would select this option.

Stacked Bar A **stacked bar graph** stacks multiple ranges of data on top of each other instead of next to one another. Different shadings are given to each range of data to differentiate among them.

Pie The **pie chart,** as the name implies, is a circle divided into wedges; it is used to depict a single data range. Because of its nature, the pie chart cannot depict multiple data ranges.

X

The **X command** defines a range of the worksheet to be used for a horizontal label of the graph. When you take the X option, you must give the addresses of or point to the cell(s) containing the label information. Often, these are row or column labels from the worksheet.

ABCDEF

The **ABCDEF commands** are used to specify up to six data ranges to be depicted on your graph. The first data range must be labeled A, the second B, and so on. You can enter the cell addresses or point to the cells to be included in each data range; then depress the Enter key when you have finished.

1-2-3 remembers each data range you specify; to respecify an existing range, reselect it and specify a new data range to be graphed. To cancel a data range, you must use the Reset option. 1-2-3 requires you to define at least one data range, regardless of the type of graph that has been selected.

RESET

The **Reset command** selects the Reset Menu for the graphing function. The options of the Reset Menu allow you to cancel either the entire graph or portions of it. The Reset Menu options are as follows:

```
Graph  X  A  B  C  D  E  F  Quit
```

Graph The Graph command allows you to cancel the entire graph. If this option is taken, the entire graph will have to be respecified to 1-2-3.

X The X command allows you to cancel the labeling of the graph's horizontal axis.

ABCDEF The ABCDEF commands allow you to cancel one or more data ranges of a graph. If you cancel all of them, 1-2-3 acts as if you do not have a graph specified.

Quit The Quit command returns you to the Graph Menu.

VIEW

The **View command** allows you to display the currently specified graph on the monitor, after which you can depress any key on the keyboard to return to the Graph Menu.

You can also obtain a display of a graph, showing the specified settings, while you are in the worksheet in READY mode. To do so, simply depress the F10 Graph function key. You can return to the worksheet by depressing any key.

SAVE

The **Save command** is used to store the currently specified graph onto a disk file. Such a file is referred to by 1-2-3 as a "graph" or "picture" file and contains a .PIC extension.

Anyone with a regular monochrome monitor must use the Save command to save a graph file, since this type of monitor is not able to display a graph. The file must then be printed using the PrintGraph option from the Lotus Access System Menu.

OPTIONS

The **Options command** allows you to dress up a graph with various options. When this option is selected, the following menu is displayed:

```
Legend  Format  Titles  Grid  Scale  Color  B&W  Data  Labels  Quit
```

Legend The **Legend option** displays a menu that allows you to specify characters for the legend to be used to represent the various ranges of data. Up to 19 characters can be shown, but as few as possible should be selected. The following menu is displayed:

```
A  B  C  D  E  F
```

You now select the appropriate data range, and 1-2-3 displays the current legend for it. If you wish to change the legend, enter the new characters; if you wish to leave it unchanged, depress the Enter key. The legend is displayed beneath the X-axis title entry.

Format The **Format option** is used to change how the specified graph is displayed—that is, what characters are used to represent the displayed data points and how those data points are connected on the graph. The following menu is displayed when this option is selected:

```
Graph  A  B  C  D  E  F  Quit
```

Graph By selecting this option, you can determine how the data are to be presented on the graph. The following menu is displayed:

```
Lines  Symbols  Both  Neither
```

Lines. This command will connect each data point within a range with a line.

Symbols. This command will display each data point in a data range with the same character or symbol.

Both. This command uses both lines and symbols in representing data points in a data range.

Neither. This command uses neither lines nor symbols, requiring the legends for data points to be specified in Legend option commands.

ABCDEF This command option allows you to select a data range. When you have done so, 1-2-3 prompts you in exactly the same way it does when you select the Graph option in this menu.

Quit This command returns you to the Options Menu.

Titles The **Titles option** enables you to label the graph with up to two lines of text; these will appear at the top of the graph. The Titles option can also be used to enter a one-line text label for each axis. When you select the Titles option, you will be presented with the following menu:

```
First    Second   X Axis   Y Axis
```

First This command allows you to enter the first line of text that is to be placed at the top of the page.

Second This command allows you to enter the second line of text that is to be placed (below the first line) at the top of the page.

X Axis This command allows you to enter one line of text to be displayed along the X (horizontal) axis.

Y Axis This command allows you to enter one line of text to be displayed along the Y (vertical) axis.

Grid The **Grid option** allows you to choose grid lines for display on a graph. When selected, it displays the following menu:

```
Horizontal   Vertical   Both   Clear
```

Horizontal This command places horizontal grid lines on the graph when it is displayed. Grid lines can be used to make the relative size of plotted points clearer.

Vertical This command places vertical grid lines on the graph when it is displayed.

Both This command places both horizontal and vertical grid lines on the graph when it is displayed.

Clear This command clears any grid lines from the display.

Scale The **Scale option** allows you to set the scaling and format of a graph for either the X or Y axis. When you have selected the axis, the following menu of options will be displayed:

```
Automatic   Manual   Lower   Upper   Format   Indicator   Quit
```

Automatic With this option, the scaling on the graphs is automatically calculated by 1-2-3 to keep the entire graph visible on the display.

Manual With this option, you select the scaling.

Lower/Upper These options must be used if the Manual command was selected. They allow you to select the upper and lower scale limits, giving you more control over how data are presented. Small differences can be made to seem much greater.

Format This option allows you to decide how numeric data will be used with scaling. When the graph is displayed, the numbers will appear in the selected format.

Indicator This option allows you to turn the scale indicators on a graph on or off when the graph is displayed to the screen via the View command.

Quit This option returns you to the Options Menu.

Color/B&W The **Color option** displays the information in colors that have been preselected by 1-2-3. The **B&W option** displays the data in standard black-and-white, with cross-hatching on the bars.

Data/Labels The **Data option** allows you to specify a range of cells whose contents will be used to label the data points of a data range (A–F). First choose the range (A–F); then specify the cells to be included in the range; then, for line and XY graphs, select the alignment of the labels in relation to the data points (Centered, Left, Above, Right, Below), using the **Labels option.** Select the Quit option when you are finished, and you will return to the Graph Menu. The next time the graph is displayed, the cell contents of the specified range(s) will be displayed as data points.

NAME

The **Name option** allows you to load in graph settings that were previously saved using the Create option of the Name Menu, reset the graph options to those for this graph, and then draw the graph using the specified features. When selected, the Name option displays the following menu:

```
Use   Create   Delete   Reset   Table
```

Use The **Use command** allows you to make graph file settings that are contained in RAM memory current by entering the name or by pointing to the file with the pointer. The selected graph will then be displayed.

Create The **Create command** allows you to save graph settings of the current graph. The graph can later be accessed via the Use command.

Delete The **Delete command** is used to delete any graph settings contained in memory. To do this, enter the graph name and depress Enter or point to the graph and depress Enter.

Reset The **Name Reset option** erases all named graphs from the computer's memory.

Table The **Table option** of the Name submenu allows you to construct a report containing all of the archived graphs in your worksheet. The pointer location is used as the upper left-hand corner of the report. Since the report actually takes up space within the worksheet, make certain that you are in an unused area; otherwise, a valuable portion of your worksheet model may be lost.

GROUP

The **Group option** allows you to specify all of the data ranges (A–F) and the X label range at one time when these ranges are in adjacent rows or columns.

Figure 7.3

The cells to be included in the / Graph Group command

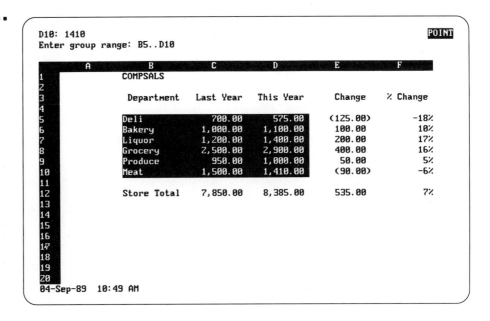

Figure 7.4

The graph generated by the / Graph Group command

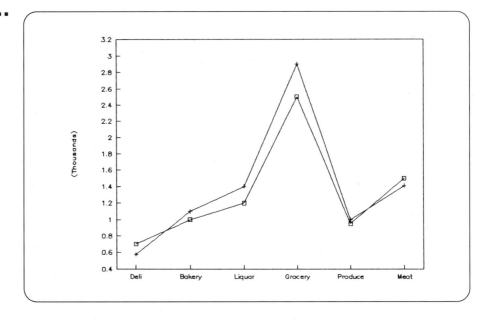

Once you have specified the range of cells to be included in the range, 1-2-3 responds with the menu:

```
Columnwise   Rowwise
```

You must tell 1-2-3 whether or not it is to divide the data in the range by columns or rows. If, for example, you had a worksheet like that depicted in Figure 7.3, in order to develop a graph of last year's and this year's sales data and have the department names at the bottom of the graph, you would include those highlighted cells in the range after the Group command was executed.

Once the range is specified, you must include information about how 1-2-3 is to use this data. In this example, a columnwise interpretation is to be used. You can now view the graph (see Figure 7.4).

Quit   The **Quit option** returns you to the Main Menu of 1-2-3.

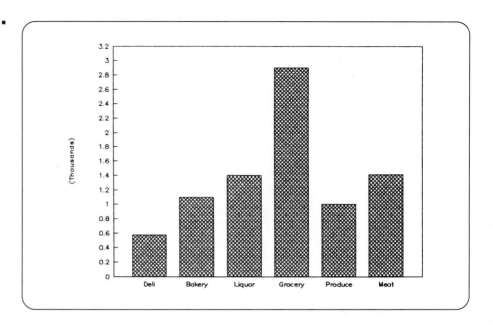

Figure 7.5
Simple bar graph of the This Year information from the COMPSALS worksheet as it appears when printed out

GENERATING GRAPHS

SIMPLE BAR GRAPHS

The first exercise below is to generate a simple bar graph using the This Year information contained in the COMPSALS worksheet. The graph you produce should look like that in Figure 7.5.

1. Load in the COMPSALS worksheet.

    | / | Gets the Main Menu |
    | F | Selects the File Menu |
    | R | Selects the Retrieve command |
    | COMPSALS | Identifies the worksheet (or you can point to the worksheet name) |
    | ENTER | Executes the command |

2. Select the Graph Menu and tell 1-2-3 to generate a bar graph.

    | / | Gets the Main Menu |
    | G | Selects the Graph Menu |
    | T | Selects the Type option from the Graph Menu |
    | B | Tells 1-2-3 to generate a bar chart |

3. Establish the X-axis label range (department names).

    | X | Indicates that the X-axis label range is to be specified |
    | B5 [by manual pointer movement or address entry] | Positions the pointer at cell B5 |
    | . | Nails down the beginning of the range |
    | B10 [by manual pointer movement or address entry] | Positions the pointer at the last cell in the label range |
    | Enter | Tells 1-2-3 that the range is established |

4. Establish the This Year column as the A data range.

A	Tells 1-2-3 that you want to specify the A data range
D5 [by manual pointer movement]	Positions the cursor at the beginning of the This Year data
.	Nails down the beginning of the range
D10 [by manual pointer movement]	Positions the pointer at the last cell to be included in the A data range
Enter	Tells 1-2-3 that the A data range is established

5. Execute the View command (V) to display the graph on the screen (see Figure 7.5). The 1-2-3 program created the scale along the Y axis based on the data (option A) being graphed.

ENTERING TITLES

Although the graph in the just-completed exercise looks okay, if you want it to mean anything at a later date, you should probably put some descriptive labels on it. Lotus 1-2-3 allows you to put a two-line title at the top of the graph and a one-line title on each axis of the graph. In this exercise, you will place the following labels on the bar chart (see Figure 7.6):

Line 1	Ed's Supermarket
Line 2	This Year's Sales
X axis	Departments
Y axis	Dollar Sales

Placing these labels on the graph involves the following steps:

1. The Options selection from the Graph Menu will allow you to place the labels on the bar chart.

O	Selects the Options Menu from the Graph Menu
T	Selects the Titles option from the Options Menu
F	Selects the First line option
Ed's Supermarket	Specifies the title
Enter	Tells 1-2-3 to accept the title
T	Selects the Titles option
S	Selects the Second line option
This Year's Sales	Specifies the title
Enter	Tells 1-2-3 to accept the title
T	Selects the Titles option
X	Selects the X-axis title option
Departments	Specifies the title
Enter	Tells 1-2-3 to accept the title
T	Selects the Titles option
Y	Selects the Y-axis title option
Dollar Sales	Specifies the title
Enter	Tells 1-2-3 to accept the title
Q	Quits the Options Menu and returns to the Graph Menu

Figure 7.6
Printed bar graph of this year's COMPSALS sales, with graph and axis titles in place

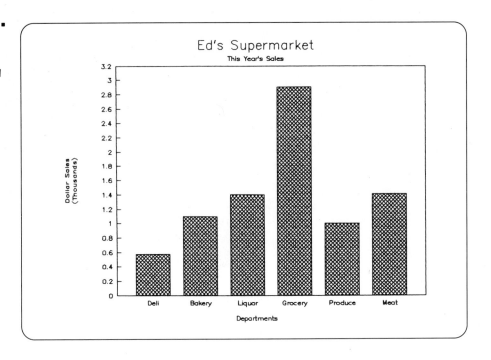

2. View the graph by depressing the V option. Your graph should now look like the one in Figure 7.6.
3. Depress any key to return to the Graph Menu.
4. Save the graph's settings onto the worksheet, so it can be easily retrieved later.

N	Selects the Name option of the Graph Menu
C	Selects the Create option
TYSALE	Names the group of graph settings
Enter	Tells 1-2-3 to accept these graph settings

If you want to take a look at this graph again, you don't have to reenter all the keystrokes; you just tell 1-2-3 to load TYSALE as the settings to generate a graph. These graph settings are also saved to a worksheet file when a save operation is performed.

CHANGING DATA RANGES

The current graph settings contain instructions for creating a graph of this year's sales for Ed's Supermarket. To graph last year's sales, the A data range and the second line of the worksheet title must be changed as follows: You have to change the A data range to the Last Year column and put "Last Year's Sales" in the second title line. The remaining graph specifications can be left unchanged.

The steps involved in performing this task are as follows:

1. Get to the Graph Menu.
2. Change the A data range.

A	Selects the A option from the Graph Menu

Figure 7.7
Printed bar graph of last year's COMPSALS sales, with graphs and axis titles in place

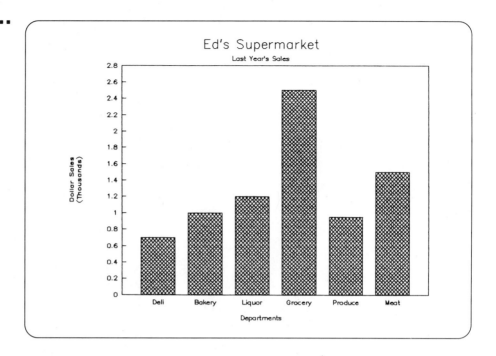

Backspace	Cancels the existing range
C10 [by pointer movement or address entry]	Establishes the first cell in the A range
.	Nails down the beginning of the range
C5 [by pointer movement or address entry]	Establishes the end of the A range
Enter	Tells 1-2-3 to accept the A data range

3. Change *This* to *Last* in the second title line.

O	Selects the Options Menu from the Graph Menu
T	Selects the Titles option
S	Selects the Second line option, causing "This Year's Sales" to be displayed
Home	Moves the pointer under the *T* in *This*
Del Del Del Del	Deletes the word *This*
Last	Enters the word *Last*
Enter	Tells 1-2-3 to accept the changed title
Q	Quits the Options Menu and returns to the Graph Menu

4. View the changed graph, using the View command (V) from the Graph Menu. The graph should now look like the one shown in Figure 7.7.
5. Depress any key to return to the Graph Menu.
6. Save these worksheet settings for later use.

N	Selects the Name option from the Graph Menu
C	Selects the Create option
LYSALE	Names the group of graph settings
Enter	Tells 1-2-3 to execute this command

SIDE-BY-SIDE BAR GRAPHS

You now have two bar graphs showing sales for this year and last year. Ed, however, wants to be able to make a direct comparison between the two years via one bar graph. Because you saved the settings of the TYSALE bar graph, all you have to do is load in those graph settings and change them in accordance with Ed's request. The following steps are required:

1. Get to the Graph Menu.

2. Replace the current graph settings with those contained in TYSALE (and stored in the spreadsheet).

N	Selects the Name option from the Graph Menu
U	Selects the Use option from the Name Menu, enabling you to replace current graph settings with previously stored settings
TYSALE	Specifies the graph settings to be stored
Enter	Tells 1-2-3 to execute the command

3. The graph TYSALE is now displayed on the screen. Depress any key to return to the Graph Menu.

4. Establish the B range as the numbers in the Last Year column.

B	Tells 1-2-3 to expect the B data range
C5 [by pointer movement or address entry]	Establishes the beginning of the B data range
.	Nails down the beginning of the range
C10 [by pointer movement or address entry]	Establishes the end of the B data range
Enter	Tells 1-2-3 to accept the B data range

5. Change the second title line of the graph.

O	Selects the Options Menu
T	Selects the Titles option
S	Selects the Second line option
Left Arrow	Positions the pointer to the right of the *S* in *Sales*
vs. Last Year's	Identifies new characters to be inserted
Enter	Accepts the new second title line
Q	Quits the Options Menu and returns to the Graph Menu

6. View the graph, using the V command. It should now look like the graph shown in Figure 7.8.

7. Depress any key to return to the Graph Menu.

8. Save the graph onto disk, so it can be printed later.

S	Takes the Save option
LYTYSALE	Names the graph
Enter	Tells 1-2-3 to execute the Save command

9. Save these graph settings for later use.

N	Selects the Name option from the Graph Menu
C	Selects the Create option from the Name Menu
LYTYSALE	Specifies the name of the graph settings to be saved
Enter	Records these settings to the worksheet

Figure 7.8
Printed side-by-side bar graphs of COMPSALS sales

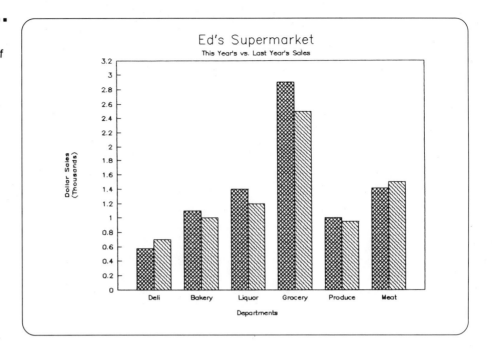

Figure 7.9
Printed line graph of this year's and last year's COMPSALS sales

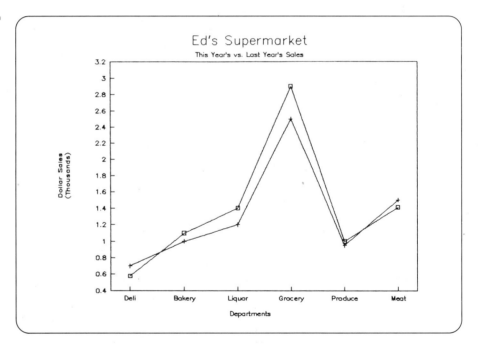

CONVERTING TO LINE GRAPHS

Ed would also like to see the bar graph information depicted as a line graph. The following steps are involved:

1. From the Graph Menu, change the graph type.
   - T Selects the Type option from the Graph Menu
   - L Tells 1-2-3 to generate a line graph

2. View the graph, using the V command. It should now look like the graph shown in Figure 7.9.

ENTERING LEGENDS

Now Ed is confused because he can't tell the difference between this year's sales and last year's sales on the line graph. You can solve this problem by providing a legend that tells which symbols represent which data ranges.

The following steps are involved when you begin from the Graph Menu:

1. Add the legends.

O	Selects the Options Menu
L	Selects the Legend option
A	Selects the A data range to hold the first legend text
TYSales	Identifies the text of the legend
Enter	Tells 1-2-3 to accept the legend
L	Selects the Legend option
B	Selects the B data range to hold the second legend text
LYSales	Identifies the text of the legend
Enter	Tells 1-2-3 to accept the legend
Q	Leaves the Options Menu and returns to the Graph Menu

2. View the graph, using the V command. It should now look like the graph shown in Figure 7.10.
3. Depress any key to return to the Graph Menu.
4. Save these graph settings.

N	Selects the Name option from the Graph Menu
C	Selects the Create option from the Name Menu
LYTYLINE	Names the graph settings
Enter	Tells 1-2-3 to save the graph settings

5. Save the graph to a file for later printing.

S	Selects the Save option from the Graph Menu
LYTYLINE	Identifies the graph to be saved
Enter	Tells 1-2-3 to execute the Save command

RECONVERTING TO BAR GRAPHS

Ed is very impressed with 1-2-3 and now wants the double bar graph to include a legend for its bars. You need to take the following steps:

1. Get to the Graph Menu.
2. Select a new graph type.

T	Selects the Type option from the Graph Menu
B	Tells 1-2-3 to create a bar graph

3. View the graph, using the V command. It should now look like the graph shown in Figure 7.11.

PIE CHARTS

Ed wants more. You will try to satisfy him by putting the original bar chart information about this year's sales into the form of a pie chart. This involves the following steps:

Figure 7.10
Printed line graph of last year's and this year's COMPSALS sales, with accompanying legend

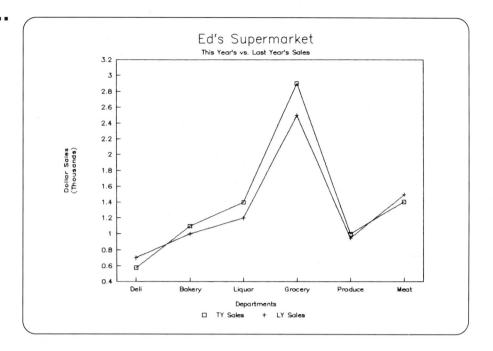

Figure 7.11
Printed bar graph of last year's and this year's COMPSALS sales, with accompanying legend

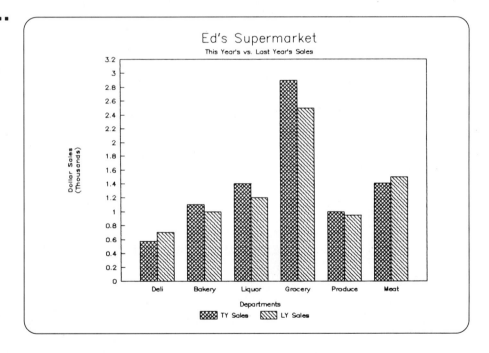

1. Get to the Graph Menu.
2. Reset the graph settings to TYSALE.

N	Selects the Name option from the Graph Menu
U	Selects the Use command, telling 1-2-3 which graph settings to use
TYSALE	Specifies the settings to use
Enter	Tells 1-2-3 to change the settings of the current graph

Figure 7.12
Printed pie chart of this year's COMPSALS sales

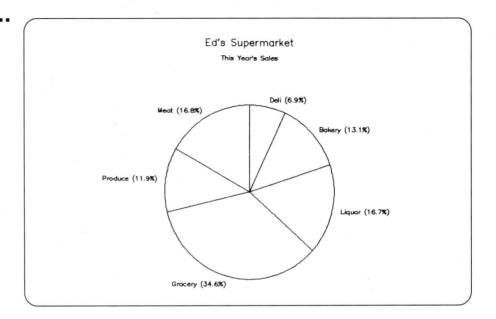

3. Get to the Graph Menu and change the graph type.

   T   Selects the Type option from the Graph Menu
   P   Tells 1-2-3 to draw a pie chart

4. View the graph, using the V command. It should now look like the graph shown in Figure 7.12. Lotus 1-2-3 remembers all of the titles from the TYSALE graph settings.

5. Save the graph to a file.

   S   Selects the Save option from the Graph Menu
   TYPIE   Names the graph
   Enter   Tells 1-2-3 to save the graph

EXPLODED PIE CHART

Lotus 1-2-3 provides you with the ability to create an exploded pie chart showing one or more slices separated from the rest of the chart. To create this effect, you must set up a separate B data range. The A range contains the values to be plotted. The B range tells 1-2-3 the colors (or patterns, if viewed on a noncolor screen) to be used and which wedges (if any) are to be exploded.

Plotting an exploded pie chart requires you to set up a new B data range in column G with values for the colors of each wedge to be plotted. These are given as single digits 0 through 8. The digits 0 and 8 are used for nonshaded wedges, the digits 1 through 7 for a shade or pattern. Add 100 to the appropriate shading value of exploded wedges. For example, if the shaded value of a wedge is 4 and you wish to have that wedge appear exploded from the pie, enter 104.

The worksheet displayed in Figure 7.13 generates the exploded pie chart shown in Figure 7.14. Don't worry if the graph appears a little "squashed"; it will appear fine when it is printed.

Figure 7.13
Worksheet for generating the graph in Figure 7.14

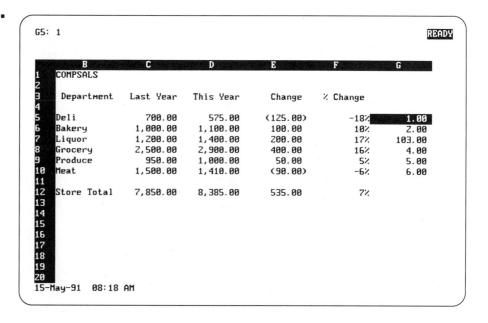

Figure 7.14
Printed exploded pie chart of the data depicted in Figure 7.13

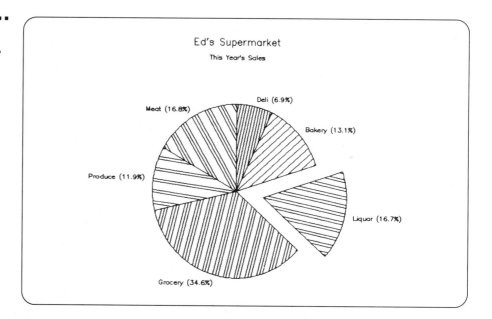

STACKED BAR CHARTS

Ed would now like a stacked bar graph showing the combined sales of each department for last year and this year. Once you have reached the Graph Menu, take the following steps:

1. Get the settings from the LYTYSALE graph that you stored previously.

N	Selects the Name option from the Graph Menu
U	Selects the Use option from the Name Menu
LYTYSALE	Specifies the graph settings to use
Enter	Puts the graph on the screen

Figure 7.15
Printed stacked bar graph of last year's and this year's COMPSALS sales

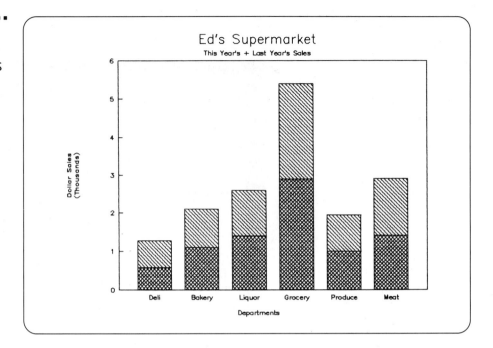

2. Depress any key to get to the Graph Menu.
3. Select a new graph type.

    T   Selects the Type option from the Graph Menu
    S   Tells 1-2-3 to generate a stacked bar graph

4. Enter a new second title line for the graph.

O	Selects the Options Menu from the Graph Menu
T	Selects the Title option from the Options Menu
S	Selects the Second title line
Left Arrow	Moves the pointer under the *v* of *vs*.
Del [three times]	Deletes the word *vs*.
+	Identifies the character to be added
Enter	Tells 1-2-3 to accept the changed second line
Q	Quits the Options Menu and returns to the Graph Menu

5. View the graph, using the V command. It should look like the graph shown in Figure 7.15.
6. Depress any key to return to the Graph Menu.

GENERATING A TABLE OF GRAPH NAMES

Ed would now like to see a table of the various graphs that have been archived to the worksheet using the Name Create commands. This is accomplished by using the Name Table command. Once you have positioned the pointer to cell C14, enter the following commands:

    N   Selects the Name option of the Graph Menu
    T   Selects the Table option of the Name submenu

Figure 7.16
The report of the various sets of graph settings archived using the Name option of the Main Menu

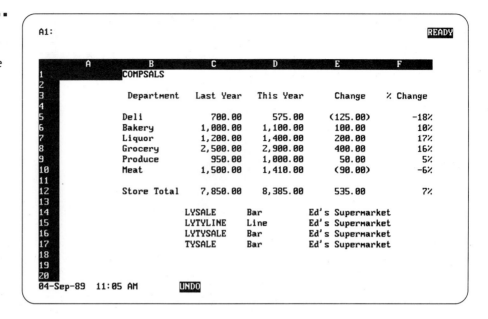

C14   Positions the pointer to cell C14
Enter   Executes the command

You should now see a report embedded within your worksheet like that depicted in Figure 7.16. Now save the worksheet file so that 1-2-3 remembers the various changes that you have made to COMPSALS.

XY GRAPHS

Up until now, Ed has been requesting only one-dimensional graphs—graphs in which only Y data points are plotted. Now Ed has come up with an application that requires you to plot a set of Y data points against a set of X data points. Ed has accumulated seven years of profit figures that he would like to compare to each year's rate of inflation. To build such a graph, you must use the XY option from the Type Menu. Ed's figures are shown in Figure 7.17.

This information has been entered in a worksheet called PROFITS. The cell that contains "1992" is cell A6. Either load or create this worksheet. At this point, the following steps must be performed to generate the XY graph.

1. Get the Graph Menu.

    /   Gets the Main Menu
    G   Takes the Graph option

2. Select the graph type.

    T   Selects the Type option of the Graph Menu
    X   Tells 1-2-3 to generate an XY graph

3. Tell 1-2-3 the A data range.

    A   Selects the A data range option from
                                 the Graph Menu
    B6 [by manual pointer   Positions the pointer at the first A range
    movement]   cell
    .   Nails down the beginning of the range

Figure 7.17
PROFITS worksheet

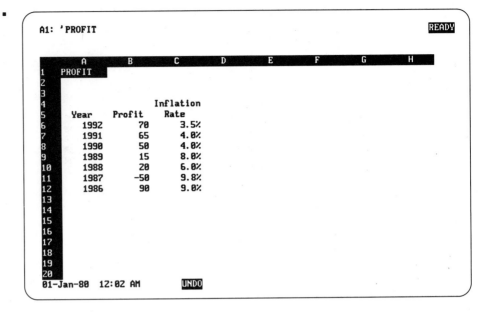

	B12 [by manual pointer movement]	Positions the pointer at the end of the range
	Enter	Submits the A data range to 1-2-3

4. Tell 1-2-3 the X data range.

	X	Selects the X data range option from the Graph Menu
	C6 [by manual pointer movement]	Positions the pointer at the first X range cell
	.	Nails down the beginning of the range
	C12 [by manual pointer movement]	Positions the pointer at the end of the range
	Enter	Submits the X data range to 1-2-3

5. Enter the titles for the graph.

	O	Selects the Options Menu
	T	Selects the Titles option
	F	Selects the First title line
	Ed's Supermarket	Identifies the first title line
	Enter	Submits the title to 1-2-3
	T	Selects the Titles option
	S	Selects the Second title line
	Profits Compared to Inflation	Identifies the second title line
	Enter	Submits the title to 1-2-3
	T	Selects the Titles option
	X	Selects the X-axis title
	Inflation	Identifies the X-axis title
	Enter	Submits the title to 1-2-3
	T	Selects the Titles option
	Y	Selects the Y-axis title
	Profits	Identifies the Y-axis title
	Enter	Submits the title to 1-2-3
	Q	Quits the Options Menu and returns to the Graph Menu

Figure 7.18
Printed XY graph comparing profits to inflation over a seven-year period

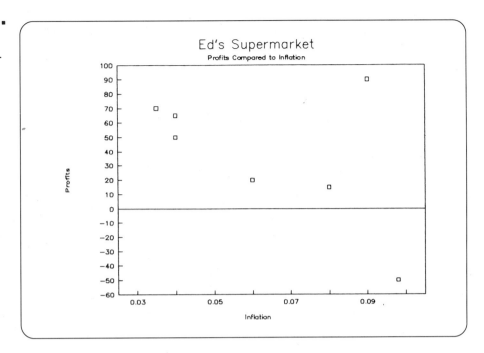

6. Tell 1-2-3 not to connect the data points with lines.

O	Selects the Options Menu
F	Selects the Format option
G	Selects the Graph option
S	Selects the Symbols option
Q	Quits the Format Menu and returns to the Options Menu
Q	Quits the Options Menu and returns to the Graph Menu

7. View the graph, using the V command. It should now look like the graph shown in Figure 7.18.

8. Depress any key to return to the Graph Menu; then save to a picture file called XY1GRAPH.

Formatting the X and Y Numeric Scaling

1. Change the format of the Y numeric scaling, that is, the manner in which the scale numbers are displayed.

O	Selects the Options Menu
S	Selects the Scale option
Y	Specifies the Y scale as the scale to be changed
F	Selects the Format option from the Scale Menu
F	Selects the Fixed option of the Format Menu
Enter	Changes the format to two decimal positions
M	Tells 1-2-3 to draw the graph based on user-specified upper and lower limits
L	Selects the Lower limit entry
−80	Enter the new lower limit amount
Enter	Depress the Enter key
U	Selects the Upper limit entry
120	Enter the new upper limit amount
Q	Quits the Scale Menu and returns to the Options Menu
Q	Quits the Options Menu and returns to the Graph Menu

2. View the graph, using the V command. It should now look like the graph shown in Figure 7.19.
3. Save to a .PIC file called XY2GRAPH.

Labeling Graph Data Points   XY graphs can sometimes be rather hard to read. The data points represented are not properly labeled because the X option (typically used for labeling the X axis) is used for plotting a set of data points. This confusion can be eliminated through the use of the Data Labels feature of 1-2-3. Using the Data Labels feature involves the following steps:

1. Establish the data labels.

O	Selects the Options Menu
D	Selects the Data Labels option of the Options Menu
A	Selects the A data range option
A6 [by manual pointer movement]	Positions the pointer at the first A range cell
.	Nails down the beginning of the range
A12 [by manual pointer movement]	Positions the pointer at the end of the range
Enter	Submits the A Data Labels range to 1-2-3
B	Tells 1-2-3 to place the labels below the data point representation (square)
Q	Quits the Data Labels Menu
Q	Quits the Options Menu

2. Tell 1-2-3 to display the graph shown in Figure 7.20.

INTRODUCTION TO GRAPH PRINTING

Lotus 1-2-3 does not provide you with facilities for directly printing your graphs from the 1-2-3 spreadsheet program. This is one of the few areas in which Lotus's integration breaks down, but if this feature had been implemented 1-2-3 would require much more RAM memory than it now requires.

To print a graph, you must leave the 1-2-3 spreadsheet software and return to the Lotus Access System Menu, where you take the **PrintGraph** option. If you have been using 1-2-3, you will be instructed to insert the PrintGraph disk in drive A. If you have previously saved your graph files and want to print them out, you can boot directly from the PrintGraph disk, which also contains a copy of the Lotus Access System.

Make certain that the disk containing the graphs you have saved is inserted in drive B, and get your PrintGraph disk ready. If you have 1-2-3 running on your computer, follow the instructions below. If the computer is off, boot the system, then insert the PrintGraph disk in drive A and with that disk start PrintGraph, skipping the instructions below. The steps involved in accessing PrintGraph from 1-2-3 are as follows:

/	Gets the Main Menu
Q	Selects the Quit option
Y	Affirms leaving 1-2-3 and in a few seconds elicits a display of the Lotus Access System Menu
P	Selects the PrintGraph option

Figure 7.19
Printed reformatted XY graph comparing profits to inflation over a seven-year period

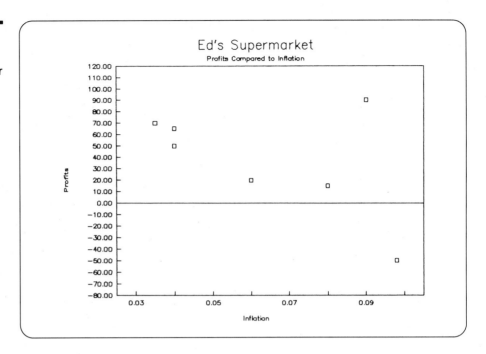

Figure 7.20
XY graph comparing profits to inflation with data labels added

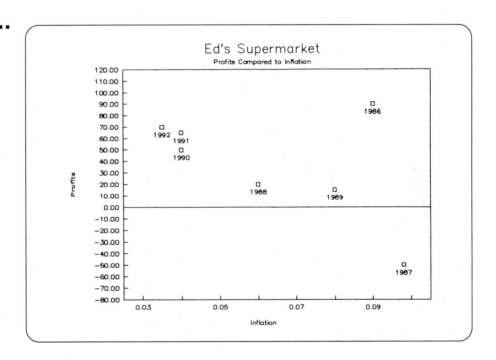

At this point, you will be directed to insert the PrintGraph disk in drive A (see Figure 7.21a), unless you have a fixed disk. Once you have inserted the PrintGraph disk, the screen depicted in Figure 7.21b will be displayed on your monitor. When PrintGraph is loaded, the PrintGraph screen shown in Figure 7.22 appears.

Figure 7.21

```
Insert PrintGraph Disk into your diskette drive

Press [RETURN] to continue or [ESCAPE] to quit
```

a

b

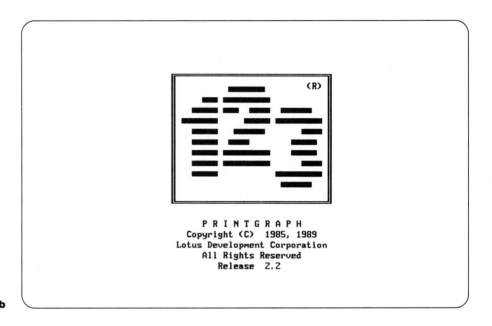

Figure 7.22
The PrintGraph Menu

```
Copyright 1986, 1989 Lotus Development Corp.  All Rights Reserved. V2.2   MENU
Select graphs to print or preview
Image-Select  Settings  Go  Align  Page  Exit

   GRAPHS     IMAGE SETTINGS                    HARDWARE SETTINGS
   TO PRINT    Size              Range colors    Graphs directory
                Top         .395  X               A:\
                Left        .750  A              Fonts directory
                Width      6.500  B               C:\123-2
                Height     4.691  C              Interface
                Rotation    .000  D               Parallel 1
                                  E              Printer
               Font               F
                1  BLOCK1                        Paper size
                2  BLOCK1                         Width       8.500
                                                  Length     11.000

                                                ACTION SETTINGS
                                                 Pause  No    Eject  Yes
```

PRINTGRAPH MENU

The information displayed beneath the PrintGraph Menu details status information about the various options used by the utility, including what paper sizes are expected, what fonts have been selected, where files are to be found, and what type of printer PrintGraph is currently configured for. When you

Figure 7.23
Menu of graph (.PIC) files

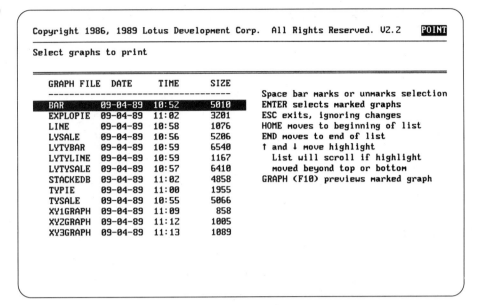

Figure 7.24
Graphs marked for printing

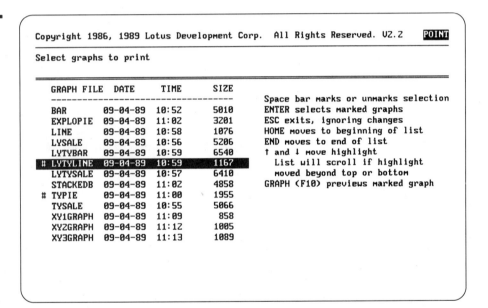

have properly started the PrintGraph utility, the following menu will be displayed:

```
Image-Select   Settings   Go   Align   Page   Exit
```

Image-Select This option is used to mark graphs for printing. When you select the **Image-Select option,** a display of all graph files contained on the disk in drive B appears on the screen. Across the top file is a wide pointer, which is moved up and down by means of the Up and Down Arrow keys. To tag or mark a file for printing, simply depress the Space Bar; a **pound sign (#)** will then appear to the left of that graph file entry. (See Figures 7.23 and 7.24.)

Figure 7.25
Settings Menu

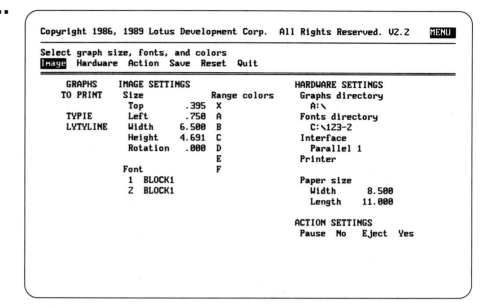

Up to 16 graph files can be selected for printing. If more than one file is selected, they are printed in the order in which they appear, from top to bottom. The computer then prints each graph in turn and automatically advances the paper for the next graph. When you have selected all the files you wish to print, simply depress the Enter key to return to the PrintGraph Menu. Depressing the Space Bar a second time will "unmark" the file.

This convenient feature, known as **batch printing,** allows you to do something else (like catching up on your reading) while your graphs are being printed.

Settings Upon selecting the Settings option, the following menu is displayed (see Figure 7.25):

```
Image   Hardware   Action   Save   Reset   Quit
```

Image The Image option (see Figure 7.26) displays the following submenu when it is selected:

```
Size   Font   Range-Colors   Quit
```

Size. This option allows you to specify the height and width of the graph to be printed.

Font. This option allows you to select up to two fonts from 11 possible fonts in generating dot matrix output. Font 1 is used only for the first line of the graph title, font 2 for any other text. Fonts are selected in the same way that files are: Use a pointer to highlight the desired option and then press the Space Bar to choose the font (see Figure 7.27).

Range-Colors. This option allows you to assign a different color to each data range. It is selected if you have the ability to generate color graphs.

Quit. This option returns you to the Settings Menu.

Figure 7.26
Image Menu

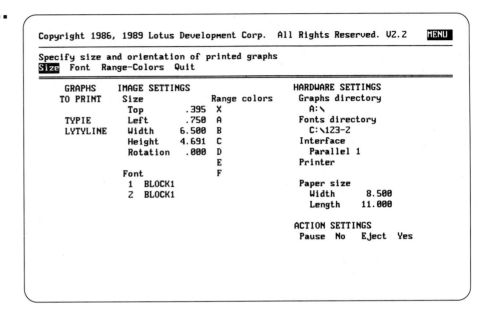

Figure 7.27
Font marked for use

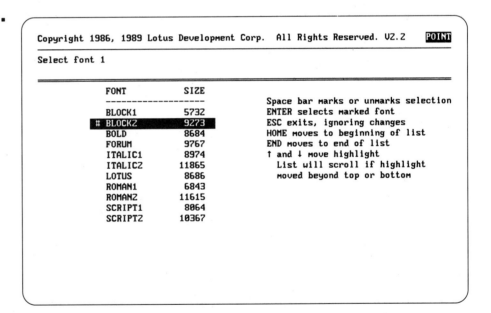

Hardware This option allows you to configure 1-2-3 to the type of print that your printer is capable of printing, as well as to tell 1-2-3 where to find the graph files and font files. Most likely these tasks have already been done for readers of this textbook, so this option—as well as the remaining options—will not be covered here.

Quit This option returns you to the PrintGraph Menu.

Go This option results in the graph being printed.

Align This option resets the top-of-page. If the graph did not print properly (for example, if there is a blank area in the middle), simply move the paper manually to a perforation and select the Align command. PrintGraph now knows where the top of the page is.

Page This option moves the paper in the printer to the top of the next page.

Exit This option allows you to go back to end a PrintGraph session. Upon being selected, it displays the menu No Yes. When you select the Yes option, you are returned to the Lotus Access System Menu. You can now take the 1-2-3 option to return to the spreadsheet or take Exit to end the session. If you select the 1-2-3 option and you are working in a diskette environment with 1-2-3 program disks, you will be prompted to insert the disk containing the 1-2-3 program in drive A.

STEP-BY-STEP PRINTGRAPH INSTRUCTIONS

To print the graph files TYPIE and LYTYLINE that were created earlier, start from the PrintGraph Menu. Then perform the following steps:

1. Move the pointer to the Image-Select option (see Figure 7.23) and press Enter.
2. Move the pointer (via the Up and Down Arrow keys) to positions at the two desired graph names. Mark them by pressing the Space Bar so that a pound symbol (#) appears to the left of each. Hit Enter when both graph names have been marked (see Figure 7.24).
3. Take the Settings selection.
4. Take the Image option.
5. Take the Font entry of the Image Menu. Select font 1 and choose BLOCK2 by pointing, pressing the Space Bar, and hitting the Enter key (see Figure 7.27).
6. Take the Font entry of the Image Menu again. Select font 2 and choose BLOCK1 by pointing, pressing the Space Bar, and hitting the Enter key.
7. You've finished with the Image; now take the Quit option.
8. Quit from Settings Menu.
9. Make sure the printer is at the top of a new page; then select the Align option.
10. You're going to accept all the defaults for printing. The next step is to take the Go option to start printing.

The following options are now executed by PrintGraph:

1. The font files are loaded.
2. The graph file is loaded, and the picture is generated.
3. The graph file is printed.

Figure 7.28

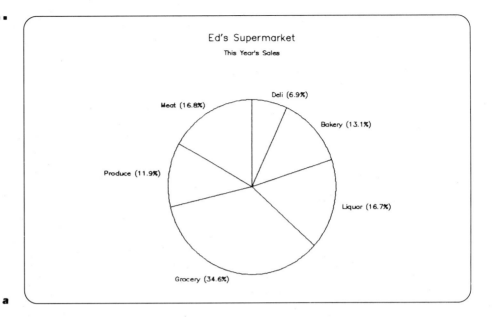

a

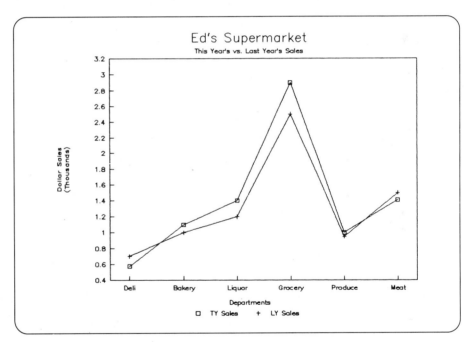

b

PrintGraph displays various pieces of status information while it prints. In the menu area it identifies the graph file currently printing, and below the current printing file it displays a list of the files that were selected for printing.

PrintGraph's printing process is very slow in comparison to regular printing because the printer has shifted to graphics mode, which is generally slower than text mode.

The files selected for printing can be seen in Figure 7.28.

CHAPTER REVIEW

To build a graph using 1-2-3, you must do the following: (1) select a worksheet file that contains information you wish to graph; (2) obtain the Graph Menu; (3) select the type of graph you want and identify the pieces of data to be included; (4) enter any additional titles, labels, and legends; (5) view the graph on the screen; (6) make any further changes or enhancements.

The 1-2-3 package allows you to develop the following graphs: line, bar, XY, stacked bar, and pie. Each of these graphs, except the XY graph, is one-dimensional—meaning that only one set of data points interacts across an unchanging X axis. If you wish to graph two sets of data points against each other, you must use an XY graph.

Each of the graph selections, except the pie chart, can use more than one set of Y data points. Each subsequent set of data points produces an additional line or bar, depending on the type of graph selected. The pie chart, by its very nature, is able to plot only one set of data points at a time.

After a graph has been finished, you can save the settings for that graph onto an area of the worksheet by using the Name option of the Graph Menu. At this point, another graph, termed the "current" graph, can be built. You can make the graph settings you previously saved become the current graph by entering the Name option and specifying which group of graph settings is to be used. The graph itself can be saved, too, but it (unlike the graph setting) is saved to disk as a separate file. After a graph has been saved onto disk, it can be printed out via the PrintGraph utility supplied by Lotus.

The PrintGraph utility, the program used to print any 1-2-3 graph that has been saved onto disk, allows you (depending on the printer that you are using) to determine the density of the graph to be printed and the fonts to be used for any text data on the graph. Font 1 is used for titles; font 2 is used for any other text data.

Printing graphs is a time-consuming process. PrintGraph's batch printing feature allows you to specify a number of graphs to be printed automatically, without your having to oversee any remaining steps in the printing process.

KEY TERMS AND CONCEPTS

ABCDEF commands
Align option
bar graph
batch printing
B&W option
Color option
Create command
Data option
Delete command
Font option
Format option
F10 Graph key
Go option
Graph Menu
Grid option
Group command
Image-Select option
Labels option
Legend option
line graph
Name option

Name
Options command
Page option
pie chart
pound sign (#)
PrintGraph
Quit option
Reset command
Reset option
Save command
Scale option
Size option
stacked bar graph
Titles option
Type option
Use command
View command
X command
X (horizontal) axis
XY graph
Y (vertical) axis

CHAPTER QUIZ

Multiple Choice

1. Which of the following graph types can have only one set of Y data points?
   a. Line
   b. Bar
   c. Pie
   d. Stacked bar
   e. XY
   f. All of the above can have more than one set of Y data points.

2. Which of the following is *not* considered to be a title?
   a. The two lines at the top of the graph.
   b. X-axis title
   c. Y-axis title
   d. Legends
   e. All of the above are titles.

3. ABCDEF are
   a. grades assigned for this exercise.
   b. X-axis data points.
   c. Y-axis data points.
   d. data point labels.
   e. none of the above.

4. Which of the following is *not* a feature of PrintGraph?
   a. Exists as a separate program available under the Lotus Access System
   b. Allows you to specify up to four fonts in a graph
   c. Allows you to batch-print graphs
   d. All of the above are features of PrintGraph.

5. Which of the following statements is *not* true about the Name feature of the Graph Menu?
   a. The stored graph settings are all active.
   b. The current graph settings can be saved onto the worksheet using this option.
   c. When the worksheet is saved onto disk, any graph settings are also saved.
   d. You can delete selected graph settings individually or all at once.
   e. All of the above statements are true.

True/False

6. The PrintGraph utility is one of the nonintegrated features of 1-2-3.

7. Once a set of graph settings is selected via the Use option of the Name Menu, the graph built with these settings is automatically displayed on the screen.

8. It is possible to reset either selected parts of a graph or the complete graph.

9. Using legends allows you to distinguish among the various sets of Y data points.

10. The XY graph is the only 1-2-3 graph type that allows you to create a two-dimensional graph.

Answers

1. c, e 2. d 3. c 4. b 5. a 6. t 7. t 8. t 9. t 10. t

Exercises

1. Define or describe each of the following terms.
   a. X axis
   b. Y axis
   c. legend
   d. scaling
   e. batch printing

2. List the steps involved in building and then printing a graph.
   a.
   b.
   c.
   d.
   e.
   f.
   g.
   h.
   i.

3. Lotus 1-2-3 automatically places the extension _____ on the file of any graph that is saved onto disk.

4. The _____ option allows you to label each set of Y data points, in order to make a graph more readable.

5. Graph settings can be saved onto the worksheet using the _____ _____ option of the Graph Menu.

6. The _____ command of the Graph Menu enables you to see the graph.

7. The _____ command is used when you wish to delete a portion or all of the current graph settings.

8. The _____ command is used to store a graph onto disk.

9. Any range can be canceled by pressing the _____ key.

10. The format in which numeric data appear on a graph can be controlled by using the _____ option.

11. The _____ axis is usually enlisted to produce labels across the bottom of the graph.

12. Explain the difference between a one-dimensional graph and a two-dimensional graph.

13. _____ bar charts combine entries into one set of Y data points; _____ bar charts allow you to see differences immediately by comparing bars.

14. _____ allows you to specify a number of graphs to be printed and then leave to do whatever you want.

15. When you are using two fonts, _____ is used for the heading, and _____ is used for the rest of the graph.

16. Basically, _____ sizes of graphs can be printed.

17. PrintGraph is separate from 1-2-3 because it takes up too much _____.

18. Explain how graphs are selected for printing.

19. You can mark graphs for printing by pressing the _____ key.

20. List the actions that PrintGraph performs in printing a graph.
    a.
    b.
    c.

COMPUTER EXERCISES

In building the following graphs, referring to the Graph command structure in Appendix A will help you greatly in locating the various graph commands.

1. Retrieve the CH3EX5 worksheet file.
   a. Generate a pie chart, using the This Year column data.
   b. Generate a bar graph, using the same data. Save these graph settings to a named area called TYEAR.
   c. Compare the two years of sales, using a line graph. Save these graph settings to a named area called TYLYSALE.
   d. Generate a bar graph of the named graph TYEAR, using all the stored graph settings but changing the column to be graphed to Last Year.

e. Generate a line graph of the named graph TYLYSALE and enter legends at the bottom of the graph. Save these settings to a named area called LEGENDS.

    f. Using the TYLYSALE settings, change the graph type to a bar graph. Save this file to a picture file using the name BAR2SALE.

    g. Enter the following headings:

Line 1	FRED'S AUTO SALES
Line 2	YEARLY SALES COMPARISON
X axis	Sales Reps
Y axis	Dollar Sales

    h. Save the graph to a picture file called BARTITLE.

    i. Save the graph settings to a named area BARTITLE.

    j. Exit from the Graph Menu. Change the contents of cells in the sales range. View the graph by depressing the F10 key.

    k. Resave the worksheet file. This will also save the named graphs.

2. Retrieve the CH3EX7 worksheet file.

    a. Graph the expenses for each year, using a line graph. Enter appropriate headings, labels, and legends. Save the file to a graph picture file called EXPENSES.

    b. Generate a pie chart for each year's expenses. Save them to files called PIE1 and PIE2. You will have to reset the B data range to accomplish this.

3. Use the PrintGraph utility to print the above graphs. Refer to the PrintGraph portion of the chapter for instructions on using this utility.

CHAPTER 8

DATA MANAGEMENT

CHAPTER OBJECTIVES

After completing this chapter, you should be able to:

- **Discuss the basic concepts of 1-2-3 data management**
- **Discuss how data management fields and records are handled**
- **Use the various options of the data management menu**
- **Define a database to 1-2-3**
- **Set up a criterion range**
- **Locate or find records in the database**
- **Understand how the Output and Extract commands interact**
- **Know how the Unique and Delete commands work**
- **Use the database statistical functions**

Data management, sometimes referred to as database, is the third integrated function of Lotus 1-2-3.

1-2-3 DATA MANAGEMENT VERSUS dBASE

The first difference between 1-2-3's database and dBASE's database is in how the two software packages store data. dBASE stores data in a disk file, whereas 1-2-3 stores records in a worksheet. The data in a dBASE application are not visible to a user; instead, file manipulation commands are issued to access or list the information contained in a file. In contrast, 1-2-3's information, since it is contained in a worksheet, is directly visible to the worksheet user.

A 1-2-3 **data management file** is composed of one or more rows containing one or more columns. This method of file storage sets certain limitations on 1-2-3 data management files, the most important of which is that file size is limited by the amount of available RAM memory on the computer. A computer with 512K or even 640K of RAM might not have enough memory for a large data file.

A 1-2-3 database can be accessed only sequentially. If a view of the file in some other order is desired, the database must be rearranged via 1-2-3's Sort feature. Unfortunately, the Sort feature is extremely slow with larger databases. A database with 2,000 records, for example, can take hours to sort using a computer with an 8088 chip.

Data management in 1-2-3 operates in **immediate mode**—that is, commands are issued from the keyboard. dBASE provides the ability to incorporate file manipulation commands in separate programs and thereafter to manipulate files via the stored instructions. A security problem exists with 1-2-3 data management files (but not with dBASE files) because all the data are immediately available to a user. Fields cannot be hidden from a user via programmed command files.

The concepts of *record* and *field* also differ in the two systems. A 1-2-3 **record** does not have to have the length and data characteristics of its component field(s) described; it is simply a row on a worksheet. The **fields** are columns in the row in which data are stored; a one-line heading at the top of each column functions as the **field name.**

Because of these limitations, 1-2-3's data management capabilities are somewhat limited. However, 1-2-3 does an excellent job with small files dealing with fairly simple applications, and its data management function is easy to use because it does not involve a separate syntax and can readily be incorporated into existing worksheets.

INTRODUCTION TO 1-2-3 DATA MANAGEMENT

Ed has requested the development of a check register application to record his checks, keep track of the balance, and help him in reconciling his checkbook. He also wants to be able to track the checks by budget category and by tax deductibility. Ed has requested that the application be placed on 1-2-3.

After an examination of the application, the worksheet appearing at the top of the next page is designed to solve his problem. Each row (record) of the worksheet holds information about a check that has been written. The information is divided into six fields of data: check number (NO.), the date the check was written (DATE), check payee (PAYEE), check amount (AMOUNT), budget category (BUDGET), and tax deductibility (TAX). The name of the application, PERSONAL CHECK REGISTER, and the current checkbook balance are at the top of the worksheet.

It is important to be aware that 1-2-3 treats the column headings as field names. Column headings play a critical role in data management and are used in just about all steps of data manipulation. If a heading contains more than one line, 1-2-3 can use only the last line.

```
PERSONAL CHECK REGISTER

                      BALANCE              338.89
-----------------------------------------------------------------
NO.    DATE          PAYEE             AMOUNT     BUDGET     TAX

       08-Feb-90  Deposit Paycheck    1,850.00
858    09-Feb-90  Jewel Supermarket     (45.60)   food
859    10-Feb-90  Stroink Pathology Lab (30.00)   med         x
860    10-Feb-90  Harjak Motors         (45.55)   car
861    11-Feb-90  Jean's Flowers        (15.00)   fun
862    11-Feb-90  Dr. Theobald          (30.00)   med         x
863    11-Feb-90  St. Joseph's Hospital (35.00)   med         x
864    13-Feb-90  Osco Pharmacy         (12.79)   med         x
865    15-Feb-90  Illinois Power        (79.84)   util
866    15-Feb-90  Osco Pharmacy         (20.00)   med         x
867    15-Feb-90  Jewel Supermarket     (75.34)   food
868    16-Feb-90  Ed Curry Plumbing    (115.00)   rep
869    16-Feb-90  General Telephone Co. (45.24)   util
870    16-Feb-90  Braden Auditorium     (47.00)   fun
871    17-Feb-90  Jewel Supermarket     (22.75)   food
872    17-Feb-90  Illinois Power - Gas (114.00)   util
873    21-Feb-90  Bloomington Federal Bank (710.00) mtge
874    21-Feb-90  Osco Pharmacy         (18.00)   med         x
875    21-Feb-90  Home Sweet Home Mission (50.00) char        x
```

 Load the file EDCHECK, or follow the set of instructions given below. The first step in building the worksheet is to set the various column widths. Use the column widths given below. Remember, the column width command sequence is / Worksheet Column-Width Set. After you've reset the column widths, enter the appropriate headings in row 4; then enter the identifying information.

Column	Width	Heading
A	5	NO.
B	10	^DATE
C	25	^PAYEE
D	10	^AMOUNT
E	2	
F	9	BUDGET
G	9	TAX

A1   PERSONAL CHECK REGISTER
C2   "BALANCE
D2   @SUM (D5.D23)
A3   (Enter dashes for this cell, and
     copy across to the other cells.)

You must now place the above checkbook entries (records) in the worksheet.

1-2-3 DATABASE COMMANDS

Lotus 1-2-3's database manipulation commands are accessed through the Data option of the Main Menu.

QUERY MENU

The Query option of the Data Menu provides the actual database capability. The **Query Menu** contains the following options:

```
Input   Criterion   Output   Find   Extract   Unique   Delete   Reset   Quit
```

Input The **Input option,** which must be selected before you choose any database manipulation commands, is used to define the limits of the database to 1-2-3. The first row of the database contains the field labels for 1-2-3. (1-2-3 treats upper- and lowercase characters the same in labels.)

Criterion The **Criterion range option** determines selection or search criteria for extracting or finding information in the database. The range will have at least two rows: one for the heading and one for the selection or search criteria. The first criterion row has one or more column headings copied from the first row of the database; it is usually better to copy these headings into the criterion range than to enter them manually. Any embedded blanks included in the database labels but not included in criterion labels, or vice versa, will adversely affect a search. The second row, which is left blank, is the row where the various search or selection criteria are entered.

Output The **Output range option** is used in defining the area that is to hold "reports" of information that meets the conditions established in the criterion range.

Find The **Find command** moves the pointer (which is expanded to appear over an entire record) to the first record that meets the conditions established in the criterion range. Any other records that meet the criteria can also be accessed by depressing the Up and Down Arrow keys. The Down Arrow key moves the pointer to the next record below the pointer's present position that meets the criteria, and the Up Arrow moves the pointer to the next record above the pointer's present position that meets the criteria. When the last record that meets the criteria has been accessed, the computer will beep. You can move the pointer to the first or last record in the database by depressing the Home or End key, respectively. Depressing the Right or Left Arrow keys moves the cursor within the pointer. Depressing the Enter or Esc key cancels the search and returns you to the Query Menu.

Extract The **Extract command** creates the reports in the output range by extracting records from the database and copying them into the report area.

Unique If several records have the characteristics specified in the criterion range, the **Unique option** allows you to have only one of each grouping copied into the output area.

Delete The **Delete command** removes records that meet the criteria established in the criterion range and then compresses the database (removes any blank rows).

Reset When selected, the **Reset option** clears any previously established input, criterion, and output specifications.

Figure 8.1
The query settings sheet of 1-2-3

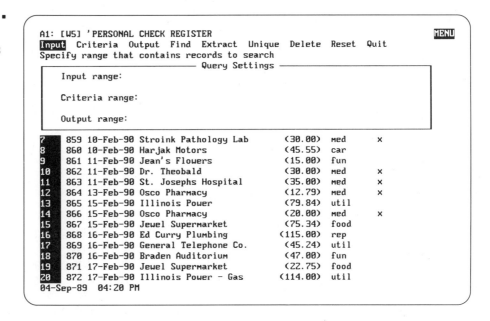

Quit The **Quit option** takes you out of the Query Menu and returns you to READY mode.

QUERY SETTINGS SHEET

Whenever the Query Menu of 1-2-3 is accessed, a query settings sheet is displayed to the screen (see Figure 8.1). This settings sheet provides information concerning the ranges needed in a 1-2-3 data management task.

BUILDING A DATABASE AND ACCESSING INFORMATION

The steps in building a database and accessing information from it are as follows:

1. The database (range) must be described in 1-2-3, and the headings row must be included in the range. This is accomplished via the Input option.
2. The criterion range must be built, and the search criteria must be specified to 1-2-3.
3. If an output report is desired, the output range has to be defined, but if you want only to locate records via the Find command, it does not.

The headings included in the criterion and output ranges must be very similar to the headings contained in the input range, because the output range headings will determine which fields are copied from the input range. If a field heading is not specified, the information in that field will not be copied from the input range to the output range.

Use the following commands to describe your database to 1-2-3:

/	Invokes the Main Menu
D	Selects the Data option

Q	Selects the Query option from the Data Menu
I	Defines the Input range of the database
A4.G23 [by entering cell addresses or by pointing]	Establishes the range of the database
Enter	Tells 1-2-3 to accept the database range

> **HINTS/HAZARDS**
>
> Lotus 1-2-3 expects the headings of the input and criterion ranges to be the same characters but does not require the case of the characters to be the same. This means, for instance, that the field name could be PAYEE in the input range and Payee in the criterion range. While the case of the characters is not important, the use of spaces is critical. The word *payee* with a trailing space is not the same as *payee* with no trailing space. If Lotus 1-2-3 encounters such a situation, it merely issues a beep without displaying an error message of any kind. This is one reason why it is important to use the Copy command to copy headings that are used in one database range to another database range.

THE CRITERION RANGE

For simple types of search (a **simple find**), the criterion range will consist of two rows: the first row holds the appropriate **criterion range headings** (field names); the second contains the search criteria, in the form of values or formulas.

Building the criterion range begins with copying the column headings contained in row 4 to another location on the worksheet (row 25). Then you must establish the criterion range by entering the following commands:

/	Invokes the Main Menu
D	Takes the Data option
Q	Selects the Query option from the Data Menu
C	Selects the Criterion option
A25.G26 [by entering the cell addresses or by pointing]	Establishes the criterion range
Enter	Tells 1-2-3 to execute the command
Q	Quits the Query Menu

In order to locate all the records in the medical budget category, you must first set up a search criterion like the following:

```
NO.     DATE        PAYEE           AMOUNT   BUDGET   TAX
                                             med
```

To find the desired records, enter the / Data Query Find command sequence and use the Up Arrow and Down Arrow keys to locate the records. Depress the Enter or Esc key when you are finished and want to return to the Query Menu.

To locate all tax-deductible records, use a Range Erase command on the budget cell and place an *x* in the tax criterion cell. The following criterion is appropriate:

NO.	DATE	PAYEE	AMOUNT	BUDGET	TAX
					x

Since the input range and the criterion range have already been established, and since the Find instruction has already been executed, a shortcut can be taken. Instead of finding these records by entering the / Data Query Find command, you can simply depress the **F7 Query function key** and move the pointer as specified above.

Now erase the contents of the tax criterion cell, using the Range Erase command, and locate all the records that contain an amount greater than $100. This task requires the following criterion range:

NO.	DATE	PAYEE	AMOUNT	BUDGET	TAX
			0		

You will notice that a zero appears in the tax entry cell, indicating that the condition for cell D5 is false. This doesn't give you much information; it would be more meaningful to have a display of the search formula used for the entire search than to have the result of the comparison for a single cell. Change the formula to text via the / Range Format Text command. Press the F7 Query function key.

Now find any checks that have an amount greater than $100 and belong to the mortgage budget category. The following criterion range is called for:

NO.	DATE	PAYEE	AMOUNT	BUDGET	TAX
			+D5<-100	mtge	

The formula happens, in this case, to go in the column (field) being searched, but it could just as easily be placed in any other field. The next criterion range example (shown below) locates any record that has a check amount greater than $100. The search formula has been placed in the Payee field, but 1-2-3 knows that you are looking for the check amount, since the column specified in the search is the Amount column (D).

Before you enter the following criterion range, make certain that you have erased the Budget and Amount criterion fields:

NO.	DATE	PAYEE	AMOUNT	BUDGET	TAX
		+D5<-100			

1-2-3 also allows you to use the following **wildcard characters** in the search criteria:

- * Finds entries that contain the same value to the left of the asterisk (Example: for* would find *fortune*, *formula*, and *fortuitous*.)
- ? Finds entries that contain the same value at every position besides the question mark (Example: c?t would find *cat*, *cut*, *cot*.

~ Finds entries that do not contain the same value at every named position (Example: ~Il* finds *formula*, *cat*, and *ignoramus*—but not *Ilium*.)

To find any record that has an entry in the Payee column starting with *Il*, the following criterion range is needed:

```
NO.    DATE      PAYEE            AMOUNT    BUDGET   TAX
                 Il*
```

To find any record having a budget entry other than *med*, the appropriate criterion range is as follows:

```
NO.    DATE      PAYEE            AMOUNT    BUDGET   TAX
                                            ~med
```

To find any record having a nonempty budget entry that does not start with the letter *m*, use the following criterion range:

```
NO.    DATE      PAYEE            AMOUNT    BUDGET   TAX
                                            ~m*
```

The above examples all illustrate how a simple search or a search using an **"and" condition** can be performed. Establishing a search with an **"or" condition** requires adding an additional row to the bottom of the criterion range after the Criterion option is selected. Before you can return to performing a simple search, the criterion range must be reduced by one row.

To find all records that have either a *med* budget designation and an amount greater than $25 or a *util* budget designation and an amount greater than $100, the criterion range is expressed as follows:

```
NO.    DATE      PAYEE            AMOUNT      BUDGET   TAX
                                  +D5<-25     med
                                  +D5<-100    util
```

What happens if you want to initiate a new search that can be ordered in a one-line criterion range, but you forget to shrink the criterion range from three rows back to two? After entering the criterion range and pressing the F7 key, you will find that every record in the database is selected. This is because a blank row tells 1-2-3 to select every record. You must shrink the criterion range back to two rows to avoid this problem.

FIND COMMAND AND EDITING/CHANGING RECORDS

Lotus 1-2-3 allows you to edit/change records after they have been located by the Find command. Once you have located a record, you can use the standard editing commands for making changes to the record. First, position the cursor to the appropriate field using the Right or Left Arrow keys and then press the F2 key. The data for this field now appear in the entry line of the control panel. Make any needed changes and press the Enter key when you are finished.

OUTPUT AND EXTRACT

The Output and Extract options of the Query Menu allow a user to compile a listing of records that correspond to certain predetermined criteria. The process of compiling the report is performed by the Extract command, but before records can be extracted, an area of the worksheet known as the output region must be defined to contain them.

The output region is formed by copying or entering the labels of the fields that you want to have in your report. For example, you can copy the labels from the criterion region and use them for the output region; then you take the Output option from the Query Menu and define the output range to 1-2-3 as the line of field headings. Any rows under the row of field headings that are needed to hold the desired records are automatically added to the output range.

After the output range has been defined, the Extract option can be used to instruct 1-2-3 to search the database in accordance with the criteria established in the criterion range and to place any records meeting those criteria in the output range. Any time the Extract command is executed, all records currently in the output range are erased; only the field headings remain from one extraction to another. The size of the output range is tracked by 1-2-3, and the only limit on it is the number of rows remaining beneath the Output headings that have been defined to 1-2-3. If 1,000 rows remain, room for 1,000 records remains in the output range.

After the output range has been defined to 1-2-3 and an extraction command has been executed, other criteria can be entered with the worksheet in READY mode. A new extraction can then be executed simply by depressing the F7 Query function key. If you want to create a hard copy listing of these various reports, you can command 1-2-3 to print out the output range between extraction commands.

On the worksheet, create an output range that contains the existing headings from the criterion range. It will also start in row 29.

/	Invokes the Main Menu
C	Selects the Copy option
A25.G25 [by entering the addresses or by pointing]	Establishes the "From" range
Enter	Tells 1-2-3 that the "From" range is established
A29 [by entering the address or by pointing]	Establishes the "To" range
Enter	Tells 1-2-3 to execute the move

Erase any existing criteria entries. Now place *food* in the budget criterion cell.

1. Tell 1-2-3 the output range.

/	Invokes the Main Menu
D	Selects the Data option
Q	Selects the Query option of the Data Menu
O	Selects the Output option of the Query Menu

A29.G29 [by pointer movement   Establishes the range of the
or address entry]   output range
Enter   Tells 1-2-3 to accept the output
                                range definition

2. Shrink the criterion range by one row.

   C   Selects the Criterion option
   Up Arrow   Shrinks the criterion range to two rows

3. Create the output report by taking the Extract option (E) from the Query Menu.

You should now see the following criterion and output ranges on your screen:

```
NO.   DATE        PAYEE                 AMOUNT      BUDGET       TAX
                                                    food

NO.   DATE        PAYEE                 AMOUNT      BUDGET       TAX
858   09-Feb-90   Jewel Supermarket     (45.60)     food
867   15-Feb-90   Jewel Supermarket     (75.34)     food
871   17-Feb-90   Jewel Supermarket     (22.75)     food
```

At this point, you can select the Quit option of the Query Menu and afterward enter new selection criteria for output records. Then you can direct 1-2-3 to extract the desired records and place them in the output area by depressing the F7 Query function key.

You may wish to see only records of tax-deductible payments. To get this listing, erase any existing criterion range entries with the Range Erase command. Then enter an *x* in the tax criterion cell, and press the F7 Query function key. You should now see the following criterion and output ranges on your screen:

```
NO.   DATE        PAYEE                 AMOUNT      BUDGET       TAX
                                                                 x

NO.   DATE        PAYEE                 AMOUNT      BUDGET       TAX
859   10-Feb-90   Stroink Pathology Lab (30.00)     med          x
862   11-Feb-90   Dr. Theobald          (30.00)     med          x
863   11-Feb-90   St. Josephs Hospital  (35.00)     med          x
864   13-Feb-90   Osco Pharmacy         (12.79)     med          x
866   15-Feb-90   Osco Pharmacy         (20.00)     med          x
874   21-Feb-90   Osco Pharmacy         (18.00)     med          x
875   21-Feb-90   Home Sweet Home Mission (50.00)   char         x
```

As you can see, the Extract option of 1-2-3 data management offers a user tremendous power to obtain different views of records contained in a database. You can use criteria as simple or as complex as you desire for extracting records.

Several large accounting firms have used 1-2-3's Extract option to examine a company's checking account during an auditing engagement. They can take the computerized records containing the checking account information and pass them to a 1-2-3 worksheet. The data management feature can then be used to extract the various groupings of records that the auditors feel should be examined. Using this feature drastically reduces the amount of time that must be spent on certain parts of an audit.

UNIQUE AND DELETE

Two other searches are provided by the data management option of 1-2-3. The first option, Unique, enables the user to print only nonduplicate records into an output range; the other, Delete, allows a user to remove any records from a database that meet certain criteria.

Unique Ed has lost his listing of budget categories and would like a new listing based on the budget entries contained in the database. This is an excellent application for the Unique command, which will allow only one occurrence of a budget category in a list.

For this application, redefine the output range to contain only the Budget category. This requires range erasing of any existing output range, followed by replacement with a single Budget field. You should also erase any entries in the criterion range—all records are to be included in this search. Now you are ready to redefine the output range as the Budget field. Select the Unique option on the Query Menu. Your worksheet criterion and output areas should look as follows:

```
NO.       DATE           PAYEE              AMOUNT      BUDGET      TAX

BUDGET

food
med
car
fun
util
rep
mtge
char
```

The blank entry above is the result of the blank Budget field entry of the deposit. As you see, none of the budget entries is duplicated.

Delete The Delete option is used to remove any unwanted or unneeded records from the database. When executed, the Delete command automatically compresses the remaining records in the database, removing all gaps and blank records (rows) in the database.

The criteria for the records to be deleted must be placed in the criterion range. It is usually safest to review records with the Extract command before deleting them. When you are certain that the Extract command has worked properly, you can feel sure that the Delete command will work, too.

Ed wrote a check to the Braden Auditorium for concert tickets. Unfortunately for Ed, the auditorium is sold out for the concert and has returned Ed's check. Ed would now like to remove the unwanted check and adjust the balance for his worksheet.

To be entirely safe, give your output area the same headings as the criterion range by copying the headings from the latter. You must also redefine the output range to 1-2-3, using the Query Menu option, in order to hold the entire heading line.

Now go to the Payee field of the criterion range and enter Bra* to select the Braden Auditorium check for extraction. Invoke the Query Menu and give the Extract command to 1-2-3. You should now have the following information in your criterion and output ranges:

```
NO.     DATE                PAYEE              AMOUNT      BUDGET      TAX
                    Bra*

NO.     DATE                PAYEE              AMOUNT      BUDGET      TAX
870   16-Feb-85  Braden Auditorium            (47.00)      fun
```

When the check to be deleted from the database is displayed, you can take the Delete option on the Query Menu. 1-2-3 then asks if you want to cancel the command or delete records, and you affirm the Delete option. The before and after views of the database are displayed below.

Before:

```
PERSONAL CHECK REGISTER

                          BALANCE      338.89
-----------------------------------------------------------------
NO.     DATE            PAYEE              AMOUNT      BUDGET    TAX
        08-Feb-90  Deposit Paycheck       1,850.00
858   09-Feb-90  Jewel Supermarket         (45.60)    food
859   10-Feb-90  Stroink Pathology Lab     (30.00)    med       x
860   10-Feb-90  Harjak Motors             (45.55)    car
861   11-Feb-90  Jean's Flowers            (15.00)    fun
862   11-Feb-90  Dr. Theobald              (30.00)    med       x
863   11-Feb-90  St. Josephs Hospital      (35.00)    med       x
864   13-Feb-90  Osco Pharmacy             (12.79)    med       x
865   15-Feb-90  Illinois Power            (79.84)    util
866   15-Feb-90  Osco Pharmacy             (20.00)    med       x
867   15-Feb-90  Jewel Supermarket         (75.34)    food
868   16-Feb-90  Ed Curry Plumbing        (115.00)    rep
869   16-Feb-90  General Telephone Co.     (45.24)    util
870   16-Feb-90  Braden Auditorium         (47.00)    fun
871   17-Feb-90  Jewel Supermarket         (22.75)    food
872   17-Feb-90  Illinois Power - Gas     (114.00)    util
873   21-Feb-90  Bloomington Federal Bank (710.00)    mtge
874   21-Feb-90  Osco Pharmacy             (18.00)    med       x
875   21-Feb-90  Home Sweet Home Mission   (50.00)    char      x
```

After:

```
PERSONAL CHECK REGISTER

                              BALANCE        385.89
     ------------------------------------------------------------------
NO.    DATE         PAYEE                   AMOUNT      BUDGET    TAX
       08-Feb-90  Deposit Paycheck        1,850.00
858    09-Feb-90  Jewel Supermarket         (45.60)     food
859    10-Feb-90  Stroink Pathology Lab     (30.00)     med       x
860    10-Feb-90  Harjak Motors             (45.55)     car
861    11-Feb-90  Jean's Flowers            (15.00)     fun
862    11-Feb-90  Dr. Theobald              (30.00)     med       x
863    11-Feb-90  St. Josephs Hospital      (35.00)     med       x
864    13-Feb-90  Osco Pharmacy             (12.79)     med       x
865    15-Feb-90  Illinois Power            (79.84)     util
866    15-Feb-90  Osco Pharmacy             (20.00)     med       x
867    15-Feb-90  Jewel Supermarket         (75.34)     food
868    16-Feb-90  Ed Curry Plumbing        (115.00)     rep
869    16-Feb-90  General Telephone Co.     (45.24)     util
871    17-Feb-90  Jewel Supermarket         (22.75)     food
872    17-Feb-90  Illinois Power - Gas     (114.00)     util
873    21-Feb-90  Bloomington Federal Bank (710.00)     mtge
874    21-Feb-90  Osco Pharmacy             (18.00)     med       x
875    21-Feb-90  Home Sweet Home Mission   (50.00)     char      x
```

Check 870 has been deleted from the database, the database has been compressed, and the checkbook balance has been updated.

HINTS/HAZARDS

Always use the Extract command before you use the Delete command. Not only do you have the opportunity to verify exactly which records will be deleted, but if you inadvertently delete the wrong records you have some form of temporary backup in the form of the records in the output range. This backup, however, disappears if another Extract command is issued.

1-2-3 STATISTICAL FUNCTIONS FOR DATABASE

In designing the data management facility for 1-2-3, the Lotus Corporation decided to include **statistical functions** for manipulating numeric data in a database. These functions are similar in nature to the regular 1-2-3 statistical functions and contain the same names with a leading @D to denote that they are database statistical functions; but they have been adapted for use in a database. The 1-2-3 statistical database functions are

@DCOUNT
@DAVG
@DMIN

@DMAX
@DSTD
@DVAR

Each of these functions has the following format:

```
@Function Name(Input Range,Offset,Criterion Range)
```

The Input Range is typically the same size as the database. Keep in mind that if you plan to copy these formulas you may have to provide absolute cell references.

The Offset tells 1-2-3 which field to use from the database in the function. A zero tells 1-2-3 to use the first column; 1 tells 1-2-3 to use the second column.

The Criterion Range portion of the formula gives the location of the criterion range specifying the criteria to be used in generating the statistics.

Ed wants some summary statistics about his checking account activity. Specifically, he wants information about the number of checks written, average check amount, high check amount, and low check amount, and he wants the summary to be in the following form:

```
Criterion     CHECK STATISTICS
AMOUNT        Number of Checks        17
              Average Amount       -86.12
              Highest Check Amount   -710
              Smallest Check Amount -12.79
```

To accomplish this, you must erase the existing criterion and output ranges. The new criterion range will consist of *Criterion* and *AMOUNT*, the latter entry telling 1-2-3 that all entries from offset column 3 are to be used in the calculations.

Enter the following information in the designated cells:

```
A25 Criterion
C25 CHECK STATISTICS
A26 AMOUNT
C26 Number of Checks
C27 Average Amount
C28 Highest Check Amount
C29 Smallest Check Amount
D26 @DCOUNT(A5..G22,3,A25..A26)
D27 @DAVG(A5..G22,3,A25..A26)
D28 @DMIN(A5..G22,3,A25..A26)
D29 @DMAX(A5..G22,3,A25..A26)
```

Format cells D26 to D29 for fixed decimals with two positions to the right of the decimal point.

You must begin the input range at cell A5 in order to avoid including the deposit record in the areas to be examined by the functions. You must also reverse the @DMIN and @DMAX functions, since you are dealing with negative numbers. The criterion range must be referenced in each formula in order to establish which parts of the column are to be included. Format the receiving cells to hold two decimal positions.

The checkbook worksheet should now appear as follows:

```
PERSONAL CHECK REGISTER

                         BALANCE        385.89
------------------------------------------------------------------------
NO.    DATE        PAYEE                    AMOUNT      BUDGET    TAX
       08-Feb-90 Deposit Paycheck         1,850.00
858    09-Feb-90 Jewel Supermarket          (45.60)     food
859    10-Feb-90 Stroink Pathology Lab      (30.00)     med       x
860    10-Feb-90 Harjak Motors              (45.55)     car
861    11-Feb-90 Jean's Flowers             (15.00)     fun
862    11-Feb-90 Dr. Theobald               (30.00)     med       x
863    11-Feb-90 St. Josephs Hospital       (35.00)     med       x
864    13-Feb-90 Osco Pharmacy              (12.79)     med       x
865    15-Feb-90 Illinois Power             (79.84)     util
866    15-Feb-90 Osco Pharmacy              (20.00)     med       x
867    15-Feb-90 Jewel Supermarket          (75.34)     food
868    16-Feb-90 Ed Curry Plumbing         (115.00)     rep
869    16-Feb-90 General Telephone Co.      (45.24)     util
871    17-Feb-90 Jewel Supermarket          (22.75)     food
872    17-Feb-90 Illinois Power - Gas     (114.00)     util
873    21-Feb-90 Bloomington Federal Bank (710.00)     mtge
874    21-Feb-90 Osco Pharmacy              (18.00)     med       x
875    21-Feb-90 Home Sweet Home Mission    (50.00)     char      x

Criterion   CHECK STATISTICS
AMOUNT       Number of Checks          17
             Average Amount        -86.12
             Highest Check Amount    -710
             Smallest Check Amount -12.79
```

CHAPTER REVIEW

The third part of 1-2-3 is data management. A 1-2-3 database is held entirely in a worksheet; there is no disk input/output involved, as there is in dBASE. A row is equal to a record, and a column is equal to a field of data. The database portion of the spreadsheet must be identified for 1-2-3.

Column headings play the important role in data management of acting as field names for the various fields in a record. They are also essential in setting up the criterion range. Any heading in a criterion range must be almost identical to the field name heading, since any difference other than character case will result in a beep from the computer, signifying that no match was found.

The criterion range is an area set up to determine which records are to be located, extracted, or deleted. At a minimum, the criterion range consists of two rows: The first contains the headings, and the second is used for establishing which records from the database are to be used. An "and" condition is specified by entering selection criteria in more than one criterion field on the same line; an "or" condition is established by expanding the criterion range by one or more rows. If any row is left blank, 1-2-3 will select all records in the worksheet.

After the Find command has been selected, the Query function key (F7) can be used to locate records in the database. 1-2-3 highlights the selected record with an expanded pointer that appears over the entire record. The cursor within the pointer can be moved via the Arrow keys.

Three wildcard characters are used in establishing criteria: The asterisk (*) works similarly to the way it does in DOS; the question mark (?) also works as it does in DOS; the tilde (˜) is a negation symbol, selecting any character string in the specified column that does not match the string it accompanies.

The output region and the Extract command work together. The output range is set up to hold any records that have been extracted from the database; records are extracted if they meet the criteria established in the criterion range. The output range also requires field names that are very similar to the database field names.

The final database commands are Unique and Delete. The Unique command reports only unique occurrences of the contents of a data field. The Delete command deletes records from the database that meet the criteria established in the criterion range.

The 1-2-3 package also provides a complete set of functions for use with a database. These functions all start with @D and are therefore easily distinguishable from other functions. The functions, too, are tied to the criterion range.

KEY TERMS AND CONCEPTS

"and" condition
criterion range headings
Criterion range option
database statistical functions
data management file
Delete command
Extract command
field
field name
Find command
immediate mode
Input option
"or" condition

Output range option
Query function key F7
Query Menu
query settings sheet
Quit option
record
Reset option
simple find
Unique option
wildcard characters
*
˜
?

CHAPTER QUIZ

Multiple Choice

1. Which of the following statements is true about 1-2-3 data management?
   a. The file is contained on disk.
   b. Disk I/O is common.
   c. A file is limited in size to 35,000 records.
   d. The entire file must be contained in RAM.
   e. Indexes are used to speed data retrieval.
   f. All of the above statements are true.

2. Which of the following statements is false about 1-2-3 data management?
   a. A record is contained in a spreadsheet row.
   b. A field is contained in a spreadsheet column cell.
   c. The amount of RAM memory can limit the number of records in the database.
   d. The column headings are used as field names.
   e. All of the above statements are true.
   f. None of the above statements is true.

3. What is the minimum number of data management "pieces" that have to be defined to find a record in the database?
   a. The input and the criterion ranges
   b. The input range, the criterion range, and the output range
   c. The input and the output ranges
   d. The input and the extract ranges
   e. The delete and the output ranges
   f. None of the above responses is correct.

4. Which commands are used together for creating reports using records from a database?
   a. Unique and Delete
   b. Output and Unique
   c. Output and Extract
   d. Output and Find
   e. Output and Criterion
   f. None of the above responses is correct.

5. 1-2-3 data management provides
   a. password protection.
   b. random access.
   c. disk file storage.
   d. fast sorting for large files.
   e. the ability to store complex programs for manipulating data.
   f. none of the above.

True/False

6. Data management in 1-2-3 is in immediate mode. This means that commands are entered from the keyboard.

7. If a line in the criterion range is blank, all records from the database are selected.

8. It does not matter if upper- and lowercase characters are used differently in the field name than in the criterion range.

9. If five fields are listed in the input range, all five field names must appear in the criterion range headings.

10. The Delete command provides an "unerase" ability to restore records that have been mistakenly erased.

Answers

1. d   2. e   3. a   4. c   5. f   6. t   7. t   8. t   9. f   10. f

Exercises

1. Define or describe each of the following:
   a. 1-2-3 data management file
   b. record
   c. field
   d. field name
   e. query range
   f. output range

2. A spreadsheet row is used to contain a database _____.

3. A spreadsheet column is used to contain a database _____ _____.

4. A database with 2,000 records takes _____ hours to sort.

5. Field names are defined by column _____.

6. The database is defined by using the _____ command.

7. The _____ range determines which records are selected or deleted.

8. The Output and _____ are usually used together.

9. List the steps you would have to perform if you wished simply to find records.
   a.

   b.

10. A blank line in the criterion range results in _____ from the database being selected.

11. The _____ command results in all database settings being erased.

12. The _____ command is used to generate a report of each "type" within a field.

13. The _____ command is used to erase unwanted records from the database.

14. List the wild cards and their functions.
    a.

    b.

    c.

15. Two lines under the criterion range headings are used for _____ _____ condition searches.

COMPUTER EXERCISES

Set up a name and address database like the following:

```
                      Name and Address Database
-----------------------------------------------------------------------
    Last       First     In       Address          City         St   ZIP
  Ghorbani     Reza      R.   4033 N. Wolcott    Chicago        Il  60712
  Ghorbani     Ann       B.   4033 N. Wolcott    Chicago        Il  60712
  Acklin       Douglas   C.   408 E. Monroe      Bloomington    Il  61701
  Walters      Barbara   A.   1981 Crestlawn     Arlington      Va  13411
  Adams        Arthur    V.   115 Ginger Creek Ct. Bloomington  Il  61701
  Davis        Russell   B.   707 Vale St.       Bloomington    Il  61701
  Acklin       Debbie    C.   408 E. Monroe      Bloomington    Il  61701
  Posio        Harvey    B.   1013 Hillcrest     San Diego      Ca  94307
  Pietrowiak   Ben       A.   3334 N. Foster     Normal         Il  61761
  Acklin       Sandy     C.   408 E. Monroe      Bloomington    Il  61701
  Ficek        Fred      R.   1215 Tamarack      Normal         Il  61761
  Decesario    Juan      C.   1214 Flores        Miami          Fl  12562
```

Use the following column widths and labels (you can center the labels using the / Range Label Prefix command after they have been entered):

A	12	Last
B	10	First
C	2	In
D	1	
E	20	Address
F	1	
G	15	City
H	2	St
I	1	
J	6	Zip

C1   Name and Address Database

Create the database, using the above data. Be sure to start each address with a single quote ('); if you do not, Lotus will try to treat the entry as a number rather than as an alphanumeric address. When you have created the database, save it to CH1GEXR1; then copy the headings and create the criterion range.

1. Find any records with a 94307 ZIP code.

2. Find any records with a ZIP code greater than 70000.

3. Find any records with a last name of Acklin.

4. Find any records that do not have an Il state designation.

5. Establish an output area, and then extract any records outside of ZIP code 61701.

6. Extract any records with a last name of Ghorbani.

7. Extract any records from Normal.

8. Extract any records outside Illinois.

9. Extract only records with a unique last name.

10. Fred Ficek moved. Delete this record, but first extract it to make sure that the selection criteria have been properly given to 1-2-3.

CHAPTER 9

SPREADSHEET MACROS

CHAPTER OBJECTIVE

After completing this chapter, you should be able to:

- **Discuss the concepts of macros**
- **Build a macro**
- **Place macros in the worksheet correctly**
- **Use special macro commands**
- **Detect and correct errors in macros**
- **Create some simple macros**

INTRODUCTION TO MACROS

The macro feature of the 1-2-3 package sets it apart from all other spreadsheets. Macros enable you to automate just about any part of your worksheet with a minimum of effort. They enable you to store keystrokes as text in a cell and then execute those stored keystrokes. A macro, more or less, is simply a repository of keystrokes.

A **macro** is only a cell of text that has a special name (range name); it is created by entering the keystrokes (or their representation) in a cell. With some of the advanced commands using the Lotus 1-2-3 command language, macros can be made to resemble programs. A macro is capable of containing complex logic that controls how a worksheet executes and of building a menu from which users can select the operations or tasks that they want to perform. Some of these advanced commands are similar to BASIC's If-Then-Else, GoTo, and GoSub commands.

Macros in 1-2-3 can have global effects on a worksheet and should be used with care. Complex macros are not recommended for the spreadsheet novice, but you do not have to know everything about 1-2-3 to use simple ones.

Complex macros that contain control logic may be easier to create if you have some programming background. It doesn't matter what language you have used. Prior programming experience enables you to solve a problem using a structured approach. Simple macros, however, can be created and used by any individual who understands how a spreadsheet's menu structure works.

If you are seated at a computer, prepare for the following example by loading (retrieving) the worksheet file COMPSALS. Set the global format of the worksheet to general.

Suppose you want to create a macro that will format the current cell to contain currency data with two positions to the right of the decimal. Before you create the macro, let's review the keystrokes you would use from 1-2-3 to accomplish this task:

/	Invokes the Main Menu
R	Selects the Range option from the Main Menu
F	Selects the Format option to change a portion of the worksheet
C	Tells 1-2-3 that you want to use the currency format to display data within a range
Enter	Tells 1-2-3 that you want to take the default of two positions to the right of the decimal point
Enter	Tells 1-2-3 that this is the only cell in the range

As you can see, the task of formatting a single worksheet cell to currency with two decimal positions requires six keystrokes. These keystrokes can be placed in a single cell and then executed. Position your pointer to any unused cell in your worksheet, such as H23, to enter the macro. The content of this cell appears below:

```
'/rfc~~
```

You enter this macro into a cell of the worksheet exactly the same way that you would enter any other label. First you type the label prefix (', ", or ^). Otherwise, the / will execute immediately to tell 1-2-3 to display the Main Menu in the control panel. Any macro that begins with a nontext character must contain a label prefix (typically '). If it doesn't, 1-2-3 will start to execute the commands.

Figure 9.1
The listing of named ranges displayed via the Run command (Alt + F3)

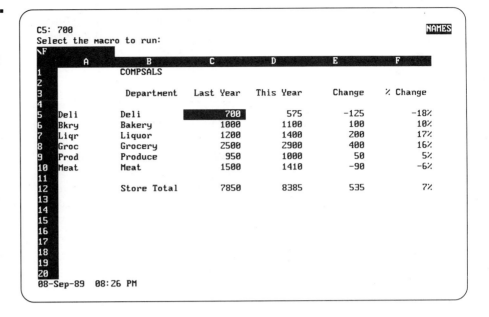

The next four characters (commands) represent the keystrokes used to create this desired format. /RFC is the same keystroke shorthand that you've seen before. It means / Range Format Currency. The two characters at the end of the macro are called *tildes*. Each represents one Enter keystroke. In the preceding macro, the Enter key is to be pressed twice. It does not matter whether the keystrokes are entered in upper- or lowercase.

Once you have entered a macro into a worksheet cell, you must give it a special range name before it can be executed. The pointer is positioned to the cell containing the macro instructions, and the / Range Name Create command is issued. Beginning with Release 2.2 of Lotus 1-2-3, a macro can be given any range name or it may consist of two characters (a method supported by earlier releases of 1-2-3). If a 1-2-3 macro name consists of two characters, the first character is always a backslash (\), which tells the spreadsheet that a macro name is to be built. The second character is a letter. Name the cell containing your macro \F (abbreviation for Format). Be sure to press the Enter key to tell 1-2-3 that this is the only cell in this range.

You can now execute this macro by positioning the pointer to any numeric cell in the COMPSALS worksheet that you want to format and then issuing the keystrokes Alt + F. This means that the Alt key and the alphabetic F key must be held down at the same time. The Alt followed by any letter tells 1-2-3 that it should find the macro with that name and execute it. If there is no macro with that name, the computer will beep, indicating that 1-2-3 cannot find the macro. You now see that the format for the contents of the cell has changed.

If you gave the macro a range name such as *save*, the macro must be executed using the Run command (Alt + F3). Once the Run command has been issued, a listing of the named ranges in your worksheet is displayed at the top of the screen (see Figure 9.1). You can now either manually enter the name of the range containing the macro instructions or you can position the pointer to the appropriate named range and press the Enter key.

Please note that if you name a macro with a backslash followed by another character, these macro names will appear at the end of the named range listing.

They can be easily accessed by pressing the Left Arrow key immediately following the Run command, which places you at the end of the listing of named ranges instead of at the beginning.

SPECIAL KEYS

By now you may have noticed that the Enter key could not be stored in a cell as a macro command without using some other special representation, in this case the tilde (~), to signify this keystroke. Many keys must have special key representations before they can be used in spreadsheet macros. These special keys are divided into three groups: function keys, pointer positioning keys, and other special keys. Below is a complete list of the special key representations recognized by 1-2-3 for use in macros.

Function Keys:

{EDIT}	Edits content of current cell (F2)
{NAME}	Displays a list of range names in the worksheet (F3)
{ABS}	Converts relative reference to absolute (F4)
{GOTO}	Jumps cursor to cell coordinates (F5)
{WINDOW}	Moves the cursor to the other side of the window (F6)
{QUERY}	Repeats most recent query operation (F7)
{TABLE}	Repeats most recent table operations (F8)
{CALC}	Recalculates worksheet (F9)
{GRAPH}	Redraws current graph (F10)
{APP1}	APP1 activates the add-in assigned to the key Alt + F7
{APP2}	APP2 activates the add-in assigned to the key Alt + F8
{APP3}	APP3 activates the add-in assigned to the key Alt + F9
{APP4}	APP4 activates the add-in assigned to the key Alt + F10

Pointer Positioning Keys:

{UP} or {U}	Moves pointer up one row
{DOWN} or {D}	Moves pointer down one row
{LEFT} or {L}	Moves pointer left one column
{RIGHT} or {R}	Moves pointer right one column
{Big Right}	Moves pointer to the right a screen at a time
{Big Left}	Moves pointer to the left a screen at a time
{PGUP}	Moves pointer up 20 rows

{HOME}	Moves pointer to cell A1
{END}	Used with an Arrow or Home key

Other Special Keys:

{DEL}	Used with {EDIT} to delete a single character
{ESC}	Used to evoke the Esc command
{BS}	Used to move the cursor via the Backspace key
{?}	Causes the macro to pause and wait for keyboard input; the macro resumes executing when you press the Enter key
~	Represents one Enter keystroke
{INS}	Used to change between INSERT and OVERWRITE mode
/, <, or {MENU}	Used to invoke the Main Menu
{~}	Used for data management wildcard searches
{{}	Used to represent the left brace
{}}	Used to represent the right brace

Representations such as these are used for all the special keys on the IBM PC keyboard. The name of the key is always enclosed in braces. If you enclose in braces a phrase that is not a function or key name, 1-2-3 returns the error message

```
Unrecognized key name {...}
```

An important special key representation is {?}, which is similar to BASIC's Input command. When 1-2-3 encounters a {?} in a macro, it pauses and waits for the user to enter data from the keyboard. Once data are typed in and the Enter key is pressed, the data are stored in the current cell.

Modifying the Macro Suppose that you want to modify the macro that was just entered to format an entire column rather than operating on just one cell at a time. In the current example, you could enter the appropriate number of {down} commands to include the correct number of cells that appear in the column. This method, however, lacks the flexibility that is needed if you want to be able to add or delete rows that might appear in the column to be formatted. How is this flexibility accomplished? Remember the role of the End key when you are moving the pointer from one position to another. In this case, the End key followed by a Down Arrow key positions the pointer from its current location to the last occupied cell in this group of cells (the bottom of the column). If you also wanted to include a TOTAL cell, you could add two Down Arrow commands. To include this ability, the macro can be changed to the following:

```
/RFC~{end}{down}{down}{down}~
```

To format a column of numbers, you now position the pointer to the beginning of the column and issue the Alt + F command. How many cells are included in the column now no longer matters. The only limitation is that the column can have no blank cells (a blank cell marks the end of the range for the {end}{down} command).

BUILDING MORE MACROS

You are now going to build a macro that can be used to save an existing worksheet, COMPSALS, to disk. You must issue the following commands from the keyboard every time you want to save a worksheet: / File Save Enter (accept the default filename) Replace.

Position the pointer to an unused cell (H25) in your worksheet. Now enter the following character string: '/FS~R. Make certain that there are no embedded blanks in the macro. A blank causes the macro to stop executing. Press the Enter key. You should now have a cell with the following contents:

```
'/fs~r
```

Use the / Range Name Create command and give this cell the name \S. Issue an Alt + S command from the keyboard to execute the macro. The worksheet should now be saved to disk. The worksheet just saved contains the macros that you have created.

Next, you are going to build a macro that can be used to insert columns in the worksheet. You must issue the following commands from the keyboard each time you want to insert a row in a worksheet: / Worksheet Insert Column Enter.

Position the pointer to an unused cell (J25) in your worksheet. Now enter the following character string: '/WIC~. Make certain that there are no embedded blanks in the macro. Press the Enter key. You should now have a cell with the following contents:

```
'/wic~
```

Use the / Range Name Create command and give this cell the name \C. After you position the pointer where you want to insert a column, issue an Alt + C command to execute the macro.

CREATING A MACRO WITH A REGULAR RANGE NAME

As you no doubt remember from the beginning of the chapter, you can, in addition to naming a macro with a backslash (\) and an alphabetic character, also use a regular range name. Remember, however, that a macro containing a regular named range must be invoked using the Run (Alt + F3) command.

The next macro allows you to set a column to a width of 25. Position the pointer to an unused cell (L25) in your worksheet. Enter the following character string: '/WCS25~. Again, make certain that there are no embedded blanks within the macro. Press the Enter key. You should now have a cell with the following contents:

```
'/WCS25~
```

Use the / Range Name Create command and give this cell the name WIDTH. After you position the pointer where you want to change the width of a column, issue the command Alt + F3, highlight the named range WIDTH, and press the Enter key. The width of the column at the pointer location should now be changed.

Most macros can be stored initially in a single cell, but some complex macros require more than one cell. Any other cells in a column that make up the macro are automatically included in the macro. A macro continues to execute instructions in a top-down, left-to-right fashion until it comes to a blank or a blank cell. There can be no embedded blanks between the commands in a cell (except label data). The blank cell tells the spreadsheet that this is the end of the macro.

HINTS/HAZARDS Be sure to check your macros to make certain that you have matching braces { } around any special words. Also, make certain that you have included tildes (~) to represent an Enter keystroke where 1-2-3 would normally expect to find them. Braces and tildes are the most frequently omitted characters in entering macros.

USING 1-2-3'S LEARN MODE FOR ENTERING MACROS

Up to this point, you have been recording macro instructions by manually entering them from the keyboard. 1-2-3 also allows you to place the spreadsheet in LEARN mode and automatically record keystrokes, at specified cells in the form of a macro, as you enter commands from the keyboard. The cells in which the keystrokes are recorded make up a **learn range.**

The Learn feature of 1-2-3 has the advantage that it allows you to both record and test a macro at the same time. Since you are actually executing an instruction at the same time that you are recording the keystrokes, the screen appears as it will when the macro executes. The Learn feature also minimizes data entry errors that can occur if you improperly spell one of the special key commands used in 1-2-3. Creating a macro using the Learn feature requires you to follow four steps:

1. Specify a learn range in which the keystrokes and instructions can be recorded in a worksheet. This range must be a series of cells within a single column.
2. Record keystrokes for a macro by actually executing the command using regular 1-2-3 keystroke commands at the keyboard.
3. Name the macro using the / Range Name Create command. Only the first cell in the learn range containing this macro needs to be named.
4. Execute the macro to make certain it works properly. If you entered some additional keystrokes that are not actually needed for proper execution, the macro can be edited and the unneeded command deleted. Make certain that there are no embedded spaces when you have finished making changes.

Creating a Learn Range Using the Learn command of 1-2-3 requires you to select the Learn option from the Worksheet submenu. The menu displayed is as follows:

Range Cancel Erase

Range The **Range option** is selected to indicate to 1-2-3 which cells will be used to hold the macro instructions.

Cancel The **Cancel option** is selected if you wish to turn off the Learn feature.

Erase The **Erase option** is selected if you wish to erase the cells containing macro commands in the learn range.

Before you can use 1-2-3's Learn feature, you must specify a range of cells in a single column that is to hold the keystrokes for the macro. If you specify several columns, 1-2-3 will take only the cells in the first column of the range. As a general rule, it is safest to include more cells than you think you will need for the macro instructions. A learn range for the COMPSALS file is created from cells N23 through N43 by issuing the following commands after you have positioned your pointer to cell N23.

/	Invokes the Main Menu
W	Selects the Worksheet option
L	Selects the Learn option
R	Selects the Range option
.	Nails down the beginning of the range
PgDn	Extends the range to cell N43
Enter	Executes the command

Recording Keystrokes with Learn Once the learn range has been created, you can activate the Learn feature by issuing the Learn command (Alt + F5). Any commands that are entered from the keyboard are placed in the learn range. If you record more keystrokes than can be held in the specified learn range, 1-2-3 automatically turns off the Learn feature and displays an error message indicating that the learn range is full. In such a situation, you may have to make your learn range larger and erase the characters in the present learn range with the / Worksheet Learn Erase command.

Suppose you wish to create a macro that will, when the pointer is placed at the first cell of a column of numbers, perform a range format of comma (,) with two decimal positions in all cells except the total cell. For the total cell of that column, the macro will execute a range format of currency with two decimal positions. When the macro is created, give it the name COLFORMT.

1. Use the Learn feature to record these keystrokes, using the following commands.

C5	Positions the pointer to cell C5
Alt + F5	Executes the Learn command to record keystrokes
/	Invokes the Main Menu
R	Selects the Range option
F	Selects the Format option
,	Selects the Comma (,) command
Enter	Selects two positions to the right of the decimal
End	Press the End key
Down	Press the Down key
Enter	Executes the command
End	Press the End key

Figure 9.2
The macro created using the Learn command

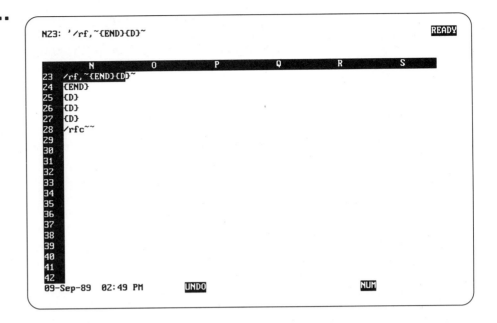

	Down	Press the Down key to position the pointer to the bottom of the column
	Down	Press the Down key
	Down	Press the Down key to position the pointer to the cell containing the total
	/	Invokes the Main Menu
	R	Selects the Range option
	F	Selects the Format option
	C	Selects the Currency command
	Enter	Selects two positions to the right of the decimal
	Enter	Formats this cell only and executes the instruction
	Alt + F5	Turns off the LEARN mode
	F5	Executes the GoTo command
	N23	Positions the pointer to cell N23 and examines the macro (see Figure 9.2)

2. Name the macro.

	M23	Positions the pointer to cell M23
	COLFORMT	Enters the command containing the macro name
	N23	Positions the pointer to cell N23
	/	Invokes the Main Menu
	R	Selects the Range option
	N	Selects the Name option
	C	Selects the Create option
	COLFORMT	Enters the name of the macro
	Enter	Executes the command

Remember, if you made any keystrokes entering the macro, they can be corrected using the Edit (F2) command. While you are editing the macro, however, make certain that you do not embed blanks or leave a blank cell.

You can now execute this macro by positioning the pointer to the first cell in a column and issuing the Run (Alt + F3) command, selecting the COLFORMT range name, and pressing the Enter key. Of course, if you had named this macro with a backslash (\) followed by an alphabetic character, you would have executed this macro with the Alt + _ command.

You should be aware that 1-2-3 does not record keystrokes using the Learn feature for the following cases or commands.

> When you are using the Learn command
> Compose (Alt + F1)
> Run (Alt + F3)
> Undo (Alt + F4)
> Num Lock
> Caps Lock
> Print Screen
> Step (Alt + F2)
> Scroll Lock
> Help (F1)

Once you have finished creating a macro using the Learn feature of 1-2-3 and want to create another macro using Learn, you must be careful to reset the learn range to another group of cells. Otherwise these new macro instructions will be added to the existing macro in the specified learn range.

EXAMINING A SAMPLE MACRO

Load the MACROSAL worksheet from the student disk. There appears to be nothing in it, but a macro called B is on the disk. This macro will build the COMPSALS worksheet that was used earlier. Execute it using the Alt + B command. After executing the macro, you should see the worksheet below:

```
COMPSALS

Department    Last Year    This Year    Change      % Change

Deli             700.00       575.00    (125.00)     -17.9%
Bakery         1,000.00     1,100.00     100.00       10.0%
Liquor         1,200.00     1,400.00     200.00       16.7%
Grocery        2,500.00     2,900.00     400.00       16.0%
Produce          950.00     1,000.00      50.00       -5.3%
Meat           1,500.00     1,410.00     (90.00)      -6.0%

Store Total    7,850.00     8,385.00     535.00       -6.8%
```

You can view the macro used to generate the worksheet by pressing the F5 (GoTo) function key and typing and entering the range name MACROS. As you can see in the following macro used to build the COMPSALS worksheet, a macro can consist of more than one cell (as long as the cells are in a column). This macro appears to be composed of three columns, but it really consists only of the entries in the middle column. Notice also that the macro shown below has blank lines between some of the entries. These blank lines have been included to make the document more readable. A "real" macro would not have blank rows.

\B	'{goto}b1~	The following 14 cells provide for entering row and column headings.
	'COMPSALS{down}{down}	
	'Department{right}	
	'LastYear{right}	
	'ThisYear{right}	
	'Change{right}	
	'% Change{right}	
	'{goto}b5~Deli{down}	
	'Bakery{down}	
	'Liquor{down}	
	'Grocery{down}	
	'Produce{down}	
	'Meat{down}{down}	
	'Store Total~{goto}c5~	
	'/wgc12~	Sets the global column width to 12.
	'700{right}	Enter the dollar sales for each department.
	'575{down}	
	'1100{left}	
	'1000{down}	
	'1200{right}	
	'1400{down}	
	'2900{left}	
	'2500{down}	
	'950{right}	
	'1000{down}	
	'1410{left}	
	'1500{down}{down}	
	'@sum(c5.c10)~	Sum last year's sales.
	'/c~{right}~	Copy this formula to the ThisYear column
	'/wgf,~	Set the global format to the comma (,).
	'pr{goto}e5~+d5-c5~	Go to cell E5 and enter the formula for the dollar change.
	'/c~e6.e12~	Copy this formula down the column.
	'{right}+et/c5~	Position the pointer to cell E5 and enter the percent change formula.
	'/c~f6.f12~	Copy this formula down the column.
	'{goto}f11~/re{left}~	Position the pointer to cell F11 and erase the garbage.
	'{goto}f5~/rfp1~f5.f12~	Position the pointer to cell F5 and format this column for percent display.
	'/rlrf5.c3~	Right-Justify the column headings.
	'/pprb1.f12~gpq	Print the worksheet, advance the page, and quit the Print Menu.
	'/fsnewmacro~r	Save the file to a new worksheet called NEWMACRO.

The leftmost and rightmost columns document the macro. The \B entry serves only to alert the user that the entries to the right contain keystrokes for the B macro. It can, however, be used with the / Range Name Label Right command to give the macro a range name. In this instance, you can position the pointer on the cell that contains the \B entry, issue the / Range Name Label command, indicate that the range is to the right of the pointer, and press the Enter key. This takes the \B range name and uses it to name the cell to the right of the pointer location. The macro is now named \B. The remark helps not only to name the macro but also to locate it on the worksheet.

The rightmost column explains the task performed by the macro instructions in each cell. Entries in this column are not part of the macro; their function is solely to make the macro easier to understand and to change.

RULES FOR ENTERING MACROS

The following rules apply when you enter macros:

1. Use a comment to name the macro. Place a backslash (\) in the cell to the left of the macro location followed by the one-character name of the macro. Remember, you can use only letters. Do not use the same character twice. Enter a single quote (') before the backslash.
2. Name the cell by using the / Range Name Create, or, because the name of the macro is already in a cell, use the / Range Name Label Right command.
3. Do not embed blanks in a macro (blanks within a label are permitted). A blank causes a macro to stop.
4. Multiple cells can be used to contain a macro as long as they are in the same column. Again, the rule about blanks applies; a blank cell in a column may cause the macro to terminate.
5. Unless an alphabetic character or brace ({) is the first character in a macro, it must be preceded by a label prefix (usually '). When you are entering numbers, for example, they must be preceded by a single quote (').
6. A cell containing a macro can have a maximum of 240 characters (the limit for any cell). A macro is much more readable, however, if you keep the number of macro commands in a cell confined to a small portion of an automated task.

PLACEMENT OF MACROS

You do not usually want to place macros inside your worksheet model. Keeping macros outside the active area helps prevent you from erasing them accidentally. You usually place worksheet macros to the lower right of your main model in an unused area of the worksheet—in the lower right-hand corner because this area of the worksheet is not affected when you delete rows or columns. This arrangement is depicted in Figure 9.3, in which the worksheet is divided into four quadrants or areas.

Many users adopt a standard cell location in worksheets for starting macros to prevent confusion in locating them for later maintenance. The easiest way to keep track of the location of macros, however, is to give the macro area of your worksheet a range name like MACROS. This allows you to use the GoTo (F5) function key. When you press the F5 key, you can type in MACROS, and the spreadsheet will place the pointer in the upper left-hand corner of that range.

MACRO DOCUMENTATION

When you write a macro, remember that you are performing a process that is very similar to programming. Good programmers place remark statements inside program code to remind themselves, and to inform others, which tasks are performed within a block of code. You should do the same with macros.

Figure 9.3
Quadrants of the worksheet

| Area of the worksheet that contains your "model" | Area of the worksheet affected by adding/ deleting rows |
| Area of the worksheet affected by adding/ deleting rows | Area of the worksheet that is "safe" for storing macros |

You can document your macros by placing explanatory text in the cell to the right of the macro instructions. Including these comments will make your macros easier to read. Your macros will also be easier to read if you make the column width of the macro column wide enough to display all macros completely so that the macro portions are visible and you can see the comments for every macro cell. This method will save you from wasting time later trying to figure out what you were trying to accomplish.

ENTERING SOME SIMPLE MACROS

The following multiple-cell macro serves no useful purpose except for allowing you to enter your first multiple-cell macro. Load the file COMPSALS from your data disk. Then move the pointer to cell G28 and enter the following macro. Be sure that you use the / Range Name Label Right command to name the macro.

```
\R    {right}{right}{right}      Move the pointer to the right.
      {down}{down}{down}         Move the pointer down.
      {left}{left}{left}         Move the pointer to the left.
      {up}{up}{up}               Move the pointer up
```

Press the Tab key one time. You can now execute this macro by issuing the Alt + R command. A rectangle of sorts appears on the screen. You can reexecute this command by issuing multiple Alt + R commands.

When you are creating macros that require pointer positioning commands, you can also use the abbreviated version of the command like those that follow:

{D} for {DOWN}

{U} for {UP}

{R} for {RIGHT}

{L} for {LEFT}

A strong case can be made, however, for using the full version of the name. This makes the macro more self-documenting and, therefore, easier to understand and maintain if it has to be used by a large number of people.

When you are using multiple pointer position commands, you are allowed to use a repetition factor inside the brackets. For example, the command {DOWN 3} tells 1-2-3 to move the pointer using three down commands. The \R macro could be entered using the following commands:

```
\R      {right 3}       Move the pointer to the right.
        {down 3}        Move the pointer down.
        {left 3}        Move the pointer to the left.
        {up 3}          Move the pointer up.
```

Using the repetition factor with pointer positioning commands actually results in making the macro easier to read and, therefore, more self-documenting.

You can use the following macro to print the worksheet; it should begin in cell G37. Be sure to name the macro. Execute the macro.

```
\P      /ppc~a                  Select print option, clear, and align.
        rb1.f12~                Tell what to print.
        oml8~                   Select the left-hand margin.
        fPage #!COMPSALS!@~q    Tell 1-2-3 to print a footer line.
        gpq                     Print the worksheet, advance to the next
                                page, and quit.
```

The next macro is used to generate a bar chart that compares the sales of the various departments for the two years of sales information contained in the worksheet. It also places legends and titles, views the graph, and returns you to READY mode. Start at cell G44. Be sure to name the macro. Now execute the macro.

```
\G      /gr~                            Select the Graph Menu and reset.
        tb                              Select the Bar Type.
        xb5.b10~                        Use Department names for X range.
        ac5.c10~                        Select Column B for A data range.
        bd5.d10~                        Select Column C for B data range.
        olaThis Year~                   Set Legend for A data range.
        lbLast Year~                    Set Legend for B data range.
        tfEd's Supermarket~             Enter title lines.
        tsThis Year vs. Last Year's Sales~
        txDepartments~                  Enter X and Y titles.
        tyDollar Sales~
        quq                             Quit Options, View, and Quit Graph.
```

PLANNING FOR MACROS

As you can see from the examples, macros often include a fairly large number of keystrokes. You may also try to incorporate a spreadsheet command that you do not know well. For these reasons, you should properly plan your macro before you begin to enter it in the worksheet.

The easiest way to plan your macro is to manually enter the keystrokes that will accomplish the task you want to perform. As you are entering the keystrokes, record them on a sheet of paper exactly as they occur.

Also keep the entries for each step of a macro as small as possible. The preceding example places each portion of the commands in a separate cell. For example, the entry used to select the graph type as Bar is in one cell, the entries used to indicate the various data ranges are in other cells, and the entries for each of the Others options are also in separate cells. Keeping the cell entries small makes it easier to find errors later.

ERRORS IN MACROS

It seems that no matter how much care is taken in entering a macro, errors will appear. Like other software that requires a user to supply the logic, macros will sometimes contain errors in logic or typing. Macros, unfortunately, do not have any error-detecting logic. A macro will try to execute a misspelled word like {rihgt} and be unable to do so. Upon reaching such a word, your spreadsheet will display the error message

```
Unrecognized key name {.......}
```

This means that you must be extremely careful when you enter macros. If even one character is out of sequence, 1-2-3 will either produce strange results or just "hang up" and wait for you to do something.

One of the easiest characters to forget in entering a macro is the tilde (~) used to represent the Enter keystroke. Another problem with spreadsheet macros is that the cell references included in them are always absolute. They do not change when, for example, cells are moved about or deleted from the worksheet. This is easy to understand. Remember that macros are simply labels in the worksheet. Do labels change when they are moved from one cell to another in a worksheet? No. Only formulas containing cell references change.

This absolute quality of macros is a good reason for using range names. A range name remains associated with the same range even if the range is moved. Range names in macros (and other formulas) will follow the cells to which they apply if the macro is copied to another location. When cell references are used, they change when moved to a different cell location in the worksheet.

MACRO DEBUGGING

Just about any piece of software has errors in it when it is first written. No matter how much time you spend on an application, some error will usually get through. The process of finding and correcting these errors is known as **debugging**.

1-2-3 includes a useful tool that makes debugging easier: the Step function. When 1-2-3 is in the STEP mode, all macros are executed one step at a time. To invoke the Step function, enter Alt + F2. The indicator STEP appears. The spreadsheet now will pause after every keystroke in the macro. After executing a keystroke, 1-2-3 waits for you to press any key to execute the next command. Thus, you can follow step-by-step with the macro as it executes. If you have text, such as a graph title, for example, you will have to press a key for each of the title's characters.

To assist you in debugging your worksheet, 1-2-3 also displays the current line of the macro being executed using the Step command in the position of your screen that held the date and time. The character of the macro currently being executed is found at the cursor location. The cursor moves as you indicate to 1-2-3 that it is to execute the next keystroke in the macro. This means that not only does the result of the command appear in any menus at the top of the screen but the macro instructions appear at the bottom of the screen to facilitate rapid debugging.

SPECIAL MACRO COMMANDS

Lotus 1-2-3 has two sets of special macro commands that cannot be invoked from the keyboard—only from within a macro. The first type can be referred to as a slash command, since this variety of command is always preceded by a slash (/). The second type is called an advanced macro command and always appears between braces ({ }). Additional macro commands can be found in Appendix A. Each of the following examples will be shown using first the slash macro commands and then the advanced macro commands.

/XG, /XI, and /XQ—{BRANCH}, {IF}, {LET}, and {QUIT}

The /XGlocation command is similar to BASIC's GoTo command. It instructs the macro to continue executing, beginning with a particular cell location (usually a range name). This command is generally used with an /XI conditional test, which is discussed later.

You can easily add this command to the \R macro that "draws" a rectangle by using the pointer. To do this, however, you must give the top cell in the macro the range name CONTINUE, using the /Range Name Create command. After you have done this, place the macro '/XGcontinue~ in the last cell of the macro. Execute the macro.

Now that control has been returned to the top cell of the macro (the CONTINUE cell), a loop has been formed. Every time control reaches the cell with the /XG command, the loop starts over. Since there is no way for control to leave this loop, it is called an **infinite loop.** The only way to stop this macro is to issue the break command (Ctrl-Break). An error message `Ctrl-Break` appears at the bottom of the screen. You must now press the Esc key to return to READY mode.

The changed macro appears below:

```
                        ┌────────────Cell named Continue
\R    {right 3}         Move the pointer to the right.
      {down 3}          Move the pointer down.
      {left 3}          Move the pointer to the left.
      {up 3}            Move the pointer up.
      /xgcontinue~      Send control to Continue.
```

The solution for this example using advanced macro commands utilizes the {branch} command. This command is used to direct 1-2-3 to execute a macro at the range name location following the command {branch}. The other implementation for this macro appears below:

```
                        ┌──Cell named Continue
\R    {right 3}         Move the pointer to the right.
      {down 3}          Move the pointer down.
      {left 3}          Move the pointer to the left.
      {up 3}            Move the pointer up.
      {branch continue} Send control to Continue.
```

Using the {branch} command in this macro results in the macro working identically as it did before. To stop macro execution, use the Ctrl-Break command.

The /XI command is the equivalent of BASIC's If-Then-Else command. It enables you to build conditional tests in the middle of a macro. This very powerful tool can be used in a variety of interesting ways. The counter macro that follows is one example of the /XI function. Its /XQ command tells the macro to quit execution; this macro is frequently used with the /XI. For example, these two commands can be linked together to form a statement like the following:

```
'/xicount>10~/xq
```

This counter macro command tells the computer that if the content of the cell named COUNT is greater than 10, it should stop executing this macro. If this command were buried in a macro, it would perform this test and either continue or stop the execution of the macro. To add this command to the \R macro, you must embed the following command:

```
'/dfcount~count+1~~~
```

This statement uses the / Data Fill command of 1-2-3 to increment a named range cell called COUNT by a value of 1 each time through the loop. We can now control the number of times the loop is executed by varying the value contained in the /XI macro command. For example, the following macro executes 10 times.

```
Named range                                                          Named range
cell Continue                                                        cell COUNT
       ↓                                                                   ↓
\R    {goto}count~0~       Initialize count to 0.                         11
   ┌─►{right 3}            Move the pointer to the right.
      {down 3}             Move the pointer down.
      {left 3}             Move the pointer to the left.
      {up 3}               Move the pointer up.
      /xicount>10~xq       If count > 10 quit, else loop.
      /dfcount~count+1~~~  Increment count by 1.
      /xgcontinue~
```

To enter this macro, make the following changes:

1. Delete the old macro name \R (/RND) and create a new \R macro name in the cell above (in this case G27).
2. Create a cell with the named range COUNT in cell K27.
3. Add the GoTo statement.
4. Add the /XI and the /DF macro commands after inserting two rows.

The solution for this example using advanced macro commands utilizes the {if}, {quit}, and {let} commands. The {if} command functions in the same fashion as the /XI command and allows you to specify a relation that, if true, then executes the instruction following the command. Be certain that you do not embed any spaces around the relational operators, since this causes an error message to appear once the macro is executed. The {quit} command functions in the same manner as the /XQ command and drops you to READY mode. The {let} command permits you to enter a number at a specified cell or named range and is used, in this example, to increment a counter. The solution appears below:

```
Cell named Continue                                                  Named range COUNT
                                                                             ↓
\R    {goto}count~0~                                                         11
    ┌▶{right 4}              Move the pointer to the right.
    │ {down 4}               Move the pointer down.
    │ {left 4}               Move the pointer to the left.
    │ {up 4}                 Move the pointer up.
    │ {if count>10}{quit}    Check if count greater than 10.
    │ {let count,count + 1}  Add 1 to count named range.
    └─{branch continue}      Send control to continue.
```

/XC and /XR

The /XCrange and /XR commands are similar to BASIC's GoSub and Return functions. /XC causes the macro to access a macro subroutine in a separate location. When that subroutine is finished, the /XR command causes processing to resume on the next line of the original macro. The /XC command is similar to the /XG command but offers a way to automatically return the macro to the point of departure, /XG does not; it is an absolute GoTo to a different part of the worksheet.

/XN and /XL—{GETLABEL} and {GETNUMBER}

/XN message˜range˜ and /XLmessage˜range˜ are input commands like {?}. They differ in that they allow a message to be displayed in the program's control panel before input is made. The message can contain up to 39 characters.

The /XN command accepts only numeric entries. Numeric entries include @ functions and formulas as well as pure numbers. /XL accepts only labels, but it will accept a number that is entered in the cell as a label.

Both commands store input in the cell specified by the range. If a named range is used, the input will be stored there; otherwise, the input will be stored in the cell where the pointer is located.

Your current \R macro requires you to change the contents of a cell in the macro if you want to alter the number of times that control is passed through the loop. The /XN command gives you more control by prompting you to enter the number of passes via the keyboard.

Before you can do this, however, you must tell 1-2-3 where to store this new piece of information called MAXIMUM. This is done by creating a named range cell at location K28 and giving it the name MAXIMUM. The following macro allows more control on the number of passes through the loop.

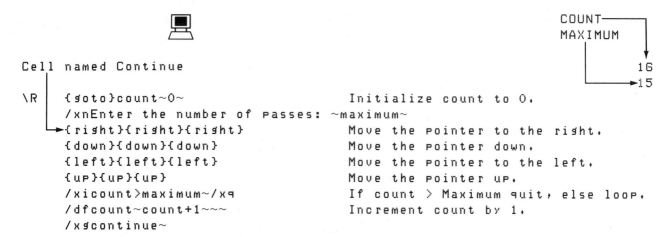

```
Cell named Continue

\R   {goto}count~0~                    Initialize count to 0.
     /xnEnter the number of passes: ~maximum~
  →  {right}{right}{right}             Move the pointer to the right.
     {down}{down}{down}                Move the pointer down.
     {left}{left}{left}                Move the pointer to the left.
     {up}{up}{up}                      Move the pointer up.
     /xicount>maximum~/xq              If count > Maximum quit, else loop.
     /dfcount~count+1~~~               Increment count by 1.
     /xgcontinue~
```

Enter the macro using the following steps:

1. Create the named range MAXIMUM at cell location K28.
2. Move the macro cells that appear under the GoTo down one cell.
3. Enter the /XN command. The character string following the /XN acts as the prompt to the user. When the user enters the number of passes, this information is placed in the cell called MAXIMUM.
4. Change the /XI entry so that the comparison is made against the MAXIMUM cell rather than against the numeric constant 10.

LOTUS 1-2-3 COMMAND LANGUAGE

Many macro commands used by Lotus can also be implemented using the built-in **command language** that is available using Lotus 1-2-3. This command language is similar to a programming language and allows sophisticated users to, in essence, write their own programs. It should be noted that these command language programs execute much more slowly than regular spreadsheet commands and should be used with prudence in a worksheet. The last example depicted above has been altered to include the use of Lotus's command language. A listing of the available commands, along with a brief explanation, can be found in Appendix A of this book.

The macro command language implementation for this example is as follows:

```
                    11 ←────── COUNT named range
                    10 ←────── MAXIMUM named range
\R   {let count, 0}
     {getnumber "Enter the number of passes:", maximum}
     {right}{right}{right} ←────── Continue named range
     {down}{down}{down}
     {left}{left}{left}
     {up}{up}{up}
     {if count > maximum}{quit}
     {let count,count+1}
     {branch continue}
```

The {let count,0} command accomplishes the same task as the {goto}count~0~ command. It places the value zero in the named range

COUNT. The {getnumber,,,} command accomplishes the same task as the /XN command; it initializes the named range called MAXIMUM to a value entered from the keyboard. The {if count > maximum}{quit} command checks to see if the value contained in the named range COUNT is greater than the value contained in the named range MAXIMUM and issues a {quit} command if it is. The {let count,count+1} command increments the named range COUNT by a value of 1 each time through the loop. The {branch continue} command returns control to the cell with that named range.

/XM or {MENU BRANCH}

This command enables you to create menus that appear while a macro is executing. Instead of the MENU mode indicator prompt, a CMD MENU mode indicator prompt is displayed. These menus look like the standard 1-2-3 menus and enable you to make choices during the execution of a macro. They are also used during processing to give messages and warnings.

All 1-2-3 menus are accessed by the /XMlocation commands. The location in the /XM command points to a menu range, which can be up to eight columns wide and two rows deep. The entries in the first row of the menu range are called *menu options* and can contain up to eight options. When the menu is executed, these entries are displayed as menu options in the control panel (much the same as regular menu options). The second row of the menu range typically contains explanatory messages to clarify each menu option. Each message can contain a maximum of 80 characters.

One or more lines of macro code appear below each menu option explanatory message in the menu range. This code will run if, and only if, the preceding option is selected. The macro instructions follow the same rules as regular macros. That is, they execute top down and left to right, and terminate when a blank is encountered in a cell or when a blank cell is located.

One of the simplest uses for a menu is to allow the user to answer a yes/no question from within a macro. For example, the following macro, called the Quit macro (\Q), asks if you are sure that you want to exit from 1-2-3.

```
\Q       /xmquit~                              Go to named range QUIT
    ┌─►Yes            No                       Menu Options
    │   Save workshe  Remain in 1-2-Message lines
    │   /fs~r         /xq                      Save file or stop
    │   /qy~                                   Quit 1-2-3
    │
Named range cell QUIT
```

After this macro is entered in your worksheet, it appears as follows:

	N	O	P	Q	R
23	\Q	/xmquit~			Go to named range QUIT
24		Yes	No		Menu Options
25		Save workshe	Remain in 1=2	-	Message Lines
26		/fs~r	/xq		Save file or stop
27		/qy~			Quit 1-2-3

Entering this macro requires the following steps:

1. Enter the name of the macro in cell N23.
2. The named range QUIT is the cell containing "Yes."
3. Since the menu entries are contained in adjacent cells, you must indicate to 1-2-3 that they are ended. Do this by changing column Q to a width of one, and then enter comments in column R.

You are not required to use the /XQ command. Remember, if 1-2-3 finds a blank or a blank cell while executing a macro, it assumes that the macro has ended. We can, therefore, simply omit the /XQ command. Upon locating a "null" or blank cell, the macro will stop.

The first line of the menu macro, /XMQuit˜, tells the macro to look for a menu beginning in the named range QUIT. The actual menu is found in the second row of cells. This menu presents two choices, Yes and No, in the third row. Notice that the first choice is in column O and the second choice is in column P. All /XM menus work this way; each choice in the menu is presented in a different worksheet column.

The labels in row 3 are explanatory messages that accompany each menu option. In the preceding example, these messages seem to run together. This is because the first message is too long to be displayed completely in the cell. When the columns are widened, it is clear that the full message is there. They then read as follows:

```
Save worksheet and exit 1-2-3    Remain in 1-2-3
```

As with regular 1-2-3 menus, you can select an option either by pointing or by entering the first letter of its name. (Make certain to choose names that begin with different letters. If two or more options in a menu have the same first letter and you try to select using the first letter, 1-2-3 will give you the first entry that has that letter.)

Suppose that you select the Yes option. The macro will continue to process the macro's instructions contained in column O. The statements in this column instruct 1-2-3 to save the worksheet file to the default name and quit from 1-2-3.

If you select the No option, the macro will continue processing in column P. This column cell contains a simple /XQ command that causes the macro to stop running.

If you create a menu that is too long for the control panel, 1-2-3 will return the error message illegal menu. The same message is displayed if the menu has more than eight options. Similarly, the secondary messages associated with each menu option can contain no more than 80 characters because the width of the display is only 80 characters.

The {menubranch location} command can be used in place of the /XM command. This menu, for example, uses the command {menubranch quit} to invoke the menu instead of the /XM quit˜ command.

PRINTING THE WORKSHEET

Menu macros can be used to automate tedious tasks that are repeated frequently, such as printing. For example, you may want several different reports. Each one will require taking several steps to prepare the worksheet for printing: You must define the output range to be printed, align the paper, and specify any options such as borders, headers, footers, and margins.

Although the actual implementation of such a macro will vary greatly from application to application, the following macro can be used as a guide for automating this task. Two different reports are required: a report in order by department name and a report in order by the dollar amounts in the Change column. The macro assumes that the print head is aligned at the top of a sheet of paper.

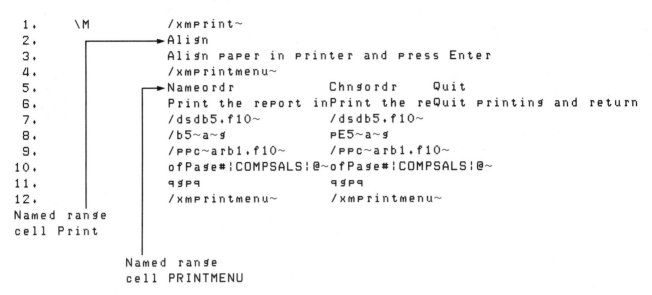

```
 1.        \M              /xmprint~
 2.                      ┌▶Align
 3.                      │ Align paper in printer and press Enter
 4.                      │ /xmprintmenu~
 5.                      │▶Nameordr              Chngordr    Quit
 6.                      ││ Print the report inPrint the reQuit printing and return
 7.                      ││ /dsdb5.f10~           /dsdb5.f10~
 8.                      ││ /b5~a~g               pE5~a~g
 9.                      ││ /ppc~arb1.f10~        /ppc~arb1.f10~
10.                      ││ ofPage#!COMPSALS!@~ofPage#!COMPSALS!@~
11.                      ││ qgpq                  qgpq
12.                      ││ /xmprintmenu~         /xmprintmenu~
Named range              ││
cell Print ──────────────┘│
                          │
            Named range   │
            cell PRINTMENU┘
```

There is not enough room to have the comment statements appear to the right of this macro. Instead, the lines of the macro have been numbered, and the following discussion of the macro commands refers to these line numbers.

Lines 1, 2, and 3   The \M is a remark statement indicating the name of the macro (M). The /XMprint~ entry tells 1-2-3 that a menu (/XM) located at the named range cell PRINT is to be executed. That menu appears immediately below the command. The menu consists of the two lines immediately below (lines 2 and 3). The object of this menu is to give an instruction to the user to align the paper in the printer. The single option is contained in the first line (line 2) and contains the word *Align,* which will be displayed on the entry line of the control panel. The second line (line 3) contains the text that further describes this entry to the user—an instruction to align the paper in the printer and press the Enter key to continue.

Lines 4, 5, and 6   Line 4 contains the /XM command, which tells 1-2-3 to execute the menu found in the named range cell PRINTMENU. The PRINTMENU cell is located in line 5. Lines 5 and 6 contain the Print Menu that is displayed on the control panel. Line 5 contains the three menu options to be displayed in the entry line of the control panel. Each entry occupies one cell. Two reports can be generated—Nameordr and Chngordr—or the user can quit the menu and return to READY mode.

Line 6 contains an explanation of each menu entry. The explanation of the Nameordr menu entry is "Print the report in department name order." The explanation for the Chngordr menu entry is "Print the report in ascending order by amount of change." The explanation for the Quit entry is "Quit printing and return to READY mode."

Line 7   Line 7 contains instructions to tell 1-2-3 to issue the / Data Sort command and specify the sort range to consist of the cells B5.F10.

Line 8 Line 8 tells 1-2-3 that the primary key is located in column B or column F and that the sort is to be in ascending order. It then tells the spreadsheet to execute the sort.

Line 9 Line 9 contains the instructions /PPC~A. The / invokes the 1-2-3 Main Menu. The first P selects the Print option; the second tells the spreadsheet to send the output to the printer. The C tells 1-2-3 to access the Clear Menu to clear the current print settings. The ~ tells the spreadsheet to take the first option of the Clear Menu and clear all current print settings. The A tells 1-2-3 to align the paper in the printer and take this print position as the top of page. The range to print is then specified for the spreadsheet.

Line 10 Line 10 contains the commands for making a footer line. The O selects the Options entry from the Print Menu. The F selects the Footer option of the Options Menu. The footer line is then entered.

Line 11 Line 11 contains the commands that tell 1-2-3 to begin printing the worksheet. The Q tells the spreadsheet to quit the Options Menu. The G prints the worksheet. The P advances the paper to the top of the next page. The Q command quits the Print Menu.

Line 12 This command tells 1-2-3 to execute the menu found in the named range cell PRINTMENU.

CHAPTER REVIEW

The macro feature of 1-2-3 enables you to store representations of keystrokes in a worksheet cell and later execute those instructions. The representations of the instructions must be preceded by a single quote ('); otherwise, the spreadsheet package will immediately start executing the instructions instead of storing them as text data. Once the keystrokes have been entered properly, a one-character name (only alphabetic characters are allowed) preceded by a backslash (\) must be assigned to the cell with the keystrokes. The macro can now be executed by pressing the Alt key plus the alphabetic character.

Keystrokes are stored as they are used in entering a regular spreadsheet command, with the exception of a number of special commands such as the Enter keystroke. A representation of such a keystroke enclosed in braces ({ }) must be used for such a command.

Simple macros will reside in one cell, but complex macros can occupy a number of cells within a column. Try to limit the number of keystrokes stored in one cell of such a macro to those necessary to perform only a single task. If too many keystrokes are stored in a cell, making any changes becomes difficult, because the task being performed may be almost impossible to comprehend.

Macros should be placed in an area of a worksheet where they will not be harmed if you add or delete rows and columns. This "safe" area is usually in the lower right-hand quadrant of your worksheet. A complex macro in this reserved area will typically consist of three columns of text data: The first column contains the macro name, the second column the macro instructions, and the third column any explanatory remarks (documentation) about the instructions stored in a cell. Only the second column is actually used by the spreadsheet; the other columns are used for documentation by the user.

In addition to entering macros manually a keystroke at a time in a cell, you can use the Learn command of 1-2-3 to automatically store instructions in the form of macro commands to the learn range as they are entered at the keyboard.

1-2-3 also provides two different types of macro commands that do not directly correspond to a key on the keyboard. These are the slash (/) commands and the advanced macro commands contained in braces ({ }). These commands provide the ability to incorporate programming constructs such as branch, goto, if, counters, and providing prompts to the user, as well as many other types of commands. Please refer to Appendix A for a further description of these commands.

KEY TERMS AND CONCEPTS

advanced macro commands
command language
debugging
infinite loop
Learn command
macro
slash commands

CHAPTER QUIZ

Multiple Choice

1. Which of the following statements about macros is false?
   a. Only the first letter of a command needs to be entered.
   b. All macros are treated as label data.
   c. Only alphabetic keystrokes (with the exception of /) are allowed in a macro.
   d. All macros must have names.

2. Which of the following statements about macro names is false?
   a. A macro name can contain up to 14 characters.
   b. A macro name can contain alphabetic or numeric characters.
   c. A macro name must have a slash (/).
   d. A macro name may contain only two characters, the second of which must be alphabetic.

3. Which of the following is *not* a special key representation to 1-2-3?
   a. {HELP}
   b. {EDIT}
   c. {BRANCH}
   d. {LEFT}
   e. All are valid special key representations.

4. Which of the following macro commands is used to exit from a macro?
   a. /XM
   b. /XI
   c. /XQ
   d. /XL

5. A macro stops when which of the following occurs?
   a. It encounters the /XQ command.
   b. It encounters a blank cell.
   c. It encounters the Stop command.
   d. It has executed for five minutes.

True/False

6. The only macro command that allows you to enter instructions across a row of cells is the /XM or {menu branch} command.

7. There is no macro command equivalent to the If-Then-Else command.

8. The Step feature allows you to execute a macro five keystrokes at a time.

9. Numeric digits are the only characters that do not have to be preceded by a single quote within macros.

10. Range names are required by a number of special macro commands.

Answers

1. c   2. c   3. a   4. c   5. a, b   6. t   7. f   8. f   9. f   10. t

Exercises

1. The keystrokes contained within a macro must always start with a _____.

2. A macro name beginning with a backslash contains _____ characters.

3. A macro name may start with a _____ and be followed by _____.

4. A macro executes from _____ to _____ in a cell.

5. One of the more common errors in building a macro is forgetting to enter the _____ command represented by a _____.

6. The _____ option of the Range Name submenu is frequently used for creating a macro name from existing text.

7. Once the macro has been named, it can be invoked by holding down the _____ key and then some other key or by entering the Run command.

8. Multiple cells can be used to contain a macro as long as they are in the same _____.

9. A cell containing a macro can store up to _____ keystrokes.

10. The special key {_____} is used to delete the character to the left of the current cursor location.

11. The special key {_____} causes the macro to pause until the Enter key is pressed.

12. The area used for storing macros in a worksheet is the _____ quadrant.

13. The _____ feature is used for debugging a macro and enables you to examine the effect of each keystroke.

14. The debug feature is activated by pressing the _____ plus _____ keys.

15. The macro command _____ requires two rows of your worksheet for holding additional options.

16. Once a macro has finished, you can invoke a menu via a _____ command.

17. List the macro commands that reference a named range.
    a.

    b.

    c.

18. The macro commands that are the same as BASIC's GoTo are _____ and _____.

19. The spreadsheet _____ or _____ is used for incrementing a counter in your worksheet on every pass through a loop.

20. The _____ and _____ macro commands enable you to display a message and then accept information from the keyboard.

21. The keystrokes for invoking the Learn command are _____ + _____.

22. Before the Learn command can be used, a _____ must be created to store the macro instructions.

23. Instead of entering five {down} commands, you can cut the number of keystrokes required by using the _____ command.

24. A macro command that can be used in place of the /XI command is the _____ command.

25. The macro command _____ can be used for incrementing counters.

COMPUTER EXERCISES

1. To complete the following exercise, retrieve the CH4EX1 (payroll) worksheet file. Create an area called MACROS that you will use to hold any macros you build. Be sure to position this area in the lower right-hand quadrant of your worksheet.
   a. Create a macro that you can use to add a blank row to receive a new employee.
   b. Create a macro that, after you have positioned the pointer to the overtime rate cell for the new employee, will automatically position to the same cell of the prior row and copy the formulas for the overtime rate, gross pay, and net pay cells to the next row.
   c. Save the worksheet file using the name CH9EX1.

2. Retrieve the 2TABLE file. Create a macro that will print the input area, the financial statement, and the table. Each report should start on the top of the page. Be sure to change the setup string for printing the table; otherwise, it will be too wide to fit on a page.

3. Retrieve the CH5EX5 file. Create a menu macro that allows you to arrange the gradebook worksheet in alphabetical order or in rank order by the final percentage. Four report options are also to be contained in the menu. Two of these options will print the entire gradebook worksheet in alphabetical order or in rank order by final percentage. The other two reports will be in the same order but will not include the summary information below the last student. After any item is selected from the menu and executed, your macro should return you to the menu.

4. This exercise is based on an adaptation of a prior case that required you to create a set of integrated financial statements. The worksheet that contains this file is CASMACRO.WKS. You are to use this worksheet to build a number of different macros for printing and other desired operations.

   The revised worksheet has a number of changes that make it adaptable for this assignment. There is no schedule of current assets. Rather, current assets are calculated to balance total assets with total liabilities.

   A schedule of sales representatives has been added. The total sales amount ties into the income statement automatically. This does away with any need to manually change the sales amount.

   The sales table has been made as flexible as possible for calculating a new year-to-date sales total for each employee. This is accomplished by adding a "dummy" column to the right of the most recent month. This column is then set to a width of one. The original @SUM function command is entered as @SUM(January.Dummy). Any new columns are now added to the left of the dummy column. This means that the @SUM(January.Dummy). Any new columns are now added to the left of the dummy column. This means that the @SUM function automatically includes any new columns in its range as long as they are added to the left (within the range of the @SUM function) of the dummy column.

   Your objective in this case is to make this worksheet as easy as possible for others to use. This ease of use typically involves using macros to cut down on the number of commands that have to be entered by the user. The macros discussed below are required for this application. If you can think of any additional macros that might be needed, include them, too.

a. *Print macro.* This macro requires a menu macro. It should prompt the user to align the paper in the printer. After this prompt has been displayed, a menu of the various reports that can be generated is displayed to the user. These reports include the following:

    A report of the balance sheet
    A report of the horizontal analysis income statement
    A report of the vertical analysis income statement
    A report of the retained earnings statement
    A report containing the ratio information
    A report containing the sales representative information

Each of the report macros should include the following:

    Reset the print parameters
    Specify the range
    Specify setup strings, if any
    Place the date at the bottom of each page
    Advance the paper to the top of the next page
    Return control back to the Print Menu

b. *Insert macro.* This macro allows the user to automatically insert a new column into the sales report. It also copies any additional information for that column.
c. *Sort1 macro.* This macro sorts the sales report in order by the Percent of Total Sales column.
d. *Sort2 macro.* This macro sorts the sales report in order by the last name of the sales representative.
e. *Graph macro.* This macro generates the pie graph displayed later in this exercise. Use the Learn command to create this macro.

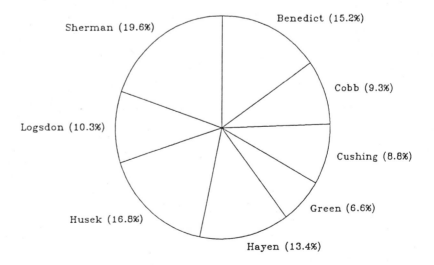

Building the preceding macros requires a generous usage of range names in the worksheet. Each of the reports should be given a different range name, as indicated below:

Report	Range Name
Comparative Balance Sheet	BALANCE1
Horizontal Analysis Income Statement	INCOME1
Vertical Analysis Income Statement	INCOME2
Retained Earnings Statement	RETAINED
Ratio Analysis Data and Ratios	RATIO
Sales Report	SALESREPORT

In addition, give range names to the various areas of the worksheet that are involved in the sorting, graphing, and insertion macros.

Make certain that you properly plan each of the above macros. This means that you should manually perform each of the above tasks first and then convert them to macro instructions. To aid you in building the required macros, planning sheets are provided at the end of Appendix A. You only need one for the printing macros, since the commands for the first print macro can be copied and changes can be made for subsequent macros.

After you have entered the above macros, test them to make certain that they work properly. Add realistic sales figures for two additional months.

Treadstone 21 Company
Comparative Balance Sheet
December 31, 1991 and 1990
Horizontal Analysis

	1991	1990	Increase (Decrease)	
			Amount	Percent
Assets				
Current assets	$667,830	$533,000	$134,830	25.3%
Long-term investments	95,000	177,500	(82,500)	−46.5%
Plant assets (net)	444,500	470,000	(25,500)	−5.4%
Intangible assets	50,000	50,000	0	0.0%
Total assets	$1,257,330	$1,230,500	$26,830	2.2%
Liabilities				
Current liabilities	$210,000	$243,000	($33,000)	−13.6%
Long-term liabilities	150,000	200,000	(50,000)	−25.0%
Total liabilities	$360,000	$443,000	($83,000)	−18.7%
Stockholders' Equity				
Preferred 6% stock, $100 par	$150,000	$150,000	$0	0.0%
Common stock, $10 par	500,000	500,000	0	0.0%
Retained earnings	247,330	137,500	109,830	79.9%
Total stockholders' equity	$897,330	$787,500	$109,830	13.9%
Total liab. & stockholders' equity	$1,257,330	$1,230,500	$26,830	2.2%

Treadstone 21 Company
Comparative Income Statement
For Years Ended December 31, 1991 and 1990
Horizontal Analysis

	1991	1990	Increase (Decrease) Amount	Percent
Sales	$1,707,025	$1,234,000	$473,025	38.3%
Sales returns and allowances	35,750	34,000	1,750	5.1%
Net sales	$1,671,275	$1,200,000	$471,275	39.3%
Cost of merchandise sold	1,095,150	820,000	275,150	33.6%
Gross profit	$576,125	$380,000	$196,125	51.6%
Selling expenses	$191,000	$147,000	$44,000	29.9%
General expenses	104,000	97,400	6,600	6.8%
Total operating expenses	$295,000	$244,400	$50,600	20.7%
Operating income	$281,125	$135,600	$145,525	107.3%
Other income	8,500	11,000	(2,500)	−22.7%
	$289,625	$146,600	$143,025	97.6%
Other expenses	6,000	12,000	(6,000)	−50.0%
Income before income tax	$283,625	$134,600	$149,025	110.7%
Income tax	124,795	58,100	66,695	114.8%
Net income	$158,830	$76,500	$82,330	107.6%

Treadstone 21 Company
Comparative Income Statement
For Years Ended December 31, 1991 and 1990
Vertical Analysis

	1991 Amount	Percent	1990 Amount	Percent
Sales	$1,707,025	102.1%	$1,234,000	102.8%
Sales returns and allowances	$35,750	2.1%	$34,000	2.8%
Net sales	$1,671,275	100.0%	$1,200,000	100.0%
Cost of merchandise sold	$1,203,318	72.0%	$864,000	72.0%
Gross profit	$467,957	28.0%	$336,000	28.0%
Selling expenses	$185,000	11.1%	$141,000	11.8%
General expenses	$100,000	6.0%	$93,400	7.8%
Total operating expenses	$285,000	17.1%	$234,400	19.5%
Operating income	$182,957	10.9%	$135,600	11.3%
Other income	$8,500	0.5%	$11,000	0.9%
	$191,457	11.5%	$146,600	12.2%
Other expenses	$6,000	0.4%	$12,000	1.0%
Income before income tax	$185,457	11.1%	$134,600	11.2%
Income tax	$81,601	4.9%	$58,100	4.8%
Net income	$103,856	6.2%	$76,500	6.4%

Treadstone 21 Company
Comparative Retained Earnings Statement
For Years Ended December 31, 1991 and 1990

	1991	1990	Increase (Decrease)	
			Amount	Percent
Retained earnings, January 1	$137,500	$100,000	$37,500	37.5%
Net income for year	158,830	76,500	82,330	107.6%
Total	$296,330	$176,500	$119,830	67.9%
Dividends:				
On preferred stock	$9,000	$9,000	$0	0.0%
On common stock	40,000	30,000	10,000	33.3%
Total	$49,000	$39,000	$10,000	25.6%
Retained earnings, December 31	$247,330	$137,500	$109,830	79.9%

Financial Ratio Analysis

	1991	1990
Plant Assets to Long-Term Liab.	2.96	2.35
Stockholders' Equity to Liab.	2.49	1.78
PROFITABILITY ANALYSIS		
EPS on Common Stock	3.00	1.35
Price Earnings Ratio	6.84	10.00
Dividend Yield	0.04	0.04

Treadstone 21 Company
Year-to-Date Sales by Sales Representative

Sales Representative		Jan.	Feb.	March	April	June	July	Total	Percent of Total
Harriet	Benedict	50,000	48,000	40,000	44,000	42,000	35,000	$259,000	15.2%
Barbara	Cobb	29,000	23,000	26,000	28,000	29,000	24,000	$159,000	9.3%
Ginger	Cushing	23,000	21,000	27,000	26,000	26,000	27,000	$150,000	8.8%
Cliff	Green	14,000	20,000	18,000	19,000	22,000	20,000	$113,000	6.6%
Roger	Hayen	37,000	40,000	38,000	35,000	39,000	40,000	$229,000	13.4%
John	Husek	125,000	27,000	35,000	33,025	36,000	30,000	$286,025	16.8%
Peter	Logsdon	26,000	30,000	28,000	27,000	31,000	34,000	$176,000	10.3%
Eric	Sherman	72,000	50,000	53,000	60,000	55,000	45,000	$335,000	19.6%
		376,000	259,000	265,000	272,025	280,000	255,000	$1,707,025	

CHAPTER 10

USING THE LOTUS 1-2-3 ADD-INS

CHAPTER OBJECTIVES

After completing this chapter, you should be able to:

- **Use the elementary features of the Allways add-in**
- **Use the elementary features of the Macro Library Manager add-in**

This chapter introduces you to two add-in packages that are provided by the Lotus Corporation when you purchase 1-2-3: Allways and the Macro Library Manager. The Allways add-in provides the ability to perform a process called spreadsheet publishing. **Spreadsheet publishing** allows you to change the size of text within a worksheet, boldface, underline, shade, and merge text and graphics on one page, and it offers many other features. The Macro Library Manager provides the ability to easily manage a separate library of macros and use them with any worksheet you have retrieved.

The intent of this chapter is merely to give some idea of the capability of these packages. If you desire more in-depth knowledge, please examine the appropriate areas of the Lotus 1-2-3 documentation.

HARDWARE AND SOFTWARE FOR 1-2-3 ADD-INS

HARDWARE REQUIREMENTS

Before you can use the Allways add-in, you must have a computer equipped with at least 512K of RAM and a fixed disk.

USING ADD-IN SOFTWARE

Before any add-in piece of software can be used, it must first be loaded into RAM memory so that it is ready any time you want to start execution. The process of attaching a piece of software—loading the software package into memory—requires issuing the command / Add-in Attach. Once this command is issued, you must indicate to 1-2-3 which add-in package is to be brought into memory. This is accomplished by highlighting the ALL-WAYS.ADN or MACROMGR.ADN file.

If, for example, you want to start Allways, you issue the / Add-in Attach command, highlight the ALLWAYS.ADN file, and then press the Enter key. If this file is not present, 1-2-3 has not been configured to integrate with Allways and the Allways Setup program will have to be run before you can attach to Allways.

Once the program has been attached, 1-2-3 displays the following menu:

```
No-Key 7 8 9 10
```

You must now indicate which function key is to be assigned to the add-in program to allow you to activate it at any time. If you select the No-Key option, you will always have to first use the command / Add-in Invoke. The numbers 7 through 10 correspond to the equivalent function keys on the keyboard, which in turn correspond to the equivalent add-in represented by that function key. These are illustrated below:

    APP1 Alt + F7
    APP2 Alt + F8
    APP3 Alt + F9
    APP4 Alt + F10

Once a function key has been assigned to the add-in package, you can invoke the program by holding down the Alt key and then pressing the appropriate function key. If you assigned 7 to your add-in, for example, that program is now invoked by using the Alt + F7 command.

Once you have finished using an add-in piece of software with Lotus 1-2-3 and you wish to free the memory used by that add-in, you can issue the command / Add-in Detach. When that command is issued, any memory that was used by the add-in software is released and available for large worksheets that you may now want to load into memory.

ALLWAYS

The **Allways** add-in of 1-2-3 provides you with the ability to perform spreadsheet publishing. This add-in package greatly increases the power and flexibility of 1-2-3 by allowing you to create presentation-quality worksheets. One of the most significant features of Allways is that you can merge worksheet and graph data on one sheet of paper as well as add many different types of enhancements to the worksheet itself. If you have any type of color/graphics monitor, you will be able to see the changes that you make to the worksheet when they appear on the screen. If you have a text-only monitor, you will be able to make the changes but you will not be able to see on the screen the results of those changes.

When you are making changes to the characteristics of how the text is to appear, Allways has two ways to create this new text. If you have a dot matrix printer, Allways can use any type of character supported by that printer. Allways also has other fonts that it can use by either downloading those fonts or by activating the graphics feature of your printer. These fonts are referred to as **soft fonts** because they are provided with the Allways package, and they include the following:

   CG Courier: the standard fixed pitch typeface found on many typewriters

   CG Times: a classic serif (embellishment of ends or corners of a character) typeface

   CG Triumvirate: a sans serif (straight lines without embellishments) typeface similar to Helvetica

DESKTOP/SPREADSHEET PUBLISHING DEFINITIONS

Before we discuss the specific operation of Allways, it would be beneficial to spend some time defining some terms that will be used in conjunction with this package. The term **typeface** refers to the style and design of the characters as they appear on the printed page. Each typeface has a different design and, therefore, a different appearance when it prints out. Some typeface styles found in the marketplace are Helvetica, Cooper, Palatine, Times Roman, and Goudy Old Style.

A **font** is a set of characters that share the same typeface and size: for example, Courier 10 point and Times 12 point. The term *point* refers to the size of the characters in the font. A **point** is equal to 1/72 of an inch. This means that a font of Helvetica 12 point is a font with characters about 1/6 of an inch high. A font of Helvetica 24 point is a font twice as big, with characters about 1/3 of an inch high. Some samples of different font sizes can be seen in Figure 10.1. Allways permits you to use up to eight fonts in any document and numbers these 1 through 8.

When laser printers or the fonts from Allways are used, the size of the font is usually measured in points. If dot matrix printer fonts are used, they are measured in characters per inch or **pitch,** which measures the width of a

Figure 10.1

The Times Roman typeface shown in several point sizes

This is Times Roman 6 point
This is Times Roman 8 point
This is Times Roman 10 point
This is Times Roman 12 point
This is Times Roman 14 point
This is Times Roman 17 point
This is Times Roman 20 point
This is Times Roman 24 point

dot matrix typeface. Pitch alternatives for a dot matrix font typically range from 17 pitch (small) to 5 pitch (wide); 10 and 12 pitch is the normal type.

A **printer font** is provided with your printer. This may be a limited font set that varies only in the size of type for some dot matrix printers. If you have a sophisticated dot matrix, laser, or postscript printer, there may be a large number of these fonts from which to select.

A **soft font** is a font that comes with Allways. Depending on your printer, a soft font is either loaded to the memory in your printer or produced using the Graphics feature of the printer. When you configure Allways using the Setup program, it places the default fonts of Times and Triumvirate with varying point sizes. If these fonts have been changed, they will, of course, be set to a different font and point size. The **default font** is font 1 and is used throughout the worksheet, except in any cells where you have explicitly specified other fonts.

It is important to use a set of like font sets (different sizes of the same font style), because this makes the document more visually appealing. Some authorities even state that you should not use more than three different font sizes on a single page.

The **spacing** is either fixed pitch (monospaced) or proportional. In a fixed pitch font each character takes up the same amount of space no matter what size it is. For example, in a fixed pitch font the characters "i" and "m" take up the same amount of space on a line. When proportional spacing is used, however, each character takes up only the amount of space that it requires, which results in more characters appearing on a line of text.

INTERACTION BETWEEN 1-2-3 AND ALLWAYS

When you have invoked Allways and are using it to make such changes to your worksheet as changing the typeface of the title, boldfacing the contents of some cells, shading a column of cells, double underlining the grand total cells of columns, or drawing horizontal or vertical lines on a worksheet, these changes are not actually made to your 1-2-3 worksheet file. Rather, Allways creates another file that it uses to place all of this formatting information and it then links this settings file to your worksheet file. A settings file used by Allways has the same file name as your worksheet file, but it has an .ALL file extension.

If you have used Allways to format a worksheet file and then later bring that file into 1-2-3 to make significant changes such as adding a new report, you must attach Allways so that it can load in the corresponding .ALL file. Once Allways is attached to 1-2-3 and you issue a / File Retrieve or / File Save command, the corresponding format (.ALL) file is loaded or saved by Allways. Now, if you make changes to your worksheet, they are automatically reflected in the Allways format settings.

HINTS/HAZARDS

Remember, you must use a / File Save command before any format changes that you make using Allways are saved to an .ALL file. If, for example, you load a worksheet file and do not change the worksheet file using 1-2-3 but use only Allways for making format changes, these changes are only saved to the respective .ALL file when you issue a Save command from 1-2-3. If you simply exit 1-2-3, all of these format changes are lost.

HINTS/HAZARDS

You should be sure to keep Allways attached while you are making any significant changes to your worksheet with 1-2-3. If you attach Allways after significant changes have been made, or you detach before changes are to be made, a mismatch between the settings file (.ALL) and your worksheet will occur. This will result in formats that might have been specified in one location suddenly appearing in another.

INVOKING ALLWAYS

Once 1-2-3 has been started and Allways has been attached (using function key 7), load the file called CH5EX1 and invoke Allways using the APP1 command (Alt + F7). The Allways screen (see Figure 10.2) appears to be very similar to the 1-2-3 screen; it too is divided into the control panel, the worksheet, and the status line.

The screen is where the changes that you make to the worksheet appear. As you make changes to the size of type displayed, for example, these changes appear on the screen.

The control panel at the top of the screen works similarly to 1-2-3. The first line contains information about the contents of the cell at the cursor location: the font, color of data, or the print characteristics such as boldface or underlined. The second line shows the address and contents of the cell; if, however, you enter the slash (/) or less than (<) symbol, the Main Menu appears here. The third line displays information about the highlighted command in the menu. The mode indicator appears in the upper right-hand corner of the screen and displays the same types of messages as 1-2-3.

The status line at the bottom of the screen provides the same information as 1-2-3; it displays the date and time along with any indicators that are needed for the display. These indicators work exactly as they do in 1-2-3.

SPECIFYING A RANGE BEFORE A COMMAND

One Allways indicator, ANC, not found in 1-2-3 deserves special attention. When the ANC indicator is on, it means that you have anchored the cell to specify a range before you enter a command.

When you are using 1-2-3 to specify a range, you must first tell 1-2-3 to execute a command and then 1-2-3 prompts you for a range. If you need to

Figure 10.2
The Allways screen

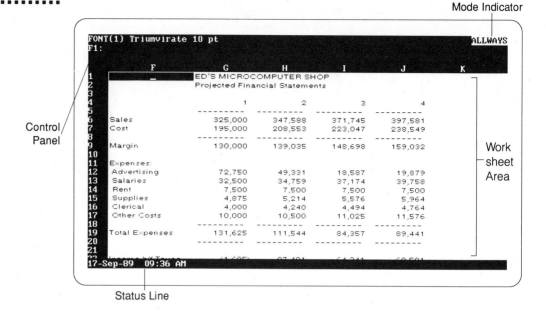

use a range of cells in several commands, you must indicate that range of cells every time you enter a command. Allways permits you to specify a range before you issue any commands, and once the range is specified, it can be used by multiple commands. Specifying a range before a command is executed requires the following steps:

1. Position the pointer to a corner cell in the range.
2. Nail down the beginning of the range by entering a period (.), and the ANC indicator will now appear on the screen.
3. Extend the range by using pointer manipulation commands to highlight the appropriate cells.
4. Select an Allways command (the range will already be in effect).
5. Continue selecting commands until you are finished with this range.
6. To cancel the existing range, either press the Esc key or move the pointer to another cell location.

ALLWAYS KEYS

Allways uses the same pointer manipulation commands as Lotus 1-2-3. Some of the commands associated with the function keys have, however, changed. The tasks performed by the function keys appear below:

F1   Help—displays an Allways help screen.

F3   Name—displays a menu of named ranges in the worksheet.

F4   Reduce—reduces the size of the display. Allows you to reduce cells down to 60% of their current size.

F5 GoTo—moves the pointer to a cell or named range.

F6 Display—switches the screen between graphics and text mode.

F10 Graph—turns the graph display on or off. This command can be used to view a graph on the screen. Press it again and only a hatched box appears on the screen to show where the graph will be placed.

Accelerator Keys Some commands of Allways that are available through its menu structure can be entered using **accelerator keys** to cut down on the number of keystrokes. These accelerator keys are two characters and start with the Alt key. Some of these commands are "toggle" commands; that is, the first command turns a feature on and the second command turns that feature off. A summary of these commands follows:

Alt + B Boldface: on/off
Alt + G Grind lines: on/off
Alt + L Lines: outline/all/none
Alt + S Shading: light/dark/solid/none
Alt + U Underline: single/double/none
Alt + 1 Sets font 1.
Alt + 2 Sets font 2.
Alt + 3 Sets font 3.
Alt + 4 Sets font 4.
Alt + 5 Sets font 5.
Alt + 6 Sets font 6.
Alt + 7 Sets font 7.
Alt + 8 Sets font 8.

EXAMPLES USING ALLWAYS

Print Enhancements In this Allways example, you are to load the CH5EX1 worksheet that you have created (see Figure 10.3). In order to get the worksheet to appear like that in Figure 10.4, you are to delete any row containing dashes or equal signs. These rows of dashes and equal signs are used to indicate a subtotal or grand total. You will be using Allways later to insert these in a cell to indicate a subtotal or grand total for the worksheet user.

After you have performed the above tasks, you are ready to prepare the worksheet using Allways. You will be making changes to this worksheet so that it appears like that in Figure 10.5.

1. Disable the Undo feature of 1-2-3 so that memory will be available for Allways and its various fonts that have to be loaded in.

   / Brings up the Main Menu for Lotus 1-2-3
   W Selects the Worksheet option
   G Selects the Global option

Figure 10.3
The CH5EX1 worksheet

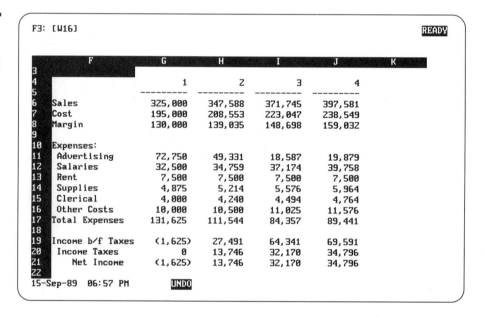

Figure 10.4
The CH5EX1 worksheet with the rows containing dashes and equal signs removed

D	Selects the Default option
O	Selects the Other option
U	Selects the Undo option
D	Selects the Disable command
Q	Quits from the menu

2. Attach the Allways add-in.

/	Brings up the Main Menu for Lotus 1-2-3
A	Selects the Add-in option
A	Selects the Attach option
ALLWAYS.ADN	Selects the ALLWAYS.ADN using the pointer
Enter	Press the Enter key to execute the command

Figure 10.5
The CH5EX1 worksheet after it has been modified by Allways

ED'S MICROCOMPUTER SHOP
Projected Financial Statements

	1	2	3	4
	---------	---------	---------	---------
Sales	325,000	347,588	371,745	397,581
Cost	195,000	208,553	223,047	238,549
Margin	130,000	139,035	148,698	159,032
Expenses:				
Advertising	72,750	49,331	18,587	19,879
Salaries	32,500	34,759	37,174	39,758
Rent	7,500	7,500	7,500	7,500
Supplies	4,875	5,214	5,576	5,964
Clerical	4,000	4,240	4,494	4,764
Other Costs	10,000	10,500	11,025	11,576
Total Expenses	131,625	111,544	84,357	89,441
Income b/f Taxes	(1,625)	27,491	64,341	69,591
Income Taxes	0	13,746	32,170	34,796
Net Income	(1,625)	13,746	32,170	34,796

Figure 10.6
The CH5EX1 worksheet as it appears using Allways

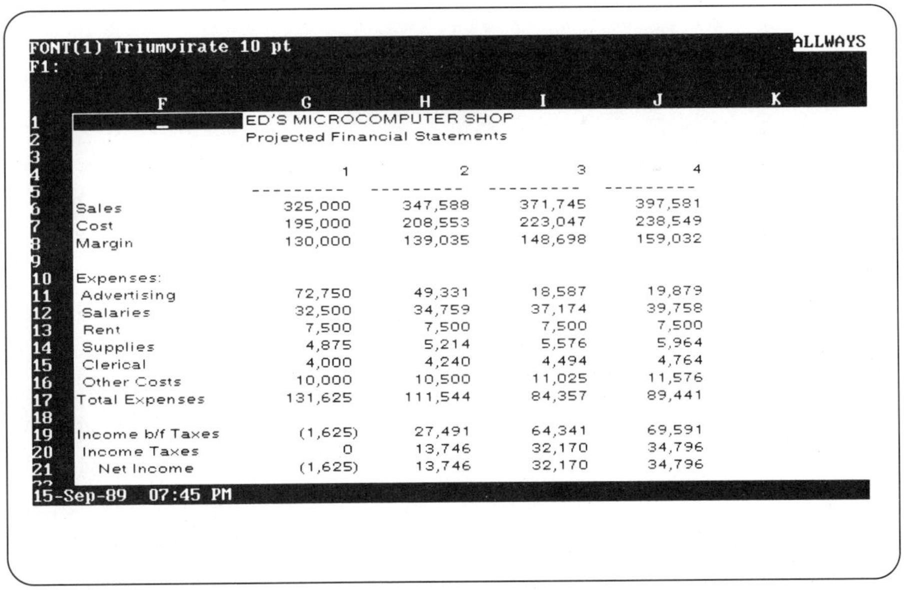
FONT(1) Triumvirate 10 pt ALLWAYS
F1:

	F	G	H	I	J	K
1		ED'S MICROCOMPUTER SHOP				
2		Projected Financial Statements				
3						
4		1	2	3	4	
5		---------	---------	---------	---------	
6	Sales	325,000	347,588	371,745	397,581	
7	Cost	195,000	208,553	223,047	238,549	
8	Margin	130,000	139,035	148,698	159,032	
9						
10	Expenses:					
11	Advertising	72,750	49,331	18,587	19,879	
12	Salaries	32,500	34,759	37,174	39,758	
13	Rent	7,500	7,500	7,500	7,500	
14	Supplies	4,875	5,214	5,576	5,964	
15	Clerical	4,000	4,240	4,494	4,764	
16	Other Costs	10,000	10,500	11,025	11,576	
17	Total Expenses	131,625	111,544	84,357	89,441	
18						
19	Income b/f Taxes	(1,625)	27,491	64,341	69,591	
20	Income Taxes	0	13,746	32,170	34,796	
21	Net Income	(1,625)	13,746	32,170	34,796	

15-Sep-89 07:45 PM

7	Assigns this add-in to the F7 function key
I	Selects the Invoke command
ALLWAYS	Selects the Allways add-in using the pointer
Enter	Starts Allways

Once Allways is invoked, your screen should appear like that depicted in Figure 10.6. Notice that Allways is indicating that the Triumvirate 10 point font is being used (this is the default font for Allways).

Figure 10.7
The font selection popup menu box

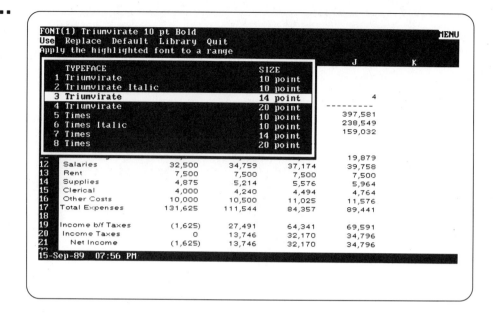

3. Change the title of the worksheet to Triumvirate 14 point and boldface it.

G1	Positions the pointer to cell G1 using pointer manipulation commands
.	Nails the pointer down with a period
G2	Extends the range to cell G2
/	Brings up the Main Menu for Allways
F	Selects the Format option
B	Selects the Bold command
S	Executes the Set command to set the range of cells to boldface
/	Brings up the Main Menu for Allways
F	Selects the Format option
F	Selects the Font option (see Figure 10.7)
14 point	Using the Arrow keys, highlight the Triumvirate 14 point option from the popup menu
Enter	Activates that font (Your worksheet should now appear like that depicted in Figure 10.8.)

4. Underline the subtotal cells in the worksheet.

G7	Positions the pointer to cell G7
/	Brings up the Main Menu for Allways
F	Selects the Format option
U	Selects the Underline command
S	Selects the Single option
J7	Extends the range to cell J7 using pointer manipulation commands
Enter	Executes the command

Figure 10.8
The worksheet with the font for the titles changes

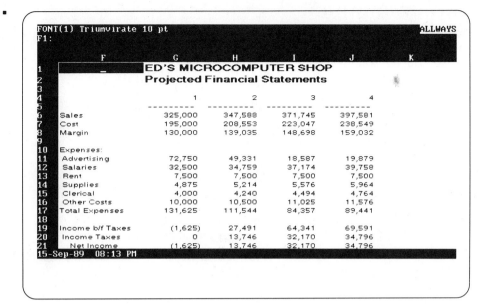

Notice that as the worksheet cells using Allways are underlined the underlined characters actually become part of the cell rather than taking up an entire row as when you are using 1-2-3. Allways accomplishes this by making the rows containing the underlining slightly taller than adjacent rows.

G16	Positions the pointer to cell G16
/	Brings up the Main Menu for Allways
F	Selects the Format option
U	Selects the Underline command
S	Selects the Single option
J16	Extends the range to cell J16 using pointer manipulation commands
Enter	Executes the command
G17	Positions the pointer to cell G17
/	Brings up the Main Menu for Allways
F	Selects the Format option
U	Selects the Underline command
S	Selects the Single option
J17	Extends the range to cell J17 using pointer manipulation commands
Enter	Executes the command
G20	Positions the pointer to cell G20
/	Brings up the Main Menu for Allways
F	Selects the Format option
U	Selects the Underline command
S	Selects the Single option
J20	Extends the range to cell J20 using pointer manipulation commands
Enter	Executes the command

Figure 10.9
The worksheet with the subtotal and grand total indicators

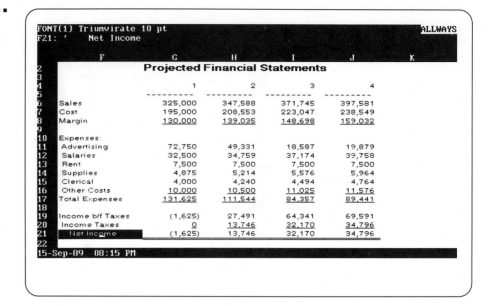

5. Double underline the grand total cells.

G21	Positions the pointer to cell G21
/	Brings up the Main Menu for Allways
F	Selects the Format option
U	Selects the Underline command
D	Selects the Double option
J21	Extends the range to cell J21 using pointer manipulation commands
Enter	Executes the command

Once you have executed these commands, your worksheet should appear like that depicted in Figure 10.9.

6. The user of the worksheet is especially interested in the figures for the second year. Therefore, to call attention to that year's projections, the column will be shaded.

H6	Positions the pointer to cell H6
/	Brings up the Main Menu for Allways
F	Selects the Format option
D	Selects the Dark Shade option
H21	Using pointer manipulation commands, extends the range through cell H21
Enter	Executes the command (see Figure 10.10)

7. Print the portion of the worksheet containing the projections.

F1	Positions the pointer to cell F1
/	Brings up the Main Menu for Allways
P	Selects the Print option
R	Selects the Range option
S	Selects the Set command

Figure 10.10
The cells for year two shaded

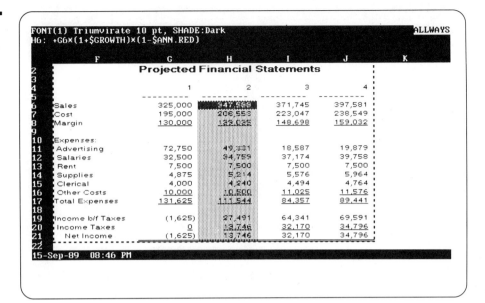

Figure 10.11
The printed worksheet using Allways

	1	2	3	4
	ED'S MICROCOMPUTER SHOP			
	Projected Financial Statements			
Sales	325,000	347,588	371,745	397,581
Cost	195,000	208,553	223,047	238,549
Margin	130,000	139,035	148,698	159,032
Expenses:				
Advertising	72,750	49,331	18,587	19,879
Salaries	32,500	34,759	37,174	39,758
Rent	7,500	7,500	7,500	7,500
Supplies	4,875	5,214	5,576	5,964
Clerical	4,000	4,240	4,494	4,764
Other Costs	10,000	10,500	11,025	11,576
Total Expenses	131,625	111,544	84,357	89,441
Income b/f Taxes	(1,625)	27,491	64,341	69,591
Income Taxes	0	13,746	32,170	34,796
Net Income	(1,625)	13,746	32,170	34,796

J21	Using pointer manipulation commands, extends the range through cell J21
Enter	Sets the range (The range is now enclosed in dashes.)
G	Executes the print operation (see Figure 10.11)

8. Use Allways to change the input variables portion of the worksheet.

Home	Positions the pointer to cell A1

Figure 10.12
The input variables after they have been placed in boxes

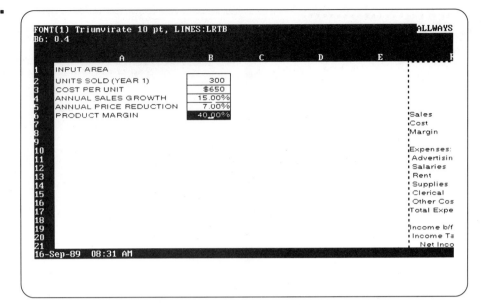

9. Use Allways to widen column A for the Allways worksheet only.

/	Brings up the Allways Main Menu
W	Selects the Worksheet option
C	Selects the Column option
S	Selects the Set-Width option
25	Changes the column width to 25
Enter	Executes the command

10. Place boxes around each input variable's value.

B2	Positions the pointer to cell B2
.	Nails down the beginning of the range
B6	Extends the range to cell B6
/	Brings up the Main Menu for Allways
F	Selects the Format option
L	Selects the Lines option
A	Selects the All option

The cells B2 through B6 should all appear to be contained in boxes (see Figure 10.12).

11. Press the Esc key to return to 1-2-3. Notice that the 1-2-3 worksheet remains unchanged; none of the enhancements that have been made to the worksheet using Allways appear on the 1-2-3 worksheet.

12. To return to Allways issue the Alt + F7 command.

13. Return to 1-2-3 and issue the / File Save command to permit Allways to create and save the settings to the CH5EX1.ALL file.

 Incorporating a Graph This sample worksheet shows you how to use Allways to merge worksheet and graph data on one report (see Figure 10.13), and it builds on the previous example. If you are doing this sample at a different session than when you built the first worksheet, go through steps 1 and 2 of the previous example before you start this worksheet.

Figure 10.13
Worksheet and graph data merged on one printed report

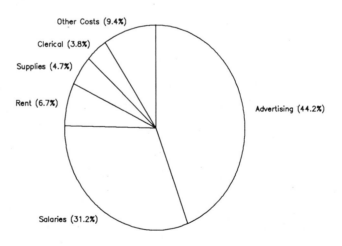

ED'S MICROCOMPUTER SHOP
Projected Financial Statements

	1	2	3	4
Sales	325,000	347,588	371,745	397,581
Cost	195,000	208,553	223,047	238,549
Margin	130,000	139,035	148,698	159,032
Expenses:				
Advertising	72,750	49,331	18,587	19,879
Salaries	32,500	34,759	37,174	39,758
Rent	7,500	7,500	7,500	7,500
Supplies	4,875	5,214	5,576	5,964
Clerical	4,000	4,240	4,494	4,764
Other Costs	10,000	10,500	11,025	11,576
Total Expenses	131,625	111,544	84,357	89,441
Income b/f Taxes	(1,625)	27,491	64,341	69,591
Income Taxes	0	13,746	32,170	34,796
Net Income	(1,625)	13,746	32,170	34,796

Ed's Microcomputer Shop
Expenses – Year Two

- Other Costs (9.4%)
- Clerical (3.8%)
- Supplies (4.7%)
- Rent (6.7%)
- Salaries (31.2%)
- Advertising (44.2%)

1. Build a pie chart for the second year's expenses while using 1-2-3. Before you can include a graph in an Allways file, the graph settings must be saved to a .PIC file on disk.

/	Brings up the Main Menu of 1-2-3
G	Selects the Graph option
T	Selects the Type option
P	Selects the Pie option
X	Selects the X option
F11	Positions the pointer to cell F11
.	Nails the pointer down with a period
F16	Extends the range to cell F16
Enter	Executes the command
A	Selects the first data-range option
H11	Positions the pointer to cell H11
.	Nails the pointer down with a period
H16	Extends the range to cell H16
Enter	Executes the command
O	Selects the Options entry
T	Selects the Titles option
F	Selects the First option
Ed's Microcomputer Shop	
Enter	Executes the command
T	Selects the Titles option
S	Selects the Second option
Expenses—Year Two	
Enter	Executes the command
Q	Selects the Quit option
V	Views the graph
S	Selects the Save option
2NDYRPIE	Enters the name of the .PIC file
Enter	Saves the file
Q	Returns to READY mode

2. Activate Allways.

Alt + F7	Activates Allways

3. Insert the graph in the Allways file.

F27	Positions the pointer to cell F27
/	Brings up the Allways Main Menu
G	Selects the Graph option
A	Selects the Add option
2NDYRPIE	Highlights the 2NDYRPIE set of graph settings to be placed in the Allways worksheet
Enter	Activates the settings

Figure 10.14
The 2NDYRPIE graph in the Allways worksheet

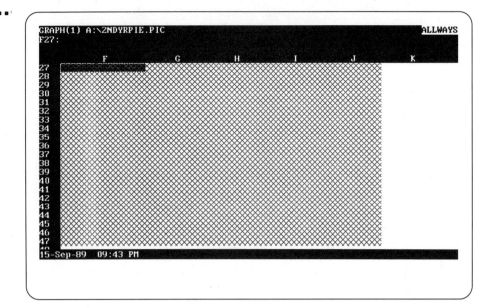

J47	Extends the range that the graph is to appear in to cell J47
Enter	Creates the graph (You may now see the hatching indicating where the graph will appear in your worksheet [see Figure 10.14].)
Q	Quits from the Graph Menu

4. If you see hatching, issue these commands to view the graph in your Allways worksheet.

/	Brings up the Allways Main Menu
D	Selects the Display option
G	Selects the Graph option
Y	Selects the Yes option
Q	Selects the Quit option (You should now see the graph as it will appear in the printout [see Figure 10.15].)

5. Print the worksheet.

/	Brings up the Allways Main Menu
P	Selects the Print option
R	Selects the Range option
S	Selects the Set option
J47	Extends the range through cell J47 to include the graph
Enter	Resets the range
G	Prints the report

You should now see a report similar to that depicted in Figure 10.13.

6. Return to 1-2-3 and save the worksheet file back to disk.

Figure 10.15
The graph visible on the screen, after the display has been activated for graphs

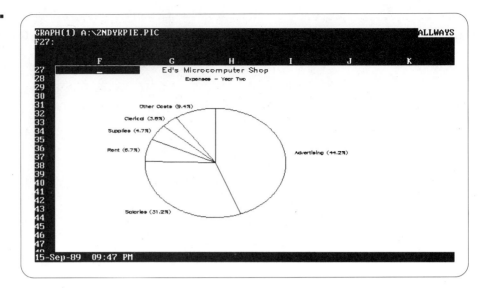

7. Verify the existence of the CH5EX1.ALL file.

/	Invokes the Main Menu
F	Selects the File option
L	Selects the List option
O	Selects the Other option
CH5EX1.ALL	Highlights the CH5EX1.ALL file, using the pointer

You should now be able to see the information for the Allways file containing the various format settings.

MACRO LIBRARY MANAGER

The Macro Library Manager permits you to create libraries of macros, store these libraries to disk, and have up to 10 of these macro libraries active whenever you are working on a worksheet. It is an add-in that must be attached before it can be used, which is accomplished using the same type of add-in commands that were used in attaching Allways to a worksheet.

A **macro library** is a range of cells that have been taken from a 1-2-3 worksheet by the Macro Library Manager, saved to disk as a library file with a .MLB file extension, and then loaded into memory in an area separate from any worksheet that you currently have in RAM. This macro library can contain a single macro, data, many macros, or both macros and data.

When a macro library is created, you must first have a worksheet loaded into memory that has information that you wish to place in a library file. You then use the Macro Library Manager to take this information from a range of your worksheet and save it to the specified library on disk, which removes the specified range of cells from your worksheet. This new library now appears on disk as a .MLB file and in an area of memory reserved for these macro libraries. Up to 10 libraries can be loaded to RAM at a time.

Macro libraries can be used to hold commonly used macros, data, formulas, or tables of information. They allow you to use macros that were specifically created for one worksheet with any worksheet that resides in memory, so that you can create a standard set of macros and use them whenever you want to.

The Macro Library Manager must be attached to 1-2-3 any time you want to save data to a library file or before you are allowed to load a library file into memory. If the Macro Library Manager is mistakenly detached during a worksheet session, any macro libraries that have been loaded to memory disappear and are no longer available to your worksheet.

LIMITATIONS OF MACRO LIBRARY MANAGER

Before you start using this 1-2-3 add-in, you should be acquainted with a number of its limitations.

- A macro library is limited to 16,376 cells.
- Whenever the Load or Save command is executed, 1-2-3 places a macro library in memory. You are limited to a maximum of 10 libraries in memory at one time.
- Macro libraries are separate from your worksheet in memory. This means that a library does not have any cell addresses, so if you want to use a macro to refer to a specific address, you must use named ranges instead of cell addresses.
- Once a macro library has been attached to 1-2-3, a macro can be invoked using the Alt key (if the macro name is two characters and begins with \) or with the Run (Alt + F3) command. When you are using the Run command, you are also permitted to use the Name (F3) command to display a screen containing all of the named ranges in your worksheet.
- If you are using 1-2-3 from diskettes, you will need a copy of the Install Disk. This disk contains the Macro Library Manager add-in drivers and software and will be needed any time you want to attach this add-in.

SAVING THE MACRO LIBRARY

When you are creating the macro library using the Save command, you must be aware of the following limitations.

- Whenever a Save command is executed, a cell in the worksheet takes up a cell in the library to be created.
- A macro library can be saved using a password. This does not, however, prohibit anyone from using the library. It does protect the user by preventing anyone from editing the macro library without first entering the correct password. If you use a password, the case of the characters entered for the password must exactly match the case of the characters used for the original.
- You can only use a macro library name once. If you try to create a new library using an existing name, 1-2-3 asks if you want the original to be overwritten.

THE MACRO LIBRARY MANAGER MENU

The options for the Macro Library Manager Menu can be seen once it has been attached to 1-2-3 by using the key sequence Alt + F_, with F_ standing for whichever function key (Alt + F8 in this text) that was assigned to this add-in. The options appear below:

Load Save Edit Remove Name-List Quit

Load The **Load option** copies the contents of a library file (.MLB) from disk into memory for use with this worksheet.

Save The **Save option** moves the contents of the cells in the specified range and any named range contained therein to the macro library in memory as well as to the specified library file (.MLB) on disk.

Edit The **Edit option** copies the contents of a macro library from memory to a range in the worksheet so that changes can be made to that library. Before you use this command, make certain that you have positioned the pointer to an unused area of your worksheet, since this command erases the current contents of the worksheet and replaces them with the contents of the specified library. Once you have made any changes to the macro library, you can use the Save command to save the changes back to the same library by responding Yes to the prompt concerning overwriting the existing .MLB file.

Remove The **Remove option** erases a macro library from memory.

Name-List The **Name-List option** enters a list of the range names contained in a library to the worksheet. Before you use this command, make certain that you have positioned the pointer to an unused area of your worksheet, since this command erases the current contents of the worksheet and replaces them with the contents of the specified library.

Quit The **Quit option** returns you to READY mode.

BUILDING A MACRO LIBRARY

This sample worksheet exercise will take the macros that have been created using the COMPSALS worksheet (see Figure 10.16) and save them to a macro library file called TESTLIBR.

1. Load the COMPSALS worksheet from disk.
2. Attach the Macro Library Manager and assign it to key F8.

/	Brings up the Main Menu of Lotus 1-2-3
A	Selects the Add-in option
A	Selects the Attach option
MACROMGR.ADN	Highlights the macro manager add-in driver (If the MACROMGR.ADN entry does not appear in the prompt line, press the Esc key and then indicate the drive or directory where 1-2-3 can find this information.)
Enter	Executes the command
8	Assigns the add-in to function key 8 by highlighting using pointer movement commands
Enter	Executes the command
Quit	Returns to READY mode

3. Position the pointer to cell G23 (the upper left-hand cell containing the macros that you want to place in a library file).

Figure 10.16
Macros from a worksheet that are to be placed in a macro library

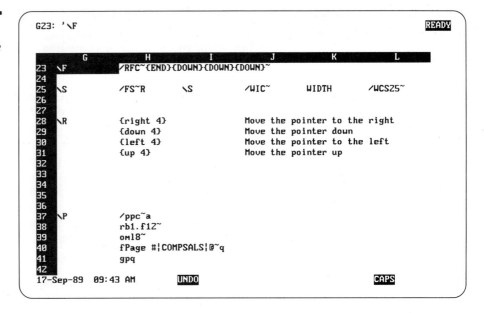

4. Create the library file called TESTLIBR.

Alt + F8	Invokes the Macro Library Manager Menu
S	Issues the Save command
TESTLIBR	Enters the name of the library to be created
Enter	Executes the command
L31	Extends the range to cell L31
Enter	Specifies the range
N	Specifies No for password protection

    The library has been created on disk. You should also see that the cells containing the original macro commands are now empty, since 1-2-3 has moved these to the TESTLIBR.MLB library file on disk as well as the library in memory. Now, retrieve any other worksheet file that you have created. Be sure that you do *not* save the COMPSALS file, since you want the original macros to remain in that file.

5. Load any file from disk (for example, CH4EX1). You can now use the Run command (Alt + F3) to execute any of the macros that currently reside in the library.

HINTS/HAZARDS

You can use the Macro Library Manager to create an .MLB file containing frequently used macro commands and then load those commands into a worksheet using the Edit command. You can now use this worksheet and its macros without having to attach the Macro Library Manager. This allows you to take the worksheet and use it on computers that are not equipped with this particular add-in of Lotus 1-2-3.

CHAPTER REVIEW

Add-in packages to Lotus 1-2-3 provide capabilities that are not found in the 1-2-3 program proper. Two add-ins that come with Release 2.2 are Allways and the Macro Library Manager. Before you can use an add-in with 1-2-3, the / Add-in command must be executed, you must indicate the add-in that is to be activated, and you must assign a function key to that add-in. Once the function key has been assigned, the add-in can be activated by using Alt + F_, where F_ stands for the assigned function key.

The Allways add-in provides the ability to perform spreadsheet publishing. Spreadsheet publishing allows you to add special print enhancements such as boldfacing, underlining, boxing-in cells, and specifying fonts, as well as many other special print capabilities. Any changes that are made to a worksheet are not included in the 1-2-3 worksheet itself but rather are stored to an .ALL file in the form of settings. Once a worksheet is loaded and Allways is activated, the corresponding .ALL file is automatically loaded into memory.

One of the most practical enhancements contained in Allways is the ability to have worksheet data and graphs appear on the same page of a printout. Before a graph can be included on a page of Allways output, a .PIC file must be created using the Save command of 1-2-3's Graph Menu. The settings of the .PIC file are loaded into the Allways copy of the worksheet, the range to hold the graph must be specified, and the graph area appears as a range of x's. To make the graph visible, you must use the / Display Graph command.

The Macro Library Manager permits you to create a set of commonly used macro commands, data, or both and save them to an .MLB file on disk. Once the Save or Load command is executed, 1-2-3 also places the library entry into a special area in memory. Up to 10 libraries can be stored in this special area. Macro commands can be executed by entering the name of the macro using the Run command or by using the Alt + _ convention if the macro is two characters in length and starts with a backslash (\).

KEY TERMS AND CONCEPTS

accelerator keys
add-in
Allways
attaching
Courier
default font
detaching
font
macro library
Macro Library Manager
monospaced spacing
pitch
point
printer font
proportional spacing
soft font
spreadsheet publishing
Times
Triumvirate
typeface

CHAPTER QUIZ

Multiple Choice

1. Which of the following commands is *not* supported by Allways?
    a. Boldface
    b. Shading
    c. Double underlining
    d. Changing fonts
    e. All of the above are supported by Allways.

2. Which of the following commands is used to invoke an add-in?
   a. Ctrl + a function key
   b. Alt + a function key
   c. Shift + a function key
   d. A function key

3. When a graph is first placed in an Allways document, the area it will occupy is indicated with
   a. x's.
   b. a box outline.
   c. the appearance of the graph itself.
   d. the appearance of the graph area in black.

4. Before an add-in can be used with 1-2-3 it must be
   a. invoked.
   b. attached.
   c. linked.
   d. none of the above.

5. Which of the following is *not* a limitation of the Macro Library Manager add-in?
   a. Each macro library must have a unique name.
   b. A macro must always have a password.
   c. A macro library can have a maximum of 16,376 cells.
   d. When a macro library is edited, a copy of that library is made at the pointer location of the worksheet in memory.
   e. All of the above are limitations of the Macro Library Manager.

True/False

6. An add-in for Lotus 1-2-3 can be activated by using the Shift + a function key without first attaching the add-in.

7. The Macro Manager Edit and Save commands can be used together to make changes to a macro library and save those changes back to the edited library file.

8. Changes made using Allways always appear in the 1-2-3 worksheet.

9. Allways requires you to issue a command and then specify a range for that command.

10. Always limits you to eight fonts within a document.

Answers

1. e   2. b   3. a   4. b   5. b   6. f   7. t   8. f   9. f   10. t

Exercises

1. Describe or define each of the following:
   a. Allways   c. Attach
   b. Macro Library Manager d. Invoke

2. Allways performs a task that is referred to as _____.

3. Before you can use Allways, your computer system must have _____ RAM and a(n) _____.

4. Once an add-in has been attached to 1-2-3, you can assign it to _____, _____, _____, or _____ function keys.

5. A font that must be downloaded to a printer is called _____.

6. The three fonts that come with Allways are:
   a.

   b.

   c.

7. A font that comes with a printer is called a _____ font.

8. The spacing of characters on a line can be in either _____ or _____.

9. Changes made to a worksheet using Allways are saved to a file with a(n) _____ file extension.

10. Once you have completed making changes to a worksheet using Allways, you must issue a(n) _____ using 1-2-3 to make certain that these changes can be accessed later by Allways.

11. Before a graph can be incorporated into an Allways document, a(n) _____ file must have been created using 1-2-3.

12. If you are defining a range to Allways before a command is issued, the _____ indicator appears in the status line at the bottom of the screen.

13. The function key _____ can be used by Allways to turn the graph display on or off.

14. _____ keys are commands that can be used by Allways to cut down the number of keystrokes needed for a command.

15. The command used by Allways to invoke its Main Menu is _____.

16. Up to _____ different macro library files can be loaded into memory.

17. The Macro Library Manager Menu command that is used to make changes to a library by copying the contents of a library to the current worksheet is the _____ command.

Figure 10.17
The YTDSALES worksheet

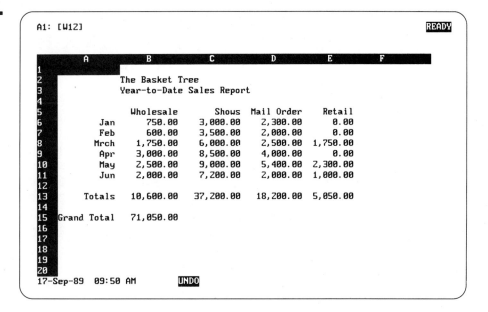

18. The _____ option of the Macro Library Manager Menu is used to create a table of the named ranges of libraries in the current worksheet.

19. A(n) _____ is a range of cells that have been copied to a file containing a .MLB file extension.

20. A macro library is limited to _____ cells.

COMPUTER EXERCISES

1. Load the YTDSALES worksheet from disk (see Figure 10.17). You will use this worksheet with and format it using Allways to generate the report depicted in Figure 10.18. Perform the following commands to format the worksheet. Save the worksheet to a file called CH10EX1.
   a. Set the first title line to Triumvirate 20 point.
   b. Set the second title line to Triumvirate 14 point.
   c. Boldface the column headings.
   d. Single underline the subtotal entries.
   e. Double underline the grand total figure.
   f. Use 1-2-3 to build a pie chart of the totals row entries.
   g. Incorporate the graph in the Allways worksheet.
   h. Print the report.

2. Retrieve the file that you created in Chapter 9 called CH9EX1. Place the macros that you entered in a library called LIB1. Retrieve any worksheet file that you have created and execute these macro commands against that worksheet.

Figure 10.18
The formatted report including a pie chart of total sales by category

The Basket Tree
Year-to-Date Sales Report

	Wholesale	Shows	Mail Order	Retail
Jan	750.00	3,000.00	2,300.00	0.00
Feb	600.00	3,500.00	2,000.00	0.00
Mrch	1,750.00	6,000.00	2,500.00	1,750.00
Apr	3,000.00	8,500.00	4,000.00	0.00
May	2,500.00	9,000.00	5,400.00	2,300.00
Jun	2,000.00	7,200.00	2,000.00	1,000.00
Totals	10,600.00	37,200.00	18,200.00	5,050.00
Grand Total	71,050.00			

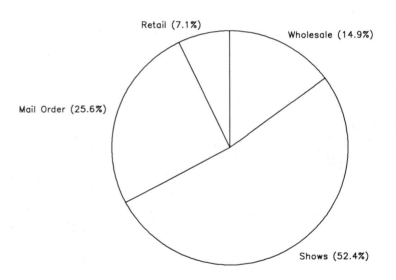

APPENDIX

A

LOTUS 1-2-3 COMMAND MENUS, FUNCTIONS, AND COMMAND LANGUAGE

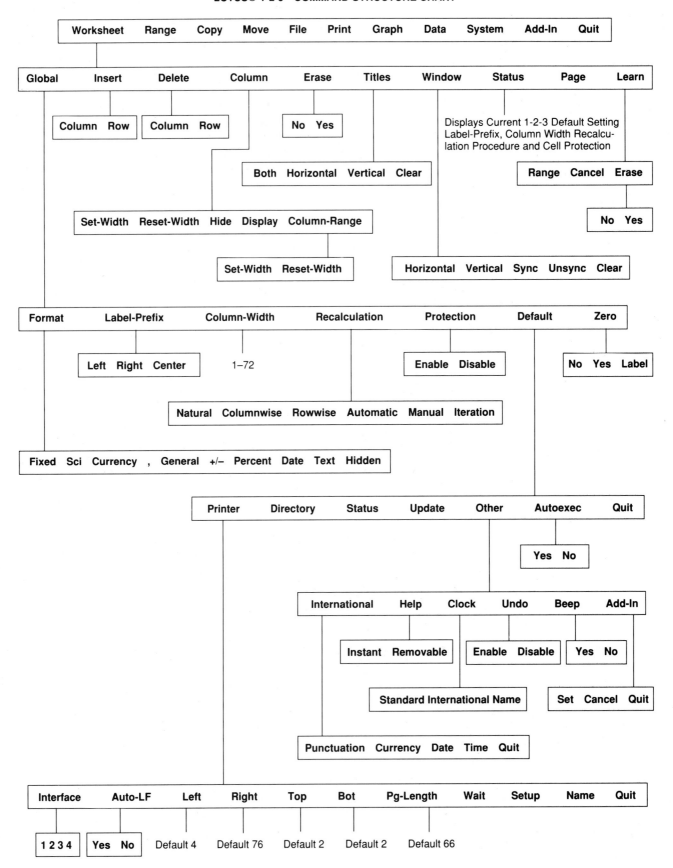

LOTUS® 1-2-3™ COMMAND STRUCTURE CHART

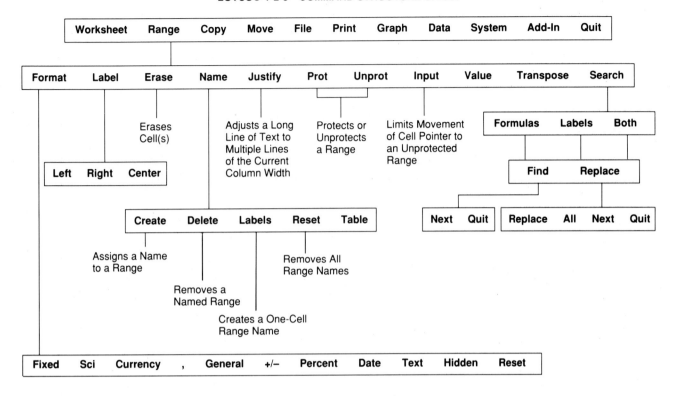

LOTUS® 1-2-3™ COMMAND STRUCTURE CHART

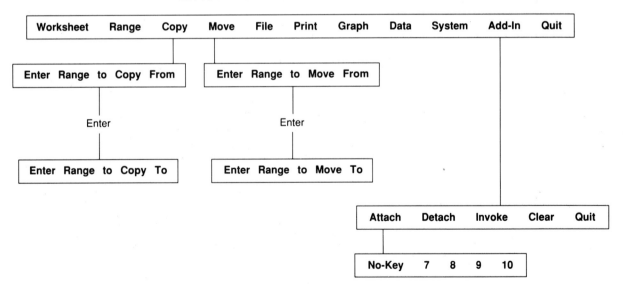

LOTUS® 1-2-3™ COMMAND STRUCTURE CHART

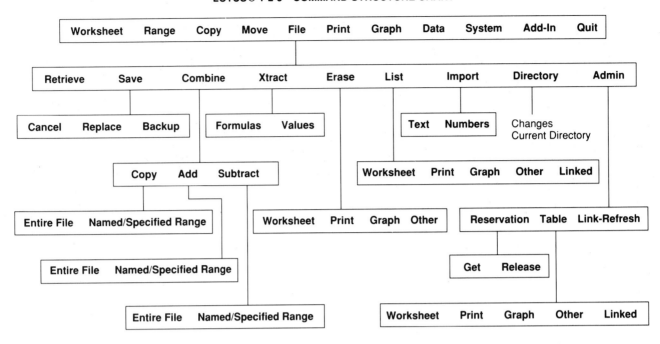

LOTUS® 1-2-3™ COMMAND STRUCTURE CHART

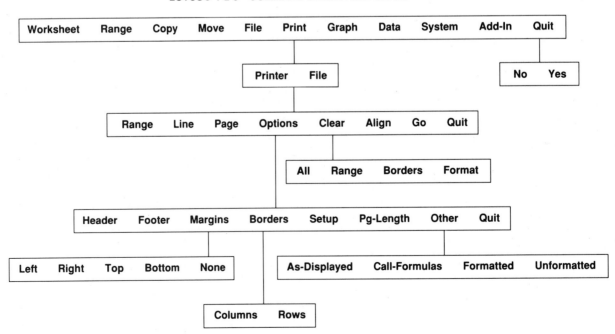

Lotus 1-2-3 Command Menus, Functions, and Command Language   A.5

LOTUS® 1-2-3™ COMMAND STRUCTURE CHART

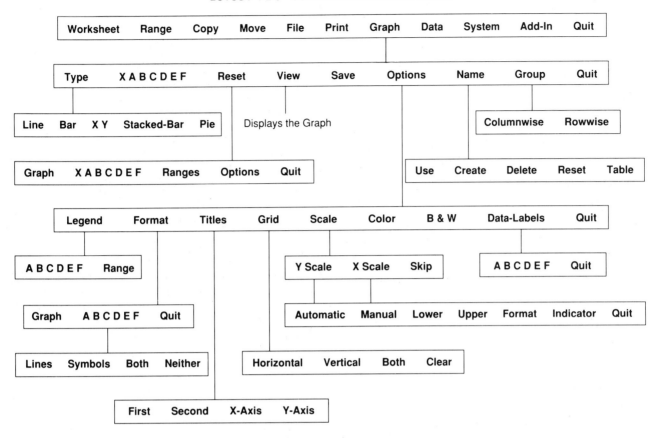

LOTUS® 1-2-3™ COMMAND STRUCTURE CHART

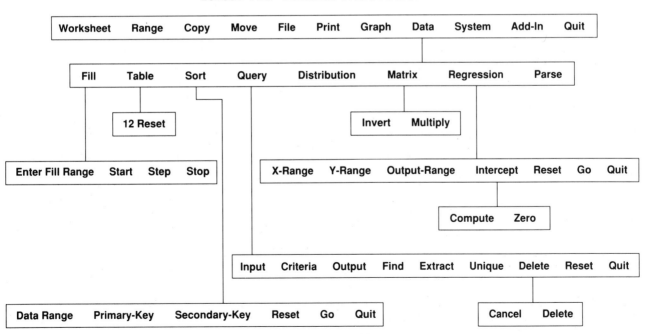

1-2-3 FUNCTION SUMMARY

The following summary of 1-2-3 functions lists those most commonly used in a worksheet environment. Functions of a more esoteric nature can be found in the 1-2-3 documentation.

DATABASE FUNCTIONS

These functions are discussed in detail in Chapter 8. Please refer to that chapter for information.

DATE AND TIME FUNCTIONS

Date functions can generate dates between January 1, 1900, and December 31, 2099. A date function returns a real number with values to the left and right of the decimal point. The value to the left of the decimal point represents a specific day, while the value to the right of the decimal point represents the time of the day. Before a date can be understandable, it must be converted to a format that is readable to a user. This is accomplished via the / Range Format Date series of commands. When the Date Menu is displayed, you may select the desirable format for display.

- **@DATE(YY,MM,DD)** The year (YY) parameter must be a number between 0 (1900) and 199 (2099). A value of 88 represents the year 1988, while a value of 103 represents the year 2003. The month (MM) parameter must be a number from 1 to 12. The day (DD) parameter must be a number from 1 to 31. Any errors that you make in entering the above parameters result in the value ERR appearing in the cell.

    After the date parameter has been entered, a numeric value appears in the cell. This value must now be changed to a readable date format.

    Once this function has been entered in a worksheet, other functions like @YEAR,@MONTH,@DAY, and @MOD (determining the day of the week) can be used against that cell.

- **@DATEVALUE(datestring)** This function allows you to enter a date string between double quotes and provides you with the numeric value for that date. For example, if you needed to determine the numeric value for the date December 25, 1988, you would enter the function @DATEVALUE("12/25/88") and receive the numeric value 32502. The difference between this function and the @DATE function is that the @DATEVALUE function uses a character string as input, while the @DATE function uses three numeric parameters as input.

    The date string must be enclosed within double quotes and can be any one of the 1-2-3 date formats. This means that any one of the following functions for the example above will return the same value:

    @DATEVALUE("25/Dec/88") = 32502
    @DATEVALUE("25-Dec") = 32502 (88 must be the current year)
    @DATEVALUE("Dec-88") = 32478

- **@DAY(date number)** This function returns the day of the month (1 to 31) of the date number. The date number can reference another date function (@DATE,@DATEVALUE, or @NOW), or it can be a cell reference.

    @DAY(@DATE(88,12,25)) = 25
    @DAY(A9) —returns the day of the month in cell A9

- **@MONTH(date number)** This function returns the month number (1 to 12) of the date number. The date number can reference another date function (@DATE,@DATEVALUE, or @NOW), or it can refer to a cell reference.

    @MONTH(@DATE(88,12,25)) = 12

- **@YEAR(date number)** This function returns the year number (0 to 199) of the date number. The date number can reference another date function

(@DATE,@DATEVALUE, or @NOW), or it can refer to a cell reference containing a date.

```
@YEAR(@DATE(88,12,25)) = 88
```

- **@NOW** This function returns the date value for the current date and time that was entered manually or by the clock calendar feature of your computer when you started your system. If you do not have a clock calendar and did not enter a date, the default value 01/01/80 is used. This function is often used to date-stamp your worksheet for printing.
- **@TIME(hr,min,sec)** This function returns the fractional value for the time entered. The parameter values are as follows: the hr parameter must be between 0 and 23, the min parameter must be between 0 and 59, and the sec parameter must be between 0 and 59. If these guidelines are not followed, 1-2-3 displays an ERR message in the cell.

FINANCIAL FUNCTIONS

The 1-2-3 financial functions require you to enter interest rates as percents or decimal fractions. If you enter 17%, 1-2-3 automatically translates that value to .17. You must also express the term and interest rate in the same units of time. If you are dealing with monthly payments, divide the interest rate by 12. If the term is expressed in years, multiply by 12.

- **@CTERM(int,fv,pv)** This function determines the number of compounding periods it will take an investment of present value *pv* to grow to a future value *fv*, earning a fixed interest rate *int* per compounding period.

  This function uses the formula $\ln(fv/pv)/\ln(1 + int)$ to compute the term.

  fv = future value
  pv = present value
  int = periodic interest rate
  ln = natural logarithm

  You have just retired and have received a lump sum payment that you want to invest in a $200,000 CD. The CD pays an interest rate of 11.75% compounded monthly. You are interested in how long it will take to double your investment.

  ```
  @CTERM(.1175/12,400000,200000) = 71.1
  ```

  This tells you that it will take 71 months (5.9 years) to double the investment.

- **@DDB(cost,salvage,life,period)** This function determines the depreciation allowance on an asset for a specified period of time, using the double-declining-balance method. The parameters are as follows: cost is the amount paid for the asset, salvage is the value of the asset at the end of its useful life, life is the number of periods for depreciation, and period is the time period for which you want to find the depreciation allowance.

  This function uses the formula $(bv*2)/n$ to compute the double-declining-balance depreciation amount for any period.

  bv = book value in this period
  n = life of asset

  Assume that you have purchased a computer system for $12,500. The useful life is considered to be 4 years, and the salvage value is $1,900. You want to compute the depreciation expense for the second year.

  ```
  @DDB(12500,1900,4,2) = 3125
  ```

  This tells you that the depreciation for the second year will be $3,125.

- **@FV(pmt,int,term)** This function calculates the future value of an investment based on equal payments. The parameters used are as follows: pmt is the value that is to be deposited each period, int is the period interest rate, and term represents the number of payment periods.

Suppose that you want to provide for the college education of a newborn child. You plan to deposit $1,200 each year into a bank account. The bank is paying 5.75% interest annually. The payment is deposited on the last day of each year. You want to compute the value of the account in 18 years.

@FV(1200,.0575,18) = 36220.45

This result tells you that at the end of 18 years you will have $36,220.45 in your bank account.

Computing the future value of an annuity due requires the formula @FV(1200,.0575,18)*(1+.0575). This example assumes that you are making the payment on the first day of the year instead of on the last day.

@FV(1200,.0575,18)*(1+.0575) = 38303.12

This result tells you that by making the payment on the first day of the year your investment would return an additional $2,082.67 over the ordinary annuity.

- **@NPV(int,range)** This function computes the present value of a series of future cash flows, discounted at a fixed period interest rate. The cash flows are assumed to occur at equal time intervals. The first cash flow, as well as subsequent cash flows, is assumed to occur at the end of the period. The int parameter is the periodic interest rate, and the range parameter is the range of worksheet cells that you use to store the series of cash flows.

Assume that the cash flows are $100 per period for 6 periods and that the interest rate is 11%. Your worksheet (cells plus their respective values) appears as follows:

E6	100
E7	100
E8	100
E9	100
E10	100
E11	100

Your NPV function is @NPV(.11,e6,e11), and the value returned is 423.05.

To find the net present value of an investment in which you make an initial cash outflow followed by a series of inflows, you must factor the initial outflow separately, since it is not affected by the interest. This is accomplished via the +INITIAL+@NPV(rate,range) adaptation of the NPV function.

Assume that your initial outflow for an investment is $5,000. Over the next six years, you are to receive flows for the first three years of $1,750 and for the next three years flows of $1,850. The rate of interest is 12%. Your worksheet looks as follows:

G5	(5000)	(Initial payment)
G6	12%	(Interest rate)
G7	1750	
G8	1750	
G9	1750	
G10	1850	

G11   1850
G12   1850

+G5+@NPV(G6,G7..G13) = 2365

- **@PMT(prin,int,periods)** This function computes the amount of the payment on a loan. Most installment loans are computed like ordinary annuities (payments at the end of the month). The parameters for this function are as follows: prin is the principal of the loan, int is the periodic interest rate, and periods is the number of payment periods.

    For example, if you want to take out a mortgage for a home and $95,000 is to be financed at a rate of 10.5% for 20 years, you would use the following formula to calculate your monthly payments:

    @PMT(95000,.105/12,20*12) = 948.46

- **@PV(pmt,int,periods)** This function computes the present value of an investment based on a series of equal payments, each of amount pmt, discounted at periodic interest rate int, over the number of periods in periods.

    Assume that you have just won the $6,000,000 Lotto. The payments for the lottery are $300,000 each year for 20 years. Each payment is to be received at the end of the year. You are also given the option of receiving a lump-sum payment of $2,700,000 instead of the annuity. You want to find out which option is worth more in today's dollars. You also know that if you were to accept the annual payments you could invest them at an interest rate of 10.25% in, compounded annually.

    @PV(300000,.1025,20) = 2,511,085

    Since 2,511,085 is less than 2,700,000, the lump sum is worth more in today's dollars.

- **@SLN(cost,salvage,life)** This function computes the straight-line depreciation of an asset for one period. The straight-line method of depreciation divides the depreciable cost (cost − salvage) over the useful life of an asset.

    Assume that you have purchased a computer system for $12,500. The useful life is considered to be 4 years, and the salvage value is $1,900. You want to compute the depreciation expense for the second year.

    @SLN(12500,1900,4) = 2650

    This means that $2,650 is the yearly depreciation allowance.

- **@SYD(cost,salvage,life,period)** This function computes the sum-of-the-years'-digits depreciation for a specified period. This method of depreciation accelerates the rate of depreciation so that more depreciation expense occurs in the early life of an asset. The depreciable cost is the cost minus the salvage value. The useful life is the number of periods over which an asset is depreciated.

    Assume that you have purchased a computer system for $12,500. The useful life is considered to be 4 years, and the salvage value is $1,900. You want to compute the depreciation expense for the second year.

    @SYD(12500,1900,4,2) = 3180

    This means that $3,180 dollars is the depreciation amount for the second year.

- **@TERM(pmt,int,fv)** This function returns the number of payment periods in the term of an ordinary annuity necessary to accumulate a future value of fv, earning a periodic interest rate of int. Each payment is equal to the pmt parameter.

You are preparing for retirement. You want to know how long it will take to accumulate $250,000 in a bank account. You plan to deposit $3,000 at the end of each year. Interest amounts to 5.75%.

@TERM(3000,.0575,250000) = 31.42

This means that it will take 31.4 years to accumulate $250,000.

MATHEMATICAL FUNCTIONS

- **@INT(x)** This function returns the integer part of x. It truncates x at the decimal point. This means that everything to the right of the decimal point is lost.

  @INT(75.35) = 75
  @INT(75.99) = 75
  @INT(@NOW)—only the whole number value is returned

  If you want to round, use the @ROUND function.

- **@MOD(x,y)** This function returns the modulo of the remainder (modulo) of x/y. Parameter x can be any positive or negative number; y must be a number other than 0. The modulo can also be used to determine the day of the week (the y parameter must be 7).

  @MOD(15,4) = 2
  @MOD(17,5) = 2
  @MOD(@DATE(88,12,25),7) = 1

  The calendar for 1-2-3 begins on Sunday. This makes Sunday day 1 and Saturday day 7.

- **@ROUND(x,n)** This function rounds a number (x) to n decimal positions. You can tell 1-2-3 to round on either side of the decimal point. A positive value for n rounds to the right of the decimal, while a negative value for n rounds to the left of the decimal a power of 10, or position, at a time.

  @ROUND(1572.2345,2) = 1572.23
  @ROUND(77.89,1) = 77.9
  @ROUND(1367.65,-2) = 1400
  @ROUND(@PMT(95000,.1025/12,20*12),-1) = 950

- **@SQRT(x)** This function returns the positive square root of x.

  @SQRT(144) = 12
  @SQRT(14) = 3.741657
  @SQRT(-15) = ERR, because x is negative

SPECIAL FUNCTIONS

- **@ERR** This function returns the numeric value ERR. Use this function to force a cell to have the value ERR. All cells containing formulas that reference this cell will also have the value ERR. This causes a ripple effect on the worksheet.

  @IF(E3>10000,@ERR,A3*B3)

  If the ERR entry appears, the value in this cell was greater than 10,000; otherwise, the value will be the result of multiplying the contents of cell A3 by the contents of cell B3.

- **@NA** This function returns the numeric value NA. This means that a number is not available to complete a formula. An NA now appears in this cell as well as in any other cells that depend on this formula. This @NA function is especially useful when you are constructing a worksheet and are not really certain what data will be involved.

  ```
  @IF(E3>10000,@NA,A3*B3)
  ```

  If the NA entry appears, the value in this cell was greater than 10,000; otherwise, the value will be the result of multiplying the contents of cell A3 by the contents of cell B3.

STATISTICAL FUNCTIONS

These functions are discussed in detail in Chapter 4. Please refer to that chapter for information.

STRING FUNCTIONS

String functions manipulate a series of characters (strings), allow you to perform calculations on strings, and produce string values. Strings can be alphabetic letters, numbers, or special characters. They must all, however, be preceded by a label prefix.

- **@LENGTH(string)** This function returns the number of characters in the parameter string.

  ```
  @LENGTH(worksheet) = 9
  @LENGTH('12345) = 5
  @LENGTH(12345) = ERR (not a string)
  ```

- **@PROPER(string)** This function converts the letters in the string parameter to proper capitalization. This means that the first letter of each word is uppercase and all others are lowercase.

  ```
  @PROPER("FOUR SCORE AND SEVEN YEARS AGO") = Four Score
  ```
  And Seven Years Ago

- **@STRING(x,n)** This function converts the numeric value x to a string with n decimal positions. Rounding takes place automatically to n positions.

  ```
  @STRING(125,2) = 125.00
  @STRING(35.6789,2) = 35.68
  ```

- **@TRIM(string)** This function removes excess blanks from the string. It removes excess blanks before and after the string, as well as any excessive blanks (more than two) within the string. Each word is still allowed to have one blank between it and the next word.

  ```
  @TRIM("  United  States  ") = United States
  @TRIM("  Dr.  No  ") = Dr. No
  ```

- **@UPPER(string)** This function converts all letters in the string to uppercase.

  ```
  @UPPER("usa") = USA
  ```

- **@VALUE(string)** This function converts the number string to its corresponding numeric value. The string can appear as a number (389.65), as a mixed number (23 3/4), or in scientific notation (2.3423E2).

  ```
  @VALUE("975") = 975
  @VALUE(42 1/4) = 42.25
  @VALUE(E9) = 15.75 if cell E9 contains 15 3/4
  ```

ADVANCED MACRO COMMANDS

When more advanced 1-2-3 macro commands are used, you must follow the syntax (grammar) specified by the Lotus Corporation. Advanced macro commands require a keyword between braces { } and may have one or more arguments following the keyword. Incorrect macro commands result in an error when you execute the macro, not when you are entering it. When arguments are used, they must be separated by a comma (,) or a semicolon (;). The four types of arguments are as follows:

- **Number** Any single numeric value, cell reference, or formula that results in a numeric value may be used. The entry 23.45 is an example of a numeric entry used as an argument. A cell reference like (M28) or a valid range name can also be used, as can a formula like (J3*K3+L3).
- **String** Any sequence of characters enclosed in double quotes up to 240 characters in length can be used. You cannot, however, use a formula in a command that calls for a string argument (exceptions are noted).
- **Location** Any range of one or more cells can be referenced. You can specify a range using either the cell address or a named range.
- **Condition** A condition includes any logical expression. The macro executes depending on the result of a true/false test specified. It compares values in two cells to determine if one is less than, greater than, or equal to another or checks the result of a specified formula.

CONTROLLING OUTPUT TO THE SCREEN

The following 1-2-3 macro commands can be used to change the appearance of the display on your monitor and to sound the bell.

- **{BEEP<number>}** Causes the computer to beep. The number argument is optional. This command can be used to signal the user that a macro that takes a lot of time has finished executing. It can also be used in conjunction with the {ONERROR} macro. The number argument (values 1, 2, 3, and 4) is used to specify the tone of the bell generated by the computer.
- **{BORDERSOFF} / {BORDERSON}** The {BORDERSOFF} macro command suppresses the display of the worksheet border (letters for columns and numbers for rows). The worksheet border remains suppressed until 1-2-3 encounters a {BORDERSON} macro command or until the macro ends.
- **{FRAMEOFF} / {FRAMEON}** These commands work exactly the same as the {BORDERSOFF} / {BORDERSON} commands.
- **{GRAPHOFF} / {GRAPHON}** The {GRAPHON, [named-graph], [nodisplay]} command has three different possibilities when it executes. {GRAPHON} without arguments displays the graph generated by the current graph settings. The following commands result in the graph disappearing from the screen: {GRAPHOFF}, {INDICATE}, {?}, {GETLABEL}, {GETNUMBER}, {MENUCALL}, {MENUBRANCH}, /XL, /XM, /XN. The command {GRAPHON,named-graph} makes the named-graph settings the current graph settings and displays this graph to the screen. The display of the graph is controlled by the rules enumerated above. The command {GRAPHON,named-graph,nodisplay} makes the named-graph settings the current graph settings without displaying the graph to the screen. The {GRAPHOFF} command redisplays the worksheet screen.
- **{INDICATE<string>}** Changes the mode indicator in the upper right-hand corner of the screen. The new mode indicator is changed to the string argument. The only way to change the new mode indicator is via another INDICATE macro with no arguments.
- **{PANELOFF}** Suppresses redrawing of the control panel during macro execution. This helps speed macro execution.
- **{PANELON}** Activates the regeneration of the control panel during macro execution.

- **{WINDOWSOFF}** Allows you to freeze the screen display so that changes are not constantly flickering across the monitor. It not only saves time but also reduces user confusion.
- **{WINDOWSON}** Reactivates the normal screen display during macro execution.

CONTROLLING KEYBOARD INTERACTION

The following macro commands provide you with the ability to create interactive macros. Such macros pause during execution and wait for the user to enter data. Once the Enter key has been pressed, execution resumes. Also included are macros that prevent users from interfering with macro execution.

- **{?}** This macro halts execution to allow you to respond to some prompt or move about on the worksheet. Once the Enter key has been pressed, execution of the macro resumes.
- **{BREAK}** The {BREAK} command works like a Ctrl-Break command and returns you to the READY mode. It does not interrupt a macro.
- **{BREAKOFF}** This macro disables the use of the Break command during macro execution. This command remains in effect until a BREAKON command is issued. *Warning:* If a macro enters an infinite loop during execution, you must reboot the system.
- **{BREAKON}** This macro enables the use of the Break command during macro execution.
- **{GET location}** This macro pauses for you to enter a single character, then stores it at the designated location. Another command that can be used for this purpose is {?}.
- **{GETLABEL message range}** This macro allows you to display a prompt (message) to the user in double quotes. The user can now enter text/label data, and, once the Enter key is pressed, the result will be stored in the named range as a label.
- **{GETNUMBER message range}** This macro allows you to display a prompt (message) to the user in double quotes. The user can now enter number data, and, once the Enter key is pressed, the result will be stored in the named range as a number.
- **{LOOK location}** This macro checks to see if you have typed a character. If you have, 1-2-3 stores the first character at the specified location. If no characters have been entered, the location is erased.
  1-2-3 is actually checking the keyboard buffer for this command. Characters in the buffer can be used in {GET}, {GETLABEL}, and {GETNUMBER} macro commands.
- **{MENUBRANCH location}** This macro command halts execution and executes the macro menu found at the range name specified by location. When a menu option is selected and the corresponding macro commands for that selection are executed, control does not automatically pass back to the main macro. Rather, a {BRANCH} command must be executed to send control back. The {MENUBRANCH} command overrides the {PANELOFF} command.
- **{MENUCALL location}** This macro command temporarily halts macro execution to let you select a menu choice from the menu, beginning at the location argument. A blank cell or {RETURN} command causes control to be transferred back to the main macro. If you press the Esc key, the menu selection process is cancelled, and control returns to the main macro. {MENUCALL} overrides the {PANELOFF} command.
- **{WAIT time-serial-number}** This macro command causes 1-2-3 to halt execution and display the WAIT indicator in the upper right-hand corner. During the interval, 1-2-3 will not respond to keystrokes. You can interrupt a

{WAIT} command by issuing a Break command, unless you issued a {BREAKOFF} command. You may want to issue a {BEEP} command after the {WAIT} to alert the user.

CONTROLLING PROGRAM FLOW

The following commands function similarly to regular programming logic flow commands.

- **{BRANCH location}** This macro command continues execution at the designated location. A single cell or a named range can be used for location. {BRANCH} acts as a "go to" command rather than as a subroutine call. This means that control transfers permanently to the new location.

- **{DEFINE location1:type1,location2:type2, . . .}** This macro command allocates storage locations and declares argument types for arguments to be passed to a subroutine. Locations 1 n are cell references for the cells in which the passed values are to be stored. Type refers to how 1-2-3 is to handle the values stored. Values will have the default type of string. You can tell 1-2-3 to evaluate how an argument is to be stored by typing *value* after it.

- **{DISPATCH location}** This macro command is used to branch to a destination that is specified in the location cell. The location can be only one cell if a named range is used.

- **{FOR counter-location,start-number,stop-number,step-number, starting-location}** This macro command controls the looping process. The counter-location is the cell that stores the current number of repetitions through the loop (tally). The start-number is the beginning value for the counter. The step-number is the value to be added to the counter each time through the loop. The starting-location is the first cell or range name of the subroutine to be executed.

- **{FORBREAK}** This macro command cancels execution of a {FOR} loop and continues processing at the first character after the original {FOR} command. This command can be used only in a routine called by a {FOR} command.

- **{IF condition}** This macro command allows you to embed logic within a series of macro commands. If the condition specified is true, 1-2-3 then executes the command following the {IF}. The IF-THEN-ELSE program construct is supported. The True condition action is found to the right of the {IF}, and the false condition action can be placed on the line below the {IF}.

- **{ONERROR branch-location,<message-location>}** This macro command branches to branch-location if 1-2-3 encounters an error during macro execution. You are also able to use the optional message-location argument to store an error message in the message-location cell. Position the {ONERROR} macro command before any error can occur. Only one {ONERROR} command can be in effect at any one time. Issuing a Break command triggers an {ONERROR} command. Once the command has been triggered, issue another {ONERROR} command in the branch-location routine.

- **{QUIT}** This macro command terminates macro execution and returns control back to the keyboard. This command is often used with an {IF} command to control execution.

- **{RESTART}** This macro command cancels the execution of the current subroutine and returns control to the calling macro. It is typically used with multiple nested subroutines.

- **{RETURN}** This macro command returns control from an invoked subroutine back to the calling macro. It is used with the commands {routine-name} and {MENUCALL}.

- **{routine-name<optional argument>,<optional argument>, . . .}** This macro command calls a subroutine and allows you to pass one or more arguments. When the subroutine finishes, control is passed to the following commands in the invoking macro. Control is passed back via the {RETURN} command.

CONTROLLING MANIPULATION OF DATA

- **{BLANK location}** This macro command erases the contents of cells in the range designated by location. No numeric formats or protection settings within the cells erased are affected. This command is often easier to use than the / Range Erase command.
- **{CONTENTS}** The {CONTENTS} command is used to copy the contents from a source cell to a target cell as a label. It has the following format: {CONTENTS target-location,source-location,[width],[cell-format]}. The optional width argument creates a label of the specified width. The width can be a number, numeric formula, or reference to a cell that contains the data.
- **{LET location:value}** or **{LET location:string}** This macro command stores an entry at the cell referenced by the location argument. Numeric data can be stored via the value argument. String data can be stored via the string argument.
- **{PUT location,col-number,row-number,number}** or **{PUT location,col-number,row-number,string}** This macro command stores a numeric or string entry at the offset referenced by the column and row entries of the specified range. If the specified range is a single cell, an error will result unless the offset is zero. A column or row offset that occurs outside the referenced range does not result in an error that can be trapped via the {ONERROR} command.
- **{RECALC location,<condition>,<iteration-number>}** This macro command recalculates the formulas of a range specified by the location argument. The optional argument condition can generate a recalculation only if the condition is false. The condition entry must contain a regular logical expression. This expression can reference a cell in the worksheet. The worksheet will continue to recalculate until the condition is true or until the iteration is exhausted (whichever comes first). The iteration argument specifies the number of times 1-2-3 is to recalculate the range. The {RECALC} command allows you to recalculate only selected areas of your worksheet. This can save quite a lot of time over the {CALC} command, which recalculates the entire worksheet each time it is issued.
- **{RECALCCOL location,<condition>,<iteration-number>}** This command recalculates the formulas of a specified range referenced by the condition argument a column at a time. The optional argument condition can generate a recalculation only if the condition is false. The condition entry must contain a regular logical expression. This expression can reference a cell in the worksheet. The worksheet will continue to recalculate until the condition is true or until the iteration count is exhausted (whichever comes first). The iteration argument specifies the number of times 1-2-3 is to recalculate the range. The {RECALCCOL} command allows you to recalculate only selected areas of your worksheet. This can save quite a lot of time over the {CALC} command, which recalculates the entire worksheet each time it is issued.

CONTROLLING FILE MANIPULATION

The following commands can be used to perform file-related tasks like reading or writing information to or from files. These commands are used only with ASCII files.

- **{CLOSE}** This macro command closes any file that was opened via the {OPEN} command. If no file is open, the command is ignored.
- **{FILESIZE location}** This macro command records the number of bytes in the file currently open at the designated cell referenced by the location argument.

The data are stored as a numeric value. If a file is not currently open, the command is ignored.

- **{GETPOS location}**   This macro command determines the current position of the file pointer in the open file and displays that as numeric data in the cell referenced in the location argument. If a file is not currently open, the command is ignored by 1-2-3. The next command in the macro is then executed.

- **{OPEN filename,access-mode}**   This macro command opens a specified file. The filename must be valid. If needed, a path can be specified. Any file extensions must also be included. The complete path name cannot exceed 64 characters. The access-mode argument can be one of the following three; it must contain the reference character.

    R   Specifies the file as read only. Use the {READ} or {READLN} commands.

    W   Opens a new file (or erases the file with this name), assigns it the specified name, and allows access via the {WRITE} and {WRITLN} commands, as well as the {READ} and {READLN} commands.

    M   Permits modifications to an existing file with the specified name and allows access via the {READ}, {READLN}, {WRITE}, and {WRITELN} commands.

- **{READ bytecount,location}**   This macro command reads the specified number of characters referenced in the bytecount argument beginning at the location of the pointer in the file. The characters are then stored as string data in the cell referenced via the location argument. The {READ} command then copies information from the file to the worksheet. The bytecount value cannot exceed 240 (the maximum for any cell). If a file is not open, {READ} is ignored by 1-2-3.

- **{READLN location}**   This macro command copies a line of characters from the open file into the cell referenced via the location argument. This command works the same as {READ} except that a whole line is read instead of a specific number of characters. The end of a line is detected via a carriage return.

- **{SETPOS file-position}**   This macro command sets a new position for the file pointer in the open file. The pointer can be erroneously positioned past the end of the file. The {FILESIZE} command is used to determine the number of the last character in the file. If no file is currently open, the {SETPOS} command is ignored by 1-2-3.

- **{WRITE string}**   This macro command is used to copy characters to the open file. It copies a string of characters from the worksheet to the current pointer position in the file. If necessary, 1-2-3 extends the length of the file to store the incoming characters.

- **{WRITELN string}**   This macro command adds a carriage-return linefeed and writes the character string to the open file.

MACRO DESIGN FORM

1. Name of macro _____

2. Overall task or objective of the macro _____
   _____

3. Range names to be used in the macro:

Range Name	Purpose
_____	_____
_____	_____
_____	_____
_____	_____

4. Steps involved in accomplishing the task to be performed by the macro:

Keystrokes	Purpose
_____	_____
_____	_____
_____	_____
_____	_____
_____	_____
_____	_____
_____	_____
_____	_____
_____	_____
_____	_____
_____	_____
_____	_____

MACRO DESIGN FORM

1. Name of macro _____

2. Overall task or objective of the macro _____
   _____

3. Range names to be used in the macro:

Range Name	Purpose
_____	_____
_____	_____
_____	_____
_____	_____

4. Steps involved in accomplishing the task to be performed by the macro:

Keystrokes	Purpose
_____	_____
_____	_____
_____	_____
_____	_____
_____	_____
_____	_____
_____	_____
_____	_____
_____	_____
_____	_____
_____	_____

MACRO DESIGN FORM

1. Name of macro _____

2. Overall task or objective of the macro _____
   _____

3. Range names to be used in the macro:

Range Name	Purpose
_____	_____
_____	_____
_____	_____
_____	_____

4. Steps involved in accomplishing the task to be performed by the macro:

Keystrokes	Purpose
_____	_____
_____	_____
_____	_____
_____	_____
_____	_____
_____	_____
_____	_____
_____	_____
_____	_____
_____	_____
_____	_____
_____	_____

MACRO DESIGN FORM

1. Name of macro _____

2. Overall task or objective of the macro _____
   _____

3. Range names to be used in the macro:

Range Name	Purpose
_____	_____
_____	_____
_____	_____
_____	_____

4. Steps involved in accomplishing the task to be performed by the macro:

Keystrokes	Purpose
_____	_____
_____	_____
_____	_____
_____	_____
_____	_____
_____	_____
_____	_____
_____	_____
_____	_____
_____	_____
_____	_____

MACRO DESIGN FORM

1. Name of macro _____

2. Overall task or objective of the macro _____
   _____

3. Range names to be used in the macro:

   Range Name   Purpose

   _____   _____

   _____   _____

   _____   _____

   _____   _____

4. Steps involved in accomplishing the task to be performed by the macro:

   Keystrokes   Purpose

   _____   _____

   _____   _____

   _____   _____

   _____   _____

   _____   _____

   _____   _____

   _____   _____

   _____   _____

   _____   _____

   _____   _____

   _____   _____

   _____   _____

MACRO DESIGN FORM

1. Name of macro _____

2. Overall task or objective of the macro _____
   _____

3. Range names to be used in the macro:

Range Name	Purpose
_____	_____
_____	_____
_____	_____
_____	_____
_____	_____

4. Steps involved in accomplishing the task to be performed by the macro:

Keystrokes	Purpose
_____	_____
_____	_____
_____	_____
_____	_____
_____	_____
_____	_____
_____	_____
_____	_____
_____	_____
_____	_____
_____	_____
_____	_____

APPENDIX

B

ALLWAYS
COMMAND MENUS

ALLWAYS COMMAND STRUCTURE CHART

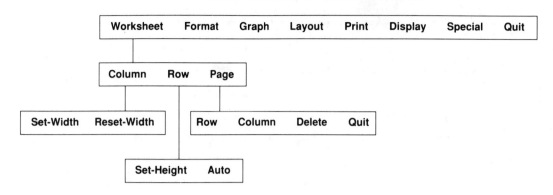

ALLWAYS COMMAND STRUCTURE CHART

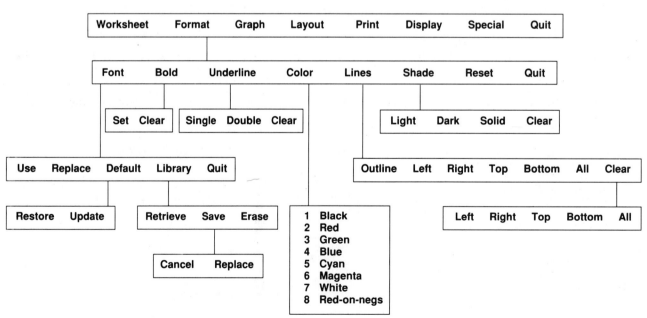

ALLWAYS COMMAND STRUCTURE CHART

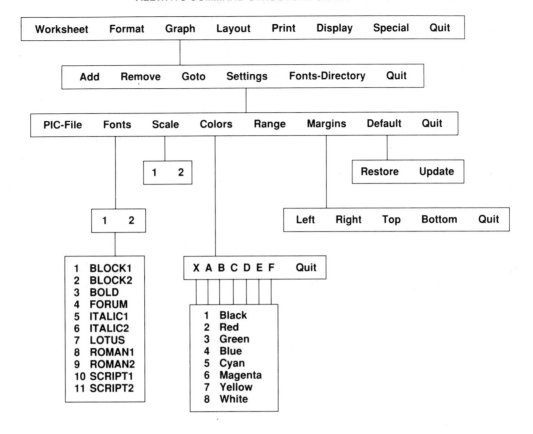

ALLWAYS COMMAND STRUCTURE CHART

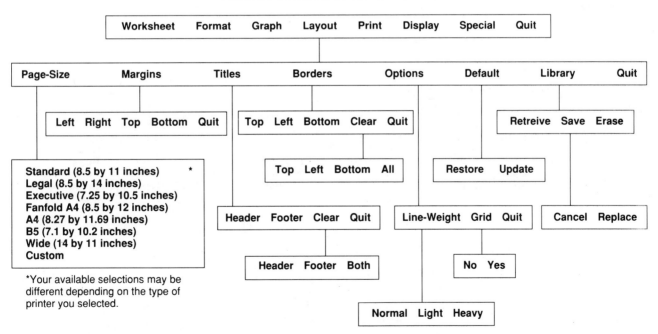

ALLWAYS COMMAND STRUCTURE CHART

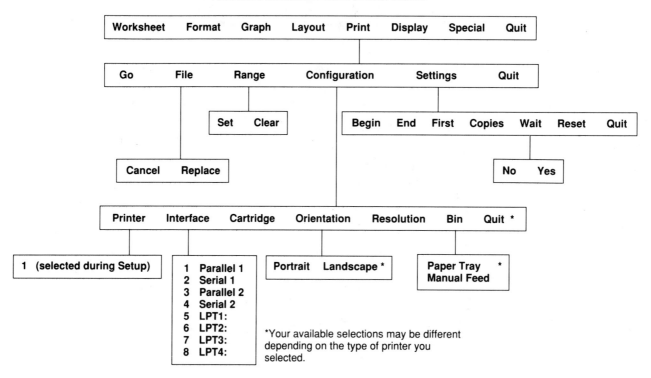

ALLWAYS COMMAND STRUCTURE CHART

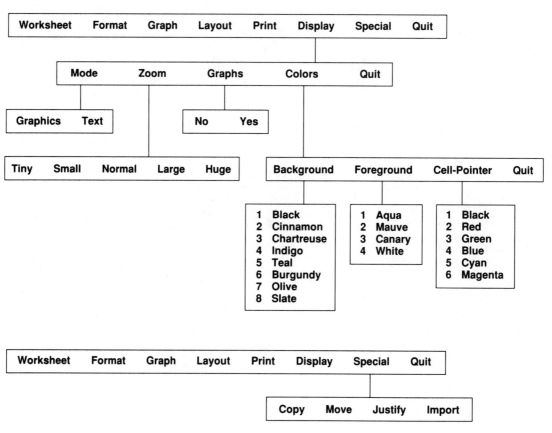

GLOSSARY

Absolute address: Cell location that does not change in the course of copying a formula to other cells. In a cell marked for absolute address, the formula contains dollar signs.

Accelerator keys: Key sequence commands of 1-2-3 that usually require Alt + some other character (for example, Alt + F3). These commands can take the place of commands that are issued via the menu.

Acronym: Word formed from letters or syllables in a name or phrase. For example, FORTRAN is an acronym for Formula Translator.

Active directory: The active directory on a disk device is the last directory that you were in via a CD command. Any files copied to the disk name (with no path specified) get copied to this directory.

Add-in: A piece of software that provides Lotus 1-2-3 with capabilities not otherwise found in it.

Address: (As a noun) number associated with each memory location; (as a verb) to refer to a particular memory location.

Align: Command that tells 1-2-3 to expect the top of page at this page position.

Allways: An add-in for 1-2-3 that provides desktop/spreadsheet publishing capability.

Alphanumeric: Contraction of the words *alphabetic* and *numeric*. A set of alphanumeric characters usually includes special characters such as the dollar sign and comma.

Alt: Key label for the Alternate key.

Alternate key: Key used for the following purposes: to create a second set of function keys in some application programs, to enter the ASCII character code directly from the keyboard, and (together with letters) to enter BASIC commands.

Alternate pitch: In WordStar, elite character spacing (12 cpi). It is invoked by issuing the ^PA command.

Append: dBASE command that enables you to add records at the end of an existing file.

Application program: Precoded set of generalized instructions for the computer, written to accomplish a certain goal. Examples of such programs include a general ledger package, a mailing list program, and PacMan.

Arrow keys: Keys (Down, Up, Right, and Left) found on the numeric keyboard and typically used to move a pointer or cursor.

ASCII: Acronym for American Standard Code for Information Interchange (pronounced *ass-key*). Often called USASCII, this code is a standard method of representing a character with a number inside the computer. Knowledge of the code is important only if you write programs.

Assembler: Program that converts the mnemonics and symbols of assembly language into the opcodes and operands of machine language.

Assembly language: Language similar in structure to machine language but made up of mnemonics and symbols. Programs written in assembly language are slightly less difficult to write and understand than programs in machine language.

ASSIGN: The DOS command that allows you to tell DOS to direct read/write requests for one disk drive into read/write requests for another drive.

ATTRIB: The DOS command that allows you to change the read-only attribute of a file. This determines whether a file can be only read or can be both read and written.

Auto-dial: Feature frequently found in modems that enables you to place a call to a specified number without having to dial it yourself.

AUTOEXEC.BAT: File that is executed by the computer as soon as the boot process is completed. This type of file is used in building a turnkey application that requires very little input from a user before starting.

Automatic recalculation: Feature that enables the worksheet to automatically recalculate itself after any change.

Available memory: Amount of RAM that is available for use by 1-2-3 in building a worksheet.

Backspace key: Key used to erase the last character typed. It is labeled with an arrow that points toward the left.

Back-up file: .BAK-extension file that Lotus 1-2-3 automatically creates as protection against loss of an original file. It can also be an additional copy of an important file created by the user via the DOS COPY command.

Banked memory: Usually two sets of 64K memory used to give a computer a total memory of 128K. Only one set of 64K can be active at a time.

BASIC: Acronym for Beginners All-Purpose Symbolic Instruction Code, a common, easy-to-learn computer programming language. The advanced version of BASIC is called BASICA. BASIC was developed by Kemeney and Kurtz at Dartmouth College in 1963 and has proved to be the most popular language for personal computers.

Baud rate: Speed at which modems can transmit characters across telephone lines. A 300-baud modem can transmit about 30 characters per second.

Bell: Sound produced by your computer or line printer, often used by programs to get your attention or to reassure you that computer processing is underway.

Big Left: The 1-2-3 command (Ctrl + Left Arrow) that moves you to the left a screen at a time.

Big Right: The 1-2-3 command (Ctrl + Right Arrow) that moves you to the right a screen at a time.

Binary: Number system consisting of two digits, 0 and 1, with each digit in a binary number representing a power of two. Most digital computers are binary. A binary signal is easily expressed by the presence or absence of an electrical current or magnetic field.

Bit: Binary digit, the smallest amount of information a computer can hold. A single bit specifies a single value of 0 or 1. Bits can be grouped to form larger values (see *Byte* and *Nibble*).

Block: Designated portion of text, consisting of one or more lines, that is to be copied, moved, or deleted.

Boldface text: Darkened text, accomplished by striking or printing the same character three or four times.

Booting: Process of starting the computer. During the boot process, a memory check is performed, the various parts of DOS are loaded, and the date and time are requested.

Boot record: Record that resides on sector 1 of track 0 of a file and contains the program responsible for loading the rest of DOS into the microcomputer.

Bootstrap (boot): Procedure used to get a system running from a cold start. The name comes from the machine's attempts to pull itself off the ground by "tugging on its own bootstraps."

Border: Set of labels for the rows and columns of a worksheet. The columns are labeled with letters, and the rows are labeled with numbers.

Bottom: dBASE command that enables you to position the pointer at the end of the file.

Break: Function for halting the program in progress. Usually the program returns to some higher-level program such as DOS, BASIC, or the main application program, but not all programs have this function. It is invoked by holding down the Ctrl key while pressing Scroll Lock.

Browse: dBASE command that displays a number of records on the screen at one time, enabling you to edit a file quickly.

B-tree structure: Structural arrangement that provides the ability to develop indexes that establish the relations for a relational database file.

BUFFERS: The DOS command that allows you to determine how much RAM is used for holding information for disk read/write operations. This command is used in the CONFIG.SYS file.

Bug: Error. A hardware bug is a physical or electrical malfunction or design error; a software bug is an error in programming, either in the logic of the program or in typing.

Bus: Entity that enables the computer to pass information to a peripheral and to receive information from a peripheral.

Byte: Basic unit of measure of a computer's memory. A byte usually has eight bits, and therefore its value can be from 0 to 255. Each character can be represented by one byte in ASCII.

Caps Lock key: Key used to switch the case of letters A through Z on the keyboard. This key does not affect numbers and special characters.

Card: General term for a printed circuit board with electronic components attached. It is also called an interface card, a board, a circuit card assembly, and other similar names.

Cartridge: Removable hard disk storage unit that typically holds 5 or 10 megabytes of storage.

Cell: Intersection point of a row and a column. It is referenced by the cell address Column/Row.

Centering command: Word processing or spreadsheet command that centers text in a document or cell.

Centering hole: Large hole on a diskette that allows the mylar plastic disk inside the diskette envelope to center on the capstan for proper rotation.

Central processing unit (CPU): Device in a computer system that contains the arithmetic unit, the control unit, and the main memory. It is also referred to as the computer.

Centronics: Standard method of passing information through a parallel data port.

Character: Any graphic symbol that has a specific meaning to people. Letters (both upper- and lowercase), numbers, and various symbols (such as punctuation marks) are all characters.

Character field: Field capable of holding any alphanumeric or special character. In dBASE, such a field can hold up to 254 characters.

Character overprint: Function that enables you to create text using diacritical marks such as tildes. It also creates special effects in printing.

Character pitch: Number of characters printed per horizontal inch of space. Twelve pitch (elite) prints 12 characters per inch; 10 pitch (pica) prints 10 characters per inch.

CHDIR (CD): The DOS command that allows you to move to another directory and make that the active directory.

Chip: Electronic entity containing one or more semiconductors on a wafer of silicon, within which an integrated circuit is formed.

CHKDSK: DOS command that checks the status of a disk and prepares the status report.

Circular reference: The situation that exists when a cell's effect depends on both its contents and the contents of other cells.

Clear screen: Procedure that blanks the screen of all characters. It can be accomplished by pressing the Home key while holding down the Ctrl key.

Closed bus system: Type of computer system that comes with plugs, called established ports, that accept device cables from the peripheral.

CLS: DOS command that clears the display monitor.

Cluster: Entity composed of two adjacent sectors. Storage is allocated to a file one cluster at a time.

COBOL: Acronym for Common Business Oriented Language, a high-level language oriented toward organizational data processing procedures.

Code: Method of representing something in terms of something else. The ASCII code represents characters in terms of binary numbers; the BASIC language represents algorithms in terms of program statements. *Code* may also refer to programs, usually in low-level languages.

Cold start: Booting process used to begin operating a computer that has just been turned on.

Color monitor: Display device that is capable of showing red, green, and blue colors.

Column: Vertical line of text.

Column Block: Command that specifies a column of data within a document to copy, move, or delete.

Combination key: Key that must be used together with another key to perform a task. Combination keys include the Ctrl, Alt, and Shift keys.

COMMAND.COM: Command processor of DOS, containing built-in functions or subroutines that enable you to copy a file or get a directory listing of a disk.

Command line: Third line of the Lotus 1-2-3 control panel. It contains the 1-2-3 commands that can be issued from the current menu.

Communications packages: Hardware packages that enable you to obtain and/or transmit information over telephone lines.

Compiler: Software that translates a program into machine language. As it performs this translation, it also checks for errors made by the programmer.

Computer: Any device that can receive and store a set of instructions and then act upon those instructions in a predetermined and predictable fashion. The definition implies that both the instructions and the data upon which the instructions act can be changed; a device whose instructions cannot be changed is not a computer.

Concatenation: Process of joining two character strings, usually accomplished through use of the + sign.

Conditional page break: Word processing technique that checks to see if a page break is going to occur in the next *n* lines and, if so, moves the specified text to the top of the next page.

CONFIG.SYS: The file used by DOS after the boot process is finished to further configure your computer system.

Configured software: Software that has been customized to the specific hardware configuration currently used.

Constant information: Information that remains the same from one document to the next.

Continue: dBASE command that finds the next record in a Locate command search.

Control (CTRL) character: Character in the ASCII character set that usually has no graphic representation but serves to control various functions inside the computer.

Control key: General-purpose key whose uses include invoking breaks, pauses, system resets, clear screens, print echos, and various edit commands. In instructions, the Control key is often represented as a caret (^).

Control panel: Top three lines on the 1-2-3 worksheet screen, consisting of the status line, the entry line, and the prompt line.

Coprocessor: Microprocessor chip that is placed in a microcomputer to take the burden of manipulating numbers off the CPU, allowing it to perform other tasks.

COPY: dBASE and DOS command that copies one or more files onto the current disk or onto another disk. In spreadsheets, it enables you to copy the contents of a cell into one or more other cells; in WordStar, it enables you to copy a block of text to another location in a document.

Create: dBASE command that enables you to build a database and describe the fields and the data type of each field.

Criterion range: Area of the worksheet on which you specify the records to be included in an operation.

CRT: Acronym for *cathode ray tube,* meaning any television screen or device containing such a screen.

Ctrl: Key label for the Control key.

Cursor (pointer): Display screen's special character (_) used to indicate where the next character will be typed, that is, where you are in a file.

Cursor control key: One of the four Arrow keys on the numeric keypad used to move the cursor left, right, up, or down on the screen.

Cursor movement: Operation of moving the cursor over the text.

Cylinder: Entity composed of all like-numbered tracks from all recording surfaces of a disk.

Daisy wheel printer: Letter-quality printer that uses a solid-font printing mechanism (the mechanism is shaped like a flower or a thimble).

Data (datum): Information of any kind.

Database: Collection of data related to one specific type of application. *Database* is often used synonymously with *file.*

Data entry: Process of placing text, values, labels, or formulas into a text document, data file, or worksheet.

Data entry window: The 14- or 23-line by 79-column area of the screen in which you can enter or edit text.

Data table: 1-2-3 feature that enables you to perform sensitivity analysis on a worksheet easily by asking multiple "what if" questions.

DATE: DOS command that enables you to change the system date.

dBASE II: Relational database package.

dBASE III: Updated version of dBASE II.

dBASE III Plus: The updated version of dBASE III.

Debug: To find hardware or software faults and eliminate them.

Default: Original (or initial) setting of a software package.

Default disk drive: Disk drive that is accessed automatically by the microcomputer when a file-oriented command is executed.

Default font: The font that is automatically used unless a font change command is issued.

Default pitch: Pitch (usually pica) used to print a document unless some other pitch is specified.

DEL: DOS command used to delete one or more files from disk.

Del: Key label for the Delete key.

Delete: dBASE command that enables you to mark a record for later deletion.

Delete indicator: Asterisk (*) that appears in a record when it has been marked for deletion.

Delete key: Key used to erase the character to the left of the current cursor position.

Delimiter: Character that indicates to the computer where one part of a command ends and another part begins. Typical delimiters are the space, the period, and the comma.

Desktop organizers: Primarily RAM-resident software packages that can include such capabilities as calculators, notepads, automatic dialers, and appointment calendars.

DEVICE: The DOS command contained in the CONFIG.SYS file that indicates which driver is to be used for the computer's operation.

DIR: DOS command that is used to list the files in the directory.

Directory: Part of a diskette that holds the names of files stored on it. The directory also contains information about file size, file extensions, their location on diskette, and the dates and times files were created or changed.

Directory (subdirectory): Like a root directory except that it is itself a file and contains DOS housekeeping entries in a regular directory; it does not have the size limitation of the root directory.

DISKCOPY: DOS command used to copy a complete disk.

Disk drive: Rectangular box, connected to or situated inside the computer, that reads and writes into diskettes.

Diskette: Square recordlike objects used for storing information from the computer.

Display: (As a noun) any sort of output device for a computer, usually a video screen; (as a verb) to place information on such a screen.

Document file: WordStar file that contains embedded codes to tell the monitor how text is to be displayed and to tell the printer how text is to be printed.

DOS: Acronym for Disk Operating System, the program responsible for enabling you to interact with the many parts of a computer system. DOS (pronounced *doss*) is the interface between you and the hardware. To perform system functions, DOS commands are typed on the keyboard, but DOS is actually a collection of programs designed to make it easy to create and manage files, run programs, and use system devices attached to the computer.

Dot commands: Special commands to WordStar that provide a user with a number of different print capabilities or perform some type of specialized task.

Dot matrix printer: Printer that generates characters by firing seven or nine tiny print heads against a ribbon.

Double-density disks: Disks that have approximately twice the storage of a single-density disk. This is achieved by using a higher-quality read/write surface on the disk, so that data can be stored in a denser format.

Double-sided disks: Disks on which data can be stored on both surfaces. A double-sided disk has been certified (tested) on both sides.

Double-strike text: Text somewhat darkened by striking or printing each character two times.

Dummy: A row or column used to end a range. This allows you to add another row or column and have that be inside the range specified by a 1-2-3 command referencing that range.

Edit: Process by which the format of data is modified for output by inserting dollar signs, blanks, and so on. Used as a verb, to validate and rearrange input data.

Editing a document: Inserting, deleting, and changing existing text in a word processing text file.

EGA monitor: A video device that is capable of presenting clear, vivid graphics. It uses a 640 × 350 (or more) dot resolution to present crisper, more colorful images.

Electronic spreadsheets: Programs used to manipulate data that can be expressed in rows and columns.

End key: Key used together with the Ctrl key to erase characters on the screen from the current cursor position to the end of the line.

Enter key: Key used to tell the computer program that you are finished typing. It is principally used when more than one character is required in the typing input.

ERASE: DOS command used to delete one or more files from disk.

Error message: Message informing you that you did not type something the program can process or that some other system failure has occurred.

Error message indicator: Brief explanation of what went wrong, appearing in the lower left-hand corner of the worksheet screen.

Esc: Key label for the Escape key.

Escape key: Key used for general purposes, usually to cause some change in computer processing. In DOS and BASIC, it is used to erase a line of input; in application programs, it is often used to transfer to another section of the program.

Execute: To perform the intent of a command or instruction; to run a program or a portion of a program.

Expansion board: Printed circuit board that can be inserted into an open bus expansion slot, expanding the computer configuration to include such items as modems and plotters.

Extension: One- to three-character portion of a filename. Extensions are typically used to indicate families of files, such as backups (.BK!), regular database files (.DBF), and indexes (.NDX).

External DOS commands: Utility commands that are not part of the COMMAND.COM command processor. They reside on disk as separate files.

Extract: Command used for creating reports from a 1-2-3 database.

Field: Subdivision of a record that holds one piece of data about a transaction.

File: Collection of data or programs that serves a single purpose. A file is stored on a diskette and given a name so that you can recall it.

File allocation table (FAT): Entity that keeps track of which sectors belong to which files and of how much available space remains on the diskette (so that new files can be created and stored in unused areas of the diskette).

File linking: The ability to link a worksheet with another worksheet by specifying the cells in the source file that are to be linked to the target file.

Filename: Unique identifier of a file, composed of one to eight characters. If an optional one- to three-character extension is used, there must be a period between the filename and the filename extension.

Filter program: Program that performs some type of data manipulation on a file, such as sorting it or breaking it down into displayable chunks.

Find: dBASE command used to locate records in an indexed file, using the index.

Find and replace: Ability of a word processing package to find a character string and replace it with another character string.

Flag character: The character that appears along the right-hand column on a WordStar screen, providing you with information about the characteristics of that line of text.

Font: Character set for printing. Pica, elite, Helvetica, Courier, and Orator are among the many common fonts.

Footer: Line of text that appears at the bottom of every page of a document.

FORMAT: DOS command that prepares a disk so that it can be used by the computer. It defines every sector of a diskette, finds and write-protects any tracks with bad sectors, sets up the directory, sets up the file allocation table, and puts the boot record program at the beginning of the diskette. *Format* also refers to how data are stored in a worksheet cell, for example, as character or numeric data.

Formula: Series of characters containing cell references and arithmetic operators for numeric data manipulation.

FORTRAN: Acronym for Formula Translator, a programming language designed for writing problem-solving programs that can be stated as arithmetic procedures.

Fragmentation: Characteristic of files whose sectors are not in adjacent locations. A fragmented file can be stored on a disk in a number of different physical locations.

Full-screen editing: Editing format that enables you to move about the entire screen using cursor movement keys. This makes changes to a worksheet, document file, or data file much easier.

Function key: One of ten keys (F1–F10) that allow special functions to be entered with a single user keystroke. Computer programs (DOS, BASIC, and so on) use these keys for different purposes.

Function key line: Bottom line on many application software display screens that identifies the task performed by each function key.

Functions: Formulas or processes built into a software package. These functions save a user a tremendous amount of effort and tedium.

Global: Spreadsheet command that allows changes entered thereafter to affect the entire worksheet.

Global characters: DOS characters (? and *) that are used to specify a number of files via a single command.

Goto: dBASE command used to position the pointer at a specific record in a file.

Graph Group: Graph command that allows you to specify the X and data ranges by indicating a range of cells in the worksheet.

Graphics: System used to display graphic items or a collection of such items.

Hard carriage return: Special carriage return recorded in a document when the Enter key is pressed, usually at the end of a paragraph.

Hard copy: Printed document on paper.

Hard disk: Rigid medium for storing computer information, usually rated in megabytes (millions of bytes) of storage capacity.

Hard page break: Convention of word processing packages to show where one page ends and another page begins.

Hard-sectored: Disks that have already had their tracks divided into sectors.

Hard space: Space inserted by pressing the Home key plus the Space Bar.

Hardware: Physical parts of a computer.

Header: Line of text that appears at the top of every page of a document.

Help level: The amount of menu-driven help displayed in the form of messages on your WordStar document screen. 0 provides the least help, and 3 provides the most help.

Hexadecimal: Number system that uses the ten digits 0 through 9 and the six letters A through F to represent values in base 16. Each hexadecimal digit in a hexadecimal number represents a power of 16.

Hidden: The 1-2-3 command that is used to hide a column so that it does not appear on the screen.

Hidden file: File that exists but does not appear to a user in the file directory. Since it is not visible in the directory, such a file is very difficult to erase mistakenly.

Hierarchical (tree) structure: Structural arrangement in which data elements are linked in multiple levels that graphically resemble an organization chart. Each lower level is owned by an upper level.

High-level language: Language that is more intelligible to humans than it is to machines.

Home: Upper left-hand corner screen position where the first printable character can be placed. This is also referred to as the initial cursor position.

Home key: Key used to send the cursor to the Home position. If used with the Control key, a clear screen results.

IBMBIO.COM: Hidden file in DOS that manages each character that is typed, displayed, printed, received, or sent through any communications adapter.

IBMDOS.COM: Hidden DOS file that handles any information to be passed to disk.

Index: dBASE feature used to order information logically within a file without physically reordering the records themselves. Indexes may be single- or multiple-field.

Indicators: Signals that appear in the upper right-hand corner of the worksheet screen, telling the user which toggle keys are currently activated.

Initialization: Process during the boot routine when the computer activates the various peripherals hooked to the computer.

Ink-jet printer: Printer that sprays ink in droplets onto paper to form characters. It is much quieter than a dot matrix or letter-quality printer.

Input line: Second line in the control panel, corresponding to a scratch area. The entry line contains any information you are currently entering for the cell location contained in the status line.

Ins: Key label for the Insert key.

Insert key: Key used to tell the computer program that you want to insert characters to the left of the cursor. The INSERT mode continues until you press the key again or until you press another special key (cursor arrows, Del, End) indicating that you want to go on to a different editing operation.

Instruction: Smallest portion of a program that a computer can execute.

Integrated circuit: Small (less than the size of a fingernail and about as thin) wafer of glassy material (usually silicon) into which an electronic circuit has been etched. A single IC can contain from 10 to 225,000 electronic components.

Integration: Process that combines a number of applications under one software umbrella. For instance, 1-2-3 combines spreadsheets, graphing, and database applications.

Interface: Adapter or circuit board containing the electrical components that connect a peripheral with the computer's bus system.

Internal DOS command: Command that is part of the COMMAND.COM command processor.

Interpreter: Program, usually written in machine language, that understands and executes a higher-level language one statement at a time.

Inverse: Command to the computer that tells it to display the characters on the screen as dark characters on a light background instead of the normal display of light on dark.

Justification: Alignment of word processing text flush with the right (and left) margins. This produces straight margins on both the left-hand and right-hand sides of a document.

K: Abbreviation for the Greek prefix *kilo-*, meaning *thousand*. In computer-related usage, K usually represents the quantity 2^{10}, or 1,024.

Key: Data item (field) that identifies a record.

Keyboard: System hardware used to input characters, commands, and functions to the computer. The keyboard consists of 83 keys and is organized into three sections: the function keys, the typewriter keyboard, and the numeric keypad.

Label: Alphanumeric information used to identify a portion of a row or column.

LABEL: The DOS command that allows you to create, change, or delete a volume label on a disk.

Label prefix: Tells 1-2-3 whether to left-justify ('), center (^), or right-justify (") text within a cell.

Language: Code that both the programmer and the computer understand. The programmer uses the language to express what is to be done, and the computer understands the language and performs the desired actions.

Language processor: Software that translates a high-level language such as COBOL or BASIC into machine-understandable code.

Laser printer: Printer that uses laser-based technology to form characters on paper via electronic charges and then places toner on the charges to display the characters. The toner is fixed in place by a heat process.

LCD monitor: Liquid crystal display frequently used on notebook-size portable computers.

Learn command: A command of 1-2-3 that enables you to record keystrokes of commands as they are entered and then place them in a cell as a macro.

Legend: Lotus 1-2-3 graph feature used to label sets of data so that a graph can be easily understood.

Letter-quality printer: Printer that generates output of a quality comparable to that produced on a typewriter.

Line editor: Low-level word processing package that allows you to work on only one line of text at a time.

Line spacing: Number of filled and blank lines that are established with each generated line. Double spacing produces one blank line after each generated line.

List: dBASE command used to display records from a data file contained on disk.

List structure: Structure arrangement containing records that are linked together by pointers.

Local area networks (LAN): Networks used to connect a number of microcomputers to share data or expensive peripheral devices.

Locate: dBASE command used to find data in a sequential file.

Lock key: Key used to cause subsequent key operations to be interpreted in a specific manner by the computer. Lock keys are toggle keys; they include Caps, Num, and Scroll.

Logged device: Disk specified to be searched automatically for any needed files.

Logical field: Field capable of holding the values of .T. (true) or .F. (false) or Y (yes) or N (no). Logical fields are always one-byte fields.

Lowercase: Small letters (*a–z*).

Low-level language: Language that is more intelligible to machines than to humans.

Machine language: Lowest-level language. Machine language is usually binary; instructions in machine language are single-byte opcodes, sometimes followed by various operands.

Macro: Entity that contains keystroke commands stored for later execution.

Macro library: A range of cells that have been taken from a 1-2-3 worksheet by the Macro Library Manager, saved to disk as a library file with a .MLB file extension, and then loaded into memory in an area separate from any worksheet that is currently in RAM.

Macro Library Manager: An add-in for 1-2-3 that allows macro libraries to be loaded into memory and executed without being part of the worksheet.

Mag typewriter: Predecessor of the computer, developed by IBM in the 1960s.

Main logic board: Large printed circuit board at the bottom of the computer.

Manual recalculation: Functional mode in which a worksheet can recalculate itself only when the F9 key is pressed.

Margin: Unused border around a page of a document.

Megabyte (meg): One million characters of storage, a quantity usually used as a measure of available storage on a hard disk.

Memory location: Smallest subdivision of the memory map to which the computer can refer. Each memory location has a unique address and a certain value.

Menu: List of commands available to anyone using a software package.

Microchannel: The bus system architecture introduced by IBM for their PS/2 line of computers. This bus system is faster than previous systems and supports multitasking (the ability to run more than one job at a time).

Microcomputer: Computer based on a microprocessor (8-bit or 16-bit) that can execute a single user's program.

Microcomputer system: Combined computer, disk drives, monitor, and input and output devices for data processing.

Microprocessor: Integrated circuit that understands and executes machine-language programs.

Microsoft: Company that originally developed PC DOS for IBM (an operating system known, with some minor differences, as MS DOS).

Minimal recalculation: Feature of Lotus 1-2-3 that recalculates only those cells affected by a change to a worksheet.

Mixed cell address: Address in which the row or column portion (not both) of the cell address can change to reflect a new cell location.

MKDIR (MD): The DOS command that allows you to create a subdirectory.

Mnemonic: Any acronym or other symbol used in place of something more difficult to remember.

Mode indicator: Status information that appears in the upper right-hand corner of the 1-2-3 worksheet screen.

Model: Symbolic representation of an entity or process that is difficult to observe.

Modem: Acronym for modulator–demodulator, a device that converts digital computer signals into analog telephone signals and reverses the procedure at the other end of the line.

Monitor: TV-like device that gives users of microcomputer equipment video feedback about their actions and the computer's actions.

Monochrome monitors: Devices similar to one-color monitors except that their pixels are much closer together, producing clearer characters.

Monospaced font: A font in which every character takes up the same amount of space on a line.

MORE: DOS filter command that displays one screen of data on the monitor at a time.

Motherboard: Another name for the main logic board.

Mouse: Hand-held controller that electronically signals the computer to move the cursor on the display screen. The same movements can be accomplished via the cursor control pad.

MS DOS: Operating system developed by Microsoft. It is the same as PC DOS except that there is no ROM BASIC provision. This operating system is used by most IBM-compatible computers.

Multipurpose monitors: Monitors capable of handling monochrome, color, and EGA signals.

Multitasking: The ability to run more than one program at one time without interrupting the execution of another program.

Nested function: Function that resides inside another function. The innermost function must be executed before any outer ones.

Network structure: Arrangement permitting the connection of data elements in a multidirectional manner. Each mode may thus have several owners.

Nibble: Slang for half a byte (four bits).

Nondocument mode: Operating mode used to create a file that has no control character sequences to provide instructions to the printer. This mode must be selected when you are creating computer programs or building data files.

Nonvolatile storage: Form of storage that does not lose its content when the system's power is turned off. It may take the form of bubble memory, or it may be powered by batteries.

Numeric data: Data consisting of the digits 0 through 9.

Numeric entry: Process of entering numbers into the computer. The numeric keypad can be set into numeric entry mode via the Num Lock key; after this has been done, numbers and number symbols (decimal, minus, plus) can be entered.

Numeric field: Field that can hold only a number or a decimal point. No alphabetic or special characters can be placed in such a field.

Numeric keypad: Section of the keyboard containing numeric entry and editing keys.

Numeric Lock key: Key used to switch the numeric keypad back and forth between numeric entry and editing.

Num Lock: Key label for the Numeric Lock key.

Object code: Machine-language code created by the compiler. It is the object code that is actually executed by the computer.

Operating system: Interface between the computer and the user that provides the user with flexible and manageable control over the resources of the computer.

Operating system prompt: Signal to the user that some type of DOS command or a command to start a program can be entered. The prompt also shows which drive has been specified as the default drive.

Orphan line: Last line of a paragraph when it appears as the top line of a page.

Outliners: Software that assists you in outlining ideas, goals, or tasks.

Output: Computer-generated data whose destination is the screen, disk, printer, or some other output device.

Output range: 1-2-3 range that holds any report generated in an Extract operation.

Pack: dBASE command that physically removes any records marked for deletion.

Page: One screen of information on a video display; quantity of memory locations addressable with one byte.

Page breaks: Marks that show where one page ends and another begins. In WordStar, they are represented by a line of dashes across the screen.

Page Down key: Key that is sometimes used to cause text on the screen to move down. Text on the bottom of the screen moves offscreen while text is added at the top.

Page number omission: A WordStar dot command that turns off the automatic page numbering of a document. This command is frequently used in preparing letters or memos.

Page number setting: A WordStar dot command that allows you to specify the page number of the first page of a file to be printed. It also allows you to reset the page number to a specific value inside a document.

Page Offset: A WordStar command that tells the printer how much of a left-hand margin is to precede the first print position in a document.

Page Up key: Key that is sometimes used to cause text on the screen to move up. Text on the top of the screen moves offscreen while text is added at the bottom.

Parallel interface: Interface arrangement that transmits all nine bits of a character at one time.

Parameter: Modifying piece of information that constitutes part of a DOS or dBASE command. It might, for example, indicate which files or fields are to be included in an operation.

Password: The 1-2-3 feature that allows you to assign a password to a file and then requires you to enter that password before access to the worksheet is allowed.

Path: The complete name for a file, including the complete subdirectory name.

PATH: The DOS command that provides the capability to automatically search specified drives or directories if the desired file cannot be found in the active disk or directory.

Pause: Computer function that can be used at any time to temporarily halt the program in use. Pause is invoked by pressing the Num Lock key while holding the Ctrl key down. Pressing any key after a Pause causes the computer to continue from the point of interruption. Pause can also be performed with one hand by pressing the key combination Ctrl + S.

Peripheral: Something attached to the computer that is not part of the computer itself. Most peripherals are input and/or output devices.

Personal computer: Computer equipped with memory, languages, and peripherals, well suited for use in a home, office, or school.

Pg Dn: Key label for the Page Down key.

Pg Up: Key label for the Page Up key.

Piping: System arrangement that allows a number of different programs to share generated input and output, since the output from one program becomes the input to another. Temporary files are created to achieve this.

Pitch: Refers to the number of characters per inch of a type style.

Pixel: Dot that is turned on or off depending on what character is being displayed on the screen.

Platen: Hard rubber roller that moves the paper in the printer.

Plotter: Device that moves a pen on X and Y axes to draw graphs or pictures. For one of the axes, the paper may move instead of the pen.

Point: A measurement equal to 1/72 of an inch.

Pointer: Reverse-video bar, sometimes referred to as the cursor. Its width is dependent on the width of the cell it is referencing.

Precedence: Order in which calculations are executed.

Press any key to continue: Message often displayed by a program when the computer is waiting for you to do something (read text or load a diskette, for example) and does not know when you will be done. Some keys are generally inactive and do not cause the program to continue when they are pressed; these include the Alt, Shift, Ctrl, Scroll Lock, Num Lock, and Caps Lock keys.

Primary key: In dBASE, the record number; in sorting, the major sort field.

Primary memory: Internal memory used by the computer for a number of different functions. It can contain data, program instructions, or intermediate results of calculations.

PRINT: DOS command used to queue and print disk-based data files.

Print echo: Function performed by pressing the Print Screen (PrtSc) key while holding the Ctrl key down. Once this key is pressed, whatever is displayed on the screen is printed. The simultaneous printing (screen and printer) continues until the key combination is pressed again. Print echo can also be performed via the key combination Ctrl + P.

Printed circuit board: Sheet of fiberglass or epoxy onto which a thin layer of metal has been applied and then etched to form traces. Electronic components are then attached to the board with molten solder, and thereafter they can exchange electronic signals via the etched traces on the board. Small printed circuit boards are often called cards, especially if they are meant to connect with edge connectors.

Printer: Device used to make a permanent copy of any output.

Printer font: A font provided with your printer.

Print screen: Function produced when the Print Screen (PrtSc) key is pressed while the Shift key is held down. When this key combination is pressed, the current information on your screen is printed.

Print Screen key: Key that, when pressed with the Shift key, results in the screen contents being printed.

Procedures: Written instructions on how to use hardware or software.

Productivity software: Software that allows a person to be more productive. These packages include such applications as desktop organizers and outline software.

Program: Set of instructions that tell the computer how to perform a certain task. DOS, BASIC, and the Instructor are all programs.

Programming language: Special means of providing instructions to the computer to get it to perform a specific task. Examples of programming languages are BASIC, COBOL, Pascal, and FORTRAN.

PROM: Acronym for Programmable Read-Only Memory. A PROM is a ROM whose contents are alterable by electrical means. Information in PROMs does not disappear when the power is turned off. Some PROMs can be erased by ultraviolet light and then reprogrammed.

Prompt line: Last line in the control panel. When a 1-2-3 menu is displayed, the prompt line contains a further explanation about a specific command.

Proportional font: A font in which a character takes up only the amount of space that it needs in a line of text.

Protected cell: 1-2-3 cells that cannot be changed by the user. The worksheet has been globally protected by the Global Protection command.

Protection: In 1-2-3, a way of prohibiting changes on either the entire worksheet or specific cells.

PrtSc: Key label for the Print Screen key.

Quit: dBASE command that returns you to the operating system.

QWERTY: Standard keyboard arrangement, first used with manual typewriters in the early 1900s.

RAM-resident: Means that once the program is loaded into memory, it stays there until either the machine is turned off or you tell it to erase itself.

Random-access memory (RAM): Main memory of a computer. The acronym RAM can be used to refer either to the integrated circuits that make up this type of memory or to the memory itself. The computer can store values in distinct locations in RAM and then recall them, or it can alter and restore them.

Range: Rectangular or square area of a worksheet.

Range name: Function used to give a specific name to a range of a worksheet; by using it, you can refer to formulas by meaningful names instead of by cell address only.

Range Search: The 1-2-3 command that enables you to find a character string and replace it with another character string in any indicated worksheet cell.

Range Value: The 1-2-3 command that permits you to take the result generated by a formula and convert that result to a numeric constant.

Read-only memory (ROM): Memory usually used to hold important programs or data that must be available to the computer when power is first turned on. Information in ROM is placed there during the process of manufacture and is unalterable. Information stored in ROM does not disappear when power is turned off.

Read/write access hole: Oval opening on a diskette that allows the read/write heads to record or access information.

Recalculation: Process by which a spreadsheet changes all cell contents that are affected by a change to any other cell in a worksheet.

Recall: dBASE command used to retrieve or unmark records that have been marked for deletion.

Record: Entity that contains information about a specific business happening or transaction.

Record number: Identification used by dBASE as the primary key for a record; the physical location in the file for a given record.

Redirection: System arrangement that allows the IBM PC to accept input from a device other than the keyboard and to send output to a device other than the display screen.

Re-form: WordStar feature that automatically readjusts text within existing margins. The manual commands are ^B and ^QU.

Relational structure: Structural arrangement consisting of one or more tables. Data are stored in the form of relations in these tables.

Relative addressing: Automatic changing of cell locations in a Copy or Move operation to reflect their new locations.

RENAME: DOS command used to rename a disk file.

Replace: dBASE command used to change several or all records within a data file quickly.

Replaceable parameters: Used in executing batch files. Pieces of information in a DOS command that might change from one use to the next. Represented by a percent sign (%).

Report: dBASE command used to create or access a parameter file modifying how a specific printed report is to be generated.

Reserved tracks: Tracks of disk storage that contain a bad sector and have been set aside so that data cannot be recorded on them.

Reset: Command that usually results in the return of a piece of software to its original default values.

RMDIR (RD): The DOS command that allows you to delete a subdirectory.

Root directory: The main directory of a disk. Subdirectories are created below the root directory on a disk medium.

Root node: Top node of a tree structure.

Row: Horizontal axis on a spreadsheet or document.

Ruler line: Line on the display screen that identifies the location of the right-hand margin, the left-hand margin, and tab stops.

Run: Action of following a sequence of instructions to its completion.

Run: The 1-2-3 command, invoked using the Alt + F3 key sequence, which allows you to highlight the range name of a macro and then automatically executes that macro.

Scaling: Description of how data values will be displayed on a 1-2-3 graph.

Scroll: Function that moves all the text on a display (usually upward) to make room for more (usually at the bottom).

Scrolling: Moving the text under the cursor. The relative position of the cursor does not have to change.

Scroll Lock key: Key that is little used in modern programs but is intended for use as a lock-type key, causing displayed text (rather than the cursor) to move when a cursor control key is pressed.

Secondary key: Defining key used to order information within the primary key.

Sector: One part of a track. For the IBM microcomputer, each track is divided into eight or nine sectors of 512 bytes each. It is the sector that holds the data.

Sensitivity analysis: Procedure used to ask a number of "what if" questions about the effect of various changes to a worksheet.

Serial interface: Interface arrangement that transmits a character one bit at a time.

Settings sheet: A screen displayed in many 1-2-3 commands that provides information about the current status of lower-level entries in a menu.

Setup string: 1-2-3 feature used to vary the pitch of printed information.

Shift key: Key used to select the uppercase character on keys that have two characters or to reverse the case of letters *A* through *Z*, depending on the status of the Caps Lock key.

Skip: dBASE command used to move the pointer forward or backward within a data file.

Slave disk: Disk that has been formatted but does not contain the operating system. You cannot boot the computer by using such a disk.

Soft carriage return: Carriage return accomplished by the word-wrap feature.

Soft font: A font that must be downloaded to your printer.

Soft-sectored: Disks that have each track divided into sectors during the format process.

Software: Program that gives the hardware something to do.

SORT: DOS filter command used to store data files; also the dBASE command used to reorder a database file physically; also a 1-2-3 command used to resequence a portion of a worksheet.

Source code: Set of program instructions written in a high-level language.

Source drive: Drive that contains any files to be copied.

Source file: A file that contains data that is to be linked to a target file in a 1-2-3 file link operation.

Spellcheck: A spelling checker package for WordStar.

Spreadsheet: Software package that can manipulate rows and columns of data.

Spreadsheet publishing: A term associated with the Allways add-in. It means that you can receive presentation-quality print enhancements for your worksheet.

Stand-alone word processors: Computers that do only word processing.

Standard input device: Device that DOS assumes will be used to enter commands or data. Unless otherwise specified, this device is the keyboard.

Standard output device: Device that DOS assumes will be used to receive any output generated by the computer. Unless specified otherwise, this device is the printer.

Standard pitch: Default pitch, usually pica, for most printers.

Status line: Top line of the control panel, which displays the cell address, the format of the data, and the cell contents.

Storage: Term that applies to either RAM or external disk memory.

Strike-out text: Text produced by placing a dash (–) over each character as it is printed.

Structured walk-through: Process of having a number of individuals review a program or worksheet and check it for accuracy, logic, and readability.

Subroutine: Segment of a program that can be executed by a single call. Subroutines perform the same sequence of instructions at many different places in a single program.

Subscript: Characters printed a half line beneath the current line.

Sum: dBASE command used to total the contents of a field for all records within a file.

Superscript: Characters printed a half line above the current line.

Synchronized: In 1-2-3, the state of having the contents of one or more windows move in a like fashion.

Syntax: Structure of instructions in a language. If you make a mistake in entering an instruction and garble the syntax, the computer sometimes responds with the message SYNTAX ERROR.

SYS: DOS command used to place DOS on a disk.

System: The command that allows you to exit a software package to DOS, issue DOS commands, and then return to the software package previously exited.

System disk: Disk that has been formatted and contains DOS. This type of disk can be used to boot the system.

System reset: System function that restarts your computer just like a power on/off. This is accomplished by pressing the Del key while holding the Ctrl and Alt keys down. Three keys are required to ensure that you know what you are doing and to avoid an accidental system reset.

Tab: Point on a line (also called a tab stop) to which the cursor will position itself whenever the Tab command is issued. Tab stops are usually represented as marks in the ruler line of WordStar.

Tab key: Key used to set automatic spacing for typing input. The Tab key has both a forward and a backward capability.

Target drive: Disk to which files will be copied.

Target file: The file that is to receive information in a 1-2-3 file link operation.

Telecommunications: Data communication using communications facilities.

Template: Form that contains the prepackaged worksheet instructions needed to perform some type of application. It can be viewed as a piece of application software on which someone has already performed the planning, design, and implementation of the logic involved.

Temporary file: File that is used temporarily in an application. Such a file will have a randomly assigned file extension such as .$$$ or .%%%. When the file is no longer needed, it is erased.

Testing: Process by which a program or worksheet is examined and tried out to make certain that it generates the proper results.

Text characters: Letters and numbers, usually in English.

Thermal printer: Printer that uses specially treated paper to "burn in" dots to form characters.

TIME: DOS command used to change the time for the system.

Timing hole: Small hole to the right of the centering hole on a diskette.

Titles option: 1-2-3 feature used to freeze text on the screen so that it will act as row or column headings.

Toggle key: Key with two states, ON and OFF, that causes subsequent key operations to be processed in a predetermined manner. Toggle keys include the Caps Lock, Num Lock, and Scroll Lock keys.

Top: dBASE command used to position the pointer at the beginning of a data file.

Track: Concentric circle of storage on a disk's read/write surface on which data are stored.

TREE: The DOS command that allows you to list all directories and subdirectories along with any files that might also be resident.

TYPE: DOS command that displays file contents on the screen.

Typeface: The style and design of the characters as they appear on the printed page.

Typewriter keyboard: One of the three main key groupings of a computer system keyboard. It contains the QWERTY typewriter keyboard, as well as some special keys such as Enter, Backspace, Tab, Esc, and Alt.

Underlined text: Text that has an underscore under every character. Usually underscores are not placed between words.

Undo: A 1-2-3 command that permits you to restore a worksheet to its prior state, allowing you to recover from many mistakes that you might make.

Unique: 1-2-3 database command used to get only one record for each data type within a database file.

Unsynchronized: In 1-2-3, the state of having the contents of the windows move independently of each other.

Upper case: Set of upper characters on two-character keys and capital letters (A–Z). Any uppercase character can be typed by holding the Shift key down while pressing the desired key.

Use: dBASE command that makes a file available for manipulation.

Variable data: Data that change from one document to the next in a mail merge operation.

VDISK.SYS: The DOS driver file that allows you to create a RAM disk using part of your system's memory.

VER: DOS command that displays the DOS version number being used.

VGA monitor: The new video adapter introduced by IBM with its PS/2 line of computers. This analog system is capable of displaying 262,144 different colors or shades of colors.

Video: Anything visual, usually information presented on the face of a cathode ray tube.

Virtual word processors: Word processors that enable you to work on a document even when it is longer than the amount of available RAM. Only the needed part of the document is in RAM at any time.

VisiCalc: First spreadsheet introduced for microcomputers.

VOL: DOS command used to display the volume I.D. of a diskette.

Volatile memory: Memory that is erased when the electrical current to the computer is turned off.

Warm start: Booting process used to restart a computer after you have lost control of its language or operating system.

Widow line: First line of a paragraph when it occurs at the bottom of a page.

Wild cards: Characters that enable you to include a number of files or fields in an operation by using only one command.

Window: Displayed portion of a worksheet or document. A window can be split into two or more smaller windows, horizontally or vertically.

Word processing: Automated manipulation of text data via a software package that usually provides the ability to create, edit, store, and print documents easily.

Word wrap: Feature that automatically places a word on the next line when it will not fit on the current line.

Worksheet: Model or representation of reality that is created using a spreadsheet software package. The worksheet is contained inside the spreadsheet border.

Write-protected: Diskettes that have been protected from having information stored on them, from being altered, or from being deleted; this is accomplished by placing a write-protect tab over the small rectangular hole on the side of a diskette.

X axis: Horizontal (left-to-right) axis.

Y axis: Vertical (up-and-down) axis.

INDEX

A> (DOS prompt), O.10
ABCDEF commands, S.197, S.198
Absolute addressing, S.113–114
Absolute range name, S.115
Accelerator keys, S.291
Active directory, O.49–50
Add-ins, S.10
   Allways. *See* Allways
   hardware requirements, S.286
   Macro Library Manager. *See* Macro Library Manager
   software, S.286–287
Advanced macro commands, S.268–271, A.12–16
Align command, for Lotus 1-2-3 printing, S.62
Align option, for PrintGraph, S.222
.ALL file extension, S.289
All option, S.96
Allways, S.10, S.287
   accelerator keys, S.291
   command structure chart, A.24–26
   function keys for, S.290–291
   incorporation of graphs, S.298–302
   interaction with Lotus 1-2-3, S.288–289
   invoking, S.289
   print enhancements, S.291–298
   specifying a range before a command, S.289–290
Alt key, with function keys, S.17–18
ANC indicator, S.289–290
#AND#, S.117
"and" condition, S.238
Application programs, O.6–7
Arithmetic functions, in Lotus 1-2-3, S.119–120
Arithmetic operations, in DOS, O.4
ASSIGN statement, O.52
Asterisk (*), O.12–13, S.237
Attaching, S.286
AUTOEXEC.BAT, O.9, O.42–43, O.45
Automatic option, S.199
Automatic recalculation, S.116
@AVG, S.66

Backspace key, O.16, S.16
Backup, S.23, S.32
Bar charts, stacked, S.211–212
Bar graphs, S.196
   converting to line graphs, S.207
   data ranges, S.204–205
   reconverted from line graphs, S.208
   side-by-side, S.206–207
   simple, S.202–203
   titles, S.203–204
Batch, O.42
Batch files, O.42–43
   creation of, O.43–44

   execution of, O.44–45
   sample, O.45
   types, O.42
Batch printing, S.220
.BAT file extension, O.42
Black box approach to functions, S.67
Boot process, O.9–10
Boot record, O.9
Bootstrap loader, O.9
Border, S.14
Borders option, S.60–61
Both command, for Lotus 1-2-3 graphing, S.199
Both option, for Lotus worksheet, S.112
Braces, S.259
{Branch}, S.268–270
BREAK option, O.52
BUFFERS option, O.52–53
Built-in functions, S.20–21
B&W option, S.200

CALC indicator, S.95
Cancel command, for Lotus worksheet, S.32
Cancel option, in Learn command of Lotus 1-2-3, S.260
Caret (^), S.70
Car loan evaluation worksheet, S.126–129
   cell contents listing, S.130
Car loan sensitivity analysis, S.163–168
   cell contents of, S.178–182
Cell contents listing
   for amortization worksheet, S.129–130
   of car loan evaluation worksheet, S.130
   of car loan sensitivity analysis, S.178–182
Cell protection, S.157
Cells, S.7
Central processing unit (CPU), O.4, O.6
Change directory (CHDIR [CD]), O.46, O.48–49
Check Disk (CHKDSK), O.17, O.20–21, O.32
Circular reference, S.20, S.91–93
Clear command, for Lotus 1-2-3 graphing, S.199
Clear option
   for Lotus 1-2-3 printing, S.62
   for Lotus worksheet, S.112, S.157
Clusters, O.15
Cold start, O.9, O.10
Color option, S.200
Column headings, S.233
Column-Range command, S.68–69
$columnrow, S.114–115
Column$row, S.114–115

Columns, S.7
   adding, S.53–55
   deleting, S.53–55
   dummy, S.104
   hiding, S.90–91
   width, changing, S.67–69
Column Width command, S.68
.COM file extension, O.42
COMMAND.COM, O.8, O.9
Command language, S.271–272
Command structure chart
   for allways, A.24–26
   for Lotus 1-2-3, A.2–5
Communication programs, O.6–7
Computer, definition of, O.5
Computer system, O.4–6
   configuration of, O.52–53
   hardware configuration of, O.4–5
Condition, A.12
CONFIG.SYS, O.52
   creation of, O.53
Control keys, O.15–16
Control panel, S.12
COPY
   DOS, O.17, O.25–26, O.32
   Lotus 1-2-3, S.49–51
COPY CON, O.43–44
@COUNT, S.66
Courier, S.287
CPU, O.4, O.6
Create command, S.200
Create option, S.98–99
Criterion range headings, S.236–238
Criterion range option, S.234
Ctrl,Alt,Del sequence, O.9
Ctrl-Break keys, O.15, O.19
Ctrl-P keys, O.16
Ctrl plus Scroll Break keys, S.16
Ctrl-S keys, O.15
Current date, S.14
Current directory, O.49–50
Current time, S.14
Cylinders, O.15

Database
   building and accessing information, S.235–236
   statistical functions, S.243–245
Database management programs, O.6–7
Data entry, S.18–19
Data Fill command, S.159–160
Data management, S.232–233
Data management file, S.232
Data manipulation, control of, A.15
Data option, S.200
Data Range option, S.107
Data ranges, changing, S.204–205
@DATE, S.66, S.119–120, A.6

DATE, DOS, O.9–10, O.17, O.31, O.32
Date functions, in Lotus 1-2-3, S.66,
    S.69–70, A.6–7
@DAVG, S.243–244
@DAY, S.66, A.6
dBASE database, S.232
@DCOUNT, S.243–244
Debugging, S.267–268
Default
    date, O.9
    disk drive, O.10–11
    font, S.288
    printing, S.63
DEL, DOS, O.28, O.32
Delete command
    in Lotus 1-2-3 database, S.234,
        S.241–243
    in Lotus 1-2-3 graphing, S.200
Delete option, in Lotus 1-2-3 worksheet,
    S.99
Delimiter, O.18–19
Del key, O.16
Desktop/spreadsheet publishing
    definitions, S.287–288
Detaching, S.287
Directory
    commands for, O.46–51. *See also
        specific commands*
    DOS, O.11, O.17, O.26–28, O.32,
        O.45–46
Directory command, for Lotus
    worksheet, S.89
Disk
    5.25-inch double density, O.14–15
    preparation of, O.13
    type, maximuum number of files for,
        O.46
DISKCOPY, O.17, O.21–23, O.32
Disk drive
    changing, O.10–11
    default, O.10–11
Disk operating system. *See* DOS
@DMAX, S.244
@DMIN, S.243–244
Documentation, final, S.154–155
DOS, O.8
    batch files, O.42
    commands, O.32–33. *See also specific
        commands*
    directories, O.11, O.45–46
    disk commands, O.17, O.20–25
    editing keys, O.16
    execution of batch files, O.44–45
    external commands, O.18
    file commands, O.17, O.25–30
    format notation rules, O.18–19
    internal commands, O.18
    parts of, O.8–9
    starting, O.10
    storage space for, O.9
    time commands, O.17–18, O.31–32
    use of 5.25-inch double density disk,
        O.14–15
    utility programs, O.29
    versions of, O.13–14
DOS prompt (A>), O.10

Double quote ("), S.70
Down Arrow, S.14
@DSTD, S.244
Dummy column, S.104
Dummy rows, S.104–106
@DVAR, S.244

EDIT, S.13
Edit key (F2), S.21
Edit option, S.304
EDLIN editor, O.52
Electronic spreadsheets, O.6–7
End key, S.15
Enter key, O.15, S.16
::entry, S.63–64
Entry line, S.12
Erase
    DOS, O.17, O.28–29, O.32, O.50
    Lotus 1-2-3, S.260
ERROR, S.13
Error messages, S.14
    Ctrl-Break, S.268
    key column outside of sort range,
        S.107
    protected cell, S.158
    unrecognized key name, S.257, S.267
Esc key, O.16, S.16
.EXE file extension, O.42
Exit option, S.222
Exploded pie charts, S.210–211
External commands, O.18
Extract command, S.234, S.243
Extract options, S.239–241

F10 Graph key, S.194
FAT (file allocation table), O.11, O.13
Field name, S.232
Fields, S.232
/File Admin Link-Refresh, S.173
File allocation table (FAT), O.11, O.13
File extensions. *See* Filename extensions
File linkage, S.172–173
    limitations of, S.175–176
    rules for, S.174–175
    sample worksheet, cell contents of,
        S.182–183
    sample worksheet for, S.176–177
/File List command, S.32
File manipulation, control of, A.15–16
Filename extensions
    .ALL, S.289
    .COM, O.42
    in DOS, O.12
    .EXE, O.42
    .MLB, S.305
    .PRN, S.59, S.65
    .WK1, S.32
Filenames, O.11–12
    global characters or wild cards,
        O.12–13
/File Retrieve command, S.32
FILES, O.53, S.13
/File Save command, S.289
Final documentation, S.154–155

Final testing, S.154
Financial functions, A.7–10
Find
    editing/changing records and, S.238
    in Lotus 1-2-3 data management, S.13,
        S.234
    in Lotus worksheet, S.96
First command, S.199
Font, S.287
Font option, S.220, S.221
Footer option, S.59–60
FORMAT, DOS, O.13, O.17, O.23–25,
    O.32, O.45
FORMAT.COM, O.18
Format +/− option, S.52
Format Currency option, S.51–52
Format Date option, S.52–53
Format Fixed option, S.51
Format General option, S.52
Format notation, O.18–19
Format option
    for Lotus 1-2-3 graphing, S.198, S.199
    for Lotus worksheet, S.51
Format Percent option, S.52
Format Scientific option, S.51
Format Text option, S.53
Formatting
    in DOS, O.13. *See also* Initialization
    in Lotus 1-2-3, S.51–53
    X and Y numeric scaling, S.215–216
Formulas, S.7–8
    entering, S.19–20
Fragmented file, O.20
Function calls, S.66–67
Function keys
    in Allways, S.290–291
    with Alt key, S.17–18
    in DOS, O.16
    in Lotus 1-2-3, S.16–17
    for macros, S.256

{Getlabel}, S.270–271
{Getnumber}, S.270–271
Global filename characters, O.12–13
Global settings screen, S.58
Go option, S.62, S.107, S.221
GoTo command (F5), S.88
Graph(s). *See also* Bar graphs
    building, steps for, S.194–195
    command, S.197
    data points, labeling, S.216
    incorporation with allways, S.298–302
    Menu, S.195
    names, generating a table of,
        S.212–213
    option, S.198
    printing, S.216–228
    settings sheet, S.196–202
Graphics programs, O.6–7
Grid option, S.199
Group command, S.200–201

Hardware option, S.221
Header option, S.59–60

Help facility, S.13, S.23–25
Help screen, S.153
Hidden files, in DOS, O.24
Hidden option, S.53
Hide command, S.90–91
Home key, S.15
Horizontal command, for Lotus 1-2-3 graphing, S.199
Horizontal option, S.156
   for Lotus 1-2-3 printing, S.112

IBMBIO.COM, O.8, O.9, O.21
IBMDOS.COM, O.8, O.9, O.21
IBM PC keyboard, location of keys for Lotus 1-2-3, S.15–18
IBM Personal Computer, disk operating system. *See* DOS
@IF, S.67, S.117–119
{If}, S.268–270
Image option, S.220–221
Image-select option, S.219–220
Immediate mode, S.232
Indicator option, S.200
Indicators, S.14
Infinite loop, S.268
Initialization, O.9
Input devices, O.4
Input option, S.234
Ins key, O.16
@INT, S.119, A.10
Integration, S.9
Internal commands, O.18
Internal line counter, S.63
Internal storage, O.4
I/O handler, O.8

/key, S.15–16
Keyboard, interaction, control of, A.13–14
Keyboard macro, S.16
Keystrokes, recording with learn, S.260–262
^KR command, S.65

Label, S.7, S.13
Label cell, S.18
Label data, S.18
Labeling, graph data points, S.216
Label option, of Zero command, S.88
Labels option
   for Lotus 1-2-3 graphing, S.200
   for Lotus worksheet, S.99
Learn command, S.13, S.259–262
Learn range, S.259
   creation of, S.259–260
Left Arrow, S.15
Legend option, S.198
Legends, entering on line graphs, S.208
{Let}, S.268–270
Line command, S.63
Line graphs, S.196
   converted from bar graphs, S.207
   reconverting to bar graphs, S.208

Line option, S.59
Linking files, S.172–173
Load option, S.304
Loan amortization worksheet, S.120–126
   cell contents listing, S.129–130
Location, A.12
Logical operations, O.4
Logical operators, and @IF, S.117
Lotus 1-2-3, S.8
   add-ins. *See* Add-ins
   command structure chart, A.2–5
   copyright screen, S.11
   data management feature, S.10
   function summary, A.6–13
   graphics feature, S.10
   parts of, S.9–10
   special purpose keys for, S.15–18
   spreadsheet, S.9–10
   starting, S.10–11
   worksheet screen, S.11–12
Lotus Access System, S.10–11
Lotus spreadsheet, S.9–10
Lotus worksheet, S.14
   column width, changing, S.26–27
   correction of errors on, S.21–22
   entering a sample, S.25–31
   movement keys, S.14–15
   retrieving files, S.32–34
   sample, S.71–79
   saving files, S.32
Lower option, S.199

Macro (Alt) key, S.16
Macro library
   building, S.304–305
   description of, S.302–303
   saving, S.303
Macro Library Manager, S.10, S.286
   description of, S.302–303
   limitations of, S.303
   Menu, S.303–304
Macros, S.254–256
   building, S.258
   creation with regular range name, S.258–259
   debugging, S.267–268
   design form for, A.17–21
   documentation for, S.264–265
   entering, S.265–266
      learn mode for, S.259–262
      rules for, S.264
   errors in, S.267
   modifying, S.257–258
   placement of, S.264, S.265
   planning for, S.267
   printing the worksheet, S.273–275
   sample, examination of, S.262–264
   special commands, S.268–273
   special keys, S.255
Magnetic disk, O.5, O.6
Main menu, S.17
   help screen for, S.24
Make directory (MD) command, O.47–48
Manual option, S.199
Manual recalculation, S.116

Margins option, S.60
Mathematical functions, A.10
@MAX, S.66
MD command, O.47–48
MEM, S.13
Memory, O.4
MENU, S.13
{MENUBRANCH location}, S.272–273, A.13
Microsoft MS DOS, O.8
@MIN, S.66
Minimal recalculation, S.116
Minus sign, S.238
Mixed cell address, S.114
MKDIR [MD], O.46
.MLB, S.305
Mode indicator, S.12–13
Monospaced spacing, S.288
@MONTH, S.66, A.6
MOVE command, help screen for, S.25
Move feature, for Lotus worksheet, S.55–57
MS DOS, O.8
Multiple printers, S.64–65

Nail down, S.49
Name-List option, S.304
Name menu, S.98–99
Name option, S.200
Name ranges, listing of, S.255
Name Reset option, S.99, S.200
Naming instructions, S.99–100
Nested functions, S.67
Network device, O.19
Next option, S.96–97
#NOT#, S.117
@NOW, S.66, S.119, A.7
Number, S.7, A.12
Numeric data, S.18–19
Num Lock key, O.16

Operating system software, O.7. *See also specific operating system software*
Operators, S.19
   order of precedence, S.118
Options command, S.198–200
Options menu, S.59
#OR#, S.117
"or" condition, S.238
Order of operations, S.19
Output options, S.239–241
Output range option, S.234
OVR, S.13

Page breaks, forced, S.63–64
Page command, S.63
Page-Length option, S.61
Page option, S.59, S.222
Parameters, O.18
Parentheses, precedence and, S.19–20
Password, S.93–94
Path, O.51
PATH, O.51–52

Pg Dn key, S.15
Pg Up key, S.15
Pie charts, S.197, S.208–210
  exploded, S.210–211
Pitch, S.287–288
Planning, templates and, S.152–153
@PMT, S.116, S.120, A.9
Point, S.13, S.287
Pointer, S.14
Pointer positioning keys, for macros, S.256–257
Pound sign (#), S.219–220
Precedence, S.19
  parentheses, S.19–20
Prefix characters, S.70
Primary Key option, S.107
Primary storage, O.4–5
Print
  command, S.58–59
  default settings, S.63
  enhancements, with allways, S.291–298
  files, passing to other software packages, S.65–66
  graphs, S.216–228
  line counter, S.63
  Menu, S.59–62
  Range option, S.59
  worksheet for macros, S.273–275
Printer font, S.288
Printers, multiple, S.64–65
/Print File command, S.65
PrintGraph, S.216
  accessing, S.216–218
  menu, S.218–222
  step-by-step instructions, S.222–223
.PRN, S.59, S.65
.PRN file extension, S.65
Program, O.4
Program flow, control of, A.14–15
Prompt line, S.12
Proportional spacing, S.288

Quadram utility QM2, O.45
Query function key (F7), S.237
Query Menu, S.234–235
Query settings sheet, S.235
Question mark (?), O.12–13, S.237
{QUIT}, S.268–270, A.14
Quit command
  in Lotus 1-2-3, S.65
  in Lotus 1-2-3 graphing, S.197, S.198, S.200, S.201
Quit option
  in Lotus 1-2-3 data management, S.235
  in Lotus 1-2-3 printing, S.62
  in Lotus worksheet, S.97, S.107
  in Macro Library Manager menu, S.304

RAM disk, O.45
Range, S.27, S.48–49
Range-Colors option, S.220
/Range Erase command, S.22

/Range Format, S.51
/Range Format Currency, S.255
/Range Format Date command, S.70
Range name, S.98
/Range Name Create, S.255, S.258
Range names
  use of, S.100–104
  verification of, S.100, S.102
Range option, S.260
/Range Search command, S.96–98
/Range Transpose command, S.94
/Range Value command, S.94–95
RD command, O.50–51
Read process, O.6
READY mode, S.13, S.65, S.274
  help screen for, S.24
Receiving ("To" range), S.49
Record, S.232
Relative addressing, S.29, S.49, S.112–113
REM, O.43
Remove directory (RD) command, O.50–51
Remove option, S.304
RENAME (REN), O.17, O.29, O.32
Repeat symbol, S.70
Replace command, S.32, S.96
Reserved track, O.24
Reset command, S.53, S.197
Reset option, S.197, S.234
Right Arrow, S.15
RMDIR [RD], O.46
RO, S.13
Root directory, O.46, O.47
@ROUND, S.67, S.119, A.10
Rows, S.7
  adding, S.53–55
  deleting, S.53–55
  dummy, S.104–106

Save command, in Lotus 1-2-3 graphing, S.198
Save option, in Macro Library Manager menu, S.304
Scale option, S.199
Scroll Lock key, S.15
Secondary Key option, S.107
Secondary storage, O.5
Second command, S.199
Sectors, O.13, O.15
Sending ("From" range), S.49
Sensitivity analysis, S.160
  changing one basic assumption, S.162–168
  changing two basic assumptions, S.168–172
  manual example, S.161
Settings option, S.220
Settings sheet, S.57–58
Setup option for printer, S.61
Shift key, S.18
Shift-PrtSc keys, O.16
Side-by-side bar graphs, S.206–207
Simple bar graphs, generation of, S.202–203

Simple find, S.236
Size option, S.220
Slash commands, S.268–271
Slave disk, O.24
Soft fonts, S.287, S.288
Software, O.6–7
Sort command, S.106
  worksheet practice with, S.107–111
Sort menu, S.106–107
Sort Reset option, S.107
Source cell, S.173
Source drive, O.19, O.21
Source file, S.173
Spacing, S.288
Special functions, A.10–11
Spreadsheet publishing, S.286
Spreadsheets
  definition of, S.4
  Lotus, S.9–10
  problem-solving steps for, S.9
  syntax, S.7–8
  uses for, S.4–7
Stacked bar charts, S.211–212
Stacked bar graph, S.196
Statistical functions, S.66–67, S.243–245, A.11
Status commands, S.91–93
Status line, S.12
@STD, S.66
STEP function, S.267–268
String, A.12
String functions, A.11
Structured walk-through, S.153–154
Subdirectories, O.46, O.47
Subprograms, O.8
@SUM function, S.27–28, S.66, S.106
Sync option, S.156
Syntax, O.18–19
System command, S.88–89
System disk, O.24
System reset, O.9, O.10

Tab key, S.15
Table command, S.161–162
Table of graph names, generation of, S.212–213
Table option, S.99, S.200
Tab plus shift keys, S.15
Target cell, S.173
Target drive, O.19, O.21
Target file, S.173
Template, S.8, S.152
  designing logic for, S.153–154
  development of, S.154
  functional parts of, S.152–153
  implementation of functions in design, S.153
  support and maintenance, S.155
  testing, S.154
Testing, S.154
Text, S.70
  repeating, S.71
Tilde, S.255, S.256, S.259
TIME, O.18, O.31–32
Time functions, in Lotus 1-2-3, A.6–7

Times, S.287
Titles
    entering on bar graphs, S.203–204
    instructions, S.112
Titles menu, S.112
Titles option, S.111, S.199
Toggle commands, S.291
Tracks, O.13, O.15
    reserved, O.24
TREE, O.46, O.50
Triumvirate, S.287
TYPE, O.17, O.30, O.32
Typeface, S.287
Type option, S.196
Type size, S.60

Undo feature, S.13, S.22–23
Unique option, S.234, S.241
Unsync option, S.156
Up Arrow, S.15
Upper option, S.199
Use command, S.200
Utility, O.18
Utility programs, O.8–9

VALUE, S.13
@VAR, S.67

Vertical command, for Lotus 1-2-3
    graphing, S.199
Vertical option, for Lotus 1-2-3 printing,
    S.112, S.156
View command, S.197
VisiCalc, S.8
VP-Planner Plus, O.45

WAIT, S.13
Warm start, O.9, O.10
Wildcard characters, S.237–238
Wild cards, O.12–13
Window command (F6), S.57
Windows, S.14, S.155–157
.WK1 file extension, S.32
Wordprocessing programs, O.6–7
WordStar, S.65
Worksheet. *See also* Lotus worksheet
    definition of, S.4
    manual, S.5–6
    practice with sort command,
        S.107–111
    protection, S.157–158
    sample, for linking files, S.176–177
    unprotected, S.158–159
Worksheet files, password-protecting,
    S.93–94

/Worksheet Global Default commands,
    S.93
Worksheet Global Format option, S.51
/Worksheet Status commands, S.91–93
Write process, O.6

X axis (horizontal), S.196, S.199
/XC, S.270
X command, S.197
XCOPY, O.17, O.32, O.30
/XG, S.268–270
/XI, S.268–270
/XL, S.270–271
/XM, S.272–273, S.274
/XN, S.270–271
/XQ, S.268–270
/XR, S.270
XY graph, S.196, S.213–216

Y axis (vertical), S.196, S.199
@YEAR, S.66, A.6–7

ˆZ entry, O.44
Zero command, S.88

DOS

Internal Commands		External Commands		Redirection	
CLS	TYPE	CHKDSK	PRINT	<	Specify input other than the keyboard
COPY	VER	DISKCOPY	SORT	>	Specify output other than the printer
DATE	VOL	FORMAT	SYS	>>	Specify output other than the printer and add this
DEL		MORE			to the end of an existing line
ERASE					
RENAME					
TIME					

DOS

Copy:

A>COPY fn B:	Copy a file from the default drive to drive B:	A>Copy *.* B:	Copy all files from a: to b:
A>COPY fna fnb	Copy a file to the same disk under another name	A>Copy file? B:	Copy any file beginning with FILE and any character in position 5.
A>COPY B:fn	Copy a file from drive B: to the default		
A>COPY B:fn fna	Copy a file from drive B: and place it on the default under a different name		

DOS

CHKDSK

			Format	
A>CHKDSK b:	Check the status of the disk in drive B:		FORMAT B:	Format the disk in drive B: w/o DOS
A>CHKDSK fn	Check the file, fn, for fragmentation		FORMAT B:/S	Format the disk in drive B: with DOS
A>CHKDSK B:*.*	Check all the files on drive B: for fragmentation		FORMAT B:/V	Format the disk w/o DOS and record a label
A>CHKDSK B:*.*/F	Check drive B: for fragmentation and fix any problems		FORMAT B:S/V	Format the disk with DOS and record a label

DOS

Directory Piping Commands

DIR!SORT	Sort the directory by file name	MORE<filename	Display the contents of filename to the monitor a screen at a time
DIR!SORT/+10	Sort the directory by file extension	DIR!SORT!MORE	Display the directory in sorted order to the monitor a screen at a time
DIR!SORT/+14	Sort the directory by file size		
DIR!SORT/+25	Sort the directory by date		
DIR!SORT>DIR1	Sort the directory and place output in file DIR1		

Lotus 1-2-3

Arithmetic and Logical Operators

+ Addition	= Equals		
− Subtraction	< Less than		
* Multiplication	> Greater than		
/ Division			
^ Exponentiation			

Functions

@COUNT(range)	Number within a range	@STD(range)	Standard deviation
@SUM(range)	Sum of a range of values	@VAR(range)	Variance
@AVG(range)	Average of a range of values	@NOW	Today's numeric value
@MIN(range)	Smallest value	@DATE(yy,mm,dd)	Get number of a date
@MAX(range)	Largest value	@PMT(prn,int,term)	Payment amount

Lotus 1-2-3

Label Prefix

'	Left justify text within a cell
"	Right justify text within a cell
^	Center text within a cell
\	Repeating label

Absolute Cell References

CR	Always come back to the same row and column location (cell).
$CR	The row can change within the address, but the columns must always remain as specified. (Any row in this column)
C$R	The column can change within the address, but the row must remain the same. (Any column in this row)

Lotus 1-2-3

Function Keys

F1 Help	F5 Goto	F9 Calc	
F2 Edit	F6 Window	F10 Graph	
F3 Name	F7 Query		
F4 Abs	F8 Table		

Edit Keys

[Backspace]	Delete character to right of cursor	[Del]	Delete character at cursor
[ESC] or [Ctrl + Break]	Erase entry	[End]	Position cursor to end of line
right or left arrow	Move cursor one position right or left	[Enter]	Record/save the changes
[Home]	Position cursor to beginning of line		

Function Keys Template

Help	Com-pose	Name	Run	GoTo	Learn	Query	APP1	Calc	APP3
Edit	Step	Abs	Undo	Window		Table	APP2	Graph	APP4

ALT +

Cut Along Dashed Line

Lotus 1-2-3 (Release 2.2)

Template Format for New IBM Keyboards

Lotus 1-2-3 (Release 2.2)

ALT+

F1	F2	F3	F4	F5	F6	F7	F8	F9	F10
Help	Edit	Name	Abs	GoTo	Window	Query	Table	Calc	Graph
Compose	Step	Run	Undo	Learn		APP1	APP2	APP3	APP4